SAINTS ON EARTH

-A Memoir

CAROLINE MATHEW

ISBN
Paperback 979-8-89446-044-4
Hardcase 979-8-89498-370-7

Dedicated

To My Parents
M. Alphonse & A. Gnana Cyril
Who had been an Epitome of
Love and Sacrifice
Throughout their Lives.

ALSO, BY CAROLINE MATHEW

- **REFLECTION**
- **TO CHILDREN WITH LOVE**
- **STORIES FOR CHILDREN**

For life goes not backward nor tarries with yesterday.
You are the bows from which your children as living arrows are sent forth.
The archer sees the mark upon the path of the infinite, and
He bends you with His might that His arrows may go swift and far.
Let your bending in the archer's hand be for gladness;
For even as He loves the arrow that flies, so He loves also the bow that
is stable.

-Kahlil Gibran (The Prophet)

"The saints are not supermen, nor were they born perfect. They are like us, like each one of us. They are people who, before reaching the glory of heaven, lived normal lives with joys and sorrows, struggles and hopes. They spent their lives serving others; they endured suffering and adversity without hatred and responded to evil with good, spreading joy and peace. This is the life of a Saint."

-Pope Francis

CONTENTS

Preface *11*

PART 1: GENESIS

1. Heartbreaking News 17

2. Abba's Childhood 23

3. Destiny Brings Abba to Andamans 31

4. Abba's Mother Departs from the World 37

5. Abba Gets Married 42

6. Abba's Wife: Amma 44

7. Abba and Amma Build Their Family 48

8. Abba Joins Land and Revenue Department 54

PART 2: WEAVING DREAMS

9. Abba and Amma's Family Grows 59

10. Abba's Village 64

11. Abba Undergoes Revenue Inspector Training 70

12. Abba is Arrested 78

13. Abba Promoted as Revenue Inspector 82

14. Abba's Father Surprises Everyone! 90

15. Abba Rejects Job Offer for Amma 95

16. Abba is Promoted as Tahsildar 103

PART 3: ODYSSEY OF LIFE

17. Amma Suffers from Epilepsy 119

18. Settlements in Mayabunder 125

19. Abba Assumes Charge of Tahsildar Settlement 138

20. Aberdeen Bazaar on Fire 143

21. Abba Decides to Build His House 146

22. Abba Undergoes Tahsildar Training 156

23. Abba Assumes Charge of Tahsildar Rangat 164

24. Abba is Posted as Treasury Officer 177

PART 4: ANTIQUITY

25. A Glimpse of British Rule in the A & N Islands 191

26. A Glimpse of Japanese Rule in The A & N Islands 231

27. Reoccupation of the Islands By british 249

PART 5: PINNACLE

28. Abba is Promoted as Assistant Commissioner 257

29. Abba Visits His Brother's Family in Sri Lanka 270

30. Abba is Posted as Controller, Andaman Labour Force 275

31. Amma's Mother Breathes Her Last! 282

32. Abba is Posted as Secretary, Port Blair Municipal Board 286

33. Abba is Posted as Asst. Commissioner Settlement 289

34. Abba Assumes Charge of Director Tribal Welfare 294

35. Abba is Appointed as Deputy Commissioner Car Nicobar 316

PART 6: THE EXODUS

36. Abba Faces CBI Inquiry and is Acquitted 333

37. Abba Assumes Charge of Director Transports 340

38. Abba Undergoes Open Heart Surgery 344

39. Abba Posted as Deputy Secretary, Pradesh Council 351

40. Abba Proceeds on Superannuation. 354

41. Abba Returns to His Village for Good 358

PART 7: REPATRIATION

42. Abba Contests Panchayat Election 365

43. Abba Faces Financial Crisis 373

44. Abba and Amma Shifting Residences 378

45. The Tsunami-Abba Visits Andamans 387

46. Abba Gets a Pace-maker 397

47. A Family Union 401

PART 8: THE SEPULCHRE

48. Abba Leaves His Village for Good! .409

49. Amma Hospitalised: Breathes Her Last 415

50. Abba's Loneliness 429

51. Family Gathering 434

52. Fateful Night: Abba Breathes His last. 437

53. Abba's Funeral. 443

Epilogue 447

Acknowledgements 451

Notes. 453

Bibliography 467

Photo Gallery 471

PREFACE

Let me tell you how I started writing this memoir. It was 7th September 2009, and I had just returned to my workplace after attending my Abba's funeral. Nine months back, in November 2008, my Amma had left for her heavenly abode. I was trembling from within; the sudden void created by Abba's departure was too painful for me to bear. But then, that is life! I sat in my office chair, dismal and grim, unable to bring myself to terms with life. Then, suddenly I felt, no, I heard my Abba calling me. I looked around, as if in a trance. Again, I heard him saying to me, "Write ma! Write something!"

I sat there in a stupor, wondering about what I had just heard. I and my Abba had planned to write a book on 'Survey and Settlement in the Andaman & Nicobar Islands' during the next summer vacation. But before that, he had left us, to his eternal abode!

I wondered what I should write! Then, on that day I decided that I would write something for my Abba, about his life. But then I did not know what to write, I was like blindfolded and left in a jungle. I really did not know what to write about my Abba! But as they say, 'When you start doing things, you would also find a way!' And I started gathering my scattered memories about my parents and wrote it all down. I started talking to my family members, Abba's friends, colleagues, office workers, and relatives, and tried to collect every bit of information, and noted it all down. Then I got the 'Service Book' of my Abba from his office, and it contained a wealth of information, about his appointment, postings, transfers, Certificates of appreciation, salary, leave sanctioned etc., and I was happy as I could see an outline of my book! Soon I set to work and the rest is history!

It has been 15 years since my Abba's departure from this world, and I too had to take a number of breaks from my writing, since the book is related to my father's life. But thank God! Finally, I could accomplish the wish of my Abba!

Abba is the protagonist of this Memoir, and Amma, his wife is his shadow. This book is all about their life. In the Indian context, Abba means father, and Amma means mother. Hence it is the story of a father and a mother. Abba and Amma had undergone great struggles in their life and had also scaled great heights. They had revealed their love through their small deeds and had endured great sacrifices to mould the lives of their children!

I have named this book 'SAINTS ON EARTH' as I believe that parents are the living Saints on this Earth. Undoubtedly, all the parents, during their life time, undergo silent sufferings and sacrifices, for the sake of their children, just like Abba and Amma. But unfortunately, many children do not appreciate their parents' sufferings and sacrifices!

I feel that parents are the same at all ages, in every country and every community, and the emotions that parents feel for their children are also the same everywhere. Time and space do not change parents' love for their children!

This story is set up mostly in the Andaman and Nicobar Islands, where Abba and Amma had built their family and spent thirty-eight years of their life, serving the people there. Hence, I have added few chapters purely on the history of the Andaman and Nicobar Islands, and about the natives of the land, to enlighten the readers about the place.

This book is a tribute to my Abba M. Alphonse (Retd. DANICS) and my Amma A. Gnana Cyril, who had undergone great griefs in their life, physically and emotionally, but had always accepted life as it unfolded to them. This book is a memoir of my parents, from my observation, acuity, and understanding. It has nothing to do with the life of any family members or relatives, and they have naturally been added into the story line as they were a part of Abba's life. Having closely observed my parents crossing different stages of life, I have tried to express my appreciation for my parents, whom I had seen struggling and growing with age. But till their last breath, their love and concern for their children did not cease!

- Caroline Mathew

PART 1

GENESIS

Chapter - 1

HEARTBREAKING NEWS

It was a bright and sunny morning in Port Blair, the capital town of the Andaman and Nicobar Islands. The ocean was mirroring a clear blue sky and the waves were dancing to their own tunes. The islands on the horizon were glistening in shades of green, while the gentle breeze appeared to be singing a lullaby. The ferry boats were busy transporting people from one island to the other, and the whole scenario was mesmerising and enthralling!

It was 2nd September 2009, a holiday for 'Onam'[1], which is the state festival of Kerala, a southern Indian state. The festival was also celebrated with great festivity in Andamans, since many Keralites lived there. Onam is celebrated to commemorate the mythical King Mahabali, who is believed to visit his people, on the day of Thiruvonam. According to legends, Mahabali was a demon king and a devotee of Lord Vishnu. He was a righteous and charitable king and there was much prosperity and the state was at its glorious era. His people adored him and Mahabali's fame was growing which alarmed the Devas, who were afraid of losing their power. Hence, they begged Lord Vishnu to help them in bringing an end to Mahabali. To help the Devas, Lord Vishnu took his Vamana Avatar, as a brahmin boy, and visited Mahabali, who at that time was doing yagna for Lord Vishnu's grace. On seeing the poor Brahmin boy, Mahabali asked him what his desire was. The boy told the king that he needed three paces of land. When Mahabali granted the boy his wish, Vamana started growing in size and soon he became gigantic. With his first two steps, he covered the earth and the sky. Seeing that there was no more land left, Mahabali bowed before Vamana and offered his head on which Vamana placed his foot and pushed him down to Patala, the netherworld. But he granted a boon of permission to Mahabali to visit his people once every year.

It is believed that ever since, every year during Thiruvonam, in the month of Chingam, the people of Kerala eagerly await their beloved king, Mahabali. Onam is celebrated for 10 days and people hold grand processions with various traditional art including music, dance, carnival floats, decorated elephants, boat races, and traditional folk dances such as Thiruvathira, Kathakali, and Pulikali the tiger dance. Families make floral decorations called pookkalam in front of their houses to welcome King Mahabali. Onam Sadhya is prepared as the main food for the celebration which is a vegetarian meal comprising of many traditional dishes and is served on a banana leaf.

Since it was a holiday, Sheryl was leisurely deciding on the work to be carried out in the garden. For a working woman like her, a day's holiday was very precious, as the pending works of the household could be taken care of and she would be able to give some time to her plants as well. Watching the speeding boats in the blue ocean and enjoying the beautiful weather, she moved on to the terrace of her house, to check the plants in the pots. She found that the weeds had lavishly grown in the tubs, enjoying the water and manure provided to the potted plants.

'I have to fix it today', she thought to herself and moved on. Sheryl and her family lived in Port Blair, in the Andaman and Nicobar Islands, an archipelago of picturesque emerald green islands, where the weather is pleasant throughout the year. Her family had just returned a day before, from their trip to mainland India, and were settling down back into their routine life. She was feeling quite happy as she had met her father, 'Abba' in Chennai, and found him quite hale and healthy, living with his younger son Ethan. It was almost after a year of Amma's death, that she had found him, normal and cheerful, in his real self!

A few days ago, Sheryl's family had gone to Tamil Nadu, the southern state of India, for the admission of their son to college, when

Abba had called up to them over the phone. He asked about their return programme to Andamans. Then Abba informed them that he had arranged the 'House Warming' ceremony of Ethan's new house and that he wanted all his children to attend the function with their families. It was an order from Abba and his children did not have the courage to say 'No' to him.

Abba had four children, two sons and two daughters. The elder two of them Sheryl and Jason lived in Andaman and the younger two children, Meryl and Ethan lived in Tamil Nadu, India. As per Abba's instruction, all his children attended the House Warming Function of their youngest brother, with their families and Abba was happy about it.

The house warming function was held on 30th August in a gala manner in Chennai. The next day after the house warming function, Abba's three elder children returned to their places of work. Soon they all got engrossed in their duties. After reaching Port Blair, Sheryl tried to call Abba over the phone, but she was told by Ethan's wife that Abba was sleeping. Sheryl thought that she would call Abba again in the evening. When she called him in the evening, then Ethan picked up the phone and told her that Abba was sleeping. Sheryl was worried about Abba, but then she became busy with her work and could not talk to Abba on that day. The next day, on 1st September too she couldn't talk to her father due to her preoccupations. She had already planned in her mind that on 2nd September she would leisurely talk to Abba without any restriction of time as it was a holiday. But then she never knew that she would never be able to talk to her Abba again!

2nd September dawned and Sheryl was in a joyful holiday mood. Her family had been invited for lunch by one of their family friends to celebrate the festival of Onam and there was no worry about cooking. Though she had got up early in the morning, but she thought that it was too early to call Abba and so she decided to prepare breakfast and then do some weeding in the garden. By then Abba would also have had his breakfast, and then she could leisurely talk to him!

Sheryl went to the kitchen and prepared breakfast for her family. She had just finished her work, when she heard her husband calling out to her loudly. She rushed upstairs and found him talking over his mobile. He was talking to Jason, her brother in Port Blair. His expression showed that something had gone wrong. He had suddenly turned pale as if the entire blood of his body had been drained out. He was muttering some words 'How?', 'When?' and was faltering over the phone, unable to express himself clearly. Sheryl was shocked and she looked at her husband, trying to understand the matter. An unknown gut fear started getting hold on her when she heard the word 'Abba'. Then her husband gave the mobile to her and asked her to speak.

With trembling hands, Sheryl took the phone and put it to her ear. She heard her brother crying on the other end. All evil forebodings were storming her mind. Her brother said to her, 'Abba is no more!'

Sheryl couldn't believe her ears! She felt the whole world whirling around, round and round, and her husband got hold of her and made her to sit down. She felt so weak and helpless! She was still not able to believe the news that Abba was no more!

To clarify the matter, Sheryl called Ethan, her younger brother at Chennai, but he was crying on the other end. He could only say, "Abba is not waking up!"

It was already 9.30 in the morning and quite late for Abba to sleep like that! Abba was an early bird! Then she knew that Abba had gone on an eternal sleep from where there would be no waking up for the mortal body!

Sheryl felt devastated and started wailing. She cried her heart out, still unable to believe that her Abba was no more……! She sensed her body going limp. She felt orphaned and could feel a sudden void within her, a void that would never be filled again. Her husband was comforting her and trying to handle the situation. At the same time, he started calling up his friends to book their flight tickets to proceed to Chennai. But it was already late and they would not be able to get the

Chennai flight as the lone Indian Airlines flight had already departed. Luckily for them, the Calcutta flight was late and would be departing by 12.30 pm. Somehow, they managed to get tickets to Chennai via Calcutta. They would be able to reach home only by late evening, after eight!

The news of Abba's death had already spread out and friends had started pouring in to Sheryl and Jason's houses to condole Abba's death. After seeing off their friends, Sheryl and Jason reached the airport with their families, to board the flight. Each family member was with a heavy heart and pain could be clearly seen on their faces. After the security check, Abba's children silently waited for the announcements. They were all forlorn and had nothing to talk!

The Veer Savarkar International Airport at Port Blair was bubbling with life. Abba's children were trying to be in their normal selves. Some known friends were surprised at their sudden journey during that time of the year and wanted to know the reason. They had to tell them about Abba's demise. More condolences were pouring in! Finally, they boarded the flight. They all got into their seats, fastened the seat belts and waited for the flight to take off.

Sheryl was very sad. Though she was very attached to her mother, Amma, but she had a special place in her heart for Abba. The smiling air hostess did not cheer her. Her mind was soaring back and so many thoughts about Abba were rushing through her mind. Nine months ago, they were on a similar journey! Amma had passed away then and she did not know how she would face Abba and how she would comfort him. On reaching home she had found Abba petrified and very silent. He did not say anything but was seated in a chair at the Veranda, surrounded by relatives and family members.

Then with trembling heart, Sheryl had moved close to Abba, took his hand in hers and started crying. She did not find words to console Abba. Then Abba spoke to her in a dejected way and said, 'Everything is over!' He was not willing to speak more and sat there with his head hung in a depressed manner.

It was almost nine months after Amma's death and Abba never recovered from that shock! He and Amma were like two love birds, constantly moving around together. After Abba's retirement, they got ample time to be in each other's company, throughout the day. One could see them always chitchatting, playing cards, cooking, joking or sometimes arguing and fighting. But after Amma's death, Abba had become very lonely and he had almost concealed himself in a shell, very silent, even angry at Amma, for having left him to suffer alone in the world!

After nine months of Amma's death, now they were going to attend Abba's funeral! The family had lost its pillars. Sheryl felt the foundations of her parents' family shaking, ready to break apart any moment. She understood that the parents were the binding factors of their family, and after them, she did not know about its future!

Thinking about Abba, Sheryl clearly remembered Abba's words, spoken just two days ago, "I have accomplished all my work perfectly. Now I can leave this world peacefully."

Sheryl wondered if Abba had premonition of his death! Why did he say that he could leave the world peacefully! A strange fear was taking hold of her, and she did not know if she would be able to see her Abba in that state, DEAD!

Suddenly there was a jerk as the plane took off and within moments it was lost in the clouds!

Chapter - 2

ABBA'S CHILDHOOD

The air hostess started announcing the customary instructions, but Sheryl's mind was soaring with thoughts of Abba. Her eyes were swelling with tears, which she tried to wipe out now and then. Seated silently in her seat, she started recollecting all her memories of Abba. Memories that she had gathered while talking to Abba, and his well-wishers and relatives. She had heard so many stories from Abba about his childhood days and of his village. It was so dreadful to think that Abba was no more. It was just impossible to believe!

Abba was born on 12th April 1936, as per his school records, but Abba used to say that he had learnt from his mother that his actual date of birth was on 12th August 1936. But for the sake of his admission to school, his birth date had been changed to April. Abba was born in a small village called Mannarpuram, which is a hamlet in Nanguneri Block under Vijay Narayanam panchayat in Tirunelveli District of Tamil Nadu. The junction of the village is also called '*Vilakku*' and it has a Grotto of Our Lady of Velankanni and it is also known as Kebi. There were a few shops selling snacks and titbits at this junction. It is a well-known place, as four main roads cross the junction of the village connecting major cities. These roads cross from Nanguneri to Tisayanvilai and from Kanyakumari to Tiruchendur. Mannarpuram village is located at the intersection of this road and INS Kattabomman, the VLF-transmission facility of the Indian Navy, is located near this place. This junction is also a known destination as all the buses stop there and people from nearby villages going to those big cities usually boarded their bus from this junction.

It is said that in the earlier days, when Abba was a young boy, several deadly accidents had occurred at the village crossing and many people had also lost their lives in those accidents. During nights people dreaded to cross the junction and come to the village as memories of those people who had died in the accidents used to haunt the villagers. People of the village who used to go to distant towns for their work and who sometimes had to return late at night, claimed that they had seen strange shadows moving in the dark and narrated horrifying accounts that used to be terrifying. Many villagers also claimed that they had seen impressions of those people dead in the accidents, at night, near the village crossing. Those stories haunted everyone in the village and people dreaded to go to the village crossing at night and they avoided such situations.

Then the villagers decided to build a grotto at the junction in honour of Our Lady of Good Health, also known as Our Lady of Vailankanni. They collected money and also donated, and the grotto was finally built and blessed. Since then, no major accident has occurred and people are safe and happy.

Mannarpuram is a peaceful village with about 250 families living there in peace and harmony. Our Lady of Rosary Church stands tall at the back end of the village, protecting the whole village, while St. Mary's Higher Secondary School stands at the entrance of the village welcoming everyone.

Abba's parents had been living in this village for generations. Abba was the youngest son and the seventh child of his parents. They were four brothers and three sisters. When Abba was born, his two elder sisters had already been married and Abba's elder sisters' children were about Abba's age. When Abba was young, his all three elder brothers went to Ceylon[2], now known as Sri Lanka, in search of jobs. Later on, the eldest brother settled in Ceylon while the other two brothers returned to the village for good. Since Abba was the youngest child and as he was still in school pursuing his studies, he stayed in the village under the protection of his mother and father.

Abba's parents were simple village folks who were very well-to-do at the beginning of their life. They had farmland and fields and dozens of cows and cattle. But after Abba was born, the family conditions started deteriorating. Suddenly one day all the cows died due to some strange illness. Then, due to some family problems, they had to sell their cattle, land and farmland bit by bit for a survival, and in their later years, they had to live a life of poverty and had to be in search of daily work to fulfil their day-to-day needs.

Abba's mother was a pious woman and she had inculcated all good values and faith in her son. Abba's father was a renowned village physician and an expert in fixing broken bones. People from far and near villages used to throng to him for treatments related to their broken bones. Many a times, he would easily fix very critical issues related to their broken bones. Whenever he would find that any bone of his patient had not been fixed properly, he would re-open the broken part and fix it again. He also had a lot of knowledge of all the herbs and their medicinal values. He could also heal people of their diseases by his prayers!

Abba's father was also a great lover of dogs and always had pet dogs with him, particularly the 'Rajapalayam breed[3]' and sometimes he used to entertain himself by going for hunting with his dogs, and used to bring rabbits and partridges home.

Abba's father was a jolly good fellow and liked to enjoy life. He liked to eat and drink and would not bother much about his future. He knew the art of talking and had the flair to be funny and make others laugh. Whenever he would make money, he would spend it on eating and drinking and then the left-out money he used to bring home, to his wife, for the family needs.

There was a popular story about Abba's father that Abba often told his children, with a smile. Once Abba's father went to a hotel at the village junction and had idli[4] and vadai[5]. Since he did not have the money to pay the bill, he told the owner of the shop that he would give him a piece of his land instead, and the shop keeper was clever enough to get the documents signed. While giving away the piece of land, Abba's father did not think about his family or his children's future needs. Later on, when Abba's mother came to know about it, she could not do anything, but only lament. Such a man was Abba's father, a jolly good fellow and so Abba's mother had to see to every need of her family.

Abba had his elementary education at St. Mary's Elementary School in the village, that was managed by the sisters of St. Anne Convent. After his elementary education, Abba had to go to a neighbouring town called Ittamozhi, for his High School.

Abba was a very religious person and since his childhood, he used to help the village priest in the church as an assistant Catechist. For this work, he used to receive an incentive of five Anna per month. This money was a great blessing to Abba because it enabled him to use it for his school needs. Abba was a God-fearing person and was always ready to help the villagers in their needs. He knew all the prayers in Latin, Tamil and English, and he was of a great help to the village priest!

St. Mary's Convent School in the village provided free education to the children of the village. The school was set on its own campus with huge Neem trees all around. The area was very shady and cool even during summer due to those trees. The sisters of that convent school were very strict about the general discipline of their students, but at the same time, they were also very loving and caring. They used to get support from American Missionaries of their congregation and would receive things like milk powder, stationeries etc., for distributing to children of the village. The milk powder was very famous among the villagers, and it was a feast to the eyes when the trucks would arrive in the village, loaded with milk powder in gunny bags, sent from America. The sisters were very generous in distributing those things to the children as well as to the villagers.

Mother Eugene was the Superior of that Convent School and she was very affectionate to Abba. Abba was a fair, cute and chubby child and was very good in his studies. Mother Eugine often used to tell Abba, "One day you will become a great man doing some big job." Abba would simply smile at that time. The Mother always used to bless Abba abundantly. After all, Abba was her favourite student! After completing education in the village school, when Abba had to go to the high school in another town, it was under Mother Eugene's guidance.

The town school at Ittamozhi was about 9 to 10 kilometres from Mannarpuram village and Abba's mother was worried about the distance of the place, as the family couldn't afford to send the child on a bus!

But Abba used to say to his mother, "Ma, don't be anxious about me. I'm a big boy now and I can walk to school. You don't worry about me!"

Hiding all her pain, the hapless mother would smile at her son. But that was not the only problem. She was also worried about the food for her son. In the village school, they provided free meals to the children but in the town school, children had to carry their own lunch. Her son would have to leave for school at dawn and would be able to return only in the evening, after walking those nine kilometres. There was no money in the house and the poor mother did not know what food she would give to her beloved son!

The distance to the town school couldn't deter Abba's enthusiasm for studies. Abba's mother somehow managed to work in the neighbour's farms and fields and with whatever grain she got as wages, she would cook food for her son. She would leave the leftover cooked rice in water at night and the next morning she would give this food, 'Pazhaya Kanji'[6] with some palm jaggery as breakfast to Abba. She would also put some Kanji in a canister and wrap some jaggery in palm leaf and give it to her son to eat for the day. Abba used to carry whatever food his mother could provide, and never complained about the food, but was very understanding. When the bell would ring for recess in the school, Abba would pick up his canister and jaggery and take it to a far-off corner of the school premises and would silently eat the Kanji and the jaggery there, alone. He tried to be away from the other children, who used to bring classy tiffin boxes and fresh food!

"There would be more water and less rice in the Kanji," Abba used to say with a smile, and used to narrate this incident to his children a number of times, remembering his childhood hardships. But Abba never regretted those adversities. Instead, he was proud of those difficulties of life that had made him a strong man!

Abba was a brilliant student of his class, and carried on with his studies with great dedication. He always scored high marks. He had a beautiful handwriting and his teachers appreciated his intelligence. He was very good in Mathematics and English. His teachers and fellow students called him 'Pythagoras' due to his mathematical skills. Abba would leave home early in the morning and would return home only in the twilight of dusk, while his mother would be waiting for his arrival by the roadside, outside the village. Many times, his legs would ache and it would be swollen due to the long-distance walking, but he would never complain about it to his mother, lest she should weep. When his mother would give him food at night and would see his tiny feet swollen, she would be filled with deep sorrow. She would sit by his side throughout the night and apply oil and massage his legs. Abba's interest in getting education was such that he never took leave and the next day morning again he would rush out for his school with all zeal!

Time rolled on and days rolled into months and years. It was time for Abba's first public examination and there was no money at home to pay the examination fees! Abba did not know how to pay those two rupees for the exam fees. Moreover, he could not bother his mother for money as he knew about his family condition!

While walking to school, Abba had seen labourers working at the roadside, carrying stones, boulders and gravel, for the construction of roads. Abba enquired those men working there and came to know that the labourers got five Anna per day for working as labourers. He also decided to work at the construction site as a labourer and earn his exam fees. Abba thought that the place was away from his village and if he worked there, his parents would never come to know about it and he would also be able to earn his exam fee. Abba knew that if his mother would learn about his working on the roadside, she would be heart-broken and cry many tears!

So, Abba met the supervisor there and narrated his need to him. He pleaded to be allowed to work in order to earn his fees. The supervisor looked at Abba, who was just a little boy, and felt sorry for him and asked Abba whether his parents knew about it and Abba got scared. Abba told the supervisor the truth, about the need for money for his exam fees, and about his family conditions. He also requested that his parents should not know about it, or else they would feel very sad! The supervisor was a kind hearted man and was impressed by the young boy's tenacity, and told him that he could start working there from the very next day onwards.

Though the next day Abba told his mother that he was going to school, but he did not go to school, instead he went to work. In Abba's village all men folk, including the young boys, used to climb the palmyra tree, to collect the sap for making jaggery, but Abba did not know to climb the palmyra tree, and he had never worked as a physical labourer like the others boys. His mother had never allowed him to do any such work. At the roadside, Abba saw the other people at work and he too took a spade and started digging the soil. Since he had never worked with the spade before, he was finding it very difficult. His palms became red and the tender skin started tearing off with sores, but he kept working for his examination fees. He somehow managed to work, and the men and women working there sympathised with Abba as he was too young to work. The workers there told Abba that they would do the digging work, and he could carry the stones. They also felt proud of him as he was working to earn money for paying his examination fees! When Abba came home in the evening, both palms of his hands were fluffy with a lot of blisters. He did not show his hands to his mother as it would break her heart!

After working on the roadside for more than a week, Abba was able to earn the needed money and paid his exam fees! He was proud of himself, and felt like a man. Abba studied very hard and passed his SSLC Examination with flying colours. Then he joined for his pre-degree course at another school in Madurai. That school was run by the priests of the Catholic Church. Abba completed his first year with very good marks, but when he was in his final year of pre-degree classes, his mother fell seriously ill and money was needed for her treatment. Abba could not carry on with his studies due to financial crisis in the family. Though the priests in the school insisted Abba to continue with his studies and that they would arrange for a scholarship for him, but Abba was in dire need of money for his mother's treatment. So, he had to put an end to his studies!

Abba's mother's health was deteriorating day by day. Abba took his mother to the hospital in a nearby town, and the doctors there, after check-up told Abba that his mother was suffering from Tuberculosis and she needed total rest and good food apart from medicine. Abba was shattered. He decided to search for a job and shoulder the responsibility of his mother.

In spite of Abba being a very bright student, he could not get higher education, and this was an ache in his heart throughout his life. Later on, Abba used to tell his children and grandchildren this story, time and again about his ardent desire for higher education but there was no one to help him. The circumstances were such that Abba could not complete his education!

Chapter - 3

DESTINY BRINGS ABBA TO ANDAMANS

Abba was one of the first few persons of the village to have completed high school. Though Abba fervently desired to get higher education, but he couldn't even dream about it! At one point of time, Abba decided to join the Seminary and become a priest. He was already working as an Assistant Catechist at the Village church and also used to lead the church prayers. The village priest, nuns of the convent and all people of the village had high regard for Abba since he was so affectionate and helpful to everyone!

One day Abba spoke to the village priest about his willingness to join the Seminary, and the priest assured him that he would speak to the Rector there, and get him admission at the Seminary. The priest kept his words and within a month told Abba to get ready to join the Seminary. When Abba informed about it to his mother, she became very sad, but accepted it as God's will!

On the appointed day, Abba left home with the village priest, to join the Minor Seminary at Madurai. On the recommendations of the village priest, he was admitted to the Junior Seminary. Abba stayed in the Seminary for about six months. But then one day he received a letter from his village priest stating that his mother was very ill in the village and his mother wanted to see him.

Abba became very sad thinking about his mother. He wanted to go to the village to see her. Reflecting deeply about his situation, he decided that he would not continue at the seminary any further. He showed the village priest's letter to the Rector and informed him about his mother's condition and his inability to continue at the Seminary. Soon he got the required permission and Abba returned to his village to take care of his mother. Abba's mother was indeed very pleased to see her son back!

In the meantime, Abba's father had been taking care of his wife, and trying to provide for the family. But Abba wanted to somehow find a job to support his parents. He thought of going to Ceylon, to be with his elder brother there. But his two brothers who had returned to the village from Ceylon told Abba about the difficulties in finding a job there, and it would be quite impossible. Then Abba changed his mind and decided to try his luck in some other place.

The next option left with Abba was to find a job in the nearby towns and cities, at his own place. He went to many places, town to town, searching for a job, but couldn't find any suitable job. Then he decided to go to Madras[7] and try his luck there. But going to Madras needed money and that was what Abba did not have! He was in total confusion about his future. Everything appeared bleak and dark to him! Though his sisters and brothers were all married and settled in life, but they were not so well to do that they could support Abba financially!

Months were passing by and the burden in Abba's heart and mind was increasing day by day. Abba's mother noticed that Abba had started remaining forlorn and sad. He was usually a cheerful and talkative lad, but now, for many days, he had become silent and appeared to be gloomy and lost. His mother understood that her son was apprehensive about something. She wanted to know the reason for his worries but Abba did not share his problems with his mother, lest she should agonize. But one day, in utter desperation, Abba told his mother that if he could only go to Madras, he would find a job for himself and would take care of the family, but there was no money in the house to go to Madras!

When Abba's mother heard about her son's problem, she decided to arrange money for her son at any cost. First, she went to a few neighbours requesting to lend her some money and instead she would work for them in their fields, but they all were in the same living conditions. How could they help her! Then she thought about the gold earrings she had and decided to pawn her earrings and fetch money for her son. She removed her gold earrings and gave them to Abba telling him to sell it and get money. But Abba was reluctant to take the gold earrings as that was the only gold ornament his mother had!

But Abba's mother insisted and said, "Take this Ayya, once you get a job you can buy jewellery for me. Don't worry about me. God will take care of you!"

Earlier Abba's mother had a lot of jewellery but then when they had hard times, one by one all her jewellery had been sold. Then she had only her 'Paambadam[8]', dangling in her long ear lobes. It was an ancient traditional jewellery made of solid gold with wax filling.

Once Abba's third sister came to her mother's village. She was married in a nearby town called Tisayanvilai. Her family was well to do and they had their own bungalow and shops in the town. But when she saw the glittering gold dangling in her mother's ear lobes, she was fascinated. She told her mother that at her age she should not be feeling so proud, wearing that jewellery! Abba used to say that she could have directly asked her mother for the jewellery and her mother would have happily given it to her. But the daughter's words pierced the mother's heart! Abba's mother did not speak a word but removed the gold from her ears and handed it to her daughter. The daughter also accepted it cheerfully. Then only after two years, Abba's father could buy a small gold stud for her and that was the last gold ornament she had. Though Abba was a young child then, but he had witnessed that incident of gold earrings of his mother and in later life, he had told stories about it to his children!

Abba sold his mother's earrings and with that money he bought a ticket to Madras. Abba was just nineteen years old then and with a heavy heart he parted from his mother. He was leaving his mother and father and did not know when he would meet them again!

When Abba was boarding the bus, his mother and father were standing there by the roadside and his mother had tears in her eyes. Abba hugged his mother and father, and left his village with great sorrow in his heart and uncertainties about his future. After reaching Madras he visited various offices in search of a job. He went to many shops too. Days were passing and the money in his pocket was also dwindling.

Finally, Abba got a job as an accountant in a warehouse. He found a dwelling place in a poor neighbourhood as he could only afford that place. He was given some salary but that was not sufficient for Abba's room rent and food. He had to work till late at night and sometimes he was also told to help in loading the goods. It was a tough job for Abba. On many nights when Abba would return from his work, he would be too exhausted and even the teashops and eateries would have been closed. Then he won't be able to buy food for himself and so he would drink tap water from the roadside and go to sleep empty stomach. Months were passing and Abba couldn't send money to his mother. Life was not a pleasant journey for him and soon Abba started searching for some other job!

While Abba was making up his mind to find another job, one day he met a group of men who were also staying in the same lodging where Abba was put up. They were five men and were talking about their voyage by some ship. Abba went to them and asked about their whereabouts. They told Abba that they were from Madurai and that they were going to Andaman by ship. They saw that Abba was just a young boy and asked Abba about his work and his studies. Abba told them that he was working as an accountant in a warehouse and was searching for another job. He asked those men whether he would be able to find a job in Andamans!

After hearing Abba's story and learning about his education, those men were very sympathetic. They told Abba that if he went to Andaman, he would immediately get a job of a clerk. Abba was filled with high hopes and happiness. Those men also took Abba to the port and Abba purchased a ticket to Andamans.

Then in the same week along with those men Abba set sail to Andaman by the vessel 'M.V. Maharaja'. The ship took seven days to reach Port Blair. For the first five days, they were in the deep blue sea. The sea was very rough as strong winds blew with thundershowers.

On the sixth day, they could see some islands far away and they were all so green and beautiful. On the same day evening, the ship reached its destination, Port Blair. But since it was late evening, the ship could not berth and was anchored at the sea. Finally, on the seventh day, the pilot came and the ship was berthed at Chatham wharf and passengers were allowed to disembark. It was raining profusely when Abba set foot at Chatham, in Port Blair. It appeared as if God was showering His blessings on Abba with a welcome rain. Abba did not know what the future had in store for him in the Andaman group of Islands!

On 4th December 1956, Abba reached Port Blair and he hardly had few rupees left in his pocket. Abba had made some good friends during the voyage and one of them advised Abba to go to the Office of the Accounts Officer, Marine and Shipping Office. The man also accompanied Abba to show him the office and left Abba there. Abba went inside the office and met the officer there. He introduced himself and told the officer that he was looking for a job.

The officer was a good man and asked Abba about his education. Abba had brought his certificates with him, ready to show, and showed it to the officer. When the officer saw Abba's certificates and found that Abba could speak English, he was impressed and told Abba that he could join the Fisheries Department from the next day itself as a Clerk. He also saw Abba's luggage; a small trunk box and asked Abba about his lodgings. When Abba told him that he had just arrived that day by ship and was directly coming from the harbour, the officer showed sympathy. He called a peon and told him to make arrangements for Abba's lodging. Abba thanked the officer and came out of the room with the peon.

After coming out of the office, Abba thanked God for all the blessings showered on him. He was in a strange land, but he had got help and also had got a job. He thanked God again! On 5th December 1956, Abba joined the office of the Fisheries Department as a Lower Grade Clerk. Everything was going well and Abba's life had found its course.

Those days, the living conditions in Port Blair were very hard and difficult, but Abba was not bothered about it. He was very happy to have got a job. He was also highly impressed by the officer who had been so kind towards him and who had helped him, without knowing anything about him. He decided that he would put in his best efforts and do his duty with all dedication and loyalty and if possible, he too would try to help the needy. When Abba received his first salary of 55 rupees, his eyes were filled with tears. He kept fifteen rupees for himself and sent forty rupees to his mother by Money Order and felt very happy. He wanted that his mother's sorrows should be over forever! Thus, destiny brought Abba to Andamans!

Chapter - 4

ABBA'S MOTHER DEPARTS FROM THE WORLD

Abba was happy with his new job and Abba's officers were very pleased with his work. He could do excellent noting and drafting in the office files. He knew to typewrite and had passed the typewriting and shorthand test conducted by the Andaman and Nicobar Administration on 3-2-1959. Thus, he had also made himself eligible for the job. Soon after, his pay at the cadre of LGC was fixed at Rs. 116/- with effect from 1-7-1959. Abba was very happy!

As Abba was a bachelor, there was no constraint of time for him and he could work till late in the evening. He had clean habits and was very affectionate and sympathetic towards others, due to which he was in the good books of his officers.

Abba's mother and father were also happy in the village as Abba was regularly sending them Money Orders and letters. Time was moving at its own pace and more than two years had rolled by, since Abba had arrived in the Andamans. Abba's mother was constantly writing to him to come home, as she was worried about her son. She knew that her son must be facing hardships in his life, and it was true. She was much worried about Abba being alone in Andaman, and she wanted that Abba should get married and settle down in his family life.

Though Abba had made some good family friends and on occasions, they used to invite Abba for lunch, but regularly, Abba was finding it hard to manage his food. He started learning to cook and was managing his food by preparing some easy dishes. His neighbours were very kind and they used to help him in his needs. Apart from food, life was very difficult in the islands. There used to be torrential rain throughout the year, the houses were wooden with mud floor and there was no electricity. Due to rain and wildernesses, the place was infested with mosquitoes, ever ready to suck the blood and centipedes were in abundance, ready to sting. There were hardly few shops and hotels. There were no proper transportation and Abba was managing his life with all adversities. Moreover, one could not go to his hometown in the mainlands when needed as the steamers used to be voyaging only once in a month, and it used to take 6-7 days to reach the mainlands. Life was indeed very difficult! In spite of all the difficulties, Abba was contented, which was the most important ingredient for a happy life!

In March 1959, two years after Abba's had joined his office, he decided to go to his village to meet his parents, and he applied for a month's leave. Abba bought new clothes for his mother and father and sweets for his relatives. The day Abba reached his village, his mother was overjoyed and she embraced her son and wept with joy! It was celebration time in the family then. Abba's father used to bring fish or meat for his son, and would ask his wife to cook it for Abba. He was happy that his son had become so responsible and was taking care of his aged parents!

Abba's mother wanted to get her son married, and soon started her search for a bride for Abba. Her all-other children were married and settled in life, and though Abba was only 22 years old, she felt it was her duty to get her son married. But his mother did not know whom to contact or meet to find the bride! Her son was handsome, young, educated and was having a government job with a good salary and she wanted a suitable bride for her son who could be a real-life partner to him.

Then Abba's mother remembered Mother Eugene of St. Anne Convent who could help her. But a few years back she had been transferred to some other convent, and she was in some other district. But Abba's mother did not give up and decided to meet Mother Eugene at any cost. She persuaded Abba to find out about Mother Eugene and to inform her about the mother's whereabouts.

Finally, on her urging, Abba spoke to the nuns of St. Anne Convent of the village and found out that Mother Eugene was working in Tiruchirappalli as the Superior Head Sister of the convent. When Abba told this to his mother, she became very happy. Then, without wasting much time, she took her son to meet Mother Eugene in Trichy!

Mother Eugene was overjoyed to meet Abba. She was very happy to learn about Abba's job in Andaman and advised him to be honest in his work and help the poor and needy people whenever it would be possible in life. When she learnt that Abba was looking for a bride, she started thinking. She knew some families with good girls. After thinking for some time, she told Abba's mother that she knew a family of a widow mother, with two daughters and they lived in a nearby village called Pothankalanvilai. They were poor people and were not very well-to-do. The elder daughter was educated and was working as a craft and needlework teacher in a government school in Radhapuram and the younger daughter was still at school. The mother was a pious woman and she had given good education and values to her daughters. Mother Eugene thought that the elder daughter would make a good wife for Abba and also told that they were poor and Abba shouldn't expect any dowry or financial help from the family.

On hearing Mother Eugene's words, Abba said, "Mother, you know about us. Money is immaterial to me and you know that we have seen worst days!"

Thus satisfied, Mother Eugine gave Abba the address of the school where the girl was working and Abba went to Radhapuram to see the girl. When Abba saw the girl, he knew that she would be his wife. She was fair, slender, tall and had long black hair. But she was very shy and did not speak much.

After Abba approved the girl, he along with his mother and father formally went to see the girl in her house in Pothakalanvillai, which was a small hamlet in the Sathankulam block. The girl's house was a small hut with thatched roof, and mud walls, similar to Abba's house. The girl's mother had made arrangements for coffee and snacks for the occasion, according to her capacity. The family of the girl was also in a similar financial status like that of Abba's family and Abba did not bother much about that. Since Abba liked the girl, it was decided that Abba would go back to Andaman and the next year, in the month of May, he would return on leave and then the wedding would be held on 9th May 1960!

Abba's holidays were nearing its end, and his ship tickets had already been purchased. So, after deciding about the marriage and fixing the date for the wedding, Abba left for his place of work in the Andamans. This time he also took his elder brother with him. As his elder brother had not completed his schooling, Abba could not find a job for him. But his elder brother remained with Abba and took care of Abba's house and food and was a great help to Abba. He was an excellent cook and Abba was happy to have his brother with him. Days were rolling by and life was moving smoothly for Abba.

During the fall of that year, Abba got a telegram from his father stating that his mother was seriously ill and the telegram was received after a week. There was a ship voyaging between Port Blair and Madras once in a month, and the ship had already departed a few days ago and there would be no ship throughout that month. Abba was shocked and overwhelmed on receiving the telegram and wept bitterly. He did not know what to do. He had never felt so helpless and miserable in his life!

The next day Abba received another telegram stating that his mother had breathed her last! Abba was shattered. He could not even go to see his mother for the last time. The steamer would be available only during the next month and by then every ritual would have been over! He wept at his inability for not being able to attend his mother's funeral. The death of his mother was the greatest sorrow in Abba's life, and he felt that ache till the end of his life!

Abba loved his mother more than anyone else on this earth. He had just returned from his holiday trip and hence could not get leave again. Even if he managed to get leave, and he went to his village, he won't be able to attend his mother's funeral and his mother won't be there to receive him. The ship would be there only in the following month and would take almost 6-8 days to reach Madras and from there it would take another two days to reach his village. Abba was devastated! The following month he arranged for tickets and sent his elder brother back to the village by ship, to take care of his father and the family. He thought that the greatest sorrow in a person's life is when death parts you from your parents! For Abba the heartache was much painful as he couldn't attend his mother's last rites!

Chapter - 5

ABBA GETS MARRIED

The following year, in March Abba applied for leave and he was granted 79 days Earned Leave from 18-3-1960 to 28-6-1960. The date for his wedding had already been fixed by his mother and father and now he had to go for his wedding. When Abba went to his village, there was no cheer or enthusiasm in his heart, as his beloved mother was not there to receive him. On reaching the village, first of all, Abba visited his mother's grave in the village cemetery, lit candles and prayed for her departed soul, and wept bitterly. Though his mother was dead but till the last day of his life, Abba always felt his mother's presence with him in all his needs. Then, with a grief-stricken heart, he went to his house to carry on with his wedding work. Though Abba's father and elder brother were there with him, but he felt a void, an emptiness, that had been created by his mother and it was a great ache for Abba!

For his wedding, Abba had bought a beautiful deep purple Banaras Silk sari for his bride, and Amma had kept it safe till the end of her life, to be buried with her, after her death. The wedding was solemnized in a simple manner in the bride's village church at Pothankalaivilai. There was also an arrangement for a chariot and a music band. As per the custom, after the wedding, the bride and groom used to be taken in the chariot, for a ride through the village, with the music band marching ahead. But the maternal uncles of the bride were not very interested in that ritual and after the wedding, they took the bride and groom directly to the bride's home from the church.

Abba was not happy at that. He was a bit annoyed and also angry with the behaviour of the maternal uncles of his bride. He thought that he had not demanded anything from the bride's family and felt that they should have carried on with the basic rituals of the wedding. He felt offended by the behaviour his bride's relatives.

Abba waited for the rituals to be over and in the evening returned to his village, with his bride, father, brother and relatives. On reaching home, he made it very clear to his bride that he would take care of her mother and sister but would have nothing to do with her any other relatives, particularly her maternal uncles. Though his bride didn't say a word, but she listened to him silently, wondering what life would offer her in future. She did not know what to say to Abba!

In the evening, Abba had arranged for a fellowship meal for all the people of his village. The whole village had assembled to bless Abba and Amma. But Abba missed his mother very much. The only comfort for him was that his mother had seen his bride beforehand and she had fixed the date for his wedding!

Abba's father was very affectionate towards Abba and his bride. He used to help Amma in cooking fish curry. While Abba and Amma were in the village, they took good care of Abba's father. But Abba was feeling a void within himself, due to the absence of his mother. He didn't want to stay in the village any longer where his mother was not there. So, even before his holidays were over, Abba left for Andamans with Amma and his elder brother, leaving his father in the village!

Chapter - 6

ABBA'S WIFE: AMMA

Abba got a devoted wife in Amma, and there could be none like her on this earth. She was slim and tall and had long black hair. A God-fearing person was she who had great faith in God. She believed in the Word of God and tried to follow it throughout her life. She knew her duties as a wife, and tried to fulfil all her duties, devotedly. She was very simple in her behaviour, kind-hearted and a peace-loving person who had a lot of compassion for others. As a child, Amma had undergone much sorrows in her life. She was the elder daughter of her mother and had a younger sister who was eleven years younger to her.

Amma's mother was a widow and she had to toil hard to give a good life to her daughters. Her mother had no family support and had to bring up her two daughters on her own. She had a small house and had also acquired a small piece of farmland from her father. She used to work in other people's farms and fields reaping the harvest, sowing the seeds, planting the paddy seedlings, winnowing, grounding the grain, pounding the spice etc. Instead of her work, she used to be paid a measure of millets, rice or grain which she would bring home and cook for her daughters. Sometimes if some rich people were kind enough, they would give her some eatables that she would never eat but would carefully wrap in some paper or banana leaf and bring home for her daughters. Once in a blue moon, she would be able to provide rice to her children, otherwise their regular food used to be millets, ragi etc., the meals of the poor!

Amma's mother had undergone great struggles and sufferings throughout her life. When her daughter was born, and she was just an infant, her husband left the village, leaving her with her baby. He had gone to Ceylon in search of a job, as was the trend in those days with men of the village. He wanted to earn money and then return home to lead a happy life with his wife and daughter. He had been gone for three years and there was no news from him. He had never sent any money to his wife and child. Once some men folk of the village had returned from Ceylon and they told Amma's mother that her husband had joined the army there. All those years, when her husband had gone, Amma's mother somehow managed her life and that of her baby daughter, by working for other people, as she had no support from her family or relatives!

Then one day Amma's mother got news from the villagers that her husband had died in the war and the Government had published his name under the list of those people who had been killed in the war. The poor woman was devastated!

Since then, Amma's mother started wearing a blue sari, as was the custom of her village, a stigma of her widowhood. But then, she started receiving a pension of 25 rupees, given by the government for being the widow of a soldier. That money proved to be a great relief to her. She would save the money to buy some clothes and necessary things for her daughter's schooling. Her daughter was growing and she started sending her to school. Since Amma was good at her studies, her mother was happy!

One day when Amma was ten years old, her father came back from Ceylon, alive! It was a great surprise to Amma's mother. The man who had been considered to be dead for so many years had suddenly returned! After all, he had not died in the war. After her husband's return, Amma's mother changed her blue sari and started wearing coloured saris, and thought that all her sorrows were over and her husband would bring colours in her life and that of her daughter. She expected that her daughter would have a bright future as the child's father had returned!

But fate wanted to have it the other way. Soon Amma's mother was with child, and the next year she delivered her second daughter. Within months of the birth of the second child, her husband again wanted to go to Ceylon to try his luck in earning money. So, after giving another child to his wife, he was again gone to Ceylon, and Amma's mother couldn't stop him!

With all sorrows in her heart, Amma's mother had to undergo more hardships and troubles in her life. Hiding her pain, she once again wrapped the blue sari around her, as a mark of her widowhood and got geared to shoulder her responsibility of a mother of two daughters! The widow pension that she was receiving from the government all those years had been stopped for her by some well-wishers of her own family, after they intimated to the office about her husband's return. There were relatives only to give her more trouble and to mock at her situation. Not a soul came forward to give a helping hand. Now she had two daughters to take care of, without any monetary help from anyone!

Amma's mother was a very humble person. She could do strenuous labour, and continued working in other people's farms, and also continued the schooling of her elder daughter. When the daughter completed her schooling, the mother did not have money to send her to college. The sisters of the convent in Amma's village advised Amma's mother to send her for a training in needlework, craft and tailoring. They also told her that, in that way, she would also get a job soon and could support her family.

Somehow Amma's mother managed to admit her daughter to a Diploma Training course in needlework and tailoring. It was very difficult for Amma's mother to manage her training as no relative was kind enough to help her. She continued working in others' farms and fields and somehow managed her life and helped her daughter to complete her training.

Finally, Amma completed her training and soon she got a job in a government school in Radhapuram as a craft and needlework teacher. This was a great relief to the family. Amma's place of posting was far away from her village and she could not return to her home every day after work. So Amma had to find a rented room close to the school. But yes, she would return home during the weekends and spend her entire time with her mother and younger sister.

Amma had joined the job of a teacher and had hardly completed six months of work when the proposal for the wedding came from Abba. There was no money in the house and Amma's mother was worried. Amma wanted to work for some more years and support her family. She thought that if she could work for another three to four years, the family would become financially sound and she would also be able to give good education to her younger sister, who had started school and whom she loved so much! Amma didn't want to get married so soon!

'But a good proposal for a daughter never knocks at your door always', said the relatives and friends. The Sisters of the convent also advised Amma's mother to get her daughter married. Moreover, the groom had a government job and was not demanding any dowry. Amma's mother convinced Amma to agree for the wedding and Amma was an obedient daughter. Thus, Amma got wedded to Abba and came to live in Andamans!

Chapter - 7

ABBA AND AMMA BUILD THEIR FAMILY

After the wedding, in June 1960, Abba brought Amma to the Andaman and Nicobar Islands and Abba's elder brother had also accompanied them. Those days the Andaman and Nicobar Islands were in unbelievable wilderness and the population was scanty, with hardly forty to fifty thousand people living there!

After the Indian Independence, the Andaman and Nicobar Islands had developed into a melting pot of ethnic diversity as people from different states of the Indian mainland had come and settled here. When Amma came to Andaman, Abba was working in the Fisheries Department in Port Blair. Then they used to live in a rented house at Prem Nagar, in front of the Catholic Church. Those days the electricity used to be supplied for a few hours. The houses were all wooden, and Amma used to marvel at those wooden buildings. Port Blair was a wild place then with pouring rain throughout the year, infested with insects and poisonous creatures. The fireflies and moths were in abundance that used to storm into the houses at dusk!

Since it was an island, fish was plentiful in the place. As Abba was in the Fisheries Department, the fishermen used to bring big fish, weighing three to four kilos for Abba's family. Amma did not know how to clean the fish but then the fishermen used to clean the fish for her. Amma would then panic as she did not know how to cook fish. Her mother had never allowed her to do any household work in her house. She used to cry at her helplessness! But Abba's brother, who was staying with them, used to help Amma in cooking. This gave her great relief. He also taught Amma how to cook fish, chicken and other dishes with traditional flavours. Gradually Amma learnt to cook. On holidays and Sundays, Abba also used to help Amma in the kitchen. Since they were only three members, Amma would cook a portion of the fish for the family and distribute the rest to her neighbours!

Abba and Amma had a humble beginning in their life, and they lived with the same humbleness throughout their life. After Amma's wedding to Abba, life had taken a turn and indeed Amma had a good life. There was no dearth of domestic help at home and Amma did not have to fret about it much. After office Abba would come home and spend his entire time with Amma, planning for their new life. Abba became an active member of the 'Tamilzhar Sangam[9]' in Port Blair. It was an organization for promoting Tamil culture among the Tamil population of the islands and Abba used to actively participate in all its activities. There were also the Hindi Sahiya Kala Parishad, Andhra Association, Kerala Samajam and Kannada Sangha, to facilitate and promote the regional culture of those states among its people.

Abba knew the importance of education and when he found that the children of his neighbourhood were wasting their time by playing around, he started tuitions for them. Abba was a genius in teaching and he used to teach all subjects. This was a free service on his part and he saw to it that the students improved in their studies. There were a few Tamil families in the neighbourhood and Amma on her part found time to teach the neighbourhood women stitching and embroidery. All the neighbours respected Abba and Amma and whenever they confronted problems in life, they often sought their help and advice.

Amma was very happy with her life with Abba. There was no dearth of eatables in the house for Amma. Abba also took care of Amma's mother and sister by sending money orders to them as and when needed.

One day Amma felt sick and Abba became worried. He took her to the lone Gobind Ballabh Pant Hospital at Port Blair. After the check-up, the lady doctor there told Abba that Amma was with child. So Amma was expecting their first child and there was happiness in the air!

Abba was very happy and started taking care of Amma even more. They together started preparing to welcome the new member to their home. Days rolled by and just a week was left for Amma's delivery due date. That day, while Amma was mopping and cleaning the courtyard and the house floor, with mud mixed with cow dung, some insect bit Amma in the palm of her hand.

This was also an ancient practice in the village of Amma and she was trying to follow the same in Andaman too! According to that ancient custom, the hearth, the floor of the house and the courtyard used to be thoroughly cleaned and then it would be sprinkled with a thick slurry of cow dung mixed with water and mud, and it would be plastered evenly and allowed to dry. It was believed that when water mixed with cow-dung was sprinkled, it would remove pollutants and kill germs. Then the traditional 'Kolam'[10], was drawn at the entrance of the house using rice flour. Amma was trying to keep some of those traditions alive in her house. But she never knew that she would have to pay for it throughout her life and soon she would have to suffer a lot, and that was the fate destined for Amma!

Amma felt the pain of the insect bite but she did not take it seriously. Soon she felt some irritation and her hands started itching. Within moments her hands became red and it started swelling with sores. When the women of the neighbourhood saw it, they told Amma to leave the cleaning work as they would take care of it. So Amma left the work in the middle and washed her hands with plain water and waited for Abba to come from the office. In the meantime, Amma's entire body started itching and it also developed rashes. When Abba returned from the office, he was shocked to see Amma's condition. Amma's whole body had swollen with rashes and she was in a dreadful state. she was also in terrible pain and the pain flowed in the form of tears from her eyes, with sheer helplessness!

All the neighbours who had gathered there were sympathizing with Amma. They suggested various home remedies and Abba followed all those remedies, but there was no ease. It was already late evening and

Abba knew there would be no use going to the hospital as it would have been closed. The next day Abba took Amma to the hospital and doctors gave her some ointment and pills but Amma's condition became worse as the rashes had covered her entire body and some of them had swelled up into blisters causing severe pain.

Amma's condition did not improve. In the next few days, Amma had her labour, and was rushed to the hospital. She gave birth to a baby daughter but by then the blisters had spread to her entire body with suppurating sores and boils. Her condition was so critical that she could not even hold her baby in her arms. The baby that she had nourished in her womb for nine months now lay in the cradle, without the touch of its mother!

Amma shed tears of helplessness as all dreams about loving her baby had been shattered. She was not able to cuddle her baby or nurse her baby. When the baby would cry due to hunger, the milk in her breasts would swell and she would weep at her vulnerability. She lamented and cried and poured out all her sorrows to God. Abba was dismayed and felt helpless and desperate. He had to search for a nursing mother who would take care of the baby till Amma was alright, but he couldn't find any. Then the neighbours tried to feed the baby with cow milk but the baby vomited. Then they had to feed the baby with powdered milk and the infant was cursed to grow with a feeding bottle for months. It was a terrible time for Amma and Abba. It appeared as if all the sorrows of the world had fallen on them and they were unable to find a way to come out of it!

Abba tried to give all type of medication to Amma, but nothing helped! Day in and day out, Amma and Abba were in and out of the hospital. Then her medicines were shifted to homoeopathy, with a lot of restriction in food, but there was no improvement. Amma couldn't wear her clothes, eat with her hands or wear slippers. While walking she had to wrap clothes on her feet to walk. Abba took great care of Amma but then he also had to go to his office and felt very helpless!

After about a month, when Abba was unable to manage the situation, he decided to take Amma to her village at the mainland so that she could stay with her mother for a few months and get treatment there. He thought that maybe, climate change would do her good. But before going to the mainland, Abba and Amma got their daughter baptized in the Catholic church and named her Sheryl Malar, after Amma's mother and St. Theresa of Child Jesus, also known as Little Flower. Then Abba applied for leave for forty-five days and took Amma and the infant daughter to Amma's village in the mainland.

After Abba brought Amma to her mother's village, he stayed there for some days with Amma's mother and sister and took Amma to the nearby hospitals. But Amma's condition did not improve much. Before returning to Andaman, Abba found time to visit his father in his village and found that he had grown old and weak. In his old age there was no one to take care of him, and he was cooking and managing his life all by himself. Abba gave him some money and then, when the holidays were getting over, Abba returned to Andaman, leaving Amma and the child with her mother.

After Abba left, Amma's mother and sister took great care of Amma and the baby. They took Amma to various hospitals. Along with that, they also visited various churches, praying hard for Amma. First, they visited the church of St. Antony in Uvari[11]. It is a very ancient church, well known for miracles and healing. Legend says that about 450 years ago the crew of a Portuguese ship contracted cholera. During the desperate situation, the crew members surrendered themselves to the Almighty God! The ship was passing off Uvari, a coastal village in South India, when the ship's carpenters made a wooden statue of St. Antony of Padua. Surprisingly all the crew members were soon recovered. The ship was docked off the shore of this village and the crew installed the statue of St. Antony in a small hut in Uvari as a token of their gratitude to the saint for saving their lives. This church soon became very famous and people throng to it on Tuesdays! Amma's mother brought Amma to this church and stayed there for a week, fasting and praying for Amma.

In the morning, Amma's mother would prepare herbal medicines by grinding neem leaves and turmeric and apply it to Amma's sores and then bandage the sores with clothes. Then she would pack food for all and they all would visit the churches. Amma couldn't wear slippers then and she had to bandage her feet with clothes to avoid the dust and sand and heat while walking. Amma's sister or mother used to carry the baby and they used to go from church to church, remain in the church for 2-3 days, worshipping and praying to God to cure Amma and only then, they used to return to their village.

Days were rolling into months and Amma's mother and sister did not give up their efforts on Amma. They continued to take her to hospitals and churches, along with the baby. After about six months, the sores in Amma's body started drying up. It did not get completely cured, but it got housed in the palms of Amma's hands and her toes. Amma would not be able to eat food with her hand, and had to use spoons which she hated. It remained like eczema in her hands and toes for many years, almost till the end of her life. Abba was constantly sending Money Orders and also writing letters to Amma and was in contact with her through letters. He was happy to learn about the improvement in Amma's health. Later, after about eight months, when Amma had almost got cured, Abba decided to bring Amma and his daughter back to Andamans!

Chapter - 8

ABBA JOINS LAND AND REVENUE DEPARTMENT

Abba was an honest and committed worker, and after joining his office as a clerk, he worked very dedicatedly, to the full satisfaction of his officers. There would not be any pending files on Abba's table for the next day, and all appreciated him. He was very humble in nature and treated his subordinate staff with care and compassion. He used to deal with the general public coming to the office with great consideration. When Abba was in the Fisheries Department, an officer had come to Andaman on transfer from Delhi. Abba happened to work with him and he was much impressed by the efficiency of Abba's office work, his noting, drafting and dealings with the common folk.

Seeing his work expertise, the officer once told Abba, "You are such a good worker. I think you should not waste your talents in this department. Here you would always remain a clerk dealing with office files. I would advise you to join the Revenue and Settlement Department as there are a lot of avenues to get promotions and you would be able to reach greater heights there."

Abba was surprised that the officer had thought about him and his welfare. He took the advice of the officer seriously and within a few months applied for a posting in the Revenue Department. Soon, vide DC's Order No. 471 dated 17-8-1961, Abba was appointed as a Colonisation Assistant in the 'Revenue and Settlement Department' in the Andaman and Nicobar Administration. Abba was very happy and joined his new office as Colonisation Assistant on 22.8.1961. Abba scaled great heights in his new office and that officer was so correct!

After joining the Revenue and Settlement Department, Abba got to meet more people in his field of work. His job was tough as he had to visit all the inhabited islands in the Andaman and Nicobar, from Diglipur to Campbell Bay, for doing survey and settlement work. It used to be so difficult to reach those interior islands, but Abba was never disheartened. Facing all hardships, he visited all those islands, and he used to see the living conditions of the people living there, and the difficulties they were facing. He had also seen the life of the Nicobarese in the Nicobar group of islands during those days, leading their ancient life!

As a Colonisation Assistant, Abba's place of posting was in Mayabunder,[12] in Middle Andaman. Accordingly, Abba had joined his office. During 1962, Abba brought Amma and his baby daughter to Mayabunder.

Mayabunder is a very beautiful Island in the Middle Andaman having more than sixty villages. During the British era, the Karen[13] Tribes who are settled here, had been brought from Burma as cheap logging labour to work in those islands. After Indian independence, refugees from East Pakistan and Bangladesh were also settled there by the Andaman administration as per the Central Government's orders. The Mayabunder Island has beautiful beaches, mangrove fringes and creeks which are so beautiful, and breath-taking!

In those days the Mayabunder Island had to be reached only by ship and shipping service was very rare, hardly once in a week. But during the monsoon and rough weather, the shipping services used to be uncertain. For about ten months there used to be torrential rains. At Mayabunder, Abba was allotted a type-II quarter near the police Thana. He had to visit all the habited villages and nearby islands to do survey work and it was part of his duty. Abba had to walk all those miles in slush and mud to reach Bajota, Chainpur, Hanspuri, Basantipur, Rampur, Tugapur, Webi etc., as there were no roads to reach the habitations. Families lived in utter poverty in those distant settlements, facing great difficulties. There were also families from Jharkand and they were the Adivasi[14] people who had come during the British era as labourers to clear the forest land. There were also the families of settlers who had been brought under various schemes of the government.

Abba visited every household on the island as part of his duty and saw the problems faced by people living there. There were no roads, hardly any schools, no electricity and there used to be heavy rains throughout the year and the place used to be infested by mosquitoes, centipedes etc. Life was very miserable for the people in those settlements. Whatever help Abba could render to those people, Abba never hesitated, but helped them wholeheartedly. Whenever he would come across poor and illiterate people, he would become a guardian angel to them and used to help them in his own possible ways!

WEAVING DREAMS

Chapter - 9

ABBA AND AMMA'S FAMILY GROWS

While Abba and Amma were living in Mayabunder, during the year 1963, Amma delivered her second child. There were complications during the childbirth, as the baby was a breech baby, being born with the feet. Moreover, the umbilical cord of the child was wrapped around the baby's neck. The doctor and nurses were all apprehensive about the parturition. Abba kept on praying for the safe delivery of the child, and his special prayers to St. Antony were heard, and the child was born, a son. Abba and Amma were overjoyed and they named him Jason Anthony, after the saint and Amma's father. There were two daughters in Amma's family, and the arrival of a male child made the family very happy, and Amma and Abba celebrated the occasion with great joy.

Since Jason was a breech baby, it was believed by some people that he had healing powers in his feet, and if he would massage people with his feet, who were having severe pain or sprain in their body, they would get cured. Some people with severe pain, also used to come home to get cured!

Both Abba and Amma were happy with their small family. They had a daughter and a son. Amma used to be busy taking care of Abba and her children while Abba used to be very busy with his official work of survey and settlement. He had to visit every settlement in Mayabunder, and Diglipur[1] and all its villages. Between 1954 to 1961 many Malayalee families had been brought to the islands and settled in North and Middle Andaman. Abba knew all those families settled in Keralapuram and Ariel Bay and Betapur. During the survey work,

Abba used to visit all those houses and he used to be treated as a family member in those houses. The Diglipur Island had Bengali settlements as well and they were settled in Kalighat, Nabagram, Kishorinagar etc.

Without any transportation, it was unimaginable how Abba used to reach those settlements that lay in the interior jungles. Abba had to walk all those miles on foot accompanied by his office staff. But Abba never complained about the difficulties he faced in his work, instead he took it as a challenge and moved on with enthusiasm.

After a few months of Jason's birth, Amma was again with child and the same year Amma delivered her third child, a daughter and she was named Meryl Malar, after Abba's mother. All three children were born to Amma within a span of four years and it was becoming difficult for Amma to take care of all her three children!

In the meantime, Abba's third brother, who had accompanied Abba earlier, had got married in the village and he had brought his wife and children to Andamans. They were settled in Kadamtala Island and he had started a shop there. He also had invited his nephew, Abba's eldest sister's son to Kadamtala to work together. The duo uncle and nephew had borrowed an amount of money from local businessmen, and had set up their garment business, and it was doing well.

As Abba's brother's business was doing well, he had also bought some land and property there. But then he fell into the company of evil friends and took to drinking and gambling. This caused a lot of commotions in his family, but he did not bother about it. After getting intoxicated, he used to be insolent to his wife and the peace of the family was gradually disappearing!

It was a Diwali day, and the friends came to invite Abba's brother to celebrate the day with them. His wife tried to stop him, but he was the man of the house, and how could he listen to his wife! He did not stop. He went with his friends to celebrate the festival. They all had drinks and also sat down to play cards, and that day, he lost all his money, property and shop to gambling. The family that was so well to do had come to the roads overnight!

Abba's brother's family was shattered and they did not know how to solve the problem. The money lenders were pressing for the loans they had given and so Abba's nephew went to meet Abba in Mayabunder. He informed Abba about what had happened to his business, and about the huge loss in their business and that everything was lost overnight. He told Abba that the money lenders had given him an ultimatum for a fortnight, and they had to pay the money or else they would face serious consequences. He also told Abba that he wanted to return to his village and requested Abba for help.

Abba didn't know what to do. He didn't have money to give to his nephew. But he went with him to Kadamtala and assured the money-lenders that the loan was on him and he would pay it as soon as possible. Abba knew those people beforehand and they let Abba's nephew to go, as Abba had guaranteed the payments. So, Abba's nephew left for his village and from there he went to Bombay to find a job, leaving the burden of thousands of rupees loan on Abba! Abba somehow managed to pay off the loan in a few years! Abba and Amma used to muse on that incident now and then in their later life!

In November 1965 Abba received his transfer order to Port Blair and Abba and Amma were very happy. While in Mayabunder, Abba had already informed his co-workers and friends at Port Blair to arrange for a rented accommodation for his family, as it would take some time to get a government accommodation. Abba's friends had found a house for him near Gymkhana ground[2] at port Blair. The Gymkhana ground is a historic ground where Netaji Subhash Chandra Bose had hoisted the Tricolour on 30th December 1943, during his visit to the Andaman Islands, before Indian independence.

When Abba and Amma reached Port Blair, the rented house had already been cleaned and set by Abba's friends and it was ready to be occupied. It was late evening and darkness had spread around and hence Abba and Amma could not see the surroundings of the house. Abba and his family occupied the house with all their luggage. But in the morning when Amma opened the kitchen window, she was shocked to see the cemetery just behind the house. She was so frightened that she immediately closed the window. She informed Abba about the cemetery and started panicking about the place. She was very timid by nature and did not dare to look behind the house. She started pressurising Abba to find another rented house as she did not want to stay in that house. But those days, finding a rented house was a mammoth task, as there were not many houses in Port Blair to be let out on rent!

Abba told Amma that he would ask his friends to look for a new house but till they found another house, they had to stay there. Amma had to agree to it! For about a fortnight they stayed in the same house and all those days Amma kept all the windows shut and never came out of the house. Then, they shifted to a rented house in Biggy Lane, and Amma was happy. Sheryl was three years old and Abba admitted her to a nearby Nursery School.

After coming to Port Blair, Abba became busy with his office work, but on Sundays and holidays, he used to spend his time with his family. Sometimes Abba's work demanded him to make a tour of the other Islands and he had to be in some faraway places. Those days he would not be able to return home as there were not many means of transports. He had to travel on the trucks carrying logs or stay in those places and would be able to return only on the next day. On such days Amma would remain indoors and would never come out of the house.

Once Amma fell ill and Abba did not know how to handle the situation. He had to take Amma to the hospital and also take care of his three children. He bought idly for the whole family from a nearby hotel 'Kerala Bhawan'. But Sheryl alone ate away the entire lot of idly. Abba just laughed, and again went to the hotel to buy more idly. Later on, this was a favourite story of Abba which he used to tell his children as how Sheryl had gobbled all the idly alone.

Abba's nature of work demanded him to go to interior islands, and he was also receiving official orders to do survey of particular islands, and submit the reports in a time bound manner. Abba had to comply with those orders. Amma could not speak Hindi, which was a setback with her and without knowing the language, she used to be confined inside the house, with the children. Abba was worried about it. He therefore decided to shift Amma and his children to his native village, as it would allow him to concentrate on his work. When he told Amma about it, she like an obedient wife, agreed.

Abba was thinking that if Amma and his children would stay in the village, they would also learn the culture of his village. At the same time, he would be able to work freely, without any worries. Abba applied for leave and during the month of May of the same year, he took Amma and his children to his village. Abba's father was very happy to see Abba and his family. Thus, Amma came to stay in Abba's village with her three children and the year was 1965!

Chapter - 10

ABBA'S VILLAGE

When Abba decided to send Amma and his children to the village, he was happy thinking that his children would also receive education in the same village school where he had got his elementary education, and he was happy!

Abba's village 'Mannarpuram' is a very ancient and typical Catholic village and Our Lady of Rosary Church with the tall steeple stands at the North end. All the houses with thatched roof and mud walls, were in four different lanes. Except for the families of the washerman, hair dresser and cobbler, all were strong Catholics. All the 250 families living in the village were related to each other in some way or the other!

The day dawned in the village with the ringing of the church bell which was followed by the records playing devotional songs. Soon all the villagers would rush out of their houses to assemble in the village church, where they would recite the 'Angelus'[3] and offer their morning prayers, thanking the Almighty for the new day. After the prayers, people would go to their houses and then to the farmlands to carry on their daily work. At noon time and again in the evening the church bells would ring for the prayers. In the evening, all the villagers, including the people who had returned from their farms and fields after the day's hard labour, would assemble in the church to offer their thanks and prayers to God Almighty. There would be the old people, the middle-aged, the youth and Children, and the entire village, and no one dared to miss the church prayers! After the prayers, all the people would assemble in the church yard, according to their age groups, and they could be seen chatting, laughing and having fun. They would discuss their day-to-day work and even discuss politics and cinema, while the little ones could be seen playing around.

As the night would deepen, gradually the villagers would start returning to their homes for supper and rest, but many old men would come back with their mats or blankets to sleep in the church yard. During summer, even the women and children would come to sleep in front of the church. The soil of the village was sandy and there was sufficient space in the church yard for everyone; the sand being so soothing for the people to lie down and rest after the day's hard work!

Most of the men of the village used to go to extract the juice from Palmyra palm to make Karupatti[4] or palm jaggery. Palmyra palm, *'Borassus Pannei'* is also the official tree of Tamil Nadu. This tree had many uses and it occupied an important place in the village life. When the tree is cut down, its hard wood is used as timber for making posts, beams or for domestic purposes. Almost every part of the tree is used. The hollow stem of the tree is used as water pipes. The leaves are used for making hand fans, mats, baskets, hats, and umbrellas; and they also made a good thatch.

Making Karuppati from the sap of Palmyra palm was a cottage industry of the village. When the palm trees would start flowering, men would climb the trees in the mornings and evenings, slash the inflorescence stalk from its top and attach small earthen pots to it so that the sap oozing from the flower stalk, drop by drop, would get collected in those pots. The pots used to be coated with slaked lime to ensure that the sap does not get fermented. The extraction of sap from the inflorescence is called tapping.

In the farmland, both in the morning and evening, men would climb the palmyra trees and collect the sap from the pots. This unfermented juice is a great summer drink; people call it padaneer. The palm leaves would be woven to form small cups to drink the sap. People used to make small sheds in their farmland with a hearth for making karupatti. Here, by early morning the menfolk would bring the collected palm sap from trees and the women folk would boil the sap of palm in big iron cauldrons for four to five hours till it turned golden brown and formed a thick syrup. When the sap would boil and start thickening, they would add grounded castor seed powder and cook it till it became very thick. The aroma of the syrup could be smelt in the air throughout the farmland. Then the women would pour the thick syrup into cleaned coconut shells that would be spread on the sand bed and let it cool for the rest of the day. The next day, they would delicately bring the solid jaggery out of those shells, by wetting the holes at the bottom in the coconut shells, and spread it on mats to let it dry in the sun. In the next few days, the palm jaggery would become solid and would be ready to be sold in the market. The whole process would be so interesting to watch! Sometimes special Karupatti would be made by adding dry ginger, nuts etc. for special occasions.

The villagers used to grow various crops in their farmland as per the season. The cultivation included growing paddy, pulses, millets, ground nuts, sweet potatoes, sugar canes etc. After the harvest of sweet potatoes, villagers could be seen sitting around a bon-fire, in their farmland, roasting those potatoes in the fire, telling stories and enjoying it. It all used to be great fun!

There were numerous Odai-trees, the *Prosopis juliflora*, those thorny trees that grew abundantly around the village and in the empty lands. These trees would be cut down by the villagers and used for firewood. The villagers would graze their cattle in those areas and the goats could be seen climbing those thorny bushes to eat the leaves. Some people used to grow those trees in their own land and made money by selling it for fire wood.

The women folk of the village did a number of works which provided them with an additional income. Traders used to come from big cities and bring different type of raw materials for the people of the village and they could work with those raw materials and give them the finished goods, and those men would come to collect it after a fortnight and pay them according to their work. This included weaving threads from cotton, making fishing nets, making beedi from tobacco leaves, weaving baskets, making lace, removing tamarind seeds from the pods etc. Those raw materials brought used to be related to the seasonal work, and even school going children used to make money by working in their free time!

The village school was run by the sisters of St. Anne congregation. The village Priest was a prominent figure and he had the right to check the wrong practices in people's lives. During festival seasons, the village would appear to be pulsating, decorated with flowers and festoons. It would look so colourful with all those celebrations and traditional rituals held there.

The village church festival of Our Lady of Rosary used to be celebrated in the month of September, for ten days, after the harvesting of crops. All the neighbouring chain of villages had their schedule of celebrating their village church festivals and it used to be celebrated one village after the other. People also attended the festivals of the neighbouring villages and enjoyed it.

The festival used to be inaugurated by hoisting the church flag by the village priest. Colourful kiosks would be set up and merchants from other cities would put up their stalls with attractive merchandise. There would be several petty shops for selling food items and sweets and savouries. All the stalls would be decorated beautifully with colourful festoons. The bangle and ribbon stalls with rainbow colour bangles were the special attraction for girls and used to be always crowded. Small children would love to throng at the sweetmeat stalls and toy stalls. Then there would be stalls selling sarees, dress materials etc. There would be various games like the giant wheel, merry-go-round, shooting the balloon etc., attracting everyone. So much cheer and happiness could be seen on every face during the festival season!

Young girls in their colourful long skirts and strings of jasmine in their hair, could be seen floating around like pretty butterflies. Those girls in half saris moving around, laughing and talking, were a feast to all eyes. Then there used to be cultural programmes in the evenings every day!

In the evenings, the women folk could be seen dancing 'Kummi'[5] the traditional dance. The woman singing and dancing in circles, carrying with tender paddy plants on their heads, sprouted in pots for the occasion, they would dance round and round in their colourful attires. The women glittering in their colourful Pattu sarees and decked with jasmine flowers would dance in circles, clapping their hands and nodding their heads. The fragrance of the flowers would fill the air and it would all be so enthralling and mesmerizing! There would also be special prayer services held every day in the church and the whole village would be assembled there!

On the last day of the festival, the chariot would be taken out with the statue of mother Mary, fully decked with flowers and lights, with all the villagers following, reciting their prayers and singing hymns. Then there would be the grand feast with chicken and mutton cooked in every household and the aroma of the traditional cuisine would fill the air. Relatives and friends would make their annual trip to the village during the festival season. Even those people who had settled in other cities or countries, or who worked in other parts of the country would make it a point to visit their village during that season and share their joy with their families.

Abba always wanted to visit his village during the festival season with his family as he would be able to meet all his family members, relatives and friends. But due to his office work and preoccupation with children's studies, he and Amma could hardly visit the village during the festival season. When he would be in Andaman, he and Amma would talk about all their memories of the festival held in the village. If someone came to Andaman from the village and visited Abba's house, it used to be such a happy moment for Abba and Amma and what a wealth of news they would gather from them about the people and relatives of their village! The news used to be about the children who had left the village in search of jobs, about those families where marriages had been celebrated for their children, about babies born in families, of girls who had attained puberty, etc. Oh! So much news they had to know about their village and for so many days they used to be munching that news! Many times, it appeared as if Abba was physically living in the Andamans, but his heart and soul were always in his land, in his village Mannarpuram!

Chapter - 11

ABBA UNDERGOES REVENUE INSPECTOR TRAINING

In May 1965, Abba brought Amma and his children to his village. Abba admitted his daughter Sheryl to class 1, in St. Mary's School in the village. Abba was very happy that his daughter was admitted to the same school where he had once got his education!

In Andaman, in his office, Abba was told by his superior officers that he had to undergo a Training for Revenue Inspector soon, and only then he would be eligible for a promotion in his career and that the training period was for nine months. There was a Training School for Revenue Inspectors in Gwalior, Madhya Pradesh. Abba had some leave to his credit and after talking to his senior officers, Abba applied for leave. Also, for that reason, for undergoing his training, Abba had to leave Amma and children in the village. Soon as per DC's order no:15 dated 23-10-1967, Gwalior was fixed as temporary Headquarters for Abba.

Abba visited his village on a short leave and after staying there for a few days he left for Gwalior, and joined his training at the Training School of Revenue Inspectors. But before leaving the village, Abba instructed Amma to take good care of the children and to bring them up with good values!

In the village, Abba had not constructed any house of his own. Abba's father had a small hut, made of mud walls and a thatched roof. But then except one or two stone houses, all the houses in the village were huts, made of mud walls and thatched roofs!

Early in the morning, women folk would be seen cleaning the mud floor and courtyard and decorating the entrance of their houses with a traditional 'Kolam-rangoli.

There were only two rooms in the house of Abba's father, with two wooden cots woven with coir, and grass mats and pillows for sleeping, and there was a room for cooking. Amma was not happy with the facilities in the village. In Andaman, her children were habituated to tables, chairs, beds, mattresses etc. But now in the village house, there was no washroom or water tap in the house. There was no electricity and studies had to be done under oil lamps. But Amma accepted the village life as a challenge. She used to get her daughter Sheryl ready in the morning and send her to school regularly. In the evening, after her daughter returned from the school, Amma used to teach her at home.

After Amma came to live in the village, her mother and sister used to visit Amma and her children in the village and that used to be happy time for the family. Abba's two elder sisters and one elder brother also lived in the village with their families but they all used to be busy with their own life. Amma maintained a good relationship with all the relatives. They always used to come to Amma for getting some or other help in the form of money or food. They had learnt that Amma was a very kind-hearted person and she would never deny them the help they needed. Abba's father was a constant support to Amma. He used to bring fish and poultry for Amma to cook and also helped Amma in cooking and taking care of the children. He used to bring special sweets for his grandson Jason, whom he loved the most!

When Abba was undergoing training in the RI's Training School at Gwalior, he made arrangements in the office to send money orders to Amma every month from his salary. Abba himself used to get a small amount of the salary and the major portion of the salary was sent to Amma so that she could take good care of the children and Abba's father.

It would be a happy time at home when Amma would receive the Money Orders. Abba's sisters would be extra caring then. They would insist that Amma went to the market with them. There was only one petty shop in the village in those days selling the basic supplies needed for daily life such as some groceries, salt, chillies, onions, pulses etc. During some urgent need, people used to purchase the provisions from that shop.

The Friday Market known as '*Chandhai*'[6] used to be put up in the nearby town of 'Tisayanvilai' and every family from Mannarpuram village used to go to that market on Fridays to purchase their weekly provisions. Fridays used to be like a festive day for all families in the village as one or other person from each family used to go to the Friday Market. The well-off ones would go in buses, some people would go by bullock carts and others would walk those eight kilometres, buy their weekly provisions and then return to their village carrying their bags and baskets.

The Friday market in Tisayanvilai was a wonderful place for selling and buying all the necessary things needed for life. It was set up in a very large area of a few acres. There would be huge crowd jostling in the market as people from many nearby villages would be flocking there to purchase their provisions. Anything that was required for the household could be bought in that market. There would be stalls for vegetables, eggs, fish, dry fish, fruits, poultry, mutton, rice, pulses, spices, eatables, clothes, slippers, nuts, earthenware, utensils etc. There would be separate enclosures for trading poultry birds, livestock, cows, oxen, etc. Every stall owner would be calling out loudly to the people to visit his stall and how his provisions were cheaper and of better quality than the other stalls. Hundreds of stalls of particular merchandise would be set in lines, selling the produce!

The market was a gala place with a bedlam of noise. The crowd consisted of rustic, common people from all the nearby villages carrying 10-50 rupees in their pockets or bags which was big money then. Most people did not wear chappals or shoes, as it was considered a luxury. Many farmers would take their farm produce to the market and barter it for other things they needed for their household.

Amma never went to the Friday Market or to any other shop. She would give money to her sisters-in-law to buy provisions for her. They would bargain and buy the goods, saving a few annas. When they would return home, they would tell Amma about their bargains and finally how the shopkeeper came down and sold his goods to them at their rates. They would also tell Amma that with the saved money they had bought something for their own family. Then account for every penny spent in the market would be given and Amma would tell them, 'No need for the accounts,' and they used to be very happy!

In the village, houses did not have washrooms. People had to go out in the local woods for attending to the nature calls. People did not use toothpaste but all people used '*umikari*'[7] for cleaning the teeth, that was made from rice husk. The husk of paddy is filled in earthen pots and burning charcoal is placed in the rice husk in the pot and slowly the entire husk would be burnt in the smoke fire. Then the burnt charcoal known as 'Umikari' is mixed with salt and used for cleaning teeth. It would make the teeth pearly white.

For bathing, people had to go to the village well. Those well-to-do ones who had pump sets in their garden or farmland, used to go to the pump set for bathing. There were two wells in the village. The first well was at the entrance of the village and the water in that well was a bit saline. The other well was behind the church and its water was sweet. People would take bath and wash their clothes in the first well and the second well was purely used for collecting drinking water.

Three families of the village, the washerman, hairdresser and cobbler were not allowed to draw water from the well directly. The family members of those three families could be seen standing near the well with their pitchers or pails, to collect water, and then somebody or other would feel pity for them and help them by drawing water for them and fill their containers. Then they would return home. Untouchability was silently being practiced in the village!

The village well was a place for all types of gossips and discussions. It would be crowded with women during day time and they would carry their pail, soaps, turmeric etc. needed for bathing. Men seldom came for a bath during that time and they had their own time in the early morning or late in the evening after returning from their fields. Women and young girls would cover their bodies by tying their skirts from under the arms, around the body and then take bath. They would wash their clothes and then would gracefully take a bath talking, laughing and enjoying all the time. Elderly women would sit on the raised stone ledges of the well and the youngsters would draw water for them. The air would be filled with the fragrance of soaps and *shikakai*[8]. After the bath would be over, the women would rub raw turmeric on the stones and make a paste of it and then apply it on their faces, arms and feet. Thus, after about one or two hours, they would return home, all glowing with the turmeric and their long hair left loose, dripping water!

Several other customs and rituals were also followed in the village. One such custom was the celebration when a girl attained puberty. When the girl would have her first menstruation, she would be segregated from the house and made to sit in a corner of a room! The well-off ones could afford a room for the girl but the not-so-well-off ones had to be satisfied by sparing a corner in a room of their house for the girl. They would also build a small enclosure for her with palm leaves behind the house, where she would be bathed. On the seventh day, she would be bathed with turmeric water, and decorated with sandalwood paste and flowers. Her maternal uncles would give her a new sari and flowers and she would have to wear them. Then fully decorated as a new bride, she would be seated on a raised platform or a chair and women from the family and neighbourhood would sing blessing songs for the young maiden. Her family, relatives and friends would pray for her bright future and also bring gifts for her. Mike sets and loudspeakers would blare out film songs as a part of the celebration. Then a fellowship meal would be arranged as per the family pocket could afford.

Abba did not like those customs and rituals. He used to say that such ceremonies were held to announce to the world that their daughter was ready for marriage so that eligible grooms may come forward to seek her hand. Abba was also dead against untouchability, and believed in the equality of all human beings. The washerman's house was close by and whenever the family members would come to collect soiled clothes for washing, Abba would invite them into the house and offer them sweets and coffee. Though they would accept the sweets and coffee offered by Abba, but they would never enter the house, and would be happy to sit on the veranda!

Abba's second brother was living in the village with his wife and they did not have children. People of the village believed that Abba's second sister-in-law had magical powers. She could be seen praying in the middle of the night and making strange noises. Abba's brother had taken seriously ill and was confined to bed for many months. He was suffering from tuberculosis and the medicines were not doing any good to him. One day Abba's brother passed away in the night. On hearing the news, all the villagers gathered to mourn his death. Amma also went with her three children to mourn the death of her elder brother-in-law. His lifeless body lay on a cot with candles lit on all sides. A wooden cross was kept by his head and his wife was crying bitterly. Relatives were coming and going, sympathizing with the deceased's wife.

In the morning, the mourners came for '*Oppari*'[9] or mourning. They were special people hired for the occasion. Whenever someone died, those people would be hired to wail and cry as per the custom. The mourning used to go on in a sing-song way as the mourners would sing about the life of the deceased, his achievements, family, life etc., one after the other. Those people who came for oppari were beating their breasts and wailing loudly, mourning in a singsong way about the life of Abba's brother. It was a very sad sight. Amma and all the villagers were crying. Then the village priest arrived and after the prayers, the body was shifted into a coffin and taken for burial to the village cemetery, which was close by.

After the burial, when the villagers returned, a pail of water was brought and poured on the deceased's wife, i.e., Abba's sister-in-law, by the village women and a blue sari was wrapped around her as a mark of her widowhood. Since that day the blue sari never parted from her. It was the custom of the village for widows to wear a blue sari. Amma was a bit afraid of that sister-in-law of Abba. She always used to remain aloof and irritated, for trivial matters she would blast up and quarrel with people, and then the quarrel used to become vulgar by throwing sand on each other and abusing with foul words. Abba used to be sympathetic towards his sister-in-law saying that she had a lonely life, and would often help her with money, but Amma used to maintain some distance from her.

Life was slowly moving in the village for Amma and the next year when Sheryl had gone to class III, she admitted her son Jason to class I, in the village school.

At Gwalior Abba's nine-month training got over. Abba had been an active candidate during his training period and the officers at the Training School were very happy with Abba. He passed the RI's Training successfully and he was awarded a Certificate by the DLR, Settlement Commission, Gwalior, Madhya Pradesh.

After his training got over, Abba went back to Andaman and joined his office. As financially he was not very sound, so he could not go to his village and meet his family. But yes, he was sending the major share of his salary to Amma in the village!

As per Abba's decision Amma was staying in the village with her children, but she was not very happy with the village life. She had lived in the Andamans for a few years and had seen the life of people there. She observed that in the village most of the youngsters were not ambitious about their life and future. Though they were talented but there was no one to guide them and they simply wasted their time and life. Amma was apprehensive about her children and their future. Abba's sisters' families were staying nearby but Amma always found herself lonely and secluded.

Sheryl was in her third standard and Amma was worried about her future. She knew the importance of the father in the children's life. She felt that her children should also be with their father and only then they would develop their potentials and grow properly.

After completing his training of Revenue Inspector, Abba joined his duty at the office of the Tahsildar, South Andaman. Amma wrote to Abba about her fears and her concerns of the future of her children and that she wanted to return to Andamans. Abba too was finding it difficult to manage his life without Amma. There were not many hotels or restaurants there and his nature of work did not give him much time to cook or do other works at home. Finally, after about two and a half years, Abba decided to bring Amma and the children back to Andaman from his village.

After a few months Amma received a letter from Abba stating that he would come home in September. Everyone was happy at that news. The children were eagerly awaiting Abba's arrival as he would bring them new clothes and sweets!

In the meantime, there was a talk going around in the village about Abba's third sister, who was married to a man in Tisayanvilai town. That man's first wife had died and he had a daughter from his first wife. Abba's that sister was the second wife to her husband, and she had four children. They were rich and had their double-storied building, printing press, shops and other businesses as well. Abba was very attached to that sister of his. There was some rumour in the village that the sister's husband had been arrested by the police for doing some illegal work. But what was the illegal work, it was not very clear, and people in the village were speaking many stories about him! Amma didn't know much about those stories but Abba's other two sisters who were in the village, used to tell Amma about the rumours they had heard about their younger sister's husband. Amma was not very happy about the news. She eagerly waited for Abba's arrival. Amidst all those commotions, one day Abba arrived in the village!

Chapter - 12

ABBA IS ARRESTED

When Abba arrived in the village, Amma, the children and Abba's sisters and relatives were all very happy and excited. The happiness could be seen on all their faces. They thronged to see Abba and the small hut seemed exploding with people. Abba was seated on a cot and everyone had to ask so many questions to Abba. It was about his life in the Andamans, the place, his journey by ship etc. Abba was trying to answer them one by one with a smile. While Abba was sitting and chatting with Amma and his relatives, suddenly some children came running from the street and told everyone that a police jeep had entered the village. It was so surprising for everyone as recently no crime had been reported in the village, then why should the police jeep enter the village!

After some time, the police jeep's siren could be heard and on seeing the crowd, the jeep stopped in front of Abba's house. The people who were assembled there started rushing out to know what had happened. A police officer stepped down from the jeep and started asking for 'Abba'. Abba came out of the house and wanted to know what the matter was!

But the officer said to Abba, "You are under arrest as we have orders to arrest you. Come with us to the station."

The words of the officer were like a thunderbolt for everyone standing there and Abba was shaken. It was hardly two hours that he had entered his village and he had not even changed his clothes! Abba tried to talk and convince the police personals but they insisted on their orders. So, Abba had to follow the orders. They didn't handcuff Abba but took him in the police jeep. While Abba was being taken by the police, Amma and the children were in tears. Abba comforted them and said to Amma, "Don't worry! I have not done any wrong and I would be back soon. Take care of the children."

The news of Abba's arrest spread like wild fire and people from other streets also started rushing out. Soon the whole village was out there and they saw Abba being taken away by the police. Nobody could understand the situation as Abba had just arrived in the village. Amma was distressed. She did not know how to help Abba. The happiness that Abba's family experienced a few hours ago had all vanished and the whole household was sunk in gloom. The condition in the house was so depressing that, no one had food that night!

The next day Amma's mother and sister came to see Amma from their village. The news of Abba's arrest had reached their village too and they had come to support Amma in her moment of grief. Amma was crying throughout and she could not tell her mother the reason for Abba's arrest. She herself did not know why Abba had been arrested!

The next day, by late evening, Abba returned to his village. He had been set free from the police station after a thorough interrogation. Abba's brother-in-law, who had been arrested by the police, had told Abba's name during the enquiry. Abba told Amma that the interrogation went on for about six hours and he could convince the police about his innocence only by showing the ship ticket and train tickets that were still in his pocket and that was sufficient proof that he had just arrived from Andamans. Moreover, his Identity Card issued by his office proved him to be a government servant. So, the authorities could find that Abba had nothing to do with the case and was innocent. So, they released Abba.

Abba told Amma that from the police station, he directly went to meet his sister's family in the town as he wanted to know their future plans about the case and also to console them and support them in their time of sorrow. He wanted to check on the possibilities of bringing his brother-in-law out of that desperate situation. So, he was late in reaching his village. Abba told Amma that his sister's family was so traumatized that any word could not console them. But on seeing Abba they felt hope. He bought food for them and made them to eat, as they had not eaten for two days!

When Abba came home, he was much worried for his brother-in-law who was in prison. The man had printed currency notes in his printing press! He had been caught with proof. His printing press with all the equipments used for printing notes were all seized and sealed. His other shops and property too had been apprehended by the authorities. A lot of money was needed to fight his case and to bring him out on bail.

The next day again Abba went to meet his sister's family in the town and found them in deep sorrow. His sister told Abba that they needed money and for that they were ready to sell their house, shops, land and property and would shift to a rented house. But it was not possible then, as the entire property had been sealed and confiscated and that they needed money. She wanted Abba to help her financially and bring them out of the situation.

But the problem with Abba was that he didn't have money to help his sister. For the next many days, every day he shuttled between his village and the town. He met a number of lawyers and tried to help solve his sister's problem and to bring his brother-in-law, out on bail. He went to many people for help but all his efforts were in vain!

Amma saw the desperate condition of Abba and felt helpless. Then one day Abba inquired Amma if her mother had any land in the village. Amma confided that her mother had a piece of farmland in her name, given to her by her father. Abba requested Amma to sell that land and help his sister's husband. In return, Abba promised that he would take care of all future necessities and endeavours of Amma's mother and sister. Abba also told Amma that once his sister's problem would be solved, they would return the money as well.

Amma's mother had come to see Amma and was in the village then. Amma being a very kind-hearted person, spoke to her mother, and told her about Abba's brother-in-law's case, and also told her about Abba's request. Amma's mother could not see her son-in-law in distress and she assured Amma that she would sell her farmland and help Abba.

Amma's mother did not wait for a second thought, but soon went to her village and sold her farmland. Whatever money she received from that sale, she brought and handed it over to Abba in full.

Abba was grateful to Amma's mother for her timely help. He was very happy and went to town, and gave the money to his sister to pay the lawyer. Then, within a week, Abba's brother-in-law was released on bail but his case went on for many years. Abba's sister kept telling Abba that soon she would pay back the money. After a few years, Abba's sister and her family sold all their property and migrated to Madras, where they purchased a plot and built a house there.

Abba had got a month's leave and more than twenty days were over in running up and down to the town for his brother-in-law's case. Once his sister's problems were solved, Abba turned his attention to Amma and the children. In a quiet moment, Amma told Abba that she wanted to return with him to Andaman. Finally, Abba decided to take Amma and the children back to Port Blair. He made arrangements for their ship tickets and took his family back to Andaman and the year was 1968!

Chapter - 13

ABBA PROMOTED AS REVENUE INSPECTOR

When Abba went to his village, he had already received his promotion order as Revenue Inspector. He was also allotted a government accommodation at Goal Ghar in Port Blair. It was a two-room apartment in the first floor, with a kitchen, washroom, small balcony, and an attic for the store. It was in a newly built colony of government quarters and all the apartments were occupied by government servants. When Abba and his family occupied the Goal Ghar quarters, there was no electricity connection, but Abba and Amma did not consider it a problem as they knew that within 3-4 months the quarter would be electrified.

The Goal Ghar colony was a hub of diverse culture and it was occupied by people from different states of India and was cosmopolitan in nature. The people spoke Hindi, Malayalam, Bengali, Tamil, Punjabi, Telugu etc. according to their mother tongue and followed different religions. But Hindi was the language for communication and people spoke to each other in Hindi. But Amma and Abba's children did not know Hindi. Abba insisted that his children should go out to play with other children of the colony so that they would soon learn to speak the language.

Abba admitted his children to Carmel School. It was an English medium school, that had recently been established and was run by the Nuns of Apostolic Carmel. Sheryl was admitted in third standard and Jason in first. In the village school, the medium of instruction was

Tamil but here the medium of instruction was English and Hindi was the second language. Amma would help the children in English but she did not know Hindi. Abba advised Amma to start learning the basic Hindi alphabets along with Jason, who was in class 1, and soon she too would be able to read and write Hindi. Abba was right as Amma soon learnt to read the basic alphabets in Hindi but she would never speak Hindi. In the evening when Abba would return from office, he used to teach his children Hindi and helped them in their studies!

Abba had set certain rules for the family. After children return from school, they should wash up and have meals and take some rest. Then in the evening they could go to play with friends for about two hours. When it would be dusk, children should return home, wash up and light the lamps and incense at the altar and then they should start studying. Before having dinner, the whole family would sit around the altar and recite the evening prayers and the rosary.

The Goal Ghar colony had many school-going children and in the evenings and on holidays they all used to play together. They used to play all sorts of games or they would simply run around the colony, chasing each other. Sometimes movies would be screened at the colony by the Field and Publicity Department and that used to be a gala time for all. The officials of the Publicity Department would start their work of arranging the projectors, setting up the screen etc., and the entire neighbourhood would be gathered there and wait patiently for the sun to set, and the movie would be screened.

The children would usually sit with their friends, the elders would sit in the company of elders, while the small babies used to be with their mothers. The movies usually screened were *'Kabuliwalah'*, *'Do Ankhein, Barah Hath'*, *'Bawarchi'*,*'Shaheed'* etc. Most people used to shed tears on seeing the movie *'Shaheed'* with the three patriots being taken to the gallows for execution singing the patriotic tune *'Aye watan, aye waten, humko teri kasam...'* After the movie would be over all would go home for dinner. Amma would not understand the movies much and later she would ask her children about the story line and they used to happily tell Amma about it. After all, they had learnt to speak Hindi!

Abba loved plants and he got a few potted plants for the balcony of his apartment. There were roses, fire in the bush, crotons etc., occupying the entire veranda. Since Abba would be late from the office, he assigned duties of watering the plants to Amma and the children.

Sheryl loved to water the plants. After waking up in the morning, the first thing she used to do was to go to see the plants and check whether any new leaf or bud had sprouted out. She loved to watch the morning dews on the flowers and leaves of the plants and would be seen sitting among the plants, enjoying it, till Amma would call out to her to get ready for the school.

Abba's mother had passed away many years ago but Abba always felt the presence of his mother in his life. He used to tell Amma and the children, "My mother is my guardian angel. She often comes to me in my dreams and she appears like an angel, with huge wings!"

One night while all were in deep sleep, Abba started making strange noises as if he was being suffocated or strangled by the throat. Amma got up and she tried to shake Abba to wake him from his slumber. Even the children got up. Abba was moaning in his sleep and uttering something which was not clear. Maybe he had a nightmare! Finally, when Abba woke up, he was sweating profusely. Amma gave him water to drink, and after drinking the water Abba told Amma,

"I had a dream and I saw my mother in the dream. She came like an angel with large wings and protected me from some danger. She did not tell anything about the impending danger, but she told me not to worry about anything as she would protect me. She wiped my tears, kissed me on my forehead and she flew away."

While narrating his dream, Abba became very emotional and started sobbing like a child. Amma and the children were shocked to listen to Abba's narration. The next day Amma was much worried thinking about Abba's dream. When Abba left for his office Amma told him to be very careful. While Abba was moving out of the house, one of

Abba's colleagues arrived on a motorbike. He invited Abba to get on to the bike as he was also going to the same office. Abba did not know to ride a cycle or a scooter. During his childhood days he had tried to learn cycling but after falling down two or three times and getting hurt, he had given it up for good. Abba accepted the offer of his friend and went with him to the office, on his motorbike.

In the evening when Abba came home from his office he was not in his usual cheerful self. He appeared to be very tired and in great tension. He told Amma that in the morning while he left for the office on his colleague's motorbike, they met with an accident. It had rained the previous night and the roads were slippery. Water was still clogged here and there on the roads. After crossing Bengali club, Abba's friend told Abba to buy a 'paan'[10] for him. He dropped Abba near a petty shop and moved ahead to park the motorbike. Abba had just arrived at the shop when the accident occurred. A live electric wire had snapped due to the strong gale of the previous night and it was lying on the side of the road. Abba's friend did not see the wire and rode over it. The wire got wound in the motorbike tyre and threw the bike and its rider some meters off the road. The rider got fractures on the leg and also had severe injuries. Abba and others hurried to the spot and the victim was rushed to the hospital. Abba had narrowly escaped the accident by a few seconds!

Abba thought that his narrow escape from the accident was because of his mother's prayers. His mother had warned him about some danger and she had also protected him like a guardian angel. When Amma heard the whole narration from Abba, she became much worried, but she also breathed peace thinking that the danger had passed off. But another disaster was lurking around, which nobody knew!

It was a Saturday. The quarter where Abba and Amma were living had four apartments, two on the ground floor and two on the first floor. Abba and his next-door neighbour, Mr. Nair lived on the first floor with their families. Mr. Nair was working in an office while his wife was a teacher. They had two children. The elder daughter was studying in class ninth while their younger son was studying in class four. Abba and Amma were very close to the Nair family as Amma could communicate with them in Tamil while they would speak to her in Malayalam and both families were able to understand each other.

Mr. Nair was working in the Public Work Department and on Friday he had to go on a field visit to an interior part of the South Andaman Island, and it was an official duty outside Port Blair. Since there were not many buses, Mr. Nair had to travel on a truck carrying logs. He was supposed to be back on Saturday. Saturday dawned and Abba got the news of an accident. The truck in which Mr. Nair had travelled, had met with an accident and Mr. Nair had died on the spot. On Saturday his body was bought home. It was a very sad day for the entire colony. The death of Mr. Nair was like the death of a family member and the whole colony mourned his death!

Abba was very sad. After the funeral was over, he told Amma, "That was my death. I should have died. But my mother's prayers saved me and my death had been diverted to the next door." Amma could not say anything. She thought that maybe it was that danger that Abba's mother had cautioned Abba in the dream and she had also protected him!

Abba was the only salaried person in his house and financially he was not very sound. There was no other source of income for the house. He had to run the family, take care of Amma's mother and her sister. Abba's father had also to be taken care of and Abba had to send money orders to him as well. It was a tough job for Amma to manage the household. Moreover, the children were going to a convent school and the fee was to be paid. The fee was Rs. 10 per month for one child and since Abba's two children were studying in the school, Abba had to pay fees for both. But later when Meryl started school, then Abba had to pay fees only for two children and fee concession was given to the third child. Somehow Abba and Amma were managing their life and were happy!

Abba was a voracious reader and buying books and reading them was a passion for Abba. He would buy a lot of periodicals and magazines for Amma and the children to read such as- Chanda Mama,

Wisdom, Rani, Ananda Vikadan, Kalki, Thuqlak, Readers Digest etc. There would be Tamil books and magazines for Amma and English books for the children. The day the magazines would arrive, all would be seen fighting to get a hand on them first, but Amma would find time to read the books only after finishing her household chores. In the evenings after completing their school assignments, the children would read the storybooks and magazines. Sometimes Abba used to purchase several other books from Readers Digest in English on various topics. He would read those books and share his knowledge gained from those books with his family!

Sundays, used to be special days! After returning from church, all would have breakfast. Then the children had to clean their school bags, fountain pens and even polish their shoes. It became a regular practice of the house till children finished their schooling. Then Abba would give oil bath to all three children, and Amma would prepare special lunch. After lunch the whole family could be seen reading books according to their tastes, or playing some indoor games such as ludo, chess, rummy etc. Sometimes, Abba used to take his family to the Cinema Halls, whenever Tamil cinema used to be screened. There were two Cinema Halls, Mountbatten Talkies and The Light House Cinema. During later years one more talkie came up in Dairy Farm and whenever Tamil movies would be screened, Abba and his family used to go to watch the movies!

Abba was a very kind-hearted man. He was very generous to people who came to him for help. Though he would not have money, but whatever help was possible from his side and he could afford, he used to help out. Once he took a fad to become a Homeopathic doctor. He also did a Diploma course in Homeopathy and bought medicines. He even purchased a number of books on homeopathy and started reading it day and night. A table was also set apart in the bedroom for keeping the medicines. There were numerous tiny bottles with powder and tiny balls of medicine in them, and the children used to be so curious about them! Sometimes Abba used to give them a few tiny balls from those bottles of homeopathy medicine that used to be sweet. But he would strictly advise his children not to touch those medicines, and they never did!

Soon Abba started treating people with the homeopathic medicine. People started coming to him for minor health issues such as cough, cold, fever, stomach problems etc., in the evenings and on holidays. Abba would listen to the problems of his patients very patiently and then used to prepare the medicines for them. He never took money from anyone as the patients who came to him were mostly acquaintances or friends and it was his hobby to help them!

Abba had got a good hand in treating people. Maybe he had got that ability from his father. Abba's treatments went on for more than six months and it was claiming an amount of his monthly budget. Amma was unable to say anything to Abba as he was the bread winner. Abba also slowly understood that his children were growing and his salary was not sufficient for the family itself, leave alone social service. So, when the medicines got over, he did not order for more medicine and Abba had to give up his hobby as it was too expensive!

While staying in the Goal Ghar quarter, there was not much money at home. There was no iron box in the house to iron the clothes. Amma would wash the school uniforms and then after drying them, she would neatly fold them and keep them under the pillows or the mattress of the bed. The next day when the children would wear the uniforms for school, they would look neat and tidy!

Goal Ghar quarters also saw Abba developing some ill habits that remained with him till his last. In the Survey and Settlement Department, Abba's friends used to insist Abba, to take drinks with them during office parties and social gatherings. In the beginning, Abba used to refuse those offers and didn't like to take drinks. But later on, as the friends pressurised and insisted him, so for the sake of giving company, Abba started obliging them. Those parties at the beginning used to be just once in a blue moon. But later on, it became as frequent as once in a month. As months rolled, Abba started bringing liquor bottle home and on weekends and on holidays he started having drinks. Amma was not happy about it. She never wanted Abba to fall a victim to the drinking habit, which she considered to be the root cause of all evils!

One day Abba told Amma that he had a party at the office and so he would be late. Amma was worried. She knew those office parties. It was evening and then night but Abba did not return. Amma gave dinner to the children and she put them to bed. She usually never ate before Abba and on that day too she did not have her dinner, and waited for Abba. As the time passed, her anger started rising at her own helplessness. Seconds were ticking into minutes and then into hours, but Abba did not return. In her anger, Amma decided to take the drink to find out what was so good about it! She took out the liquor bottle that Abba had kept in his cupboard and poured a glass full, and gulped it down. Then she sat there crying and waiting for Abba to return. She had taken the drink neat, without mixing any water, and soon felt intoxicated. In her intoxication, she also fell asleep and did not know when Abba returned. It was about midnight when Abba came back from the party. He knocked at the door and kept banging, but no one opened the door for him. The neighbours heard Abba banging on the door and they opened their door. Abba went into their house and through the balcony of their house, Abba entered the balcony of his apartment and finally came inside the house. It was good that Amma had left the balcony door open. After entering the house, Abba found Amma lying asleep on the floor, in the front room. He tried to wake Amma but she was so intoxicated due to the liquor that she slept like dead, and Abba left her to sleep!

The next morning when Amma woke up, Abba told her that the party at the office went on till late and he could not come out. He was angry at Amma for having taken liquor as it could damage her, and Amma could only smile helplessly. This story became a folklore in the family which Abba used to tell his children to tease Amma now and then!

Chapter - 14

ABBA'S FATHER SURPRISES EVERYONE!

Life was going on smoothly in a routine manner for Abba and Amma at Goal Ghar quarters. The Children were working hard in their English medium school and Abba and Amma were constantly helping them.

One fine day after sending the children to school, Amma went to the kitchen to prepare lunch. She had just entered the kitchen when she heard a knock at the door. Amma was alone at home, as Abba had also left for his office. She was reluctant to open the door as she did not know who would be there at the door!

On many such occasions, whenever Amma used to be alone at home and the door-bell would ring, she would never open the door. She had bad experiences of people talking to her in Hindi and she could never reply to them. They would ask her questions and she would not know how to answer them. During such situations, she used to be so embarrassed. Then if someone would ask the questions in Tamil, she would breathe peace. Later, when Abba would return from office, she would narrate those incidents to Abba. Listening to Amma's hitches, Abba would laugh and tell her to try to speak in Hindi as only then she would be able to learn the language. But Amma never learnt to speak the language, though she could understand it!

Standing near the door, Amma was deciding whether she should open the door or not, when she heard her name being called out. She was so surprised as it was Abba's father's voice. Amma was thinking as how it was possible, as Abba's father was in his village. She again heard the door banging and her name being called loudly, and she finally opened the door.

Amma was amazed to see Abba's father standing at the door, with a bag in his hand. He was in his traditional white dhoti, loose shirt and a towel on his shoulder. His grey walrus moustache covered his mouth and cheeks and he appeared tired and worn out. Amma took the bag from her father-in-law's hands and led him in. She made him comfortable, gave him hot water for a bath, then gave him breakfast and asked him to rest. Abba would be arriving from his office only in the evening and there was no means to inform Abba about his father's arrival. So Amma waited patiently for Abba to return.

In the evening when the children returned from school, they were surprised to see their grandfather at home. They knew him from the village, and were overjoyed to see him and troubled him with all their questions. In the evening, when Abba arrived home from the office, he was very surprised to see his father at home! Abba couldn't believe his eyes! He was so happy to see his father! Abba's father was about seventy-five years old and could not walk properly. Due to his old age, he couldn't control his walking, and could not walk steadily. Sometimes, he would stumble and fall or he would start running due to nerve problems. His ardent desire to see his son's place of work had brought him to Andamans!

Abba's father told Abba that he came to Madras and asked some people about the ship's sailing programme to Andaman. Then he managed to reach the port and bought a ticket to Port Blair. At the port, he met some people who knew Tamil and they told him that they were also going to Andamans. When he enquired about Abba to those men, they told him that they knew Abba. While on the ship, those men took good care of Abba's father. When the ship reached Port Blair, they arranged a taxi for him and told the driver to take him to Goal Ghar. The driver was a kind man and he brought Abba's father to Goal Ghar quarters, enquired about Abba's apartment, located the quarter and brought him home. Abba's father was not able to climb the stairs of the apartment as it was too steep. But somehow, he crawled and managed to climb it and reached his son's house on the first floor. Such was the determination of the old father!

In the evening it was celebration time for all at home as Abba's father had come from the village. Special dishes were prepared and the whole family enjoyed their supper together. The children hung around their grandfather who was willing to tell them hundreds of stories. Even when the children were in the village, he used to regularly tell them stories! He continued those threads and told stories of kings and queens, fairies and bandits and war. There were so many stories in his head and the children were amazed at his stories. Whenever the children would find their grandfather free, they would climb onto his lap and pester him to tell stories. He too never got tired of telling stories of treasure hunts, warriors and monsters. Amma used to scold the children to allow their grandfather some rest but the grandfather would set her aside and always enjoyed the frolics of his grandchildren!

After coming to Port Blair, Abba's father's health improved a lot as Abba and Amma took very good care of him and were very careful in giving him a good diet at proper time. He was a pure non-vegetarian and Abba arranged for eggs, chicken, meat and all varieties of sea food for his father. At night Abba would give his father a peg or two of whiskey and that cheered the old man!

Abba took his father to the Catholic Church and in and around Port Blair along with his family. After staying with Abba for about six months, one day Abba's father told Abba that he wanted to go back to his village. Abba tried to convince him to stay back for a few more months and when the school would close for summer vacation, all could go to the village together. Abba was worried that in the village there was no one to take care of his father or give him food on time. But Abba's father did not agree to it and so Abba had to give in.

Abba bought new dresses for his father, gave him money and sent him back to Madras by ship with a family friend who was also going to his hometown. Thus, Abba's father returned to his village, well-satisfied that his son was leading a happy and respectful life in Andamans. What else do parents need from their children!

After his father's departure, Abba always talked about his father who had only visited a few nearby villages and towns and who by his sheer courage, will power and determination, had reached Andamans all by himself, at the age of 75, to see his son's workplace. Abba was very proud of his father!

Just a few months had passed after Abba's father had returned, when Amma's younger sister, *Chithi*[11] came to Andaman from the village to live with Amma and her family. She had completed her pre-degree course and there was not enough money at home to send her to university.

After *Chithi* had completed her studies, she wanted to become a nun. She told about it to her mother, but her mother did not agree to her wish. *Chithi* was not happy about it and told her mother that she did not want to stay at home and that she wanted to stay in the convent. Her mother thought that she was irritated and unhappy and once her anger would pass off, she would return home, and so she allowed her to go to the convent. So *Chithi* went to the convent and told the sisters there about her desire. They were happy and allowed her to stay in the convent. Then *Chithi* became a *Novice*[12] there, and spent her time in prayers. When it was time for her to take her first wows, the sisters in the convent informed Amma's mother about it, and Amma's mother was totally shocked to learn about Chithi going to take her first vows, as she was unaware about those developments!

Amma's mother wrote a letter to Amma about her younger daughter who had joined the novitiate, and requested Amma to write to the Superior of the convent expressing her unwillingness about Chithi becoming a nun. Accordingly, Amma wrote a letter to the Sister Superior stating about her mother's concern and to send Chithi back home. She also wrote about Chithi having 'Sleepwalking' disorders since her childhood!

Chithi used to have sleepwalking disorder. When she was young, sometimes, she used to walk in her sleep. At night, she used to get up and start walking and sometimes would even go out of the house. Once she sleepwalked and was found walking around a well near the house, when her mother had found her on time and saved her life!

The sisters at the convent received the letter sent by Amma, and they decided to send Chithi back home. On that day after midnight, the nuns went to Chithi's room with a torch light. When they flashed the torchlight on Chithi's face, she got up, and thinking that it had dawned, took her toothbrush and toothpaste and went to the washroom to freshen up.

The sisters at the convent took that as an excuse and sent Chithi back home. Now Chithi was very depressed and was not at all happy at home. So Amma's mother had written a letter to Amma asking if she could send her younger daughter to Andaman, to be with her. Amma told about her mother's request to Abba and he too agreed to the idea. Then Abba sent money for Chithi's journey and also arranged for the ship tickets and for her safe arrival at Port Blair. When Chithi came to Port Blair, it was again a happy time for the children. She brought lots of homemade sweets, all prepared at home by Amma's mother!

Chithi was fair and pretty and looked like a film actress. She had long curly hair and spoke softly. She loved reading books and reading novels was her addiction. Whenever she would be reading novels, she would forget everything else. When Abba would bring the weekly magazines and story books, she would be the first person to grab them and read. She would help the children with their homework, and play indoor games with them. Chithi loved cooking and trying new dishes was her hobby. She was indeed a great help to Amma!

Chapter - 15

ABBA REJECTS JOB OFFER FOR AMMA

It was the year 1969, and by late December people started talking about the appearance of a new comet. The news was spreading like wild fire and on radios as well as in the newspapers, the news was published and people had nothing else to talk. The comet was named 'Comet Bennett' after its finder and by mid-January 1970 the comet became visible to the naked eyes!

The comet had a long tail and it could be clearly seen in the pre-dawn skies. People had many religious beliefs attached to the comet. Many people even thought that the comet would bring ill luck in their lives. To avoid it, people started chanting their prayers in the early morning hours and they could be seen offering water and flowers to the comet. Some people would blow the conch and ring bells and chant mantras. Each one behaved as per his own belief and a lot of activities could be seen early in the morning in Goal Ghar colony, with the appearance of comet Bennett.

Abba educated his children about comets and told them that comets are heavenly objects moving in space and are made up of dust, ice and gases. When far away from the sun they are like rolling stones but when they come closer to the sun, the heat of the sun evaporates the comets' gases causing them to emit dust and micro-particles which take the shape of a tail. Abba would show the children pictures of the comet from books and newspapers and try to teach them some science.

It was 1st January 1970, a Wednesday and holiday for New Year. Abba and his family attended the morning service in the church and were back home. Amma and Chithi prepared special lunch and sweets to celebrate the day. After lunch was over, Abba gave 20 paise to his children and told them to go to a petty shop at Goal Ghar and buy paan for all. Those days one paan used to cost less than five paise. The children came back home with the paan and returned a balance of ten paise to Abba. Then Abba asked them about the accounts. Now and then, Abba would send his children to the shop to buy some petty things and used to ask for the accounts. He used to do that to teach his children how to handle money and also to develop in them the skills of purchasing and getting back the correct balance. While the elders were enjoying their paan, suddenly they heard a very loud noise. It was a huge rumble and all the people of Goal Ghar colony and nearby areas heard it and were stunned. Nobody knew what had happened!

Abba put on his shirt and came out of the house with the others. There he saw the people running towards Goal Ghar junction and Abba also rushed to that direction. People from nearby places were running towards Goal Ghar in large numbers and all were talking about some accident. When Abba reached Goal Ghar junction, he saw that a bus had met with an accident and had turned turtle, with all its four wheels on the top. People were trapped inside the bus and were wailing for help. A policeman had also arrived on the scene and with the help of local people he was trying to rescue the passengers and trying to bring them out of the bus safely.

It was a major accident. People were bleeding, crying, and sobbing. One lady was crying bitterly with a pointed glass stuck in her throat and blood was oozing from it. Amma and Chithi also reached the accident site with the children, but couldn't withstand the sight of blood and so they all returned home. After some time, an ambulance arrived and the volunteers started transporting the victims one by one to the hospital. Abba was there with the volunteers, helping the victims and he returned home only after it was dark.

Amma had done her Diploma Training in Craft and Needlework and she was also an expert in embroidery. She used to teach her elder daughter needlework and embroidery and Sheryl was interested in needlework. while staying in Goal Ghar, Keeping Amma's interests in mind, Abba bought a sewing machine for her. Abba also knew to stitch. During Christmas Abba would buy clothes and Abba and Amma could be seen cutting and stitching the frocks for Sheryl and Meryl till it would be completed. Then Amma would do the finishing works of hemming and fixing the hooks and buttons. Even otherwise, Abba would come out with excellent ideas of frock designs and would try to execute it for his daughters. Later, for his daughters, he used to design and stitch different types of dresses, even after they started their college. From where he had learnt all those skills, only he knew!

One day, a priest who was also the Manager of a Convent High School came to meet Abba. It was evening time and Abba had returned home from his office. Abba knew the priest as he was a good friend of Abba. Whenever there would be any problem regarding school matters, he used to seek Abba's advice.

The priest was in need of a craft teacher for his school and he had learnt that Amma had got formal training in needle work and craft. Moreover, she also had work experience, and had worked as a craft teacher in a government school in her native place. The priest spoke to Abba about the vacancy in his school and offered Amma the job of craft teacher and wanted Amma to join the school from the next day itself. Abba looked at Amma, who was standing nearby, and asked her what she had to say on the matter and if she wanted to do a job!

But Amma never had to say anything on her own. She always respected and followed the words of Abba. This time also she looked at Abba for his opinion and simply told him that she did not know what to do. Abba then told the priest that Amma could not take that job since she had to take care of their three children. The priest tried to persuade Abba but Abba was very specific and adamant in his opinion and told that his children were very young and they needed their mother's care at home, and the children were their priority. Moreover, he could earn for his family and his wife need not earn for him. The priest's all efforts to persuade Abba was in vain!

Though Abba was very strict about his family matters, but he was a loving person. Sometimes he would become very romantic. Whenever the family would be invited for some occasion, Abba would see to it that all the children and Amma were neatly dressed. Amma had long thick black hair that flowed down to her knees. Sometimes Abba would make Amma seated on a chair and comb her long hair very delicately, and by folding, unfolding, twisting and turning the hair, he would make a beautiful bun out of it! From where he learnt all those hairstyles, nobody knew. Then he would decorate it with strings of jasmine flowers which he would have already brought. Then he would bring the hand mirror and ask Amma to look at herself and would also ask the children, "How is Amma looking?" Then Abba would bring perfume and spray it on all the family members turn by turn. Thus, the family would go out happily, laughing and talking!

Though Abba was a devout Catholic, but he respected all the other religions as well. He had good knowledge of the various festivals celebrated by people of other religions and used to educate his children about it. Abba had many Muslim friends who paid visit to Abba's house and Abba too used to visit their houses with his family during Eid celebrations. In Port Blair, there is a *Dargah* or Mazar situated at Mazar Pahad, near the sea shore at South Point and it has two graves- one of Allama Fazal Haq and the other of Liyaqat Ali. They both were freedom fighters of the First War of Independence and had been transported to the Andamans. People used to throng to the Mazar to pray to the sacred souls seeking divine intercession and on fulfilling their *mannat,* they used to offer a sacred feast at the Mazar. Whenever, Abba used to be invited by friends to the Mazar, he would visit the Mazar with his family.

In the evenings, while it would be study time, Amma would make the children to sit in different corners of the living room to do their homework and study. But the children used to be very playful and would start talking and teasing each other. Sometimes they would even fight with one another. Amma would get angry at that and threaten them saying that when Abba would return from office, she would complain about them. But when Abba would return home, the scenario would be totally different. The children would pretend to be keenly learning their lessons, and they would also look at Amma from the side of their eyes, now and then, to see if Amma was going to complain about them. But Amma would never complain about them. After Abba would change and freshen up, he would also sit with the children and ask them questions from the lessons of their books and if they would not give a perfect answer Abba would scold them and sometimes even beat them. He would never compromise with their studies!

Once Sheryl got a zero in a class test in mathematics. When Amma saw the test paper, she was very upset. She was afraid that Abba would beat the child for such a mark. She took a wooden ruler and started beating Sheryl. To escape the beatings, Sheryl tried to get under the bed and the ruler got broken by hitting on the bed post and the broken ruler hit Sheryl at her nasal bridge, and she started bleeding profusely.

When Amma saw the blood, she became frightened. Amma somehow managed to stop the bleeding and told the child that she wanted to save her from Abba's anger and his beatings, and so she had beaten her. She tried to bring the child out, but Sheryl would not come out from under the bed, and stayed there till Abba returned from office. When Abba returned from the office, he learnt about the happenings from Amma. He called out to Sheryl who immediately came out of her hiding and started crying. When Abba saw the injury of Sheryl, he got angry at Amma. He told her to beat the child on the hands or legs, but not on the face. Amma was very sad as she had given a permanent scar on her daughter's face!

It was a Saturday and Abba was at home. While the children were returning from school, Abba was standing in the veranda. Abba called out to one of Sheryl's classmates who was also living in the same colony and asked her about her studies. The girl told Abba that she had done well in the class test. She also told Abba that she got the test papers and had scored good marks. When Sheryl reached home Abba asked her about her marks. Sheryl became afraid as she hadn't got good marks.

She took out the answer paper from her bag and silently handed it to Abba. Then she went to the bedroom to change her school uniform. Abba saw the test paper of Sheryl and became very angry as she had scored less marks. Abba went to the bedroom with a cane in his hand and started beating Sheryl. He was shouting at her as to why she had not learnt her lessons on time. Amma was crying and wanted to protect the child but she too got a cane. Then Abba pulled Sheryl towards him and she fell down, her head banged against the bedpost and blood started oozing from her head. Seeing that Abba stopped his beatings.

Abba told Amma to take care of Sheryl's injury and to apply some coffee powder on the place where it was bleeding and to press it so that it would stop bleeding. Amma brought coffee powder but she was not able to see the injured place. The entire head was sticky with blood. She told this to Abba and he brought the scissors, cut the hair around the bleeding part and then Amma pressed all the coffee powder into the child's head. This soon stopped the flow of blood but it did not stop the child's tears!

On watching Sheryl being beaten by Abba, the younger children got so scared that they huddled in a corner. Abba called them and told them that if they did not study well, they too would face the same punishment. All the members of the household were scared and there was total silence in the house. That day Abba did not talk to anyone at home. He was very sad!

The next day while Sheryl was reading her lessons, Abba told her to close the book. He came close to her and asked if her wound was giving her pain. He also examined the wound carefully. He asked Amma to bring hot water and he cleaned the wound and applied some medicine to the affected part. Then he advised his daughter to study well and not to compromise with her studies. The child took the advice of Abba very seriously and decided in her heart that she would never fail in any of her exams in future. That was Abba's nature. Sometimes, he used to get angry on the spur of the moment, but would later regret his behaviour!

On holidays or evenings, Abba would sometimes sit with the children and teach them the lessons from their books. Then he would ask them questions from the lesson. If they wouldn't be able to answer properly, he would get angry at them. Usually, Sheryl and Jason would succeed to answer the questions asked by Abba, and would manage to escape Abba's anger but Meryl would not be able to escape Abba's beatings. On seeing Abba, she would be so scared that words won't come out of her mouth. When Abba would ask her questions, she would not be able to answer due to her fear, and then Abba's anger would wreck on her. Even Amma and Chithi wouldn't be able to stop Abba from beating Meryl. Those incidents had hurt Meryl a lot and she became an introvert and seldom spoke about her feelings to anyone!

Abba used to say that Meryl looked like his mother and he had also given his mother's name to her. He used to call her by different names for her dusky skin, but then that used to be just for fun, but Meryl used to feel low at those times and considered it an insult and used to remain sad and forlorn as everyone at home also used to tease her by those names! Even Abba used to tease Meryl by saying that she was picked from a dustbin, or she had been purchased for a sack of chaff! Then the siblings used to tease her and Meryl would weep for hours, while Amma would scold everyone, to stop the teasing!

Then Amma would console Meryl and try to make her understand that Abba was simply having fun, or if he was angry, it was because of her being so slow in all her work. She should learn to do things fast and only then she would grow into a good girl. Even the elder siblings would be very considerate and try to console Meryl. But Meryl wouldn't understand all those talks and she used to weep silently. She slowly started thinking that Abba did not love her and that she was an unwanted child!

Abba was financially not very sound. But he never showed it to anyone. With a single person's salary, he was unable to fulfil all the necessities of the family. Chithi had come to stay with them and Abba had to send money orders to his father also. All those tensions would sometime make Abba desperate and helpless. Then in the evenings he would take a few pegs and vent out his anger on Amma or the children.

During those days whenever Abba used to be very angry, Amma used to calm the children by saying that Abba wished good for them and that he wanted them to do well in their life. She would also convince the children that Abba had a lot of responsibilities in his life and that made him irritated and angry at times. She would advise them to follow Abba's instructions and never to be disobedient and they should study well and try to make Abba proud. The children too would assure Amma that they would study well!

With all the internal struggles, life in the family went on smoothly and Abba and Amma were happy with their family life.

Chapter - 16

ABBA IS PROMOTED AS TAHSILDAR

It was the year 1970. Abba's children had become comfortable in their English medium school. Abba made it a rule that children should speak in English at home and the children too followed Abba's orders and had started conversing in English and Abba was happy.

On 17.10.70 Abba received his transfer order and he had been transferred to Mayabunder Island. He had got a promotion as a Tahsildar and hence it was a promotion transfer, which he had to comply with. Abba's children were studying in an English medium school at Port Blair, and in those days, there were no English medium schools on any other Island in Andamans!

Abba was a bit worried about his children's education due to his transfer to Mayabunder. His children did not know good Hindi and education in the government schools was imparted purely in Hindi medium. Amma did not know to speak Hindi properly, though she had learnt the basic alphabets from her children's books while teaching them. But Abba accepted his transfer as a challenge and considered it as a part of his service and decided to take his family to Mayabunder by steamer.

It was a bright day when Abba and his family set sail to Mayabunder. The place could be reached only by boat and the only steamer available was S.S. Cholunga. Abba and his family got a cabin and the captain and his crew were very kind and hospitable towards Abba's family. Amma could not withstand the smell of the ship and felt sea sickness, but Abba enjoyed the voyage well. Most of the time he would take the children out of the cabin and would be in the captain's cabin or the wheelhouse of the ship. From there the children could see the blue ocean with the dashing waves. It all used to be so wonderful. The crew of the ship entertained Abba's children by teaching them about the function of the wheel of the ship. The children were able to see dolphins in the ocean following the steamer and used to be very excited. Abba told his children stories about dolphins rescuing humans from drowning and there were a number of reports of dolphins coming to the help of swimmers or sailors who were in distress, and they even helped them to safety.

On the way to Mayabunder, the ship anchored in front of Strait Island[13] and the tiny island could be seen shining far away. All the passengers came upon the deck of the steamer to watch the natives. Abba told the children that the island yonder was the Strait Island and one of the ancient tribes of the Andaman Islands, the Great Andamanese[14] had been settled there.

The Great Andamanese are one of the ancient aboriginals living in Andamans since time immemorial. It is said that during the 18th century they were the largest tribe in the Andaman Islands and their population was estimated around 8000 natives. But after the British occupation, by the late 18th century, their number had decreased drastically in trying to defend their territories from the British invaders. Hundreds of Andamanese were killed and thousands more were wiped out due to epidemics such as measles, influenza, syphilis etc., brought to the islands by the outsiders. By the early 1900s, the population of the Great Andamanese had decreased drastically to around 600. Then in 1969, they were just 23 surviving members and those surviving Great Andamanese were rehabilitated in Strait Island by the A & N Administration.

The serene white beach of Strait Island was sparkling bright in the morning sun. The government authorities had brought coconut, papaya, bananas and other essential commodities for distributing it among the Andamanese. All the goods brought for the natives were lowered in a small boat and the officials waited for the Great Andamanese to arrive. Soon some Andamanese could be seen coming in a canoe to collect their gifts. The excitement among the passengers was increasing as the natives came closer to the boat in their canoe. They were not hostile but appeared friendly to the group of people who provided them with the gift items. The passengers also saw a few canoes anchored near the shores. Soon one more canoe started moving towards the ship.

When the canoe reached close to the steamer, people saw a few youngsters of the Andamanese tribe in the canoe. Their black skin glistened in the sunlight against the blue waters. They looked exactly like the African Native Tribes with tiny curly hair on their head. Their loins were covered with red cloth that had been provided to them by the administrative officers. Those youngsters were in a very cheerful mood, laughing and talking to each other in their language. Suddenly someone from the steamer tossed a coin into the sea, and immediately a boy jumped from the canoe, to collect the coin and in no time the fellow surfaced with the coin in his mouth. He climbed onto the canoe and showed the coin proudly to his friends. Soon, other passengers started tossing more coins into the sea and the youngsters dived from their canoe one after the other to collect them. This was fun and game for them. While this was going on, suddenly a big bellowing siren was heard, and the anchor of the ship was lifted. Soon the steamer started moving.

Abba arrived at Mayabunder with Amma, Chithi and the children. On 17-10-1970, Abba reported for duty and took charge of his office. Mayabunder is a town and a Tehsil in the northern part of Middle Andaman Island. This beautiful island is well lined with mangrove tidal creeks, beaches and attractive picnic spots. It is said that this island was settled during the British colonial period by migrants from Burma and ex-convicts from Mainland India.

Abba was allotted a Type-II government quarter close to his office. The school session was in the middle and Abba admitted his children to the Primary School in Mayabunder. Sheryl was admitted to class five, Jason to class three and Meryl to class one. The school was housed in a wooden building, built on stilts. In those days all the buildings in the Andaman and Nicobar Islands were wooden.

Abba's children were the shining stars of the school since they were so fluent in English, and they were the children of the Tahsildar. The school was a Hindi medium school and since the children did not know Hindi, they were finding it difficult to cope up with the studies. But the teachers were very kind and cooperative and helped the children in their lessons. They showed extreme patience in teaching the children the Hindi language.

There was a small bazaar in Mayabunder which was about a kilometre from Abba's quarters. Sometimes Abba would send his children to the bazaar to buy some provisions from the shops. While the children would be walking to the bazaar, as per Abba's orders, they used to talk only in English and people on the roadside would stop and stare at them. They would wonder at such young children speaking in English!

In Mayabunder, Abba's neighbour was one Mr. Pillai's family, and they were from Kerala. Both the husband and wife worked in the government office. They had a daughter who was about two-three years old. When Mrs. Pillai would go to office, she used to leave the child with Amma. Amma used to take care of the child and also feed the child from time to time. Soon the child became very attached to Amma and she always wanted to stay with Amma. Even when the parents would return from office for lunch, the child did not want to go to her parents. The parents were not very happy about that and soon they arranged for a nanny and stopped sending the child to Amma. This made Amma very sad but Abba advised Amma not to interfere in the family matters of others and that the parents had the authority over their child!

There was a huge backyard behind Abba's quarter and Amma had set a poultry over there. One could see colourful chickens of all sizes cocking around in the backyard. During morning and evenings, Abba and Amma could be seen giving feed to the chickens. The passenger Ferry used to make a trip to Mayabunder once in a week from Port Blair. During those days when the ship would arrive at Mayabunder, Abba would have guests at home and Amma and Chithi would be very busy preparing extra lunch for four to five people. The guests used to be Abba's friends or acquaintances such as the captain of the ship and his family or the captain and his officers or some merchants who were on a trip to Mayabunder etc. Amma would prepare special lunch for the guests according to the availability of fish, chicken etc.

Those days there were no poultry farming done in the islands and no one in Andamans had heard about broilers. Amma had three to four coops in the backyard and thirty to forty chickens. The hens would lay eggs regularly and Amma would store the eggs of particular hens, while the rest would be consumed at home. When some hens would stop laying eggs, and become broody, Amma would set a basket cushioned with sack and straw and set all those eggs, nine, eleven, thirteen always odd numbers, in the basket. Then she would make the broody hen sit on those eggs to incubate and hatch chicks. She would not allow the children to go near that hen then. After twenty-one days, the hen would start breaking the eggs. The hen knew which egg was ready to hatch and with its beak would break the eggs, one by one. The children used to count the days by marking it on the calendar. Then after twenty-one days, now and then, children would start loitering around the coop. After returning from school, their first work would be to check on the chicks. Sometimes Amma and Abba could be seen breaking the left-out eggs of the hen, that used to be one or two and release the chicks as they would still be trapped in the shells.

Then Amma would carry all those chicks in a basket, along with the mother hen, to a corner in the backyard and keep them safe by covering them with a bamboo basket, and with feed and water. The chicks would be so adorable in pleasant sunny colours! The children would request Amma and want to hold the chicks and Amma would give them one chick each to hold for a sometime. Those were lovely days for Amma, Abba and the children!

That year, the Census work had started and Abba was given special duty of Charge Superintendent during 1971 Census, to carry out the Census work in Middle and North Andaman. It was hectic time for

Abba, but he carried out the work very meticulously with the help of his assistants. He conducted House to house survey in all the remote and interior villages and islands with habitation, from Diglipur to Baratang. It was a very hard-hitting time for Abba! Every individual household, scattered in all those islands of North and Middle Andaman had to be visited for the survey. The documents and forms had to be filled and collected and then compiled for the census work. It was a mammoth task that had to be completed in a time bound manner. Abba personally visited all those remote villages with his assistants and supervised the survey. There was no Sundays or holidays for Abba during those days. Moreover, the climatic conditions were very disruptive, with pouring rain and cyclonic weather, it would be so difficult to reach those remote settlements. But nothing could break Abba from completing his work!

During the survey work, on many days Abba used to reach home very late, and he would be totally drenched. He would be sneezing throughout the night then Amma could be seen giving him steam and massaging his legs with oil. But next day, early morning, again Abba would leave the house to carry on the survey work with his team. Many times, Abba and his assistants had to trudge the interior villages of Diglipur, Mayabunder, Kadamtala or Baratang, late in the night and they had to use bamboo torches for light. Since there was no road to many of the settlements, they all had to walk those miles, but Abba never complained about the difficulty of his work. He would walk hand in hand with his subordinate officials.

There were many interior islands where some police personals were posted, and there were also some small islands where people were settled by encroaching the land there, and Abba had to visit those islands by canoes. Narcondum Island, Ross and Smith Island, Landfall Island, Interview Island were such islands and Abba visited all those islands for his survey work.

Many times, Abba had to travel at night in canoes and after returning home, Abba used to tell Amma and his children about the magic of the sea, 'Bioluminescence'. While his visit to Long Island, he had seen the ocean sparkling bright at night, with every wave, while the waters broke on the shore or the oar of the canoe hit the waves, the water used to shine like the spilling of diamonds, sparkling bright. Abba also told that in many islands in Andamans this magic of bioluminescence could be seen in some particular season, on very dark nights. Abba used to say that the mesmerising marvel produces ethereal blue glow as the waves break on the sandy shore. Bioluminescence in Andaman Islands is caused by microscopic organisms, that casts the waters around the Andaman Islands with radiance, bringing the night sea to life in a constellation of sparkling light.

Seeing the enthusiasm of Abba's way of handling his work, his assistants too would become motivated, and they too never complained about the hardship of their work. Trudging those jungles, crossing those swamps, reaching the distant islands in canoes, or walking in knee deep slush and mire, working day and night, finally, Abba could complete his census survey work and submit all the reports and documents on time.

The Census Commission of India recognised Abba's hard work and Abba received a letter with a certificate of appreciation and a Silver Medal from the Census Commission. It stated:

'M. Alphonse, Tahsildar was discharging the duties of Charge Superintendent during 1971 Census and he is awarded with a Certificate of Honour by the Census Commission of India on 15-8-1972 in recognition of the outstanding zeal and high quality of services rewarded by him during the 1971 Census of India and the President of India had been pleased to confer upon him the 1971 Census Silver Medal.'

It was a proud moment for Abba and of course for the entire Survey and Settlement Department. At the home front too Amma, Chithi and the children were very happy for Abba and Amma told Abba that his hard work had got him the reward!

Abba always remained updated about the happenings in the world and also used to talk about it with his family members. He was an ardent listener of 'Radio Ceylon' and the broadcast of Tamil Songs by the Radio. The history of Radio Ceylon dates back to 1925, then it was known as *Colombo Radio*, launched on 16 December 1925. Colombo radio was the first radio station in Asia and the second oldest radio station in the world. Radio Ceylon became a public corporation on 30 September 1967 and the station's name was changed to the Ceylon Broadcasting Corporation. It was said that soon after conquering Mount Everest on May 29, 1953, Edmund Hillary and Tenzing Norgay turned on their transistor radio – and the first thing they heard was the All-Asia Service (English) of Radio Ceylon, more than 3,000 kilometres away.

Abba used to listen to the All-India Radio news regularly and 'Spotlight' was his favourite programme. In 1971 there was a surmise that there might be a war between India and Pakistan. Even it was discussed in the All-India Radio news and Abba used to inform Amma and the children that soon there would be a war and all at home would be worried about the war. In the evening prayers, Abba's family especially started praying for peace in the country and that there should be no war. On the evening of 3rd December 1971, Pakistan launched air strikes on 11 airfields in the North-Western India, including Agra, under Operation Chengiz Khan[15]. Abba listened to the radio news and informed his family about the war. He also informed them that the Pakistani troops had targeted Indian Airbases and within forty-five minutes of those strikes, they had shelled India's western frontier and were reported to have crossed the border at Punch in the state of Jammu.

The whole country was in the fear of war. On the same evening of 3rd December, shortly after midnight, Mrs. Indira Gandhi, the Prime Minister of India, addressed the nation on radio, saying, "A war has been imposed on us." She ordered a reply air strike. The Indian Air Force immediately replied with similar air strikes, starting on the same night. The war had started!

It is said that in order to save the Taj Mahal from the enemy attack, it had then been covered with burlap and camouflaged with a forest of twigs and leaves as the white marble shone brightly as a white beacon in the moonlight, and was easy for the enemy to destroy. When the war was declared, all the members of Abba's house used to listen to the war bulletins on radio to know the updates of the war.

During the Indo-Pakistan war[16], Abba had got special duties to shoulder as a Magistrate. Abba had been given additional charges of law and order and to check the mock drills being carried out in the schools and villages in case of air strike. During those days of the war, India's Flag Ship INS Vikrant[17] used to take shelter in the bay near Mayabunder and Diglipur Island. The ship could be seen anchored at a distance from Mayabunder and the residents of the inlands used to marvel about the immensity of the ship. The presence of INS Vikrant in the bay was a silent message to the islanders about the seriousness of the war. Abba told the children that Mayabunder and Diglipur areas were safe anchorages for the Flag Ship to escape Pakistani submarines. At nights, the Flagship would leave for war and would be gone. People talked that during the night the ship would silently move out of its safe harbour in Andaman to destroy several Pakistani submarines and ships and it would silently return and in the morning, it could be seen anchored safely near Mayabunder and Diglipur islands.

As the Magistrate of Mayabunder, Abba was invited to visit INS Vikrant, the Flagship of India and was taken on a guided tour of the ship by the naval officers. He was so astonished to see the ship from inside. The Flagship played a vital role in enforcing the naval blockade of East Pakistan. INS Vikrant was a massive, majestic and magnificent aircraft carrier and the pride of the Indian Navy. It had an overall length of 700 ft. a beam of 128 ft. and a mean deep draught of 24 ft. It was armed with sixteen anti-aircraft guns and its aircraft consisted of Hawker Sea Hawk and Sea Harrier jet fighters, Sea King MK42B, Chetak helicopters and anti-submarine aircraft. The flight deck of the ship was designed to handle aircraft up to 24,000 lb. The ship was designed in such a manner that the submarines moving underwater could all be easily seen in a special room. When Abba told his family about the ship, they all were proud of India's Flagship!

Since Abba was in contact with the naval officers, he knew many things happening around, related to the war. He used to share some of the matters about the ongoing war with Amma and the children. On many days Abba would come home very late and the children used to be very scared and would cuddle around Amma, praying for Abba's safe return. The impact of war could be seen everywhere in Mayabunder.

In the Primary School of Mayabunder, during morning assembly, the headmaster announced about the Indo-Pakistan war and all the children were terrified. They went to their homes after the school and informed their parents about it and the news of the war spread out like wild fire. In the meantime, near the primary school playground, huge trenches had been dug on all sides, for people to hide, in case there was a war. It was announced to children and the general public that when the sirens would be blown, all of them should leave the classrooms and homes and run towards the playground. Then they should jump into those trenches there and sit on their haunches till the next siren would be blown. People living in the quarters nearby should also join in those mock drills. That was an exercise to save the people in case the Pakistani aircrafts dropped bombs on the island.

As a part of the mock drill, the siren used to be blown out, and then there would be panic and mayhem in the school. All children would run hither and thither, pushing each other, thinking that Pakistani aircrafts would soon drop a bomb on them. They ran for their lives. On reaching the playground they would all jump into those ditches, falling on each other like autumn leaves. They would sit there holding their breath, waiting for the siren to be blown again. Only when the sirens would be blown again, would they get back their breath. But then the little ones could not come out of those ditches as the ditches were six to seven feet deep. The teachers and the elders would help the children and bring them out of those trenches. Abba's children also participated in those mock drills and after returning home, they used to tell stories about those drills and their fears and anxieties about the war to Amma!

Then there was an announcement that at night time the sirens would be blown and there should be an immediate blackout. It was also announced that people should put off all the lights and they should not burn candles or lanterns. There was a fear that enemy planes might operate air raids at night and if they spotted lights, they would be able to figure out the Islands and would drop bombs there. As soon as the sirens would be blown, Amma, Chithi and the children would blow off the candles and the lanterns! It would be pitch black and all would be so scared to move from their places. They used to huddle together and silently tell their prayers!

The war went on for only thirteen days but to the common people, it appeared to be like thirteen years. Life had come to a standstill during those days. On 16th December in the evening, the Pakistani army surrendered in Dhaka. The Prime Minister of India, Mrs. Indira Gandhi ordered an immediate ceasefire and addressed the nation saying that India had won the war and East Pakistan had been liberated and a new country, Bangladesh was born. When the war ended, people took a sigh of relief. How proud all were of the Indian Prime Minister Indira Gandhi and the Indian Army!

Abba had wonderful language skills. He loved to read books and newspapers. He would listen to the radio news and the panel discussions held regularly on radio. He would make the children to sit with him and listen to the news. On days when Abba would be out on tour to interior villages in Mayabunder, he would assign duty to the children to listen to the news. The next day, he would ask the children to tell him the news in English. Whenever Abba would be on duty, the children could be seen sitting with pens and notebooks, listening to the radio and writing down the news.

Christmas in Mayabunder used to be very fascinating. The making of stars with bamboo sticks and colour papers would begin much early in the church and at homes. The carol singing would begin a month before Christmas. Along with the priest, all the parish people, including the elders and the children would visit distant villages in groups, singing carols and enjoying. Abba used to join the carol groups sometimes, but he would send his elder children to join the carol rounds, and Meryl would stay back with Amma as she would not be able to walk all those miles. Sometimes it would be past midnight when the groups would return after the carols. The groups used to cover the carol rounds on foot and while returning they would make bamboo torches out of dry bamboo, that were available in abundance in those jungles, and with the light of the fire of those bamboo torches, they would cross those pitch-black jungles. It used to be so thrilling and mesmerising to watch the fireflies everywhere shining in the dark night and the twinkling stars shining in the sky above!

Chithi was interested in cooking and would try new dishes now and then. There always used to be a good stock of sweets and savouries at home, including achappam, murukku, adirasam etc., all prepared by her. As Chithi had reached her marriage age, Amma was worried about her wedding. It was Abba's responsibility to find a groom for her and get her married. There was a young Malayalee chap working as a clerk in the Asst. Commissioner's office, and one day he approached Abba expressing his desire to marry Chithi. Abba was okey with the alliance but Amma did not like it and did not accept it. She told Abba to find a boy from their own community for her sister and not someone from outside their community. But Abba did not know how to find a groom for Chithi from their own community and was tensed about it!

After a few months another proposal was received for Chithi from another young man and he was from Amma's own village doing trade in Andaman. The lad was not much educated, but Amma knew him from Port Blair as he used to visit Abba's house at Gol Ghar and bring vegetables for them. When Amma came to know about the alliance, she became happy. She knew the boy from her village and he had clean habits. Moreover, Amma knew that there would not be any demand for dowry from the boy's side. In the beginning Abba was not interested in the alliance as the boy did not have much formal education. He strictly told Amma to look for an educated groom for Chithi. But Amma kept on talking in support of the boy as he belonged to their village. Moreover, Amma argued that in Andaman it would be difficult to find a suitable boy for her sister from their community. After months of persuasion, Abba finally agreed to the proposal brought in by Amma. Soon a day was fixed for the groom's family to visit Abba's house in Mayabunder, to see the bride. The children of the house were very happy as a wedding was to take place in the family. For them, the wedding meant new clothes, lots of sweets to eat and no studies!

PART 3

ODYSSEY OF LIFE

Chapter - 17

AMMA SUFFERS FROM EPILEPSY

Chithi's wedding talks were in full swing and Abba, Amma and the children were all very excited about it. The would-be groom was to visit with his parents in a few days to see the bride. The whole house-hold was neatly arranged for the bride seeing ceremony. On the appointed day, the groom came with his mother, father and a few friends to see the bride- Chithi. The groom's mother and father had come all the way from their village, Pothankalanvilai. Finally, the would-be bride came holding a tray with coffee and sweets for all. She was fair, slender and was wearing a silk saree. She had jasmine flowers in her hair and she looked very pretty and graceful. She kept the tray on the teapoy and greeted the grooms' parents with folded hands and the groom's family liked her. The would-be groom's mother gave a saree to Chithi and also gave her flowers to wear, as per the custom, stating that they had accepted the bride. Then a sumptuous lunch was served to the groom's family with sweets and gifts. The bride seeing ceremony went well and there was fun and happiness everywhere. The wedding was fixed for 6th February, and six months were left for the wedding. It was decided that the groom would arrive at Mayabunder with his parents and relatives, a few days before the wedding and Abba agreed to make arrangements for their boarding and lodging. After fixing the date, the groom and his parents left for Port Blair.

Days were rolling by and Abba and Amma started making arrangements for the wedding and prepared a list of the works to be carried out which included printing invitation cards, distribution of wedding cards, purchasing jewellery and clothes and gifts for the bride, purchasing clothes for the family members, the menu for the wedding feast etc. Accordingly, they also started following the work-schedule.

As the day of the wedding started nearing, the tension and worries in Abba's household started increasing. Abba had withdrawn money from his savings bank to make jewellery for Chithi. He also had to arrange money for other expenses such as clothes, decoration, vehicles, the wedding meal for guests etc. He was afraid that he would not be able to manage the financial burden and started feeling tensed. In his tension he started venting out his anger and irritation on Amma. Abba even started threatening Amma saying that if any problem should arise during the wedding, he would run away from the house. Abba was afraid that the groom might make some sudden demands during the wedding and he might not be able to fulfil them due to lack of money!

As Abba's worries and fears started rising higher and higher, Amma too started feeling the stress. She started thinking deeply about the various adverse possibilities and became much worried about Chithi's wedding. She became obsessed with all the fears and worries of Abba and started remaining silent and gloomy. She did not pour out her fears on anyone like Abba did, but kept it to herself, in her heart, praying silently to God and to Mother Mary that the wedding should go on smoothly. But the cheer and joy of the household were silently vanishing from Abba's house, which no one noticed!

With the marriage date nearing, Abba and Amma became more and more nervous and tensed. Amma became an easy prey for Abba to vent out his worries and rage. Among all those developments one day Abba received a letter from the would-be groom, stating that his mother had passed away at his village on the mainland. But the groom did not want any changes in the wedding date. He wanted the wedding to be held on the same day as per the calendar. Unaware of the pressure gathering in the house, the children enjoyed, playing with Chithi, teasing her and having fun!

It was the day of Chithi's wedding. All had new dresses and were very happy. Abba had designed the frocks for his daughters and Amma had herself stitched it at home. The rest of the clothes were stitched by a tailor. The groom with his father and relatives had reached Mayabunder three days before the wedding and they were put up in a guest house. There was happiness and cheer everywhere. Sweets were being made, guests were being received, and there was laughter and fun all over. The fragrance of fresh jasmine flowers, glittering jewellery and Kanchevaram[1] saris could be seen all over the place. Ten cooks had been arranged by Abba to prepare the wedding feast. Abba had bought twenty-one goats, lots of chicken, vegetables, spices, onions, Ghee etc. and the preparation for the feast started on the eve of the wedding.

The wedding was solemnized at St. Thomas Church at Pokhadera, in Mayabunder and it was a grand wedding attended by Abba's family members, relatives and friends. The wedding feast too was well arranged and Abba's office staff, friends, neighbours and people from the parish were all invited. A huge pandal had been erected around Abba's quarter which was well decorated with palm leaves, festoons and flowers and the loudspeakers were blaring out film songs. Guests were being received, food was being served and people were talking and laughing and enjoying the feast. Among all this, the children had a wonderful time playing, running around, eating and having fun. In the evening when Chithi was to leave with her groom, there was a lot of emotional exchanges with crying and hugging. Amma was crying with Chithi and the children were also crying. Abba too became emotional!

While Chithi was departing, Abba said to her, "You are my eldest daughter. If you face any problem in your life, you can always tell to me and I would be there for you. This is my promise to you. You are always welcome to this house."

So Chithi departed with tears in her eyes. Even years after her wedding, she always used to remind Abba that she was his eldest daughter and Abba too would tell her that he knew it!

The wedding of Chithi went on well without any hindrance as Abba or Amma had feared. That evening after the bride and groom had been sent off, the whole family sat together, with Abba, Amma, the children and their family friends. The elders were all discussing about the wedding that was so well arranged and all appreciated the food and Abba's management of the wedding work. Abba and Amma were very satisfied and happy that everything had gone well. Then they all had dinner together. Since everyone was dead tired, so after dinner, all went to sleep. Some young men who had been working for the wedding had stayed back and they all slept under the pandal, and soon all were fast asleep.

It was after midnight when Abba heard some loud noise and then he heard Amma's cries. Abba got up and looked for Amma, but she was not in the bed. There was no electricity and Abba tried to find the matchbox to light the candle. After lighting the candle Abba went towards the washroom and found that Amma was lying unconscious in front of the bathroom door. Abba tried to call Amma, but when there was no response from her. Abba called out to the children and they all got up. Abba placed the candle on a nearby table and asked Sheryl to fetch water. But she was too afraid to go to the kitchen all alone. She called Jason and they both went to the kitchen and got a jug of water. Abba splashed a little water on Amma's face and after some time, Amma opened her eyes. But within moments, she again became unconscious!

On seeing Amma's condition, the children started crying. Abba tried to console them. Then Abba with the help of the children lifted Amma to the bed. Amma's condition did not improve throughout the night. Amma would come to consciousness for some time, with her whole-body trembling and jerking, then she would mutter something and again she would swoon. This went on for some time. Finally, after about two hours Amma slept but Abba did not sleep!

The children were frightened and they stood watching the condition of Amma, weeping all the while. Though Abba made the children to go to bed, but he stayed awake to help Amma, praying all the while and waiting for her to come back to her senses.

The next day dawned and there was deep sorrow in the household. Abba decided to take Amma to the hospital. There was an Adivasi cook at home to help Amma in the kitchen and so Abba did not worry about the food. He got the children ready, gave them breakfast and sent them to school. Then he called for the office jeep and took Amma to the lone government Hospital there. The only doctor there attended Amma but he could not find the reason for her illness. In the evening when the children returned from school, they came to know that Amma had been admitted to the hospital and they became very sad. Abba took all of them to see Amma. The hospital was away and it was on a hillock in Mayabunder. When the children reached the hospital, Abba took them to the room where Amma was admitted while he went to meet the doctor.

Amma was lying on the bed and she seemed to be lost. Her hands and her body were trembling and she was muttering something. She looked afraid and had turned pale. She was pointing towards the ceiling and was telling that something was flying over there. The children were all terrified at Amma's state. When they looked up, they could see nothing on the ceiling. They started crying at Amma's condition. The nurse consoled them and told them not to cry as Amma would get well soon. But how soon no one could say!

It was the next day after Chithi's wedding when Amma was admitted to the hospital. Chithi was in Mayabunder with her groom. They were supposed to leave for Port Blair by the steamer that night. When she came to know about Amma's health condition, she rushed to the hospital with her husband. She tried talking to Amma, but Amma was not in her senses. Since the steamer was leaving after a few hours, so Chithi could not stay there for long and she soon left with her husband. But she was very sad. She had been a constant support to Amma all those years but now Amma was alone. Chithi wept at her inability to stay back with her sister and take care of her. She lamented at her plight. She had to leave Amma in such a condition. She could only shed tears, and could do nothing!

Amma's condition did not improve. She was not in her real self. She appeared to be very afraid. She kept calling out to nurses saying that something was flying over her bed and that it was going to kill her.

Then Amma was given an injection, maybe some sedative and soon Amma slept. The doctor told Abba that due to lots of worries and mental tension, maybe Amma had developed some nervous disorders and that with proper rest and sleep, she would get well soon.

Amma remained in the hospital for about a week. The children were very sad and depressed without Amma and Abba took care of them in the absence of Amma. Abba felt that Amma was the lifeline of the house and without her, the house did not feel like a house at all. The children went to school in the morning but after school they waited eagerly for the evening when Abba would return from office and take them to see Amma in the hospital. After three days Amma became a bit normal and she spoke to her children and their joy knew no bounds. Abba and the children thanked God for giving Amma back to them. After a week when Amma returned home from the hospital, everyone was happy!

After a few months Amma got cured of her illness but now and then she would have those fears and nervous breakdowns. People in the neighbourhood started talking strange stories about that quarter where Abba's family was living. They told that Amma must have seen some ghost or spirit in the bathroom that night when she had fainted. They also told Amma and Abba that many years ago, a lady had committed suicide in that bathroom by hanging herself and maybe Amma had seen her impression. After learning about those stories Amma was more frightened and Abba decided to change the house. He applied for another accommodation and soon got an independent house, a bit away from the one where they were presently residing. Abba and his family soon shifted to the new quarter.

Chapter - 18

SETTLEMENTS IN MAYABUNDER

The new quarter allotted to Abba was a sea facing bungalow. It had a huge independent campus, big lawn and enough space for the children to play around. In the corner of the garden, there was a Japanese bunker[2] also known as a pill box and a huge banyan tree had grown by its side. So there always used to be shade on the bunker.

Abba told his children that the Japanese had occupied the Andaman and Nicobar Islands during World War II. They had constructed those bunkers on the coast across the Andaman and Nicobar Islands to keep watch on the sea for British Ships and planes and to attack it. The bunkers were made of solid concrete and were of a square shape. It was 12'X 12' in size with ten feet height and the children found it difficult to climb on it. Yet somehow, they would manage to climb on it and used to play there for hours. The bunker had two small entrances dug from the side, in order to get inside it. On the top, at the centre, there was a square hole of 10 inches from where the Japanese could shoot their enemy aircrafts. On all the four sides there were small square openings on the wall for sunlight and also from where the Japanese soldiers could shoot at their enemies. The bunker was divided from inside, and people said that the Japanese soldiers used to store their food, bed, arms and ammunition inside it.

The children would lie on the top of the bunker and used to look inside it in turns. They never dared to go inside the bunker through the side entrance as the weeds had covered it and they were also afraid. Moreover, the servants told stories of cobras and snakes living inside the bunker and in some bunkers, they had also seen motor bikes, left behind by those Japanese soldiers!

Abba loved gardening. Within a few weeks of his shifting to the new quarter, he got labourers to clear the land to make a garden there. In front of the house, he planted flowers of all types and in the backyard, he had a vegetable garden. The house was on a raised land and in front of it, there was a steep slope. Abba decided to do terrace farming there, on the slope. He got the entire area cleared and the land was dug in small steps to make a terrace garden. On the sides, he also planted banana trees.

Soon seeds were sown in the land and plants sprouted. In the evening it used to be time to water the plants and Abba and the children used to thoroughly enjoy that time, but the children used to be more focused on splashing water on each other and playing. Soon the garden started yielding a good harvest of vegetables and Abba would tell Amma to distribute a portion of it to the gardeners, neighbours and to the office peons. At night children would be given duties to look for snails and pick it in pails. At night, the children would all walk with torch lights, as if on a mission, and search for snails that would be creeping on plants or eating the leaves. In the beginning, the children felt repelled to pick those sticky, creepy snails but then Abba announced a one-paisa incentive for picking one snail and soon children started picking it up very enthusiastically. All the collected snails would then be dumped into a hole dug in the earth for the purpose and buried with salt. During the daytime, the snails would rarely be visible but at night they came out like an army from the underworld to destroy the crops. Many times, the children used to ask Abba about the snails and Abba would tell them that snails are nocturnal creatures and they slept under the soil or in some damp places during day time and used to come out at night to hunt and feed themselves.

When the banana trees would bear fruits and would be ready to ripen, Abba would get the banana hand cut from the tree. Then he would get a sack and put the banana hand in it with straw, to ripen fast.

On some occasion, Abba would get the soil dug, and the sack with straw and banana hand would be buried in it for a few days. Then when the sack would be unearthed, the banana hand would be all yellow and ripe, which Abba would distribute among the gardeners and servants, after keeping a few bunches for the family.

In front of the house there was the beach. The place where Abba had made the step farming, the land was very steep and it landed at the sea beach. Sometimes during holidays, Abba's all three children would get permission from Amma and go down to the beach to play. Though Amma would give permission, but she would strictly tell them that they should return home before Abba returned from his office for lunch. Happily, the children would go down to the beach carrying their towels and water bottles and play there in the sea beach for a long time.

One day Abba's children found a raft on the beach, tied to a tree on the shore. It was a Burma bamboo raft, flat bottomed and made of bamboo stakes that was lashed together with rope. Long bamboo poles were also tied to it that could be used as oars. The shores had shady mangrove trees and as it was high tide, the sea had crept up and encroached the entire beach. The raft was moving up and down, with the moving waves, as if inviting the children. The children were very happy to be on the beach and decided to call it their own beach, as it was in front of their house!

The children left their water-bottles and towels on the shore and started running and playing on the soft white sand. After playing there for some time they started splashing sea-water on each other. But then they were tempted to get into the water that was so cool! They decided to enter the serene waters holding hands, advising each other not to leave hands, to be very careful and not go too far. So, holding each other's hands, they carefully entered the water. It was so chill, and refreshing in the hot sun. Suddenly Meryl slipped and fell in the water. Sheryl and Jason tried to pull her out but they too slipped and fell into the water. The water was shallow and so there was nothing to worry about. Since the children's dresses had been drenched, they decided to take bath in the chill sea water. They did not know swimming, but they lay in the shallow water, and kicked it with their legs and moved their arms and splashed the water with hands, laughing and giggling all the time. Then the children decided to climb onto the raft. They helped each other to climb the raft and then untied the rope of the raft. Then with the help of the bamboo poles, they started pushing the raft in the water.

There was no one in the vicinity, and a gentle breeze was blowing that made the raft to move slowly. Seeing the raft moving, the children were very excited and clapped their hands and laughed. They were so happy to see that they could row the raft themselves. It was high tide and the raft started moving faster. The children were giggling and enjoying on the raft. The sun was shining bright, the breeze was blowing on their faces, and making their hair to fly and the children were laughing with the wind! They were enjoying, but they did not think what they would do if the raft got into deeper waters.

Suddenly they heard a man shouting at them from the shore. The raft belonged to that man and he was the owner. He was fishing near the beach when he suddenly noticed that his raft was moving, and was shocked. On seeing three young children on the moving raft, he was terrified and shouted at the children to return. The man was running on the shore, keeping pace with the direction of the raft and was yelling loudly, calling out to them to return. The children were very frightened on hearing the man shouting, but they did not know how to turn the raft and come back!

The man understood the problem of the children and he entered the water. He started swimming towards the raft and soon caught the rope of the raft. He pulled the raft to his side and started swimming back with it. With great effort he brought the raft with the children to the shore and tied it to a tree. Then he brought the children down, one by one, from the raft. He was very angry at them and scolded them severely. He shouted at them and wanted to know about their parents, to complain about them. The children were terrified and were near to weeping. All the smile, cheer and happiness vanished from their faces!

And the fear of beatings and scoldings from Abba made them shudder. They hesitatingly pointed their fingers to their house, on the top of the hillock. The man knew that it was the Tahsildar Sahib's quarter and he understood that they were Abba's children. After that, he did not shout at them, but advised them not to play with the raft in future as it might be very dangerous. Then the man went away advising them to go home. The children breathed peace and the smile returned on their faces!

But the children were not willing to go home so soon. They wanted to play and enjoy on the beach for some more time. Moreover, their clothes were all wet and they also had to dry their clothes before going home, or else Amma would scold them. Moreover, she would never allow them to go to the beach in future. So, they started playing on the beach by chasing each other and pushing each other on the sand.

The pure silky white sand was gleaming in the sunlight and the beach was strewn with colourful corals and shells of different shapes and varieties. There were so many conches, Glory of the cone shells, Lion's paw Scallop shells, Scotch Bonnet shells, Murex shells, Cowrie shells, Nautilus shells, tritons, clams, Queen Conch shells, King shells, queen shells, corals and shells of different colours, shapes and sizes. It appeared as if the sea had brought out its entire wealth to decorate its beach! What a variety of shells were strewn on the beach for miles and miles in shades of hues! The children were mesmerised at the wonder of the sea and loved it all.

The beach was so enthralling that the children did not want to return home. They enjoyed watching the hermit crabs crawling around on the sand with their shells and it was a very pretty sight. In the shallow waters, the live corals were shining brightly, waving like bunches of flowers in the ocean. The colourful fish in the water moving among the corals was all so enthralling to see. The children got into the shallow waters and tried to catch the fish, by silently stalking them, but the moment their hands would be in water, fish would escape and they couldn't catch any.

Then they started wading in the water. Suddenly Sheryl stepped on some black thick piece which appeared like a dry piece of wood.

It was soft and then the children noticed that it was a huge leech. But Sheryl had unknowingly stepped on it and it got pressed by her feet and it started spitting out, and immediately the entire water surrounding it was covered with something resembling white vermicelli noodles. The children were scared. Then they did not know that those creatures were sea cucumbers. But then it became a game for the children to find those sea leeches and press them with their tiny feet, with all their strength and then move away immediately, while the creatures would spit noodles into the water, and the children would laugh, clapping their hands. This game went on for some time, till they got bored!

There were also starfish of different colours and sizes in the shallow waters of the beach. They saw the balloon fish all puffed up, but they were scared and did not pick it up. Jason found a tiny sea horse and he wanted to take it to school. But then he put it back into the sea as Sheryl told him that it might not survive till the next day. The low water of the beach was alive with varieties of creatures such as sea urchins, colourful fish, corals, clam-shells, crabs etc. The children felt that it was such a wonderful place to spend their holiday and they should visit it regularly.

After playing on the beach for some time the children started collecting shells and conch and tied them to their towels. Then they heard Abba's Peon calling out to them from the garden. The children were afraid of a scolding and they all rushed back home, with the bundle of collected shells. They were afraid that Abba would get angry at them. Amma had already told them to reach home before Abba returned for lunch but they had lost count of time!

As they entered the house, the children found Abba having his lunch. He asked them where they had been and they told him that they had gone to play on the beach, in front of the house. Abba did not scold them, instead, he told them to show him what they had collected from the beach. The children opened their bundle and showed Abba their collection of shells. Abba took a look at all the shells and then laughed at their tan skin. He told them to have a bath and have their lunch. He also advised them to be careful in the waters as the shells and corals might cut their feet. Then after finishing his lunch Abba went off to his office.

The children were very happy at their discovery of a new beach and had thousands of stories to tell Amma. They also requested Amma to accompany them to the beach the next time. Though Amma agreed, but she never went to the beach with the children.

While in Mayabunder, Abba had to go on tours to different far-off islands and villages. The office jeep would take him only to a certain distance till where the road stopped. To reach those settlements, Abba had to walk for miles with his men. Some places could be reached by canoes for a certain distance, but then they had to walk through the creeks in the marsh and swamp for miles and it used to be so difficult!

Abba always used to plan out his office works in advance about visiting those distant settlements. He visited those places with his team, wearing his gumboots and raincoats, carrying all the equipments for his work, as per his schedule. On some days when he would return from those inspections, his legs would be swollen due to those blood-sucking leeches that had got on to his legs. On some days one or two leeches would still be there on his legs sucking blood and Amma would put salt on them to kill them. The moment salt would be put on them they would drop down like ripe fruits from trees. The place where the leech had been sucking blood would be red and swollen and Amma would massage Abba's legs by applying all sorts of oils to ease his pain.

While going for survey work through the marshy swamps on rafts or canoes, the boatmen would tell Abba that those creeks and swamps were very dangerous as there were crocodiles in the water that would be waiting patiently, submerged in shallow waters to pounce on the prey. Many stories about people killed by crocodiles had been heard by Abba from the local people. The jungles were also the home of wild elephants and one had to be very careful while crossing those forests. Those elephants had been brought during the British era to help logging. But later on, some of those elephants were left out in the jungles of North Andaman, and they had turned wild. Whenever Abba would go on a tour, Amma would panic and fear and would breathe peace only after Abba would return home.

Mayabunder also had a Bengali settlement and they were the settlers brought from East Pakistan. They used to celebrate Durga Puja in high spirits for ten days. According to Hindu mythology, the demon Mahishasura had received a boon of invincibility from Lord Brahma, which meant that no man or God could ever kill him. After receiving the boon, Mahishasura attacked the Gods and chased them out of heaven. To fight off the demon king, all the Gods came together and worshiped Adi Shakti. It is said that the divine light that came out of all the Gods during the puja created Maa Durga!

The fight between Maa Durga and Mahishasura had lasted for ten days. Goddess Durga slayed the demon king on the tenth day, and hence the day is celebrated as Vijaya Dashami, symbolising the victory of good over evil. On the last day, devotees immerse the idol of Goddess Durga in the holy water of river Ganges. It is known as Durga Visarjan. Before the immersion, long processions are carried out by worshippers accompanied by the beating of drums, singing and dancing, with a lot of fanfare.

In Mayabunder also Pandals used to be erected in all Puja sites. The beautiful idols of Goddess Durga used to be installed at all pandals. The beautiful idol of Maa Durga, looking very angry, with ten arms, holding different instruments such as a conch, discuss, lotus, sword, bow and arrow, trisula, mace, thunderbolt, snake and flame, and one foot on Mahishasur the demon, could be seen in all the pandals. The devotees would be seen worshipping and singing bhajans. Prasad would be prepared and distributed to all devotees. The celebration would go on for ten days. People in their new dresses would throng those Puja Pandals with their families and friends. With the thumping of the 'Dhols' and brass cymbals, men, women and children could be seen dancing in front of the idol of Goddess Durga. Sometimes they would dance with fire. They would dance holding earthen pots, with burning coal in both their hands. Frankincense would be added to the burning embers and the smoke would rise and fill the pandals. The men would dance in a mad fit and more people would keep joining in the dance and it would go on till late at night. On the last day, the idol of Goddess Durga would be carried to the sea and immersed in the water while young boys and men would jump along with the idol and try to get hold of something from the idol and preserve it in their homes. It was considered auspicious and people believed that it would bring good luck to them!

There were also Adivasi settlements in Mayabunder. The Adivasis are tribals of Jharkand who were brought to Andamans during the British era through the Catholic Mission, and they had been brought to clear the forests. After Independence, most of them stayed back and continued to work in the Forest Department.

Once Abba and his family attended a wedding of an Adivasi couple in Bajota in Mayabunder. Bajota is an interior village that had to be reached by canoes. The wedding was carried out at the church of the bride's house and then the groom's family brought the bride to their house after completing all the rituals there. While bringing the bride and the groom into the house, they placed baskets before the bride one after the other and the bride walked in it softly while the relatives carried the groom on their shoulders. Then they made the bride and groom stand together in one basket and gave them a bow and arrow asking them to shoot together at the vegetables kept at the other end. After that, the groom had to carry his bride crossing a small brook and take her into the house. At the entrance, the elders washed the hands and feet of the groom and the bride and took them in. The celebration went on throughout the day till late evening with fun and festivity and all the people joined the traditional dance and danced to the thumping of drums, singing songs. A sumptuous meal was also served with 'Handia'[3] the traditional rice beer drink of the Chota Nagpur Tribals.

While in Mayabunder, Abba used to take his family on picnics to nearby islands and beaches. There Abba used to show the German Jetty to his children and say that the jetty was said to have been built by German engineers during the Second World War. It was said that the jetty was once a centre for repairing submarines during the war. Just like the Japanese Bunkers and the Cellular Jail, the German jetty is also a reminder of the tragedy the island had witnessed in the past. The jetty is situated close to APWD Guest House and one could have a wonderful view of the small islands nearby. Avis Island was one of the favourite destinations of Abba for enjoying family picnics. It is a very beautiful island with a lot of coconut trees and could be reached in half an hour by boat from Mayabunder jetty. The coconut plantation of the island and the pristine clear waters and its beach would mesmerise anyone visiting the island. Whenever Abba and family would visit the island, Amma would already pack food and carry it with her. It would then be fun time for the children playing on the beach. Then there were those beaches at Karmatang and Rampur where Abba used to take his family for spending holidays. Abba knew many families there and would also visit their houses with his family. It all used to be happy days!

In Mayabunder there was also the Karen[4] Settlement and they were settled in a village called Webi. Historically saying, in 1925, thirteen families of the Karen community had been brought to Mayabunder in Andaman from Burma and the next year another fifty families were brought and settled there. Those people were given land for settlement and free rations for one year. Then they founded the 'Webi Village' which means hidden village. The Karen people are great agriculturists and they love fishing and hunting. Their population soon spread beyond Webi village but they have maintained their unique culture.

Most of the Karen people follow Christianity, and they celebrated Christmas with great fanfare. They love music and sing melodious carols. The Karen people are expert craftsmen and skilled in making bamboo, cane and wood works. Baskets woven by the people, also known as 'Chey' are found in every household in different sizes.

Abba had some very good friends among the Karen people. He used to be invited with his family to their houses on special occasions. When oranges used to be harvested during the season, those friends used to send baskets of oranges for Abba. Those used to be the best oranges of the country, big in size and very sweet like honey. They also cultivated special 'Burma Rice', brown and white in colour which they used to bring for Abba.

It was the year 1972 when a very sad incident occurred in Betapur, under Rangat Tahsil. All the Tahsils of North and Middle Andaman were under the office of the Assistant Commissioner Mayabunder, which was also the headquarters. Abba was in his office, when a wireless message was received from Rangat office which stated that a boat carrying school children had capsized at CFO Nallah River. Immediately Abba arranged for his jeep and left for CFO Nallah with other officials, the place where the incident had occurred. When Abba and his team reached the place, they saw total mayhem there, people who had lost their children were wailing and mourning. Though it was raining heavily, but the rescue operations had started and people were thronging the place to see the rescue operations.

The Revenue officials and Police personals from Rangat had already arrived at the spot. They informed Abba that all the passengers in that fatal boat were girls and they were school children studying in Rangat Higher Secondary School. After their school got over, the girls had returned by bus and they got down at Betapur and then they boarded the dinghy to cross the nallah to go to their houses in the interior villages. It was raining heavily and the nallah was flooded. But then, during rains, that river used to be always flooded!

According to eye witness, after the children got into the dinghy, the boatman started rowing the boat against the stormy tide. The current of the water was very strong and the torrential rain was pouring which made it difficult for the boatman to row the boat. The water in the river was increasing every minute and when the boat reached midway, it suddenly capsized in the strong tides and undercurrent. Everyone in the boat fell into the roaring river and there was a turmoil of cries and shouts for help. The current was carrying away the girls and the boatman could not help anyone. Some men of the village happened to watch that deadly sight, and they jumped into the flooded river to save the drowning girls. They could rescue some girls but many were still missing!

Abba saw the rescue operations that were being carried on. Divers had been brought to search the missing girls. Finally, bodies of five girls could be found and two girls were still missing. Night had fallen by then which made the rescue operations to halt. The family members of the girls felt miserable and were lamenting the death of their children. No words could console them!

Abba reached home late that night and informed Amma about the accident. The next day, by early morning Abba again left for CFO Nallah. On that day, bodies of the two missing girls were also found. The flooded river had carried their bodies a few miles away. Seven girls had drowned in the accident and all the villages of Middle Andaman were drowned in gloom!

Those days the CFO Nallah had to be crossed by boats as no bridges had been constructed to cross the river. It was always risky to cross the river by boats during monsoons. And it used to be raining 9-10 months, so people could not set aside the canoes. They lived in interior villages and had to cross the river for some or other work. Children who studied in higher classes had to go to Rangat School and there were no other means except crossing the river in canoes.

In 1989, a 'Bailey Bridge' was constructed across CFO Nallah and it was inaugurated by the then Lt. Governor of the islands on 5th September 1989. The bridge was named 'Rama Devi Bridge', in memory of those children who had lost their lives in capsizing of boat in 1972. The children who drowned in the fatal accident were- N. Rama Devi, J. Chari Ka, Susheela A, Omana, Prabhavathi, Shiva Prathayini and K. Indira Devi.

In December 1972 Abba received his transfer orders to Port Blair. He was given a warm send-off by his office staff and the common people of Mayabunder. He used to be very kind towards the poor and needy. He was easily approachable to the common man and they could come to him with their problems. If it was within his reach, he would surely help them. If the problem could be solved by his senior officers, he would write such supporting notes, quoting rules in the files, that the senior officers would be convinced to sign the files. Such a man was Abba and hence the poor people regarded him a lot. While Appa was leaving Mayabunder, many people arrived at the jetty to bid him adieu. There were the office staff, friends and common folk. While Abba got into the steamer some of them were very emotional and so too was Abba!

Chapter - 19

ABBA ASSUMES CHARGE OF TAHSILDAR SETTLEMENT

After getting relieved from Mayabunder, Abba and his family came to Port Blair. Abba joined his duty as Tahsildar on 23-12-1972, at the Office of Settlement. After reaching Port Blair, Abba also applied for government accommodation. Till the accommodation was allotted to him, Abba made arrangements for Amma and the children to stay with Chithi and her family, who were staying at Goal Ghar in Port Blair, while he himself decided to manage in the Government Guest House. It was decided that in the evenings, after office, Abba would visit Chithi's house and Amma agreed to the arrangement.

Abba admitted his children to Nirmala School, which was a Hindi Medium convent school. The nuns of the previous English medium Carmel School came to meet Abba and requested him to admit his children to their English medium school, but Abba did not agree to them. He was quite adamant there and argued that in the Andaman and Nicobar Islands there were no English Medium Schools in any other Islands. If he admitted them in English medium school then, maybe the next year if he would again get a transfer to some other island, it would be difficult for his children to again switch back to the Hindi medium of studies. So, he told the nuns of the school that his children should be in the Hindi medium school. Even the nuns of the Convent School felt that Abba was right and they returned. Abba used to take wise decisions and his decision to admit his children in Hindi medium was right because within three years Abba was again transferred to another island.

After about two weeks of arriving at Port Blair, Abba was allotted a type II Quarter in the Delanypore colony. There were eight double-storied buildings in the colony with four apartments in each building. The quarter allotted to Abba had two apartments on the ground floor and two on the first floor. Four families lived in the block, two families were from Kerala, one was a local Muslim family and Abba was from Tamil Nadu. Abba's apartment was on the ground floor, by the side of the road.

Abba's father was living in his village and Abba used to regularly send money orders to him. One day, few months after coming to Delanypore quarter, Abba received a telegram from his village stating that his father had passed away. The telegram had been sent a few days ago. Abba couldn't go to his village as there were no ships to the mainland for the whole fortnight.

In the evening, Abba came home with the telegram and showed it to Amma and his children. He was very sad as he was unable to attend the funeral of his father. He wept out his sorrow and narrated to his children the hardships his father had faced in his life, and lamented that during his last days Abba was not there to take care of him. He lamented that the greatest sorrow of living in Andamans was that the place was cut off from the mainlands and one was unable to attend the funeral of his parents. Abba couldn't attend his mother's funeral, and now his father had passed away and again he was unable to attend the funeral. A pall of gloom spread in the household. Everyone was sad!

After joining his office, Abba became busy with his work. He was also assigned the Rehabilitation work of settlers brought under various schemes of the government. Now and then, Abba used to be out on his duty of survey and settlement and land records. Abba had also developed the habit of smoking and taking alcohol frequently due to which Amma was not very happy. The peons of Abba's office used to come for domestic help and sometimes Abba would also provide them drinks. Amma would get angry at that and sometimes there would be a row in the house. During such situations Abba too would get angry and shout at Amma telling her not to teach him what to do and what not to do, and Amma would become silent, and then in a day or two the matter used to subside.

But on one occasion, the matter went beyond control. It was a holiday and during the afternoon Abba had a few pegs of whisky. Again, in the evening, he took more drinks. A peon of Abba's office had come home for some domestic help and Abba offered drinks to him. That peon was a young man and he used to call Amma as 'Akka', meaning elder sister. When Amma came to know that he had taken liquor, she got angry at the peon and scolded him not to fall into such bad habits. But the peon instead told Abba that Amma had scolded him for taking drinks. This made Abba furious, and in his anger, he shouted at Amma asking how she dared to talk to his office people against him! He then slapped Amma on her face, in front of the peon.

Usually, whenever Abba used to get angry, Amma used to keep quiet, but on that day Amma did not keep quiet. She wanted to know why she was being beaten and what her mistake was! At that, Abba lost all his control and started shouting at Amma that she should not advise him. He brutally pushed Amma and she fell down. But Abba didn't stop there, he seemed to be in a mad fit, and felt that Amma had insulted him in front of his office staff. The intoxication caused by liquor was taking a hold on him and he started brawling with Amma and her Sari got torn in the tussle. When the children saw that, they came to rescue Amma and they also got beatings. Jason pushed Abba down, and Sheryl and Meryl tried to lift Amma up. The situation was taking a sad turn, when the office peon silently escaped from the scene!

The sun had set and it had started getting dark outside but Abba's anger was not calming down. He shouted at Amma to get out of his house and also pushed Amma and the children out of the house from the backdoor and locked the door from inside. The children were all desperate and were crying and they huddled close to Amma, who was also crying. Even in that desperate situation, Amma told her children to hush their voices, lest it should be heard by the neighbours and it would bring a shame to Abba and the family. Soon the children quietened and cuddled to Amma and they all sat silently on the back steps, behind the house and did not make any noise. But Amma's heart was totally shattered. She felt so desperate about herself, and sad for being born a woman! She spent that whole night outside the house, hugging her children and weeping silently at her helplessness!

Throughout that night, Amma and the children remained outside the house, in the cold, being bitten by mosquitoes, embracing each other. At first, Amma thought that Abba would open the door after some time. But she was wrong. Abba had slept off in his intoxication and did not wake till early next morning.

Though Amma was very hurt by Abba's behaviour, but while talking to her children, she blamed the liquor for all the brutality shown by Abba. She told the children that if Abba had not been drunk, he would never have behaved in such a cruel way. That was Amma! She always supported Abba in all situations of life.

When Abba woke up, he saw that Amma and the children were not in the house. It took him some time to recall the happenings of the previous evening. When he understood that Amma and the children had spent the entire night outside the house, Abba felt ashamed of himself. He opened the door and saw Amma sitting outside and the children sleeping beside her. He called out to Amma and told her to come in. The children were all sleeping, cuddled to Amma, and Amma woke them up and took them inside the house!

The next day Abba was very sorry for his inhuman behaviour. He was not able to look at Amma and his children at their face and felt embarrassed. He promised Amma that he won't touch liquor again and would never behave in such a way. As promised, Abba did not take liquor for a few months. Gradually, within a week, the household was normal once again. But Amma had undergone such mental trauma that night that she once again developed those nervous breakdowns, and epilepsy. All of a sudden, she would go blank, her body muscles would go stiff, her entire body would start trembling, then her arms and legs would twitch, her mouth would froth and she would have convulsions and would faint. It would take six to seven hours for her to return to normalcy. Abba was very worried about Amma and he took her to the hospital for treatment.

During the summer of 1973, Abba told Amma to go to his Village with the children and spend the summer vacation there. He wanted that Amma and his children should be in touch with his relatives in the village. But Amma did not like the idea. Abba's father had passed away and Amma did not want to go to the village as Abba did not have his own house there. She told Abba, "First you build a house there and then I would go to stay there in the village with the children."

On hearing Amma's words, Abba became very furious and he shouted at Amma and asked whether she had brought dowry with her to enjoy such a luxurious life after marriage. He also told her to ask for money from her mother to build the house. This time Amma did not speak a word, she only shed silent tears. The row between Amma and Abba went on for more than a week and Abba did not talk to Amma!

After that Amma started remaining gloomy. She told her children that she had been offered a job as a craft teacher in a convent school, but Abba did not allow her to accept the job. Had she accepted the job, she too could have financially helped Abba and the family. She also told the children that Abba was angry because he was very distressed as he did not have money to build a house. All of Abba's salary was spent on the family and Abba could not save money to build a house. She told her daughters to study well and try to find good jobs, so that they should not be dependent on others for money, and they should be financially independent. Though Amma used to be very sad at Abba's behaviour, but she always compromised with the situations and tried to keep the family happy. She always remained a dutiful wife and mother!

Chapter - 20

ABERDEEN BAZAAR ON FIRE

It was the year 1973, and life was moving at its own pace for Abba and Amma. Children were doing well in their studies in their new school. At the home too, they were all adjusted to the new colony as there were many children there to play with. They all used to play together making a lot of noise, and the colony was a happy place!

After Abba and his family had shifted to Delanypore quarters, a very sad incident was witnessed by people of Port Blair. One of those nights, Aberdeen Bazaar, the main bazaar of Port Blair town was gutted down in fire. It was past midnight and on those days Port Blair town used to become silent by 7.00 p.m. People had all gone to bed and there was silence everywhere. The lights in houses were all put off. By midnight there was a big rumble. The cows of the neighbour's house started mowing loudly. Abba was a light sleeper, and the noise woke Abba and he got down from his bed. He opened the back door and went out to see what had happened. There he saw the sky glowing in crimson and was surprised. He called out to Amma and the entire household woke up, even the neighbours, had all come out. From there they could see Aberdeen bazaar on high flames!

Delanypore is on a hillock and is about two kilometres from Aberdeen Bazaar. All people from the neighbouring areas had gathered there and they could see the fire from the main road. All were scared to see the deadly sight. The sky had turned red and the heat of the fire could be felt till Delanypore. Throughout the night oil drums and paint drums were bursting into mid-air and igniting the night sky, the sight of which terrified the residents. People had all woken up and there was a big crowd at Delanypore junction, to watch the fire. It was a massive fire!

The sirens from the fire engines could be heard from Delanypore and there was a lot of noise coming from the bazaar and none could muster courage to go to the fire-affected area and help the people there!

Amma was worried about Chithi and her family who were then living at Babu Lane in Aberdeen Bazar. Abba went inside the house, changed his clothes and told Amma that he was going to Aberdeen bazaar to find out about Chithi and her family and also to help the people there. He told Amma to take care of the children and that he would try to return soon.

But Abba returned only the next morning and he told Amma that Chithi and her family were safe. The fire had not reached their place. Amma breathed peace. But throughout the night, Chithi's family and all the people of Babu Lane were in utter fear and panic and they all spent the night outside their houses, fearing the spreading fire. They were just a few streets away from the site of the fire. After assuring that Chithi's family was safe, Abba spent that night helping the people at the fire-affected area, trying to evacuate them to some safe place.

Abba told that many shop owners of Aberdeen Bazaar had lost their complete life-savings in the fire and the sad part was that most of the shops were not insured! The firefighting trucks arrived but they were unable to douse the fire. Most of the shops in the bazaar had been burnt to cinders. Abba also told that during the crisis, there were some greedy and covetous fellows, who wanted to make money from the situation.

While the shopkeepers brought out their goods and tried to load them in some vehicles to send them to their warehouses or some place of safety, those lorry or taxi owners did not take the goods to the warehouses of the shopkeepers. But they transported it to their own places of choice and looted the entire loads of goods. There was total pandemonium at Aberdeen Bazaar! Amidst the fire leaping forth and gutting shop after shop, the owners couldn't identify the drivers who had loaded their goods in trucks. Some shopkeepers who heard about those incidents were unwilling to take out the goods from their own shops. They told the rescuers that they would better see their goods burn down to ashes in shops, rather than see their properties looted. They did not open the shops, lest their goods should be robbed. With tearful eyes, they stood watching their shops burning and turning to ruins. The fire had not spread to those shops till then, and they could have easily saved their goods, but they allowed their shops to be gutted in the fire and willingly lost everything. It was a terrible sight!

Abba was there in the bazaar throughout the night and he had also watched some of those incidents. He could help a few shopkeepers to get back their goods. He was very angry with those people who had raided the shopkeepers, for showing such inhuman behaviour at a time of crisis and for being so selfish and greedy!

After a week of the fire accident, Abba took Amma and the children to Chithi's house. They had to walk through the main road of Aberdeen bazaar and the heat of the fire could still be felt. It was so heart-wrenching to see the burnt skeletonic structures of shops after braving the fire! Rubbles from the fire lay in heaps on both sides of the road and smoke was still escaping from those heaps! A small path had been cleared for people to walk through. Many people had come to see the condition of the Bazaar and were feeling very sad at the sight. The shop owners were clearing the debris from their places. The place appeared to be a burning ghat! The Aberdeen bazaar that always used to be bubbling with life, lay paralyzed like a burnt serpent. The entire bazaar was heaped with wreckages and rubble and there was sorrow and silence in the air.

Chapter - 21

ABBA DECIDES TO BUILD HIS HOUSE

Along with the passing time, Abba became very busy with his office work. But at the back of his mind, he could always hear Amma's words ringing about not having a house in the village and asking him when he would build his house. Abba finally decided to build a house in his father's land, in his village and decided to start the construction work during the summer vacation of that year. He told his plan to Amma and she was happy. They both started saving penny by penny, by all means, for their house. Abba also started arranging for money and he withdrew all his savings from his account, got salary advance, took a loan from his Provident Fund and also got a house-building loan from his office. He could collect around nine to ten thousand rupees. Then he got his leave sanctioned and during the summer vacation, set out for his village with Amma and the children. All were happy!

Before starting the construction work, Abba took his family to St. Anthony's Church at Uvari. It was a Tuesday and the church was overcrowded with devotees. There were the sick people and those people who were possessed by evil spirits. The Sacred Oil was blessed and kept on the Altar. People could apply the oil on their eyes and sit there and pray. If anyone was possessed, the evil spirit would come out of the person and leave. Abba told Amma to apply the oil on her eyes, as she used to have epilepsy. The children were worried thinking if Amma was possessed, what would they do. Amma applied the Holy oil on her eyes and sat in front of the church. There were devotees who were possessed, and they were shouting and telling so many stories as how they got possessed. Then those devotees started jumping in their places, begging to some unknown power telling, "Don't burn me! Don't send me to hell! I'll leave this person! etc.". Then those possessed people would run around the church five to seven times and then jump into the sea, that was just on the side of the church and would faint. The family members would be with the possessed person all the while and would bring the person out of the sea. Then, when the person would come to senses, the demon would have left its victim and the person would have become normal. Hundreds of devotees were getting cured in that way and were taken back home. Such prayers used to be held only on Tuesdays. Amma sat there for a long time with the Holy Oil applied on her eyes, but nothing happened to Amma and the children were happy, thinking that Amma was not possessed!

When Abba arrived at the village, he found that his elder brother's widow had built a small house on a piece of the family land and was living there alone. She had no children. Sometimes her brother's children used to come from another village and stay with her in her house. All her neighbours in the village were afraid of her due to her irritable nature. But she always used to be in good terms with Abba, as he always sympathised with her and also helped her with money. When Abba told her about his plans of building a house in the village, she was happy.

On an appointed day, the foundation stone for Abba's house was blessed and laid by the village priest, amidst prayers in the presence of Abba's family and relatives. Soon raw materials were bought, and sand, stones, brick, cement and timber filled the courtyard. Labourers were hired and Abba told his children also to assist the workers in the house-building work. As the construction work started, the entire area throbbed with activities. In the evenings when the workers would be given their daily wages, Abba would also give his children some money and would advise them to save the money.

Truckloads of river sand were brought for the construction and was dumped in heaps in front of the construction area. At night the whole family of Abba, Amma and children would spread mats or bedsheets on the sand bed and sleep there. There would be story sessions and Abba would tell stories about the ancient past to his children. Sometimes Abba's sisters with their grandchildren would also join Abba and his family. Then stories of the past would go on and on and children used to enjoy it.

The stories would be about the people of the village, the neighbouring villages, about the crimes committed in the village and people who had been bailed out with the help of money; or about people who had got treasures such as pots of gold from the waste lands and had suddenly become rich, of robbers attacking the village, the whirlwind that had lifted a child into the sky etc.

One famous story that was often told by Abba was about the ancient times when dacoits used to come on horsebacks to loot villages, one after the other, and people lived in fear of those dacoits. The dacoits used to enter villages and take away all precious belongings with them. The villagers used to feel helpless in front of their weapons. Sometimes they used to bury their loots of gold and silver in earthen pots in some waste land. In Abba's village too a few people were lucky to have discovered such buried treasures of pots of gold in wastelands and had suddenly grown rich!

Once, very long-ago, dacoits had entered the village of Mannarpuram. This incident had happened when Abba's grandfather was an infant, and it had then been spread by word of mouth from one generation to the other. It was after midnight when the dacoits had attacked the village. Two very old women were still awake and were talking about the ancient times. Nobody in the village knew their age and people believed that they must be about a hundred years old and as they say, in old age, even sleep becomes an enemy and doesn't want to embrace you. Those women were also spending sleepless nights, and were sitting in a corner of the courtyard and talking in a low voice about the times of yore. By then, the bandits had entered the village, and had started raiding the houses.

Some bandits found the two crones awake and talking in the corner of a courtyard. They got hold of the two women and dragged them out. They decided to have some fun with those old women. The women were frail and resisted the bandits. But the bandits got a lock and locked their long earlobes together. The women struggled and tried to free themselves but they could not release themselves, while the dacoits started laughing and having fun by teasing them!

Both the old women were afraid and started pleading to the dacoits to do no harm to them and to leave them, when miraculously, all of a sudden, the church bell at the steeple tower of Our Lady of Rosary Church started ringing on its own, continuously. The ringing went on and on, loudly and it aroused the whole village. The dacoits were shocked to hear the church bell ringing and they immediately came out of the houses they were raiding, leaving all their loot behind. The bandits who were teasing the old women till then, pushed them down and got on to their horses, and called out to their companions to escape and they all left the village in a haste!

The people of the village heard the church bell ringing continuously and all got up from their sleep and rushed out of their houses, panic-stricken, wanting to know what had happened. Usually, the church bell used to ring so continuously during some emergency or during the funeral toll, to announce the death of any villager. The uproar of the villagers had already made the bandits to escape from the village. The villagers assembled at the church yard, wanting to know who had rung the bell and the reason for the ringing of the bell from the steeple at that time. Some villagers found out the two old women whose earlobes had been locked together and brought them to the church yard. Then they somehow unlocked their earlobes.

The old women narrated to the villagers about the dacoits who had started raiding houses and how they locked their earlobes together, when suddenly the church bell started ringing on its own, saving the village from the dacoits. The old women told the villagers that it was the church bell that had saved the village that night. All the people thanked their

Maker, and for the miracle that had saved the village. After that incident, the faith of the villagers in their God and Church grew stronger!

Abba's story sessions used to go round and round and Abba's sisters used to join those sessions and tell their own stories. The children used to enjoy those story sessions and would fall asleep in between! Another story told by Abba's elder sister was incredible. Once there was a great cyclone. Strong gales were blowing and people took shelter inside their houses. The thatched roofs of huts were being flown away by the windstorm. On that day, a small child, about two years old was playing in the mud outside the house. No body remembered that the child was playing outside. Suddenly the storm turned into a whirlwind, and the child was lifted up into the funnel of the wind along with leaves and dust. Within moments, the child was in mid-air, and then was lost to view. Some people had seen the child being carried by the wind and soon the news spread in the village. Parents and the villagers started searching for the child and later on, the child was found a few miles away from the village. The stories told were all very interesting, and Abba's children loved those story-sessions!

During the day time, Abba used to be very busy, as he used to be providing the materials to the workers at the construction sites. Whenever some materials got finished, he would have to go to the town for procuring it and he would take Jason or his nephews with him. Jason used to feel so grown-up and responsible at those times, while going to town with Abba. As the work progressed, the building started getting a shape. It was a small bungalow made of bricks and cement, with a living room, two bedrooms, a Kitchen, a dining space, a room for pantry and an open terrace which could be reached from behind, by stairs from the left side of the house. To the surprise of all the villagers, there was a washroom within the house and there was also a washroom in the backyard of the house, within the campus. There was a compound wall, fencing the whole place with an iron gate. Abba told Amma that he was thinking of giving a name to the house and asked Amma if 'MALARAGAM' was alright! Amma agreed to the name as it meant 'Abode of Flowers', in Tamil.

Many villagers came to see Abba's house and they all admired it. By the time summer vacations drew to an end, Abba's money had also dwindled and he had to stop the work as he had to return to Andaman. A major part of the work had been completed but the woodwork and final finishing were yet pending. Thus, without finishing the house work, Abba and his family decided to return to Andamans. But before leaving the village, Abba spoke to his brother-in-law that after reaching Andaman he would send him money for completing the pending work of the house and his brother-in-law too agreed to take care of the work.

A few days before the end of the holidays, when Abba was getting ready to return to Andaman, a cousin of Abba came to meet him from the nearby town of Tisayanvillai. Abba's mother and that cousin's mother were sisters and so they were closely related. Abba told Amma and his children that once upon a time his cousin's family was very well off, but then, they were facing some financial crisis. Abba's cousin told Abba that his elder son had completed his Diploma in Education but was unable to find a job as a teacher in his town. With folded hands he requested Abba to help his son and to find a job for him in the Andamans.

Abba was moved by the pleadings of his cousin and told him, "Anna, (elder brother) you don't worry. I would take your son with me and I will try to find a job for him. I have three children and he would be the fourth child in my house. He can share our food and stay with us."

On hearing those words, Abba's cousin was overwhelmed and tears rolled down his eyes. He hugged Abba and blessed him!

On the appointed day Abba and his family were ready to leave the village. Abba's cousin and his son had already arrived. When the bus arrived, Abba and his family along with the young man, boarded the bus from the village junction. They reached Chennai and stayed in Abba's elder sister's house.

This was the same sister's family who used to live in Tisayanvilai village. The family had sold their land and property in Tisayanvilai, and had shifted to Chennai for good. They had purchased a property in Chennai and had also constructed a house there. Abba had sold Amma's mother's land for that sister when her husband had been trapped in a case. Whenever Abba used to visit his sister's house in Chennai, she would say to Abba that the house in which she and her family were staying belonged to Abba and one day she would hand it over to him. Abba used to simply smile at his sister as he knew that such a day would never come in his life!

The ship tickets for Abba and his family were already booked in M. V. Nancowry, so Abba purchased a ticket for his cousin's son. It was a bright sunny day and the weather was good when the ship set sail for Port Blair from Chennai Port. Abba had cabin tickets for his family and his children enjoyed the voyage thoroughly. They would go to the deck and watch the blue sea and the dancing waves, and even count those waves! Chennai coast was visible only for a few hours and then the ship entered into the deep ocean. Amma did not leave the cabin as she had sea sickness. But when the children would come down from the deck, they would tell her stories of the ship and the sea. For breakfast, lunch and dinner Abba used to take his children to the dining saloon, which used to be so neatly arranged for the cabin passengers and food was served there. For Amma, Abba arranged for food to be served in the cabin. The bunk passengers had to buy tokens and stand in a queue with their plates, to get their food!

The ship was a moving town with numerous facilities for the passengers. There was a recreation hall where people could play indoor games and every evening movies used to be screened there. There was a library-cum-reading room where cabin class passengers could spend their time reading books and magazines. There was also a dispensary with a doctor and nurse to treat the sick. Then there was the engine room with boilers and bellowing machines. It would be very hot over there. Abba's children used to go around the ship, observing each room and watching the activities going on there. Then they used to sit on the deck and watch the waves, sometimes they would watch the flying fish and would be excited. Flying fish are a wonder of the ocean. The entire shoal would leap out of the sea, fly for some distance and then would together fall back into the sea. The children would watch all those amusements and tell stories about them to Amma!

The ship had been sailing for two days, and on the third day at noon, the ship was suddenly stopped. Bells were rung continuously for a few minutes. All the passengers rushed to the deck to find out what had happened. The crew members in their sparkling white uniforms also were seen rushing to the deck and they all fell in a line. Some people were talking about a ship that had sunk in the ocean at that place many years ago, and to pay homage to it, the ship had been halted in the ocean. But Abba told the children that it was an emergency drill training. The training was for the crew to carry out the rescue operation, in case of some disaster. After about an hour the ship set sail again and the passengers were happy.

The next day, one of the passengers on the ship had a heart attack and his condition became critical. Even the best efforts of the doctor and medicines were not being able to steady his condition, and his life could not be saved. Within a few hours, the man passed away. Two more days were left for the ship to reach Port Blair, and the body of the deceased could not be preserved till then!

The ship was brought to anchor, and stopped in mid-ocean. Sirens were blown and prayers were read out. The dead body of the man was covered in a white shroud and placed in a coffin and then the coffin was lowered into the sea with some pieces of iron tied to it. It was a very sad sight. The family members of the deceased were wailing and mourning, unable to bear their grief. After about three hours, the anchor was lifted and the steamer continued on its voyage!

On the fifth day, the green islands could be seen and a cheer spread on all the faces of the passengers as they saw the emerald green islands spreading out in lush green colours, against the blue sea. Birds could be seen in the sky and leaves and twigs could be seen floating in the waves. As the ship crossed Ross Island[5], which stood as a sentinel at the entrance of the harbour, the furnace blared out a loud siren and smoke and soot escaped from the funnel of the ship. The pilot came in a boat to lead the ship to the harbour and then the ship was berthed at Haddo wharf. The passengers came on the deck and started searching for their relatives and friends at the harbour. When they could locate them, they waved at each other and expressed their joy. There was a melodrama of mixed emotions in the air!

Abba and his family finally reached home with a new member, a young man of twenty-two. Abba had willingly decided to bear the additional expenses of a new family member, just to help his cousin. Though Abba had a big heart and wanted to help everyone, but many times there would not be much money in his pocket to provide help. On the first of every month, Abba would bring his salary home and also sweets and savouries. Everyone would be very happy on those days. Abba would hand over the entire salary to Amma and he would tell the children that he had handed over his salary to the Home Minister of the house! Then whenever he would need money, he would ask money from Amma for his expenses, thirty to forty rupees, and Amma would quietly hand over the money to him.

After receiving the salary money in her hands, Amma would prepare a list of provisions to be purchased for the entire month and give it to the servant boy along with some money. The servant would procure all the things and bring them home in cardboard cartons. Then Amma would check the items with the bills, one by one and tally the bill amount. Sometimes the children would pester her for some sweets and she would buy it for her children. Then Amma would clean all the items and fill them neatly in bottles and containers that would have already been cleaned and dried, and arrange them on the kitchen racks.

The beginnings of the months used to be pleasant for Amma as she would have sufficient money for buying provisions, vegetables, fish, poultry etc. But by the second half of the month, Amma would be very careful and stingy with the money she had to spend. At the beginning of the month, she would cook fish and chicken on Sundays and holidays. But towards the end of the month, she would be satisfied cooking dal and vegetables, to be served with pickles. Sometimes when there won't be money to buy vegetables, then Amma would manage with dal and coconut chutney. Coconuts were always available at home as one or another friend of Abba who had farmland would bring it for Abba's household.

Sometimes, by the end of the month when there would be no money at home, Abba would be angry and there would be a row in the house. Abba would shout at Amma blaming that she had spent all the money lavishly. But he also knew that she never spent money lavishly but only for the family's needs. Those were very hard days!

Amma would never throw the old clothes but stitch out pillow covers from it. Uniforms used to be purchased for Sheryl and Jason, once in two years. For Meryl, Amma used to stitch uniform out of Sheryl's old uniform that would have become small for her. Amma would carefully remove the stitches from the old dress and get the cloth from it. Then she would turn the cloth as its top side would have been faded. Then by turning the cloth upside down, she would stitch a new dress for Meryl. The dress would look quite new and Abba would appreciate Amma for her creativity and thoughtfulness. But Meryl used to be sad as she usually got the old clothes of her elder sister, who would have grown out of it!

After the arrival of a new member at home, Amma had to face more problems in managing the house. But she would smilingly feed the young man and never allowed a frown to appear on her face. Sometimes Abba would tease Amma saying, "Amma, your Dal is running like a river!" And Amma used to smile as she would have added more water to the dal to manage it for everyone!

After about six months, Abba was able to get a job for his cousin's son and the young man got appointed as a Primary School Teacher and was posted to a primary school in Rangat. When he left home for joining his duty, Abba managed to give him some money and sent him off with blessings!

Chapter - 22

ABBA UNDERGOES TAHSILDAR TRAINING

Amma's seizures had not got fully cured yet, and Abba's family was struggling with Amma's ailment. She was unable to take in any happy or sad news, and she would have convulsions. On one occasion when Amma had her fits, Abba took her to the G. B. Pant Hospital, in Port Blair and admitted her there. Abba had taken Sheryl also with him to take care of Amma. Leaving Amma and Sheryl in the female ward, Abba went to meet the Head doctor. Abba knew most of the people of Port Blair including the doctors. While Abba had gone out, the lady doctor who was on duty came on rounds. She came to Amma's side, and started asking many questions to Amma in Hindi and when she found Amma dumb, she started shouting at Amma. Amma was confused as she did not understand so much Hindi. The lady doctor was from Kerala and Amma tried to express her problem in Tamil. But the lady doctor did neither listen to her nor sympathise with her and started scolding Amma.

Amma burst into tears and looked at Sheryl for help. Sheryl had been watching the behaviour of the lady doctor and she got angry. She tried to explain Amma's problem to the doctor in Hindi, but the doctor was arrogant and did not want to hear anything. She looked down at Amma in such an inferior way! Sheryl was just twelve years old but she defended Amma and told to the doctor, "You should be kind to the patients. You are a doctor and you don't even know how to talk to a patient!" This annoyed the doctor and she left the place immediately, red-faced. Amma was in tears and felt so helpless. She told Sheryl that she did not want to stay in the hospital and got down from the bed. She asked her daughter to collect her belongings, and walked out of the ward.

Amma was walking out of the female ward and Sheryl carrying the bag followed Amma. When they reached the entrance of the hospital, they saw Abba coming with a doctor. When Abba saw Amma, he was surprised and wanted to know why Amma was not in her ward. Amma could not say anything and Sheryl explained to Abba what had happened in the ward. She also told Abba that Amma did not want to be admitted and wanted to go home.

The doctor who was standing with Abba was the Head doctor and when he learnt what had happened in the ward, he was quite unhappy. He wanted to call in the lady doctor for an explanation, but Abba stopped him from doing so and told him that all such behaviours are normal in human life and that maybe the lady doctor had some personal problems due to which she had behaved in that way. Then the Head doctor took Amma and Abba to his chamber, examined Amma and wrote the prescription for her. After collecting the medicines, Abba brought Amma home. The children were happy as Amma was not admitted in the hospital. Amma was very proud of Sheryl for defending her and replying to the lady doctor about her inhuman behaviour and at home Amma proudly narrated the incident to Abba and her younger children.

In the year 1974, Abba received an order from the Administration, vide no. 1870 dated 10-7-74 to proceed to Katni in Madhya Pradesh for Tahsildar's training for 6 months. When Abba had to go for his training to Katni, he was much worried about Amma, as he did not know how Amma and the children would manage their work in his absence. Every day Abba would give instructions to his children about how they should behave, take care of Amma, study well and help Amma in the household chores. Abba also gave special instructions to Sheryl to take care of her younger siblings and Amma!

Amma was the sweetest and gentlest mother one could ever have. But for the past few years she had been suffering from epilepsy and the healthcare facilities were not so good in the Andaman and Nicobar Islands. Whenever she would be overjoyed or over sorrowful, she would have an attack of fits. She would suddenly swoon and foam in her mouth. Her entire body would go stiff, twisting and wilting and then she would become unconscious. She would not come to consciousness for about 5-6 hours during those times. The children would panic and wail and Abba used to console them and take care of Amma as well as the children. This was the constant worry of Abba while leaving for his training.

Chithi, was in Port Blair with her family and when she came to know about Abba's training, she told Abba that she would always be available for Amma's help. Abba also told his problems to his office staff and they were kind people. They assured Abba that they would visit Amma and the household regularly and provide the necessary help needed. Thus, being satisfied, Abba left for the training.

After Abba's departure, Amma had those fits again and Amma would faint while all her three children used to be sitting by her side throughout the night. Sometimes Chithi would come and stay with Amma for the night, but then she had her family and children to take care of and so she would have to return in the morning.

When Amma would be alright, she loved to chat with her children and listen to their stories about their school and friends. Washing clothes was her favourite chore and every day she would collect all the dirty linen of the household and wash them, spread them on the line and after they had dried, she would fold them and keep them in the cupboards.

One day while Amma was drying the clothes on the line in the backyard, the line snapped and hit Amma in her left eye. She sat down, unable to tolerate the pain. Her left eye became blood red with blood clotting. When the children returned from school, they saw Amma's blood clotted eye and her pain, and they were frightened. They thought that Amma had lost her left eye. They did not know what to do and did not know anyone in the hospital. Neighbours and friends who came home, suggested different types of medicines to cure the blood clot in Amma's eye. One family friend was an elderly Muslim uncle, who regularly visited Abba's house. In Abba's absence, he had visited the house on that day and saw Amma's condition. He advised the children to pour the blood of a live chick into Amma's eye, to cure her and after some time, he also brought a live hen, slit one of its hocks, and poured the blood into Amma's blood-clotted eye. But the blood clot in Amma's eye did not cure!

Those days, the pastoral care of the Catholic Church of the Andaman & Nicobar Islands was entrusted to the Priests of the Society of Pilar, Goa. The children knew a Malayalee priest in the church who was also a doctor. He always used to give medicine to the people of the parish who were sick and whoever sought his help. So, the children decided to take Amma to that priest. The priest saw Amma's blood clotted eye and applied some ointment to her eyes. He also gave the ointment to the children and told them to apply it carefully to Amma's eyes, three times a day and to take care of Amma. The children brought Amma home and carefully applied the ointment to Amma's eyes and also took care of Amma. After about a month, Amma's eye got cured!

While Abba was under training in Katni, he used to regularly write letters home. There used to be separate letters for Amma and the children. In his letters he would advise the children about their studies, discipline, going to church, obeying Amma and being good children with good conduct. The children too would write back to Abba about the family, about their achievements and progress in studies. Abba Once sent his photograph that was taken in Katni. He had thick black beard all over his face and was in a woollen coat and he looked handsome. Whenever any family friend would come home, the children used to show Abba's photo to them and used to feel proud and happy for Abba!

It was about three months after Abba had left for his training. One day when the children returned from school, they found Amma depressed and having those symptoms of having fits. They did not know what to do. Amma's hands were trembling and her eyes and face were twitching. Amma's all three children were standing beside her bed, feeling helpless. Amma had cooked lunch for the children and it was all kept on the dining table. Though Amma was very feeble and unable to get up and serve the children food, but whenever she would come back to her senses, she would try to tell them with her expressions to have their lunch, but the children had lost all their appetite! They were worried at Amma's condition and started discussing how to take care of Amma. They thought of taking her to the hospital, but then for that, she should be able to walk! The afternoon passed taking care of Amma and her condition did not improve.

In the evening the Muslim uncle visited Abba's house. When he saw Amma's condition, he told the children that may be Amma was possessed by some evil spirit. He also told that he would bring his Imam who knew to cure such type of illnesses which happens due to demonic possessions. The uncle left the house and after some time, he returned with the Imam. He also brought many things with him for the prayer. The Imam set all the things on a table, and started telling his prayers. He asked for a jug of water and then prayed with it. He sprinkled the water around the house and also sprinkled it in the room where Amma was sleeping. Then he took an egg, a few betel leaves and a nail and after praying for about half an hour, set out of the house with all those things. He crossed to Prem Nagar and went to a banyan tree there, which was about a few hundred meters away from Abba's quarter. He then kept the betel leaf at the foot of the tree and prayed for some time. Then, he broke the egg at the root of the tree and also drove in the nail into the trunk of that banyan tree. Jason had accompanied the Imam and uncle and had seen all the happenings and after returning from there he told his sisters about it. Then the uncle assured the children that Amma would be well soon, since the demon had been nailed to that banyan tree. That banyan tree was near to the children's school. While going to school and returning from school, they used to feel so scared on seeing that tree and always talked about the demon nailed to that tree!

But Amma did not get cured, in spite of all those prayers. Usually, she used to recover within a day or two, but that time it was more than three days and she was in a semi-conscious state. Chithi had come to see

Amma and she became much worried at Amma's condition. Whenever she would get time, she used to shuttle up and down from her house to take care of Amma.

One of the neighbours saw Amma's condition and brought home a staff nurse. The nurse gave Amma an injection and left back a vial with medicine, telling the children that the next day Amma had to be given the injection again and they should arrange for someone to give the shot, as she had her duties and won't be available. It was the next day and the injection had to be given to Amma, but the children did not know what to do as they did not know any other nurse!

There was an injection syringe and other paraphernalia at home and sometimes, when Amma used to be sick, Abba used to give her injection as per the doctor's advice, and the children had seen that several times. The children discussed the matter seriously and then Jason gave his opinion that Sheryl should try to give injection to Amma since she was the eldest. Even Meryl supported her brother and they showed their confidence in their elder sister that she could easily do it.

Though Sheryl was afraid, but she gathered all courage, and broke open the vial, filled the syringe with the medicine and praying to God, injected the hypodermic into her mother's arm. But the needle would not enter the skin and blood started flowing out and she was so terrified that she pulled out the needle immediately. Jason and Meryl, who were standing by her side, kept coaxing her to try again, at the same time all three of them were crying. Tears were rolling down their eyes. The two younger children held their mother's arm tightly and once again Sheryl tried to pierce the needle into her mother's skin with all her strength. This time she was successful and she emptied the medicine in the syringe into her mother's body! God, she had done it! All three children hugged each other and wept bitterly while their mother lay in an unconscious state, unaware of her children's sorrow!

That day, by evening Amma returned to her normal sense. Later on, when Chithi and her husband came home, the children told them about the incident of giving injection to Amma, and they got very angry at the children, saying that it was too dangerous. They told the children that the needle could have got broken inside Amma's body and it could have claimed her life. The children were very scared on hearing that. They had not thought about it. However, the incident became a folklore of the family!

At Port Blair, at Abba's household, the period of 6 months passed struggling with Amma's illness and the day today problems of life. At Katni, Abba's training got over on 31-12-74. After completing his training, Abba arrived at Port Blair by January 10, 1975. He brought sweets and dresses for all his children, saris for Amma and Chithi and he also brought a sari for Sheryl.

Those days Amma hardly had two or three good saris which she used to wear while going to church or while attending some functions. Once in a year Abba used to buy some cotton saris for Amma to wear at home and she used to maintain her clothes very well, using starch and was always neat. Sheryl was in class ninth and Abba thought that she would have grown up to wear a sari and so he had brought a sari for her too!

Amma and the children were happy at home as Abba had returned. Now no one had to worry about anything, anymore, as Abba was there to shoulder all the responsibilities of the household!

During those days, one of Abba's close friends was facing some family problems. He was a Keralite and Abba knew him from the early days of his coming to Andaman. Abba had been a great help to him then, in finding a job for him. One day the friend told Abba that his wife was suffering from some psychological problems and she was behaving strangely at home. His children were very young and they were frightened to see their mother in that state. The doctor had advised him to change her place of residence for a few days and it would do her good. Since he considered Abba like a brother, he shared his problem with Abba.

When Abba heard about it, he told his friend not to worry and that he would help him. He also told his friend to bring his wife to stay with his family for a few days, for a change of place. The friend was very grateful. The same day evening, he brought his wife to stay in Abba's house. The lady was a kind hearted person and Abba's family knew her well as they were family friends, and used to visit each other's houses. After coming to Abba's house, the lady was normal in her behaviour for some time, but then suddenly she started singing nursery rhymes, clapping her hands and dancing like a small child. Amma and her children became anxious to see her like that. Though Amma was very frightened, but since the children were at home, she did not worry much. But the next day, after Abba had gone to his office and the children had left for their school, Amma was alone at home with the lady and the domestic help. Amma started panicking when the lady suddenly started laughing very loudly, nonstop, and then she started calling out the names of her children. Amma was unable to control her and was very frightened. With the help of the domestic help, Amma managed to silently lock the bedroom door so that the lady wouldn't be able to go out. The lady started banging on the door and started shouting loudly, calling out to Amma, but Amma did not open the door. Though Amma was very frightened, but she waited patiently for Abba and her children to return home!

When the children returned from school, they too heard the aunty singing the nursery rhymes loudly and calling out her children's names and they did not know what to do. When Abba returned from office, he was shocked to find Amma and the children standing in the veranda, waiting for him. When he entered the house, he too heard the lady's shouting, her singing and dancing in the room and Amma's worries. Abba became worried that Amma might have her seizures again! He sent words to his friend, and he came after some time and took his wife back with him. This was Abba, always ready to help others!

In 1975 Abba again received his transfer order and he had been posted to Rangat[6] as Tahsildar. Abba told Amma to pack up all the things soon, as they would be leaving for Rangat in a fortnight.

Chapter - 23

ABBA ASSUMES CHARGE OF TAHSILDAR RANGAT

On receiving the transfer order, Abba started making arrangements for packing all the household things. Peons from Abba's office came to help him in the packing. After about a week the packing was completed. It was the month of June, and the monsoon had already set in and was raining cats and dogs. Since there were no roads available connecting South Andaman with North Andaman, all luggage had to be transported to Rangat by a steamer.

On an appointed day Abba with Amma and the children left for Rangat in the steamer called 'T.S.S. Yerawa'. Abba got a cabin booked and that was comfortable for the family, but the sea was very rough. Children could not go on the deck due to the torrential rains. The waves were high and with every coming wave, the steamer was being tossed up and down. Those who were on the deck would roll right and left along with the waves. Along with passengers, the cattle, baskets with poultry and other goods being transported to Mayabunder would also roll from here to there. Sometimes with every dip of the prow of the ship, water would be splashed on the deck. Many times, people would be very scared and they would pray to their Gods to take the steamer safely to its destination!

On the way to Rangat, the ferry stopped at Havelock Island and Abba told his children that the place was under South Andaman district, and the population consisted mainly of Bengali Settlers and many of them had their origin from East Pakistan, as those people were given settlement by the Indian government after the Partition of India in 1947. Abba had already conducted survey work in the island and told that there were six villages in the island: Govinda Nagar, Vejoy Nagar, Shyam Nagar, Krishna Nagar, Radha Nagar, Shyam Nagar and Krishna Nagar. In December 2018, the island has been named as Swaraj Dweep, as a tribute to Netaji Subhas Chandra Bose. The island is known for its pristine beaches. Radhanagar Beach on the western coast, also known as Number 7 Beach, is one of the most popular beaches on the island.

After about an hour the ferry left for Neil Island, which is known for its mesmerising deep blue waters surrounding the island. This island with beautiful beaches is located between Havelock and Ross Island. Abba told his children that he had conducted survey work on Neil Island as well, and the vast majority of settlers at Neil Island were refugees from erstwhile East-Pakistan, following their migration prior to that country's war of independence in 1971. The villages on Neil Island are Sitapur, Bharatpur, Neil Kendra, Lakshmanpur and Ram Nagar. In December 2018, Neil Island was renamed as Shaheed Dweep as a tribute to Netaji Subhas Chandra Bose. Abba bought Rosagolla for his children from the island and after about an hour the ferry moved towards its next destination.

During the later part of the day, the rains stopped, and children went on the deck to enjoy the blue sea. After a few hours, the steamer reached Nimbutala and Amma and the children were happy. They got down the steamer and found that Abba's office Jeep was at the jetty to pick them up. A lorry had also been booked to carry the luggage. After the luggage was loaded, Abba and his family left for Rangat which was more than 10 km. away from the place.

The journey from Nimbutala to Rangat was very pleasant. The winding roads passed through the lush green forests, with the sunlight playing hide and seek through the thick foliage. Tall trees, bamboo shoots, orchids hanging from trees, the blue-sky visible among the thick vegetation, everything was enthralling to the eyes and the soul. Abba, Amma and the children spotted wildlife in abundance in the forests such as deer, wild goat, boar and monitor lizard and a variety of birds cooing and chirruping from tree top and they enjoyed their journey thoroughly. Since the children were enquiring about the places, the driver kept telling the names of places to them now and then and he also described the specialty of those places. Abba knew all those places as he had visited those settlements many times for survey and rehabilitation work. There were also green paddy fields on either side of the road which were captivating the minds. Suddenly Abba would tell the driver to stop the jeep in front of some house and he would get down. The people there would be overjoyed to see Abba and they would heartily welcome Abba and his family into their house and they would also serve them sweets and savouries. Abba knew so many families there!

Abba reached Rangat with his family in the evening and the next day morning, on 11-6-1975 Abba took charge of his office as Tahsildar, Rangat. The town of Rangat is situated in Middle Andaman, around 210 km from Port Blair and it is 70 km to the south of Mayabunder. It is one of the three tahsils of the North and Middle Andaman district including the villages of Rangat, Bakultala, Dashratpur, Kadamtala, Kaushalyanagr, Long Island, Nilambur, Nimbutala, Paransala, Sabri, Shivapuram, Sundargarh, Urmilapur and Uttara. Rangat itself is a small town nestled amidst greenery everywhere.

The town had a small bazaar with decrepit stretch of petty shops on either side of the road for various utilities. A small nallah flowed on the side of the town and during rains it used to be flooded. The earmarked Tahsildar's quarter was on a hillock next to the Government Guest House and the Tahsildar's office. From there one could have a bird's view of the whole town of Rangat.

The quarter allotted to Abba was a wooden bungalow on stilts. It was in an independent campus with a huge lawn carpeted with green grass and Abba's children loved to roll and play on the green grass there. There were four big rooms in the main building, and the kitchen and pantry were at the back, in a separate building that was connected to the main building with wooden stairs. The doors had glass panels at the top half side and wooden planks at the bottom half side. Since the building was on tall stilts, there was ample space under the building for children to play all sorts of games!

Behind the backyard of the house, there was the dense forest with tall trees swaying with climbers. A brook flowed through the forestland singing its way and ended in a small puddle behind the backyard of Abba's bungalow, covered with wild plants and bushes. During summer season, wild goats could often be seen there, drinking water from the puddle. When the wild goats would be seen drinking water there, Amma would hush the children and tell them not to make noise, lest they should be frightened and run away. There was a big garden surrounding the house with fruit-bearing trees and a bedlam of birds chirruping throughout the day. The tamarind and mango trees at the back of the kitchen used to be full of fruits during the season and those days, Abba's children, after school, loved to spend their time on those trees, eating tamarind or mangoes with chilli powder and salt. Throughout the year, a variety of birds could be seen in the garden which would be so fascinating!

By evening the whole scenario would change and insects would take up the stage. Crickets would start singing from the trees and from the surrounding jungle, while moths, butterflies, and beetles would lavishly enter the house through the windows and occupy all the walls. Sometimes the flying ants would swarm into houses and Amma would tell the children to close all windows and doors to avoid those ants. She would also predict that it would rain soon, and it would really rain, which used to amaze the children!

At night the fireflies could be seen teeming in the garden and on the trees in the jungle behind the house, glowing their tiny light in the darkness. They would also enter the house and children would catch them and put them into bottles or matchbox and play with them. But Amma always used to be against it and would insist that the children should set the fireflies free. Abba would tell the children that those insects glowed to attract its mates and they lived only for about two to three weeks. By late night all the fireflies would settle in the guava tree in the garden and the entire tree would look like a bright Christmas tree, glowing throughout the night! Abba's children used to watch the tree at night, through the windows and marvel at it. Such a heavenly sight it used to be to see the clear star-laden sky above and the fireflies glowing everywhere in the garden below!

Rainy season used to be terrible in Ragat and it would pour night and day, for days together, with thunder and lightning reverberating the skies. It used to appear as if the skies were expressing their fury and vengeance on the earth below. There used to be news about trees burning and exploding due to striking of lightnings and people standing near those trees being killed by the lightning. Abba used to tell his children that houses were fitted with lightning rods, to protect it, in case lightnings strike on houses. Since the lightning bolt hits the tallest point, those rods are fixed at the highest point of the building, aiming to attract the lightning bolt. When the lightning bolt strikes, the rod safely channels the millions of volts of energy through copper or aluminium cables into the earth.

In Rangat Abba got his children admitted to the government schools there. There were two schools, one was a Higher Secondary school having classes from VI to XI, offering education in Hindi and Bengali medium, while the other school was a primary school having classes from I to V offering education in Hindi, Bengali, Tamil and Telugu medium. Since Abba's children were already in Hindi medium school, so there was no problem with their studies. In the school Jason had joined the Junior NCC group, and on the days, when he would have NCC classes, he used to feel so proud, wearing his NCC uniform and cap.

Abba was a great administrator and shouldered all his responsibilities well. Everyone in Rangat office, appreciated him for his passion for work. He was also the Magistrate of Rangat and had a court in his office where he used to settle the family quarrels and land related disputes of people belonging to Rangat Tehsil. Family disputes also used to be brought to him about quarrel over the property, taking care of the elderly parents, fight between children for the parental property, the husband-wife quarrel, etc. Abba used to hear all those cases patiently and used to settle those cases wisely and amicably. Sometimes he used to share some of those cases with Amma. At home, Abba used to read out the Proverbs from the Bible, and tell tales of King Solomon and tales from Panchtantra to his children. He would advise his children to be wise in life. Since Abba's office was the Magistrate's office, the National Flag had to be hoisted every morning and the same had to be lowered every evening during sunset and Abba used to attend to all his duties very sincerely.

Abba was a great artist and loved to act. In his younger days, he was devoted to the stage. He was an ardent admirer of 'Shivaji Ganeshan'[7] the famous actor of Tamil cinemas. In a jolly good mood, Abba would speak out the dialogues from the movies of 'Shivaji Ganeshan' with all emotions and entertained Amma and the children at home. He would also sing the film songs of life and death from the movies of that great actor. He was very creative too. It was his hobby to decorate the house with curtains, furnishings and flowers. He would also design and decorate the 'Altar'[8] at home, with the help of his children.

In Rangat Abba used to be invited as Chief Guest for cultural programmes organized by various communities living there. Since there were people from Tamil Nadu, Kerala and West Bengal, many festivals used to be celebrated there. Abba used to attend all those cultural programmes with his family, celebrated on the occasion of Pongal, Onam, and Durga Puja and also attended the 'Jatra'[9] and 'Villu Pattu Kachcheri'[10] till late at night and enjoyed it.

There was a temple of Lord Karthikeyan, also known as Murugan Temple built on the rocks, in the centre of Rangat town. The 'Panguni Uthiram'[11] festival used to be the most important festival celebrated in that temple by the Tamil Hindus. The devotees used to fast for ten days, spending their time in prayers, and preparing themselves for the festival. On the last day, many devotees would walk on the fire, with milk pots or 'Kavadi'[12]. It would be a mega event of the year and many people from distant villages would throng to Rangat to see the 'Fire walking Festival'.

The fire pit would be the size of a volleyball court and it would be got ready from many days. The place would be dug to about three to four feet depth. People would start gathering huge logs in the pit, days before the event. On the day of the festival, since early morning, those logs would be burnt and the red-hot embers would be spread in the pit. More and more logs would be burnt throughout the day so that the entire pit could be completely filled with embers. By evening the fire pit would be ready with a cushion of glowing embers red-hot. Men could be seen turning the embers from time to time so that they do not get extinguished. Those men would be sweating profusely, and could be seen pouring water on themselves, from the barrels that would be arranged near the pit. A boundary would be made with ropes around the fire pit and the spectators would not be allowed to cross the lines.

The 'Idumban Puja' used to be held on the eve of the fire walking festival. According to Tamil Hindu mythology, Idumban is considered to be an asura, who was a devotee of Lord Karthikeyan. According to the legend, Sage Agastya is said to have wanted two hills, Shivagiri and Shaktigiri, to be transported to his abode in the south, and he commissioned the asura Idumban, who was his disciple, to carry them. Idumban obeyed to the orders and he bore the hills slung across his shoulders by inventing a tool called the kavadi. The tool was made out of the staff of Lord Brahma and it was employed as a pole, and the two divine serpents were employed as ropes for the pole. When Idumban became fatigued after carrying the hills, he placed the kavadi near Palani to rest and revive. Meanwhile, Murugan who had journeyed to Palani after losing the fruit of wisdom to his brother Ganesha, claimed the hills to be his own. Unable to lift the hills and resume his journey, Idumban confronted the deity and was killed in the combat, but was resurrected on the request of his wife, Idumbi, and the sage Agastya. After having restored to life, Idumban wished to serve at Murugan's shrine. Thus, Lord Murugan declared that Idumban would stand guard at the foot of the hill, and also announced that every devotee who worshipped him at the site would first adore his dwarapala or door guard, Idumban.

Before entering the fire pit, water mixed with turmeric used to be poured on the feet of the devotees. Some devotees would have tiny Vel[13] pierced into their bodies, cheeks and tongues. It would be an amazing sight to see the devotees in yellow clothes, white vibhuthi dusted on their bodies with vel pierced, and all devotees shouting 'Vel-Vel'. After all the devotees had crossed the fire pit, the last devotee would enter the fire pit pulling a chariot that would be attached to his body with iron clamps.

The Vel has got a special significance in Hindu Mythology. It is believed that Goddess Parvati presented the Vel to her son 'Karthikeyan' as an embodiment of shakti. Thus, Murugan is also known as Vel Murugan. After the celebration would be over, people would extinguish the fire of embers the next day by using milk and water.

While in Rangat Abba bought a Jersey cow and there was no dearth of milk and curd at home. A man was appointed to take care of the cow and Abba paid him some money every month. He would milk the cow in the morning and evening. The children would enjoy watching the man milking the cow. Amma would boil the milk and collect the cream from the milk. Then she would make butter and ghee from the cream for home use.

One day Abba brought two pairs of Guiney Pigs home. One office staff of Abba's office had been transferred and he had left his Guiney pigs with Abba. Since the house was on stilts, there was enough space under the building for all those animals. Soon the Guiney pigs started breeding and their numbers reached more than forty. The children enjoyed counting them and feeding them with grass and chapattis.

It was 2nd October 1975, and there was news on the radio about the death of a popular leader Kumaraswami Kamaraj[14] due to cardiac arrest. On hearing the news, Abba became very sad and wept like a child. He told his children that Kamarajar was a great leader known for his simplicity and integrity. He had served as the Chief Minister of the Tamil Nadu and had played a major role in developing the infrastructure of the State, and had worked to improve the quality of life of the needy and the disadvantaged. He had made immense strides in education and trade. New schools were opened, so that poor rural students need not walk more than three kilometres to their nearest school. Better facilities were added to existing ones. No village remained without a primary school and no panchayat without a high school. Kamarajar fought to eradicate illiteracy by introducing free and compulsory education up to the eleventh standard. Amma told the children that the system of education geared up in Tamil Nadu state because of the efforts of Kamarajar. Abba went on talking about the achievements of the great leader throughout the day and mourned his death. He was very sad and told his family that the nation had lost a great leader and a great soul!

One day Abba brought a spotted deer home, it was a fawn and it was caught by some men while it had entered their farmland. Animals such as deer and wild goat were in abundance in the jungles and now and then would enter the farmlands and paddy fields and destroy the crops. The farmers would set traps to catch those animals. If any deer was caught, they would kill it and distribute the venison among their neighbours and friends. But on that day, the farmers found a young fawn in the trap, and they did not feel like killing it. There was no zoo in Rangat to keep the fawn and when Abba learnt about the fawn, he sent his men to bring it home. The huge lawn in front of Abba's quarter appeared complete with the fawn grazing there. After school, Abba's children would spend a lot of time playing with the deer. They would collect tender grass and feed the deer and used to be very happy. The deer was there for a few months and when Abba was transferred and was leaving Rangat, he handed it over to the Forest Department officials with the request to send it to the zoo at Port Blair.

Winters used to be very cold in Rangat. The entire place would be foggy by evening and people could be seen moving with shawls and sweaters and the place would appear like a hill station. The coconut oil in bottles would freeze and it had to be melted by keeping the bottles near the hearth or in the morning sun. As Abba loved gardening, soon he planted roses, lilies and other ornamental plants in the garden and had the best garden with all varieties of flowers blooming there. He loved to walk on the garden lawn early in the morning and collect roses and lilies for the vase. Sometimes he would tell his daughters to collect flowers for the vase and decorate the house.

As a part of his duty, Abba also visited other villages or islands. Once during the Durga Puja holidays, Abba had to go to Kadamtala Island on duty for a week. Since the puja holidays had started for the children, Abba decided to take Amma and the children with him so that they could also enjoy their holidays. He booked rooms in the Forest Guest House at Kadamtala and left for the tour with his family, in his office jeep. The journey was through the Reserved Forest and was dangerous. The forest was the home of one of the native tribes -the Jarawas[15].

The Jarawas are one of the ancient aborigines of the Andamans and lived in the forests of Kadamtala and South Andaman. They were pitch dark in colour with short curly hair and belonged to the Negrito stock. They were similar to the Great Andamanese. An entire stretch of forest area was marked as a reserved forest for the safety of the Jarawas and there were check posts with police personnel at both the ends of the forest. Only people having permits were allowed to enter those forests, after proper checking of the documents.

The Jarawas lived on the western coasts of the South and Middle Andaman Islands. They were very hostile and were still in the primitive stage of their life on earth, and were hunter-gatherers in the true sense. They entirely depended on the forest and sea for their food. Wild boar, monitor lizard, fish, fruits, honey and tubers were part of their main food. Both male and female Jarawas used to remain completely naked. They loved to decorate themselves with clay, shells and palm leaves.

After the British conquered these islands, the Jarawa population decreased to a great extent. Later, when the settlers from East Bengal and Burma made their settlement in the allotted land of South and Middle Andaman, the Jarawas turned very hostile as it was their land that had been occupied by the settlers.

The Jarawas regularly attacked the people of the settlements and took away goods, utensils and food items. Whenever people dared to pass through the forest, the Jarawas used to hide on the trees and attacked those people with their poisonous arrows. Many people had already been killed by the Jarawas who had tried to venture into those jungles. The Jarawas always carried their bows and arrows with them. People from the settlements did not dare to venture alone into the Reserved Forest area.

While travelling through the Reserved Forest, a bush police personnel also accompanied Abba and his family in the jeep, holding his rifle. On reaching Kadamtala, Abba left Amma and the children in the Forest Guest house and went on his tour to the nearby villages. The children and Amma had a gala time by playing indoor games and having fun. In the evenings, when Abba would be free from his work, he too would join Amma and the children and played Ludo, Chess or Rummy with them. Nights in the guest house were frightening as there were no houses nearby and the fear of 'Jarawas' was in the minds of Amma and the children. The jungle used to become alive at night with the crickets chirruping in chorus and the fireflies flashing their lights. At night sudden cries of animals could be heard, that used to make the children cuddle with fear!

One afternoon while Abba and his family were in the forest guest house, suddenly there was an uproar and people could be seen running on the roads. It was lunchtime and Abba had come for lunch. Someone told Abba that a PWD truck that was transporting labourers through the Reserved Forest had been attacked by the Jarawas. The Jarawas had tracked the truck and had attacked the truck by showering arrows on the men. One labourer had died in the attack and about 10 men had been injured. The driver somehow managed to escape with all the labourers in the truck. The Jarawas knew every inch of the jungle, and were also aware of every movement of poachers or settlement people moving in the jungle. They were experts in climbing trees and moving from tree to tree, faster than the monkeys. They would silently stalk the vehicles or people who crossed the forest and when they would get an opportunity, they would kill those people using their bows and arrows. People said that the Jarawas used to wet the arrows with their spit and shoot at people. It was believed that since they did not consume salt, their spit worked as venom on those arrows.

After learning about the incident, Abba called his driver and immediately left the place to meet the victims attacked by the Jarawas. Abba saw that there was a crowd as people had come to see the men who had been shot by Jarawas. Arrows were still stuck in the bodies of some men. The corpse of the man who had died in the attack was kept separately on a cot, covered with a white shroud. After some time, the doctor arrived and he asked the people to move away from the victims. At first, he checked the wounded men and provided them with first aid and medicines.

The children also had followed Abba to see what had happened but Amma had stayed back. After sometime the children returned to the guest house and told Amma that some men still had arrows stuck to their bodies and they were bleeding profusely. Amma was much frightened on hearing that.

Abba remained with the victims for a long time, talking to them and encouraging them. The villagers had gathered in large numbers crowding there and they complained to Abba about the regular Jarawa attacks and how the Jarawas looted their houses at night times. They requested for police protection and Abba assured them help.

After the first aid was given to all the injured men, it was time for the doctor to do the postmortem of the man who had been killed by the Jarawas. But the doctor was very nervous. He was a young man, very new to his profession and he was quite anxious. He requested Abba to accompany him during the postmortem. Abba did not know what to do. But seeing the delicacy of the situation and the condition of the doctor, Abba decided to accompany him. Abba stayed with the doctor throughout the postmortem giving moral support to the doctor. Finally, after a few hours the medical examination got over and Abba returned to the guest house. Abba told Amma that he had accompanied the doctor to the postmortem, and Amma appreciated Abba's courage. In the evening the doctor came to meet Abba at the Guest House and expressed his gratitude for supporting him!

In Rangat, Abba used to take his family to the beaches and he used to tell them that most of the beaches hosted turtle nesting grounds. Some of the famous turtle breeding beaches are Amkunj beach, Cuthbert Bay and Dhaninallah beach. The Karmatang beach at Mayabunder is also known for turtle breeding. Jason and Sheryl told Abba that boys from their school used to bring turtle eggs collected from the beach and play with it. Those eggs looked like tennis balls, and used to be soft. But Abba told his children that it was not right to play with turtle eggs.

Rangat was a wonderful hamlet and Abba enjoyed his work in Rangat. He was a perfectionist and liked to work in a time-bound manner. He had a cordial relationship with the officers of various departments and they all admired Abba's skill and work ethics. He was a very humble person and was always very kind and considerate towards his subordinate staff. After a year, in 1976, Abba received his transfer order to Port Blair.

Chapter - 24

ABBA IS POSTED AS TREASURY OFFICER

In 1976, Abba came to Port Blair with his family and he again admitted his children to Nirmala convent school. He could not get accommodation immediately, as allotment of government quarter used to take some time. One of Abba's junior officers a Malayalee chap, who was also a friend of Abba, had been allotted a government accommodation in Goal Ghar but the man had not shifted into it as his family was on the mainland India. His wife and children were supposed to return only after a year. When he came to know about Abba's problem, he told Abba that he could occupy his quarter, till Abba was allotted his own accommodation. Abba thanked him for his generosity and soon shifted into the quarter with his family.

The quarter where Abba had shifted with his family was very close to the convent school and the Catholic Church. Abba too assumed his office as Treasury Officer, Andaman and Nicobar Administration.

At Abba's village, the construction work of Abba's house could not be completed due to financial constraints. Though Abba had told his brother-in-law that he would send money to complete the pending house work, but he couldn't do so. Finally, after three years, Abba could arrange for the money and the work had got completed. After Abba came to Port Blair, he received a letter from his brother-in-law stating that the construction work of the house had been completed. Abba was happy and decided to visit his village. But the session had started and children could not accompany him due to their school. So, Abba was confused.

When Chithi and her husband came to know that Abba wanted to go to the village, they told Abba that they need not worry about the children as they would take care of them.

Soon Abba applied for leave and went to the village with Amma. Abba and Amma were very happy as the construction of their house had been completed. Now, they had their own house in the village. A house warming function was held in a simple way and Abba christened the house 'MALARAGAM' after his daughters, meaning abode of flowers. Then Abba and Amma returned to Chennai, and Abba took Amma to a hospital and got her medical check-up, as her seizures had not got cured. Amma was given medicines and soon after, they returned to Port Blair.

After about six months Abba was allotted a type-II government quarter in Junglighat, in front of Chowdhary saw mill that was close to Junglighat jetty and playground.

The Junglighat colony had eight blocks of houses with four apartments in each block. 32 families were living in that colony and the people hailed from various states of India. Most of the families were from Kerala. There were also families from Tamil Nadu, Andhra Pradesh, Uttar Pradesh, Bihar, West Bengal and Karnataka. People followed various religions and the colony was a perfect example of 'Mini India' with communal harmony and national integration. All the festivals were celebrated by the residents of the colony with equal enthusiasm. During Diwali people living in all the houses would light 'Diya', the earthen lamp or candles and children would burn crackers together. A star would twinkle in every household during Christmas and Holi was played by all the children of the colony together. They would mix colours in big buckets and splash them on everyone who crossed the colony. They never spared anyone. With the same fervour, the residents also celebrated Durga Puja and Eid. During their own festivals, people distributed sweets to all the houses in the colony and it was a tradition followed by each house.

The Junglighat jetty was very close to the colony and fresh fish would be available during mornings and evenings at the jetty, for people to buy. Children of the colony used to go for walks at the jetty. Whenever the ferry would arrive with passengers from Dundus Point or Namunaghar, it would be a heart-warming sight. School students, college students and office going people would be transported by this ferry. There also would be vegetable vendors travelling in those ferry boats who brought vegetables from their farmland, to be sold in the colonies, carried on shoulder poles, balancing two cane baskets suspended from each end. They used to bring seasonal vegetables and fruits and it used to be very fresh, and all the womenfolk of the colony used to buy vegetables from those vendors.

In the colony, there were two to four children in each household and evenings used to be very noisy there. All the children would assemble either in the yard of the colony or in the playground and play various games according to the season such as 'Gilli-Danda, Kite flying, marbles, kabaddi, Ce-buddi etc., and there would be a bedlam of noise and shouting. During the season of kite flying, Jason used to be very excited and Amma and his siblings used to help Jason in making kites, using bamboo and paper, attaching the sails as well as the tail to the kite. But preparing the twine for the kite would be a tedious job. Jason would want to firm the kite using glue. Sometimes, powdered glass mixed with flour glue would be applied to the strings and then it would be left in the sun to dry and become firm. He used to tell Amma that it would make the string strong and his kite would be able to cut the strings of the other kites. While flying the kites, there used to be a lot of competition among the children and when they would be able to cut another person's kite, how happy they used to be! Sometimes boys from other colonies also used to come for kite flying and sometimes there used to be a row between the colony boys and the outsiders. How happy Jason used to be when he would win a kite-fight by cutting an opponent's line and bring home a kite that he would have won! Then there were the football matches held in the ground among the boys. Amma always used to become a child with her children and enjoyed all their games!

Various programmes and activities used to be held at Junglighat grounds. During Dussehra festival a pandal used to be set and the puja would take place there. People would throng the pandal with families and it used to be a wonderful sight. Then there used to be those magic shows by magicians from mainlands, and all people would crowd to see those magic shows. Sometimes a cyclist would come from the mainlands and the ground would be decked with festoons and blaring loudspeakers. The cyclist would begin cycling at day break and go on and on throughout, pedalling his cycle till late night. He would drink tea or water, and even have his meals while cycling, and people used to encourage him by pinning rupee notes on to his shirt or garlanding him with rupee notes. Sometimes there used to be films screened by the Field and Publicity department, which used to be an entertaining pass-time for people. During the rainy season, the children of the colony would assemble within houses and play all types of indoor games, and sometimes they would simply sit and chat. While the children used to be playing, mothers would assemble in groups and chit-chat about cookery or their children's studies, while men folk would be seen discussing politics or their office problems. Those were good old days as people had time for their neighbours! But when it would be time for the lights to be on, all would disperse, and the children would run back to their homes to study their lessons.

Amma got some good friends in the colony who could speak Tamil. There was a family from Coorg with two sons and the lady of the family could speak Tamil. She was very close to Amma and they visited each other's house and used to have chit chats over a cup of coffee. Since Abba was the Treasury Officer, there was a telephone installed in the house and Abba also had an office jeep that used to take him to the office and bring him back home. Abba was regarded with high esteem by everyone in the colony and Amma was also looked up to with dignity. Whenever somebody in the colony faced any problems, they used to meet Abba and seek his advice.

While staying in the colony, one day Abba got a pet dog. He loved dogs and could be seen caring for the dog and feeding it regularly. It was an ordinary stray dog, pitch black in colour and Abba named it Blackie. After a few years the dog died in an accident. Later Abba got another dog and named it Caesar. Amma would say that Abba had got fondness for dogs from his father, as Abba's father always used to have pet dogs!

While staying in Junglighat colony, a tragic incident happened. A Malayalee Christian family in the colony had three children, two sons and a daughter, and the children were in their primary classes. Both the parents were working in government office. The father used to be very strict with his sons while the mother was very kind hearted, but she often used to be ill. In the afternoon, after the children would return from school, the parents would give them lunch and then leave for their office. They used to give proper instructions to their children to do their home-work and not go out of the house till they returned. Even the children used to assure their parents that they would stay inside the house and would not go out. But the moment the parents would leave the house and would be out of sight, the boys would rush out of their house to play, leaving their little sister at home as she was very young. They would play with cycle tyres or simply chase each other by running around the quarters. The people of the colony used to watch the boys playing and would smile at their innocent antics!

On that day, just after the parents had left for their office, both the brothers ran out of their house to play. It was drizzling lightly. Behind the sea-facing quarters of the colony, huge pits had been dug for the construction of a new building. While both the brothers started running around, the younger brother took a short cut and ran behind the buildings, in order to overtake his elder brother.

By then the elder brother had reached the main road in front of the colony, but he did not find his younger brother behind him. The elder brother ran around the quarters to search for his brother, but could not find him anywhere. Then he asked the other children of the colony if they had seen his brother, but no one had seen the child!

It was evening 5.00 pm and the parents of the boys returned from their office. They saw the elder son and daughter at home but the younger son was not there. They asked the elder son about his younger brother and he replied that he must be playing somewhere. It was getting late and when the child did not return home, the elder son told the parents that he had been searching for his younger brother for about two hours and the parents were shocked!

They soon rushed out of the house and started searching for the child frantically. The news spread everywhere and soon all the people of the colony came out of their houses and started searching for the child. They looked for him everywhere but all was in vain. They went to the sea shore in front of the colony and started looking for him in the waters. Some unknown fear started taking hold of the mother and she started wailing, while the women of the colony tried to comfort her. Some people went to a pundit to find about the child and he assured that the child was alive and he was in a distant place. But those words could not bring any comfort to the parents. Throughout that night the parents remained awake, and along with them their neighbours, all worrying about the lost child!

The next morning Abba had woken up early and was sitting in the veranda and sipping his coffee, his pet dog Caesar sitting near him, when men from the municipality came to clean the colony. Abba told them that a child was missing since the previous evening and no whereabouts were known about him. One of the men told Abba that there were deep pits dug behind the quarters which were filled with rain water and he asked Abba if they had checked in those pits. Hearing that Abba became apprehensive as no one had checked in those pits. Soon those men got long bamboo poles and started checking all those pits filled with water. In one of those pits, the men could feel that the pole was hitting on something. Soon the news spread everywhere and people from the colony and nearby colonies also started gathering there. There was fear and worry on every face!

A worker from the municipality removed his shirt and got into the pit. Holding his breath, he entered the water and felt something was trapped in the bottom of the water there. He came out of the water and informed everyone about it. He again went inside the water and tried to pull out that thing. But it was stuck and buried in the slush, at the bottom of the pit. The man came out for a breath and again went down, pulling hard on that thing from the slush. This time he succeeded to pull it out and found that it was the body of a child!

The man came out of the water and informed Abba and others that the child had drowned in the pit!

Soon there was wailing and weeping and every one was mournful. The man finally brought the body of the child out from inside the pit. The previous evening, when the child had taken a shortcut and ran behind the quarters to get ahead of his elder brother, maybe he had slipped and fell into the pit. As he fell into the pit full of water, his both hands and legs had got stuck in the clay at the bottom of the pit and he could not budge!

The whole colony became grief-stricken and the funeral of the child was attended by all the people of the colony. It was a very miserable incident which put a halt to the games of the children of the colony and for many days children did not come out of their houses to play! The colony that used to be bubbling with life, suddenly became very silent!

One of Abba's neighbours in the colony had brought a maid from the mainland to help them in the housework. Though the family was from Kerala, the maid was from Coimbatore in Tamil Nadu. Theirs was a small family of four members, husband, wife and two daughters. Both husband and wife were working as clerks in government offices and the children were in school. The maid was a young girl of about fifteen years, plump and dim in colour. She would do all the work of the household including cooking, mopping, washing etc. Before going to the office, the mistress would assign her a lot of work and see to it that the girl had sufficient work to do for the day, so that she wouldn't find time to gossip with neighbours.

After Abba and the children would leave, sometimes when Amma would find time, she used to talk to the girl in Tamil and the girl used to feel very happy. Amma felt sad about the young girl's condition. One day Amma asked the girl whether she knew to read and write and the girl told Amma that she had never gone to school and that she had lost her father when she was very young and her mother had to work in some household in Coimbatore to run the family. Amma felt sorry for the child and asked her if she wanted to learn to read and write. The girl was very excited about it and said that she wanted to learn to read and write. So Amma told the girl that in the afternoon, after lunch, when her master and mistress would return to their office, she should finish her household chores fast and then she could come for the classes and Amma would teach her. The girl was overjoyed and became very excited. Amma also told the girl that she need not worry about the books and notebooks as Amma would arrange it for her.

Accordingly, after her masters' departure, the girl would eat her lunch, finish her cleaning work and then by 2.30 pm, she started to come to Amma's house to study. The lunch hours in the office used to be from 1 pm to 2 pm and by then Abba also would have left for his office after lunch. So Amma managed to find some time to teach the girl.

Amma on her part started collecting old notebooks of her children to be used for the girl. Usually, Amma used to have a nap in the afternoon but she sacrificed it for the sake of the girl. Amma started the classes and taught her the basic alphabets in Tamil and English and also taught her the numerals. The girl was very intelligent and learnt her lessons fast. Amma was very happy with her progress. She used to share about the girl's studies with Abba and her children. She used to give homework and the girl used to complete it regularly and she told Amma that she did her homework after 10 pm, after completing all her household chores and after her masters went to bed.

One day, the mistress of the girl's house returned early from office, around 3.00 pm. Usually, the husband and wife used to return from the office only by 5.30 pm. When the lady found the house locked from inside, she rang the doorbell and also called for the girl. When the door was not opened, she banged on the door and started calling the girl's name loudly, but there was no response. When the girl heard her name called loudly, she rushed out of Amma's house from the back door in great panic and crossed her master's garden by climbing the rails, entered her quarter from the back door and opened the front door. The mistress was very angry and shouted at her for being lazy. She even slapped her for not opening the door immediately. Amma was watching the entire incident from the bedroom window and did not have the courage to go and talk to the mistress. But when Sheryl and Jason returned from their school, she told them about the incident.

The next day the girl did not come for her class and Amma was worried. After three days the girl came to meet Amma and told her that she was not keeping well. She was very careful not to be noticed by anyone and was very afraid that somebody would see her. The same week the girl's mistress found the books and notebooks of the girl from the store room. She learnt from the girl that Amma was teaching her to read and write. She beat the child black and blue and then dragged her out of the house by pulling on her long hair. Then she called Amma and started shouting at her for spoiling her maid!

Amma was a very gentle and docile person who could never shout at anyone. Amma tried to convince the lady but could not pacify her. The lady threatened Amma to stop her teachings or she would have to face severe consequences. Though Amma's children came to her rescue but couldn't withstand the lady who was very loud and overpowering. In the evening when Abba came home, he found Amma very sad. When Abba asked her what had happened, she broke down and told Abba about her student, the servant girl and the evening row with the neighbour.

Abba heard Amma patiently and then in a convincing way said to Amma, "We should have cordial relations with our neighbours and should not get into any row." Abba knew that Amma was teaching the girl but he never expected that it would take such a turn. Abba made it clear to Amma that it was their internal problem and that Amma should not interfere in it. Thus came a sad end to Amma's classes!

Abba was very interested in cooking and trying new dishes. On Sundays or holidays, he would take the charge of the kitchen and ask Sheryl to assist him. He liked to prepare chicken and pulao or coconut rice etc. Abba's all-time Favourite food was 'Kanji'. Amma used to prepare Idli, Dosa, Chappati etc. for breakfast but Abba always preferred to eat Kanji, the leftover rice of the previous night soaked in water.

Once Abba had to go to Calcutta on duty and while he was leaving the house he saw Amma cooking dried fish curry with brinjal. He smilingly told Amma that the curry smelled good, and left for the airport. Abba reached the airport, and also checked in his luggage, just a suitcase. Then he was told by the staff at the airport that the flight was delayed by two hours and the flight would depart by 12.30 pm. Abba looked at his watch and saw that it was only 8.30 am., so, he decided to go home. Abba called his driver and told him that he wanted to go home, as the flight had been delayed, and he would return after two hours. Abba's house was hardly ten-minutes' drive from the airport, and Abba soon reached home.

Amma was surprised to see Abba. When she asked Abba about it, he told Amma that the flight was delayed and he had checked in his luggage. He told Amma to cook food soon as he would have his lunch at home and go to the airport. Amma soon cooked rice and served food to Abba with dry fish curry. While Abba was eating his lunch, Amma heard the noise of the airplane above the house, and told Abba about it. But Abba ate his food at his own pace, relishing the dry fish curry. Later when he reached the airport, he was told by the authorities that the flight had already departed. Abba informed the authorities about his baggage and they assured Abba that he would get it the next day. Again, Abba went home and the next day he took another flight to Calcutta. This became the folklore of the family as how Abba missed his flight for eating dry fish curry!

During that trip to Calcutta, Abba got a chance to visit the Mother House of Missionaries of Charity and could also meet Mother Teresa[16]. He was much impressed by the humility and kindness shown by the mother. The Mother asked Abba about his place of living and work and was happy to learn about the Andamans from Abba. Then he was taken to see the orphanage run by the missionaries and Abba's heart melted for those children and he donated some money for them. While Abba was leaving, Mother Teresa blessed him and prayed for him. After Abba returned from Calcutta, he had so much to talk about Mother Teresa!

Life was going on its own speed and Abba's children had reached higher classes. But during the summer of that year, Amma missed her periods. She was about 39 years old and thought that she had had her menopause. But with the passing days and months, Amma felt that she was gaining weight. Even Abba noticed that Amma was putting on weight and one day Abba took Amma to the Hospital for a check-up. A lady doctor checked Amma and told Abba that Amma was on her family way and was four months pregnant. Abba told the doctor that they were wondering if Amma had done off with her menstruation!

After the check-up when Abba and Amma came home, Amma was very upset and embarrassed about how she would face everyone. Her children were all grown up, the elder daughter was fifteen years old and the younger two were thirteen and twelve respectively. Abba and Amma seriously thought of aborting the child. They sat together and discussed about it for days, whether to have the fourth child or not! Then, after a week they both went to the hospital to consult the doctor. Abba expressed his worries and told the doctor that they wanted to abort the child. The doctor checked Amma again and told Abba that it was too late for an abortion and it might even be dangerous for Amma's life. So, Abba and Amma had to give up the idea of aborting the baby!

Now Abba started thinking differently about the baby. He thought that Amma was always sick, and maybe by delivering the baby she would be cured of all her diseases. So, with no other option, Abba and Amma decided to give birth to the child. The same day evening Abba called all his three children and told them that soon they would have a baby in the house. He also advised the children to help Amma with the household chores. Though Abba had advised the children to help Amma, but Amma never allowed her children to do any work as she thought that there were servants for domestic help and so there was no need for the children to help in her work.

Amma's mother had been living alone in her village. Chithi's family was growing and they had two children. So Chithi brought her mother to Andaman a few months back and Amma's mother was staying with her. She and Chithi used to visit Amma once in a while and Amma too used to go to meet them. When Amma's sister came to know that Amma was pregnant, she regularly visited Amma and took care of her.

Abba was much worried about Amma's health and thought that there could be complications during the childbirth as Amma was forty years old. Moreover, Amma had not got cured of her epilepsy. But the labour was normal and in December Amma delivered her fourth child, a son and they named him Ethan Antony. Everyone was happy at home and Abba took great care of Amma. The children were happy to have a younger sibling and all poured a lot of love and affection on the child!

PART 4
ANTIQUITY

Chapter - 25

A GLIMPSE OF BRITISH RULE IN THE A & N ISLANDS

Abba was a voracious reader. He had a great quest for gathering information and to improve his knowledge on various topics. He always liked to collect books. He enjoyed reading books on literature and on other subjects as well. After coming to Andamans he had collected a lot of literature on the Islands and used to read it to learn about the history of the islands. He had many good friends among the local people, the Pre-42 settlers, the Moplah settlers, the Karen settlers and the settlers from Burma. They used to visit Abba for some or other work and even Abba used to visit their places for his survey and settlement work or during some special occasions. There they used to discuss about the life and living conditions of people in the Andamans during the pre-independence era, and the atrocities done by the British and the Japanese on the islanders.

Abba believed that people should have proper knowledge of the place they live in, and used to educate his children about the islands and its history!

GENERAL DESCRIPTION OF THE ISLANDS:
The Andaman and Nicobar archipelago is a Union Territory of the Indian Union, consisting of 572 islands, islets and rocks. These islands are positioned between 6° and 14° North latitude and 92° and 94° of the East Longitude forming a long chain. It is supposed to be a continuation of the Himalayan ranges that pass in an arch through Myanmar's Arakan

Yoma southwards into Sumatra. These Islands are about 150 km north of Aceh of Indonesia and are separated from Thailand and Myanmar by the Andaman Sea, and they are bounded by the Bay of Bengal towards the west. The length of the Andaman Group of Islands is about 467 km. and its maximum width is about 52 km.

The Great Andaman and the Little Andaman form the Andaman group of islands. Four narrow straits —the Austin Strait between North and Middle Andaman; the Homfray's Strait between Middle Andaman, Baratang and the north extreme of South Andaman; the Middle Strait between Baratang and South Andaman; and the Macpherson's Strait between South Andaman and Rutland Island divide the Great Andaman group of islands.

The Andaman Islands are closely surrounded by the Landfall Island to the North, Ritchie's Archipelago in the East, Rutland and Cinque Islands to the South, and the Labyrinth and Interview Islands; and the South and North Sentinel Islands on the West. There are two volcanic islands in the Andaman group, the Barren Island with the only active volcano in the Indian Sub-continent, rising to 1,168 feet, lying to the North-East of Port Blair; and the Narcondam Island, with an extinct volcano, lying to the east of North Andaman, rising 2,330 feet out of the sea.

The Little Andaman Island, forms the southern edge of the Andaman group, and lies south of Rutland Island across Duncan Passage, in which lie the Cinque and other islands, forming Manners Strait which is the main commercial seaway between the Andamans and Madras Coast. The Andaman Islands have a number of safe harbours and tidal creeks. Great Andaman consists of a mass of hills enclosing very narrow valleys, and is covered by an exceedingly dense tropical jungle.

The Ten Degree Channel separates the Andaman group of islands from the Nicobar group. Towards the south of this channel there are twenty-two islands forming the Nicobar group, out of which twelve are inhabited islands while the remaining ten islands are devoid of human habitation. To the northern end of the Nicobar group is the coral island of Car Nicobar. The small island of Batti- Malv is located to the south of Car Nicobar, and it is followed by another coral island called Chowra Island which is to the north of Teressa and Bompoka Islands, placed close together across a turbulent passage. Towards the East and south of these islands are the islands of Camorta, Trinkat, Katchall and Nancowry, forming a close group, creating the magnificent Nancowry Harbour. To the north of Kamorta and to the East of Chowra island are the Tillangchong island and a small island of Man. Lying across the Nancowry group of islands are Kondul, Little Nicobar and the Great Nicobar Island, and a few outlying islands including the Pulo Milo, Menchal and Megapod which also brings an end to the Nicobar group of islands. The length of the Nicobar Group of Islands is about 259 km., and its maximum width is about 58 km.

In the North Andaman and Middle Andaman, there is one stream each- the Rangat is a small stream while the Kalpong is a perennial river. The Kalpong river originates from Saddle Peak and flows towards the north before merging into the Andaman Sea near Aerial Bay. The Great Nicobar Island has four perennial streams, namely the Galathea, the Dak Aniang (Alexandra), the Dak Tayal (Dagmar)and the Amrit Kaur, all originating from Mt. Thullier. The Galathea is the longest river which flows towards the south and merges into the sea at Galathea Bay.

HISTORY: HOW THE ISLANDS GOT ITS NAME?

Since time immemorial, the aborigines have been living in the Andaman and Nicobar Islands and they are the original inhabitants of the land. Records reveal that the Andaman and Nicobar Islands were identified by the ancient traders and travellers across the world since age-old times as it is positioned on the trade route from India to East Asia.

The Census of India 1901 of the Andaman and Nicobar Islands III, states that in the first millennium A.D., the Chinese and the Japanese had known these islands respectively as Yeng-t'O-mang and Andaban. During the second century, a geographer of the Roman empire, Claudius

Ptolemy, located these islands in his map, in the Indian Ocean and named them as 'Agmatae'. Records also reveal that between the second to the sixteenth century, several travellers and traders, happened to have touched the shores of these islands, and had identified it with different names. The Chinese monk I-ching of the 7th-century had described the inhabitants of the Andamans as cannibals. The great Chola king, Rajendra II is said to have conquered these islands and had called it 'Nakkavaram' which is translated as naked man's land in Tamil. In the great Tanjore inscription of 1050 A.D. the Andamans are mentioned under a translated name along with the Nicobars, as 'Timaittivu, or Islands of Impurity". Marco Polo, a Venetian merchant, who travelled from Europe to Asia in 1271-95 had referred to these islands as 'Necuvarum'. Niccolo de Conti, in 1430 had refered to these islands as 'Andemania'. It is said that after Conti, the eastern travellers started using the name Andaman, for these islands. The Malays are said to have been pirating these islands for many centuries for getting slaves for their own country as well as Siam (Thailand). They called these islands as 'Handuman' which possibly referred to the Hanuman of the Indian Epic *Ramayana*, that had been passed down to the Malays in stories. It seems that in order to keep the other travellers away from these islands, they had spread stories about the inhabitants of the islands to be cannibals. The Native Andamanese called the Orientals including the Malays, Burmese and Chinese, as 'Chauga' or the ancestral ghosts, as they knew them well, for often raiding their islands for collecting trepang or sea-slug and valuable birds' nest as well as for trapping slaves.[1]

INVASION OF THE NICOBARS BY VARIOUS COUNTRIES:

Records reveal that the Nicobar Islands had been invaded by the European countries from the sixteenth century. George Whitehead in his book- 'In the Nicobar Islands' states that 'In the sixteenth century the Nicobar Islands would form part of Portuguese possessions, in charge of Viceroy of Malacca; but we know nothing further, except that Portuguese Missionaries were soon at work in the islands, and that there are a few Portuguese words incorporated in the language.'[2]

In January 1711, two French Jesuits were said to have landed in Great Nicobars and after preaching the Gospel for about two and a half years, they proceeded to other islands and in 1715, their death had been reported to their Mission. Missionaries from the Moravian Church from Tranquebar also tried for a settlement on the Nancowry Island, but due the death of a great number of missionaries, their Mission had to be relinquished.

The Danes tried to occupy the Nicobar Islands many times. At first the Danish East India Company took possession of the Nicobar Islands on 1 January 1756, and colonized the Nicobars in December 1756, and also christened the islands as Frederick's Islands after their king. But the tropical disease of malaria brought death to many settlers and in March 1760, the settlement was abandoned. Again, in 1768, another attempt was made by the Danes and again they made a settlement in Nicobars, but the settlement was repeatedly abandoned due to the outbreak of diseases. In 1783, the king of Denmark took over the rights and administration of the Nicobars from the Danish East India Company and it is said that from 1793 to 1807, the Danes kept a small sentry in the Nicobars. In 1845, the Danes made their last attempt to occupy the Nicobar Islands, but finally renounced the islands in 1848.

The Austrians tried to form a settlement on the Nicobar Islands twice, but there was no permanent result. It is stated that between 1864 and 1865, Italy also tried to buy the Nicobar Islands from Denmark but it could not happen. The British purchased the right to all the twenty-four islands of the Nicobar from the Danish government on 16 October 1868, and Denmark's presence in Nicobar formally ended. Then, the British took formal possession of the Nicobar Islands and established a penal settlement known as the 'Nancowry Harbour Settlement' which was under Port Blair, in the Andaman Islands. It is said that the main objective of the British to occupy the Nicobar Islands was to put an immediate end to piracy and to the number of murders taking place of the ship wrecked crews whose ships touched those islands.

FIRST SETTLEMENT BY THE BRITISH:

During the 18th Century, the British government wanted to establish a penal colony in the Andamans that could serve as a harbour of refuge for the British Navy. Accordingly, the then Governor General, Lord Cornwallis, commissioned Lieutenant Archibald Blair of the Indian Navy to survey the Andaman Islands and he was given two ships named 'Elizabeth' and 'Viper' for the assignment. Lt. Archibald Blair reached Andaman on 29 December 1788 with his group of men. He surveyed the coast of the Great Andaman Island. During this expedition, Blair is said to have had encounters with the native tribes of the Andamans.

After returning to Calcutta, Blair submitted his report related to the coastline with harbours and geographical features of the Andaman, and about the best location for the settlement. In June 1789, he was commissioned to set up a colony in Andamans, in the harbour of his choosing and Christian it *Port Cornwallis*. With him on this expedition, were Lieutenant Colebrooke and Lieutenant Wales and a detachment of about 200 mechanics, craftsmen, sepoys and labourers[3]. Blair reached Andaman with his companions, and selected Chatham Island with an area of 12 acres for the first settlement. Since the island was connected to the main island by a walkway, Blair considered that it would be easy for them to shield themselves from the hostile natives who lived in the vicinity there.

Soon he started the work and by the end of October 1789, a major portion of the island was got cleared. Huts for dwelling and a hospital for treating the sick were also built. Soon vegetable and fruit trees were planted. The Higher part of the island was sown with grass. Provisions were brought from Penang and Calcutta. Blair considered the possibility of timber trade. A jungle road was cut from top of Phoenix Bay to Navy Bay, now called Haddo, to serve as a line of demarcation for the natives.

A wharf was then constructed at Chatham, and completed in February 1791, to felicitate the landing of 500 tons of naval stores imported at that time for use. By 1791, the settlers were allowed to take their families to the new colony.[4]

In the meantime, Blair and Colebrooke made a hydrographical survey of the coastline of all the islands and made some significant discoveries. Blair also submitted his report to the authorities, drawing their attention to the North Andaman for having a better harbour, and recommended it to be a worthy place for the settlement. During this period, Captain Blair had tried to make some friendly relations with the aborigines. M. V. Portman, the officer in charge of the Andamanese in his book 'The History of our Relations with the Andamanese', states that Captain Blair had taken two Andamanese to Calcutta, and they were Jarawas.[5]

SETTLEMENT SHIFTED TO NORTH ANDAMAN:

In November 1792, shortly after receiving Blair's report, the government issued orders to shift the settlement of Port Cornwallis from Chatham Island to North Andaman. The Governor General also ordered to set sail four ships under Blair's command - *Union, Juno, Cornwallis and Sea Horse* to carry 360 settlers with supplies for six months for the new settlement. All the four ships set sail from Calcutta, and it is said that due to violent storms, *Juno* along with her crew of 90 settlers and huge measure of provisions, sank in the Bay of Bengal and only rest of the three ships could reach the new settlement.

Work was soon started in the new settlement of Port Cornwallis in North Andaman and the policy and plans adopted in the first settlement were also carried out in the new settlement. In 1773, Captain Kyd took charge of this settlement and he found that the settlers were suffering from various diseases. Soon after, more artisans and labourers arrived, as also 200 convicts. A couple of months later, 113 additional sepoys and settlers came, and, in May 1773, 72 labourers.[6]

Though Workers and convicts were brought in to develop the settlement, but the pouring rains brought more diseases such as jungle sores, malaria, infection and death. More and more death of the settlers became a matter of grave concern to the government. In 1796, when the surgeon of the settlement died, the settlers became desperate and no one wanted to stay back on the island.

The matter was taken up with the higher authorities and on February 8, 1796, orders were issued to withdraw the settlement from North Andaman. At the time of abolition, the settlement in Port Cornwallis had 270 convicts on its roll, besides 550 men, women and children, including those belonging to the European artillery. The convicts, with their provisions and stores, were sent to Penang; the others were sent to Calcutta.[7] Thus came an unhappy end of the settlement of Port Cornwallis in North Andaman!

REVIVAL OF THE PENAL SETTLEMENT:

In 1857 the Great Indian Mutiny broke out, and the British once again considered the Andaman Islands for transporting the convicts, sentenced for their crimes of mutiny and revolt. On 15 January 1858, orders were issued to Captain Man, directing him to proceed to the earlier site of the settlement at Chatham Island in Andaman. The settlement this time was to be known with a new name, called Port Blair, in acknowledgement of the extraordinary works of Lt. Archibald Blair for setting up the first settlement in the islands.

It is stated in the Imperial Gazetteer of India 'Persons transported to Port Blair are either murderers who for some reason have escaped the death penalty, or perpetrators of the more heinous offences against the person and property. Their sentences are chiefly for life; but some with long term sentences are also sent from time to time. Convicts are not received under eighteen years of age or over forty years of age and they must be certified medically fit for hard labour before transportation.'[8]

The treatment of prisoners at Port Blair was adopted from the original colony in the Straits Settlement, where convicts were divided into four classes and promoted from one class to another after definite periods of good behaviour or reduced to a lower class for any lapse of good conduct, the best behaved being selected as 'sirdars' or 'tindals' with a certain amount of authority over their fellow-convicts.[9]

Soon, Captain Man was appointed as the Commissioner of the settlement and was given full judicial and executive authority throughout the Andamans. Man was instructed to receive the convicts transported for their crimes of revolt at Port Blair and they should immediately be put into convicts of third class. Ater observing their conduct, the best among the group were to be promoted to the second class and employed as overseers over the other convicts. But any convict showing rebellion or adamant behaviour should be degraded to the fourth class with imposition of iron chains and severe punishments.

Man is said to have left with his group for the Andamans on the *Semiramis*, and after going around all the islands, reached Chatham Island and found it to be the best spot for the settlement. On 22 January 1858, the British Flag was duly hoisted starting another chapter of the penal settlement in the Andaman and Nicobar Islands.

Soon Dr. James Patterson Walker replaced Man, as the Superintendent of the settlement. He was an experienced Jail Superintendent. Dr. Walker arrived at Port Blair by the *Semiramis,* on 10 March 1858, accompanied by the first group of 200 convicts, an overseer, two doctors and a guard of 50 naval brigades-men, under an officer of the Indian Navy, and soon after more convicts were sent to the Andamans. It is also said that later more convicts joined, but many could not survive in the settlement.

In honour of this day, 10 March is celebrated as Andaman Day in the Andaman Islands.

SETTLEMENT HEADQUARTERS SHIFTED TO ROSS ISLAND:

As per the Local Gazetteer, the Andaman and Nicobar Islands, published in 1908, "Dr. J. P. Walker soon started his work of clearing the Chatham and the Ross Islands, and started clearing at Haddo and Atlanta Point. He fixed the headquarters at Ross Island where they have been ever since. He worked under enormous difficulties, and with great energy, and his inadequate staff induced him to be very severe. In addition to the natural difficulties of his position, he had to contend with constant escapes and attempts at escape and repeated attacks from the Andamanese."[10]

Portman in his book 'The History of our Relations with the Andamanese' reports about the convicts at the settlement, who tried to escape when they got a chance. "Convict No. 61, Narain, attempted to escape from Chatham Island, by swimming to the mainland, and nearly succeeded. He was caught, brought to trial and sentenced to suffer death and executed. On the same day, convict 46, Naringun Singh, committed suicide by hanging himself, at a secluded spot-on Ross Island. On the night of 18th March, 21 convicts escaped on a raft from Ross Island to mainland, in the hope of being able to reach the continent of India by a narrow neck of land supposed to connect the Great Andaman to Burma. On 23rd of March eleven convicts escaped from Ross Island.[11]

The cruel dealings of Dr. Walker compelled the prisoners to make efforts to escape, and on such situations, many of them got killed by the natives in the forest. The rest would be caught by Walker's men, and they used to be brought back and executed mercilessly. Within a span of five months, on 16 June 1858, Walker submitted his report about the convicts' declaration and it stated that out of the 773 convicts received at the settlement, 61 had died in the hospital, 140 had escaped and were believed to be dead, 1 committed suicide and 87 were hanged to death on attempt to escape. The report created much concern among the higher authorities and Walker was strongly advised to stop his inhuman dealings with the prisoners.

It is said that in July 1858, the sick rate of the settlement had increased very high, and during that month, 28 inches of rain-fall was recorded on the settlement. The convicts did not have proper living places and by November 1858; to accommodate 1000 convicts, huts were built at Ross Island, raising it five feet from the ground.

Dr. Walker soon developed Ross Island with the help of convicts and the Island had all the comforts and facilities for a developed civilization. The Chief Commissioner's Government House was built there. Fruit trees of different types were planted on the island which grew well. Ross Island stationed several Head Quarters of several Departments. On the island were also located European Troupes, the Madras Sappers and some free police. It is said that along with the Commissariat supplies, the Stores of Executive Engineer and Marine were all situated there. Along with that, there were also 2330 free and prisoner population on the island.

Ross Island was so well developed and maintained that it came to be known as the 'Paris of the East'. There was a church, barracks for troops, officers' mess, water treatment plant, and a club. There were also shops, a swimming pool, a bakery, schools for children, officers' quarters, and a cemetery.

THE BATTLE OF ABERDEEN:

Those days the native Great Andamanese, the real people of the land, lived in and around Port Blair and their camps were spread across to Port Mouat. Walker wanted to expel the aborigines from the land and he is said to have fired ammunitions and grenades from his liner on the Andamanese settlements. His naval brigades also raided their camps and killed numerous people. But the government was not in favour of it and rejected the plans of Walker. But Walker kept on clearing the forests from the harbour to Port Mouat, posing a threat to the natives.

On 8th October 1858, Viper Island was occupied by four sections of convicts, and a guard of the Naval Brigade. The Andamanese gathered in large number near the encampment, but there was no collision.[12] The Great Andamanese became very apprehensive of the British encroaching their land. Whenever the convict parties worked in groups for clearing the jungles, they were attacked by the aborigines.

M. V. Portman describes the attacks of the natives: "On 6th April 1859, 248 convicts were employed in digging wells, constructing huts and clearing the jungles at Haddo, opposite of Chatham Island, when they were attacked by around 200 aborigines who were armed with bows and arrows. Three convicts were killed on the spot, and one was severely wounded who died in the hospital the next day. The savages carried off the convicts' working tools, clothes and utensils. On 14th April, when the convicts of the two divisions were engaged in cooking, about 1500 aborigines armed with axes and knives and bows and arrows, suddenly attacked the convicts. After having killed three convicts on the spot and six seriously wounded, they were obliged to retire into the sea under the protecting fire of the Naval Guard boat, moored off the landing place, while the savages remained in the encampment, and carried off the working tools, clothes and cooking vessels of the two divisions. There were 446 convicts present and 12 had fetters on. These the savages selected and having removed their fetters, carried them off into the jungle, and they have not been seen since. The convicts later on told that the aborigines did not show any disposition towards the convicts with a mark of imprisonment, but were anxious to attack and murder the section gangs-men, the sub-division gangs-men and the division gangs-men, who were marked by wearing a red turban, badge and coloured belt. They called the convicts to come and dance with them, and the convicts obliged due to fear."[13]

Again, the Andamanese showed themselves at Aberdeen in small groups, but when the convicts turned to attack them, they disappeared. On 14th May the aborigines again attacked and this war is Known as 'the Battle of Aberdeen', in which many of the Andamanese were killed. M. V. Portman gives a vivid picture of the attack: "On the 14th May 1859, the aborigines attacked Aberdeen and Atlanta Point. Owing to timely warning from two escaped convicts who had been travelling with the aborigines, the attack was provided for and the plunder of tools on a large scale prevented. The Naval Guard was landed at Aberdeen; the

Charlotte anchored between Ross and Atlanta Point; Lieutenant Warden, I.A., landed a party of naval men, and marching to the top of Aberdeen hill put the convicts in his rear for protection; while the *Charlotte's* men stopped the aborigines who were coming from the shore. Lieutenant Warden was attacked from the jungle, and, owing to the numbers of savages, retreated into the boats, from whence he protected the convicts who had gathered on the pier, and in the water, by firing on their heads. The Charlotte's guns too opened fire on the savages, who held possession of the convict station for over half an hour, plundering everything worth carrying off. Lieutenant Hellard, I.N., with a party of Naval Brigade-men, Dr. Walker's crew, and a number of convicts rushed up the hill and drove off the aborigines. None of the convicts were wounded but several of the savages are supposed to have been dead. A few days afterwards, another attack was threatened, but though the Andamanese entered the place where the convicts were clearing, but they did not follow them when they retreated to the station. The above-mentioned fight was afterwards known in the settlement as the Battle of Aberdeen."[14]

It is said that in this battle, the British won the war as Walker had already received the news of the attack through a runaway convict named Dudhnath Tewari. Due to numerous deaths of the natives in the war, the Andamanese withdrew into deeper jungles and the Great Andamanese could never reclaim their land again.

It was the year 1859, when about two hundred Punjabi convicts, conspired to murder Walker, for the cruelties inflicted by him. But Walker received prior information about the plot through some of his spies and escaped with the help of two convicts. Later, all the conspirators were seized and severely punished.

On 26th March 1859, Walker was promoted to the rank of surgeon in the army, and he resigned his appointment as Superintendent of Port Blair. On 29th July 1859 Captain J. C. Haughton was appointed to succeed Dr. Walker.

STORY OF DUDHNATH TEWARI, CONVICT NO. 276:

Dudhnath Tewari was a life convict, who had escaped from Ross Island immediately after his arrival. In *Chambers' Journal* for *March 1860*, the statement of Tewari was published which is given here[15]: "Dudhnath Tewari, a Sepoy of 14th Regiment of Native Infantry, having been convicted of mutiny and desertion, was sentenced by the Commission at Jhelum, to transportation for life and labour in irons. He was received at the Penal Settlement at Port Blair, by ship *Roman Emperor* from Kurrachee, on the 6th April 1858, and was given the number 276. He escaped from Ross Island, Port Blair, on the 23rd April, 1858, and after a residence of one year and twenty-four days in the Andaman jungle, with the aborigines, voluntarily returned to the convict station at Aberdeen, on the south side of Port Blair, on the 17th May 1859.

He escaped, with ninety other convicts, upon raft made from felled trees bound together with tent ropes, Aga, a convict gangs-man with limited geographical knowledge, having assured them that the opposite shore was within ten days march of the capital of Burmah, under the Rajah of which place it was his intention to take service.

On reaching the mainland of Andaman, and after penetrating through the jungle for two days, they were joined by a large body of convicts, who had escaped at the same time from Phoenix Bay and Chatham Island. Aga appears to have been in command of the entire body of runaways who numbered 130. For fourteen days they moved very slowly in the jungle without knowing any direction. The food was all lost in the beginning, and for eight days they ate nothing. Then they climbed some trees and managed to get some jungle fruits. Water was scarce and they had to leave twelve men on the way to die for want of food and water. On the fourteenth day by noon, they were surrounded by 100 savages armed with bow and arrows. The convicts offered no resistance and only supplicated for mercy by signs and attitudes which were disregarded. An indiscriminate slaughter of them by the savages took place, and there were a great number killed and wounded, when Dudhnath Tewari took a flight in the dense jungle, with three bad arrow wounds, on the eyebrow, on the right shoulder and on the left elbow. Two more convicts had joined him in the escape and they spent the night in the jungle.

The next day, they were seen by a group of aborigines who were embarking in five canoes. The aborigines chased them and killed the two convicts, while Tewari feigned death. The aborigines pulled him out by his leg from his hiding place while he begged for mercy. They shot at him at the wrist and his hip. Tewari again feigned death a second time, but the aborigine archer pulled the arrow out from his hip and aimed another shot. Tewari again pleaded for mercy, and this time, they did. Then they helped him into a boat, and put red earth moistened with water round his neck and nostrils, and a lighter coloured earth on his body and wounds, and took him to a neighbouring island of Tarmugli, which is one of the Labyrinth Islands south of Port Mouat. The tribe who captured him was the *Aka-Bea-Da* Tribe of the Great Andamanese.

During the entire year, Tewari was wandering with the aborigines, from island to island, never staying long in one place. While he was with them, he wore no clothes, shaved his head, and in all respects conformed to their customs, enjoyed throughout the best of his health. Most of his wounds healed in about a month, except the elbow wound that remained sore for three months. The aborigines never extracted service from him, but for a long time looked upon him with great suspicion, and never permitted him, even in sport, to take up a bow and arrow.

After living for about four months with the aborigines, Pooteah, one of the elder natives, made over to him as wives his daughter Leepa, twenty years old, and Jigah, sixteen-year-old, the daughter of Heera. In the Andamanese tribe, if the seniors think that a young man and a young woman should be united, he sends for them and gets them married himself. Towards evening the bride, having painted her body in stripes with the fingers smeared with turtle oil, sits on leaves spread on the ground, by way of carpet or bed, while the bridegroom similarly painted, squats on his carpet of leaves, a few paces off. They sit in silence for an hour, when the person united them comes from his hut, takes the bridegroom by the hand, and leads him to the bride's carpet, and having seated him on it, presents him with five or six iron-headed arrows, and then returns to his hut, leaving the newly married couple who sit there in perfect silence, until it is dark, when they return to their private residence.

In Tewari's case, there was no ceremony of arrows. He was seated by Pooteah, one fine evening, between Leepa and Heera, to whom the Chief pointed with his hand, and addressing the young man observed 'Jirie. Jog'! and left the spot immediately. They were not painted as per the custom.

Tewari travelled with the attacking party, along the sea coast, and set Dr. Walker on his guard, just on time. Tewari had left the Andamanese tribe so that he might give information of an intended attack by the savages upon the convict station at Aberdeen."

Later, on October 5, 1860, Dudhnath Tewari, convict No. 276, was granted free pardon for his good services by the Governor General and was allowed to be sent home to Calcutta, by the first opportunity. It is said that in December 1866, Tewari was sailing from Calcutta to Rangoon with Major Wraughton, and when the ship halted at Port Blair, Mr. Homfray, the officer in-charge, took Tewari to the Andamanese Home at Ross Island. The Andamanese immediately recognised Tewari, and they abused him for abandoning his wife Leepa. But Tewari did not meet Leepa. It is said that the aborigines changed Leepa's name to 'Modo Leepa', meaning a 'deserted bride'.

ANDAMAN HOMES AND ORPHANAGES FOR THE ABORIGINES:

Captain Haughton, after assuming charge, followed peaceful methods toward the convicts. He believed in reforming the convicts rather than punishing them. He voyaged to various islands and tried to make friendly contacts with the natives. It is said that because of his peaceful policies, the Penal Settlement at Port Blair became the first reforming

Penal Settlement in the world. He also stopped the indiscriminate clearing of jungles, as he thought that the land would soon grow back into jungles if not utilised, and so only land required for building or cultivation was cleared. This saved the hunting places of the aborigines. Soon the aborigines also stopped attacking and massacring the run-away convicts, and were satisfied with only looting them of the metal they had.

In 1862, Lt. Colonel R. C. Tytler took charge of the settlement from Captain Haughton. Tytler followed the same policies of Haughton. He is said to have cleared about 76 acres of land around Mount Harriet[16] with the help of convicts and self-supporters. His achievements include building a pier at Ross Island and starting a ten horsepower Chatham Saw Mill[17], at Chatham Island. Built in 1883, the Chatham Saw Mill is considered to be Asia's oldest saw mill.

During Tytler's period, the relationship with the Great Andamanese showed noteworthy development. The Andamanese Home was started at Ross Island during this period. It was a free asylum to which any Andamanese was admitted. He could stay as long as he pleased, and go when it suited him. There he was fed and taken care of, and for the sick there was a good and properly maintained hospital. From the home, they could take small necessaries and luxuries for their friends at a distance. Rev. Henry Corbyn, the Christian priest of Port Blair was made in-charge of the Andaman Home and within a short period, Corbyn was able to influence about twenty-eight Andamanese to stay in the Home for short periods. There were men, women and children in the Andaman Home, where they made basket, women stitched and children were taught the English alphabets by instructors.

It is reported by Portman that 'during the month of December 1864, about 100 Andamanese lived in the Home of Ross Island and gave no trouble.' Apart from Ross Island, there were Andaman Homes at other places as well. Records say that 'By 1874, there were new Homes at Mount Augusta, Rutland Island, Brigade Creek, Kyd Island, Pirij, and Gop-laka-bang, in addition to one at Viper Island, which was directly under Humfray's charge. The other ones were mainly under the control of convict pehrawallahs.'[18]

In 1870, the Andaman Orphanage[19] was started and continued till 1896 when it was merged with Andamanese Home due to circumstances. Along with the Andamanese, there were also Nicobari children in the orphanage. It is said that the Nicobari boys were admitted to this orphanage so as to educate them and bring them out of their superstitious beliefs due to the impact of the witch doctors. The orphanage was then shifted from Ross Island to Haddo and Mr. Vedappan Solomon[20], who was a Catechist, was appointed as the in-charge of the orphanage.

The residents in the home were employed to help in catching runaway convicts, in collecting edible birds'-nests and trepang and other natural produce, and in making curios. The small income derived from that was spent on them. 'The procedure was then officially adopted, and carried out with great success by Messrs. Corbyn, Homfray, Man, Godwin-Austen, and Portman in succession, was the simple one of providing the home and visiting the people in their own haunts, as opportunity arose, with suitable presents.'[21]

Thus, the government's objective for establishing friendly relations with the native tribes had started taking a course.

FEMALE CONVICTS IN THE SETTLEMENT:

The proportion of female convicts was very less, compared to their male counterparts in the Settlement at Port Blair.

The female convicts received at the settlement were classified in two classes-those who were in the Female Jail and those who were out of the Female Jail. Every woman life convict had to live in the jail unless in domestic employ by permission or married and living with her husband. Women were eligible to marriage or domestic employ, after five years in the settlement. If they get married, they could leave the

Settlement after fifteen years, with their husband. All married couple had to wait for each other's full term to be completed for the release. Unmarried women had to wait for twenty years. But they could all rise from class to class and become petty officers.[22]

Though the government tried many ways, but not many women offered to come to the settlement. Then female convicts from other prisons were persuaded to come to Port Blair. It is said that in 1860, 35 female convicts from Bengal expressed their willingness and they were transferred to Port Blair settlement. In order to grow the settlement, the authorities made announcements that if a female at the settlement married a male convict, she along with her husband would be given the status of self-supporters. This was a great enticement and in no time, a number of marriages started taking place at the settlement. It is said that the newly married couples were settled in Shadipur at Port Blair, and thus the place got its name.

But the marriages held in the settlement did not serve the purpose. It was observed that after the marriages, when it was time for the term-convicts to be released, they left behind their wife and children in the settlement. It was also noted that some life convicts in the settlement married the female convicts, only to become self-supporters. It was also reported that there were about 400 female convicts in the settlement who were anxious to get married, but due to the existing rules, they could not marry. All these led to immoral practices among the convicts and a number of cases of murders were reported in the settlement, where the self- supporter convicts had attempted to murder the female convicts for having been unfaithful.

The 'Report of the Indian Jails Committee 1919-20, at page 276, states, "Free passages for the conveyance of convict's family to the Andamans were not granted, nor was any propaganda seriously attempted to induce the wives of the released convicts to join them in the islands. Local marriages, were allowed to be contracted between self-supporting male convicts and female convicts who had served a certain number of years of their sentences in the Female Jail. The number of female convicts available for these local marriages was altogether inadequate. In the year 1918 there were only 233 female self-supporters as compared with 1,304 male self-supporters, or a proportion of one woman to six men. It has been said that men often accept the position of self-supporter with a wife from the female prison in order to live upon her immoral earnings." Thus, the Committee was of the opinion that "No self-respecting prisoner would consent to bring his women into this polluted atmosphere, even if the women were ready to come and if their relatives would let them do so."

THE FIRST JAIL AT VIPER:

The first Jail of the penal settlement was built in Viper Island during 1864-67. This jail had solitary lockups, whipping stands, gallows, etc., and the penal settlement's cruel judgements were accomplished here. It is said that during 1868, the system of chain-gang was started. According to this system, the convicts condemned to chain-gang were involved in hard labour during day time and at night the convicts were chained with iron fetters, binding them all together. This made it impossible for the prisoners to escape from the island at any cost. It is also said that when a convict first came to the settlement, he was kept in the Viper Jail for a month in order to become adapted to the various types of punishments.

The Handbook for the Andaman and Nicobars up to 1st April 1877, states at Page 34-35 that 'The jail on Viper Island is intended for the reception of local prisoners and such convicts of the punishment chain-gang as from time to time may be sent there. A ward and cells shall be set apart for the reception of refractory convicts of the punishment chain-gang, who will be tasked at works in a shed near their ward, and not allowed to leave their own enclosure; they are required to keep perfect silence, and are to be under the constant supervision of petty officers, and will be visited two or three times a day by the jailor.' The posting of supervisors was:

1 Jemadar to each station containing 400 convicts and upwards.

1 First Tindal to every 200 convicts

1 Second Tindal to every 100 convicts.

1 Peon to every 50 convicts.

1 Orderly to every 25 convicts.

SHER ALI MURDERS THE VICEROY:

The history of this penal settlement would be incomplete without the mention of Sher Ali[23]. Sher Ali was from Kabul and a Wahabi convict, 30 years old, strong and had a well-built physique. In a family feud, he had killed one of his relatives named Hydur at Peshawar and later he pleaded for his innocence but he was convicted on April 2, 1867, with a sentence of death, which was reduced to transportation for life to the Andaman Islands. Sher Ali reached Andaman Penal Settlement in May 1869 via Karachi and Bombay.

Lord Mayo, the Viceroy of India, visited Port Blair in the first week of February 1872. He visited Mount Harriet in the evening on 8 February and while returning from Mount Harriet, many other officers were following him in his descent. Sher Ali had slipped inside the security cordon of the Viceroy at Hope Town Jetty. At about 7 pm, he succeeded to ambush Lord Mayo near Panighat, at Hope Town. The moment the Viceroy reached the small boat, Sher Ali jumped out of the dark and with his knife stabbed Lord Mayo twice. The Viceroy wobbling with deep wounds, fell into the sea. Sher Ali was caught forthwith and the Viceroy was taken out of the shallow water. On the way back to Ross Island by Flagship Glasgow, the Viceroy died of excessive bleeding.

Sher Ali was later tried and on March 11, 1872, he was hanged to death at the Viper Gallows.

The memorial erected in honour of Sher Ali, at the place he murdered Lord Mayo, could be seen at Hope Town, Port Blair even today.

INSPECTIONS OF THE SETTLEMENT:

Since the death rate at Port Blair settlement was on the rise, the government delegated Robert Napier, in 1863, to examine the causes of the increasing death among the convicts. Napier visited the settlement and saw for himself the sufferings of the convicts and the unhygienic condition of the settlement's dwelling places. The convicts had no proper shelter, they had inadequate clothes for changing after getting wet in the rain, no proper food, they were suffering from mental depression and had no personal hygiene. He reported that since 1858, around 8,035 convicts had been sent to Port Blair, and out of them 2098 had died and 612 had abandoned the settlement, who could be presumed as dead. He submitted his report expressing the view that much of the mortality could have been prevented by providing better arrangements and shelter to the convicts. Insufficient supply of nutritious food was noted to be a major cause of ill health and death in the settlement.

Dr. L.P. Mathur in his book 'Kala Pani'[24], History of Andaman & Nicobar Islands with a study of India's Freedom Struggle' gives a vivid description of the Inspection of the Settlement by various Committees. Sir Henry Norman was sent by the Home Department in 1874, for an inspection of the penal settlement at Port Blair. After visiting the settlement Norman reported that as on June 1, 1874, there were 7820 male and 895 female life convicts and 888 term convicts in the Andamans. He also reported that there were 500 married couples with 578 children and 1167 tickets of leave convicts. Norman recommended that marriage among the male and female convicts should be encouraged as this would improve the moral state of affairs of the settlement, which was in a disgraceful condition. He also advocated in favour of the convicts with tickets of leave, to be encouraged to bring their wives or husbands from the mainland. On the line of these recommendation, the government introduced the system of remission of sentence of a convict in the settlement and that the life convict after a stay of twenty or twenty-five years could protect his release by earning remissions.

During 1890, C.J. Lyall Esq., C.I.E., and Surgeon Major A.S. Lethbridge, M.D. submitted their 'Report on the Working of the Penal Settlement of Port Blair', and at page-2 it states, "Our visits to the Alipore and Presidency Jails and our inspection of the stations of the Penal Settlement have left no doubt in our minds that confinement within the walls of an Indian prison is now a much more severe form of punishment than transportation, and we are convinced that this fact is well known to the criminal classes. The causes which have led to this change of opinion in regard to the once dreaded 'Kalapani'. In spite of all difficulties, convicts were willing to go to the Andamans.

BRITISH OCCUPATION OF THE NICOBAR ISLANDS:

After making a settlement with the Danish, the British had formally occupied the Nicobar Islands and established a penal settlement at Nicobar in June 1869 known as 'Nancowry Harbour Settlement'. As per government directions, the Superintendent of the Port Blair Settlement, used to depute an Assistant as the Officer-in-charge to the Nancowry Settlement to take care of the administrative work there.

It is reported that the pioneers of the settlement lived in a small ship named *'Blenheim'* for five years, till April 1874 which was anchored in the harbour.[25] The convicts sentenced to a term were sent to Nancowry and every convict was required to pass three years in the Nicobars before being transported back to Port Blair. By 1884, the authorities tried to establish a permanent colony at the settlement by encouraging the self-supporter-convicts. It is also reported that the British brought Chinese and Burmese settlers, by inducing them with free-ten- year land lease, free ration and a free passage to their homes, but those Burmese and Chinese settlers did not show any interest in their work and were also not willing to stay in the new climatic conditions and soon left.

It is said that 'the Penal Settlement in Nancowry Harbour consisted on the average of about 354 persons: 2 European and 2 other officers,

Garrisons-58, Police-22, other free residents -35, Convicts-235. They were employed in public works similar to those in the Andamans.'[26]

The government gradually started focussing more on development of trade with Nicobarese and also got the forest land cleared for agriculture so that the settlement could become self-supporting. It is said that the trade included edible bird's nest, trepang, ambergris, split-cane and beetle-nut. In exchange for these items the Nicobarese liked to get iron and iron implements, rice, cloth, liquor, tobacco, sugar, silver and pottery items.

In the meantime, the British wanted to have dominion over the Nicobar Islands. For this they permitted the Assistant Superintendents to contact the 'Menluanas[27]' or the 'Witch- Doctors' and influence them with small gifts or by monetary benefits, to carry out the orders of the British officer in the Nicobars. But later on, the government learnt that these 'Menluanas' did not have much influence over the Nicobarese, but the 'Captains'[28] were considered to be more influential than the witch doctors. Soon the government started focusing more on trade and new regulations were imposed that imports and sale of foreign spirits, arms and ammunitions could be sold only with license. This had a positive effect on the Nicobarese as they liked to indulge in merry making and celebrations.

After nineteen years of the British occupation of the Nicobars, the government felt that the objective of making the settlement at Nancowry was achieved as during those nineteen years of occupation, not a single attempt of piracy had been attempted or reported. Moreover, the colony was facing monetary impediments. The government then thought that the Nicobarese were no longer a threat to the waterways, and the trade relationship could be maintained in the same way from Port Blair as well. Thus, in 1888 the settlement from Nancowry was packed up.

But the British Administration kept a hold on the Nicobarese with the help of two local government agents, and one of them was a paid agent. His duties were to report on the affairs of the Nicobars, give and take port clearances and maintain meteorologic registers. The unpaid agent used to be a trader who would collect information during his visit to the island of Nicobar. The Deputy Superintendent or his officers used to visit the island to settle disputes and dispose the cases related to crimes.

During the British occupation of the Nicobars, it is said that formal appointments of all Chiefs were made by the Government, as per people's selection, and they worked as Government agents. Each Chief received a formal Certificate of appointment, and an annual suit of clothes, a flag (Union Jack), and a blank leather-bound book. The Chief was bound to produce all these during his official visit to the village, and to hoist the flag at the approach of every ship, and produce his book so that the Commander might write his remarks and reports.

It is said that during the First World War, in 1914, a German warship 'Emden' arrived at Nicobar. On sighting the warship, Rani Islon[29] courageously hoisted the Union Jack. The commander of the warship thought that there might be some battalions hidden in the jungle and so they left the harbour. Later, the Rani was rewarded by the British for her faithful services. Thus, the British ruled over the Nicobar Islands in an indirect form, through Chiefs and elders.

In the orphanage at Port Blair, only Nicobari boys were left as the inmate Andamanese had gone away or had died. Since the Nicobari boys were homesick and wanted to go back to their island, Vedappan Solomon volunteered to go to Nicobar with the boys. Then with due permission, he landed on Car Nicobar on 15 March 1895, and established the S. P. G. Orphanage at Mus Village on Car Nicobar. His wife also accompanied him and she was a great support to him. In addition to her evangelistic work, she taught the Nicobarese girls many useful arts, such as cooking, sewing and embroidery, housekeeping and many other similar things. It is said that Solomon established the first Anglican church at Mus village in Car Nicobar and his wife also started a school there. Due to their efforts, several inhabitants of Car Nicobar were converted to Christianity. In the book 'Sons of Light' John Richardson recounts about Solomon, "These Car Nicobarese boys felt their exile; some of them tried to escape in an open boat and were all lost in the sea. To avoid such an occurrence again Mr. Solomon was sent to open a school at Car Nicobar. A bungalow and a small school were built for him. He collected his old boys and conducted prayers on Sundays. By force he collected twelve young boys of school age, of whom I was one."

In the beginning, Solomon was assigned with a number of duties on Car Nicobar, such as, to be Government Agent, Port Officer, Meteorological Observer, school master, unofficial Magistrate and amateur doctor. In his official capacity he used to board the vessels that called at the port and request the captains and crews not to trade goods in exchange for 'intoxicants'. Slowly the tireless efforts of the Solomons started changing the Nicobarese society. He also made a thorough study of the Nicobarese language, customs and habits, and his reports were considered so valuable ethnologically that they were sent to the Royal Society for publication.

Solomon's approach made the islanders to abandon their savage customs, to cultivate vegetables and fruit for their consumption, to drink tea instead of toddy, to sew and to do carpentry. Their former customs of infanticide, devil murders, felling coconut trees on the death of their owner, dragging about the bodies of deceased persons, burying them with live animals and so on, were altogether given up in the principal village of Mus, where the mission station was, which were gradually followed by other villages on Nicobar as well.

In the orphanage, among the Nicobari boys, there was a boy named *Ha-Chev-Ka,* who later on came to be known as Bishop John Richardson[30], the greatest leader of Nicobar. V. Solomon saw great leadership qualities in the boy. He baptized him and christened him with the name John Richardson. He also sent John to Burma in 1906 to a school at S.P.G. Mission in Mandalay. After his schooling, Richardson was ordained in Rangoon as the first Nicobarese Anglican Priest. He then returned to Car Nicobar in 1912 and worked as a teacher. John

Richardson is said to have worked as Honorary Tehsildar between 1925 and 1945. He also worked as Conservator of Port between 1920 and 1933. Richardson wrote the first Car Nicobarese Primer using the English alphabets, during 1923. He had also authored the Book of Common Prayer, with a few selected Psalms, and the translation of the four Gospels and the Acts of the Apostles and the remaining parts of the New Testament in the Nicobarese language.

CONSTRUCTION OF THE CELLULAR JAIL:

It was noticed by authorities that more and more prisoners at the mainlands were allured to go to Andamans instead of their home prisons. Hence the Home Department assigned Charles James Lyall and A. S. Lethbridge to examine the condition of the penal settlement at Port Blair. They both submitted a report stating that the punishment of transporting the convicts to the Andaman Islands was failing to achieve the purpose as the criminals preferred to go there rather than be confined in Indian jails. Lyall and Lethbridge recommended that a 'penal stage' should exist in the transportation sentence, whereby transported prisoners could be subjected to a period of harsh treatment upon arrival. As per their recommendation, it was decided to build a prison and construction of the Cellular Jail[31] was started.

The construction work of the Cellular Jail was started in 1896 and it was completed in 1906, and it took ten long years for the completion of the jail. The jail was built on the pattern of the Madras close prisons, and no prisoner could see another during the confinement. It is said that the building materials for the construction of the jail were brought from Burma and it took 600 convicts ten long years for the completion of the prison work. Iron grills, chains, fetters, shackles, flogging stands, and oil mills for the jail were brought from England. The Cellular Jail was built as a three-storied building and it was spread over seven wings, which appeared much like the spokes of a bicycle wheel, which initially had 663 cells, and later 30 cells were added to it. It had a central tower in the middle from where a single guard could keep watch over all the seven wings from its vantage point. When the jail work was completed, it was designed to accommodate prisoners on solitary confinement. Each cell was 4.5 by 2.7 metres (14.8 ft × 8.9 ft) in size having a single ventilation window that was 3 meters above the floor.

CONVICTS' TENURE AT THE SETTLEMENT:

'The life convicts were received into the Cellular Jail for six months, where discipline was the severest but the work was not very hard. They were then transferred to the Associated Jail for 18 months where the work was very hard, but the discipline was less irksome. For next three years the life convict had to live in barracks, locked up at night, and went out to labour under supervision. He did not receive any reward for his labour. During the next five year he would be a labouring convict, but was eligible for petty posts and easier forms of labour, and also got a small allowance for little luxuries or to save in the special Savings Bank. After having completed ten years of transportation, he received a ticket-of-leave and became a Self-supporter. In this condition, he earns his own living in a village; he can farm, keep cattle, and marry, or send for his family. But he is not free, has no civil rights, and cannot leave the settlement or be idle. After spending 20-25 years in the Settlement, with approved conduct, he may be absolutely released. While he is a self-supporter, he is first assisted with house, food and tools, and pays no taxes or cesses, but after 3-4 years, he is charged with every public payment, which would be demanded of him, were he a free man.'[32]

JAILOR BERRY'S CHASTISEMENTS IN CELLULAR JAIL:

Records of freedom fighters reveal that the Cellular Jail was a hell of a place where prisoners were tortured brutally. There was a Jailor named David Barry, who was very notorious and he never missed any opportunity to perpetrate tortures and cruelties on the prisoners. The prisoners dreaded him as they suffered inhuman sufferings in the Cellular Jail which were excruciating at times. There was no provision for latrines in the cell and the cell was like an open lavatory with an open earthen pot, smeared with coal tar and kept in a corner to serve the purpose. The prisoners were made to work like animals as they had to extract oil at the oil press in the jail premises. If they paused while working or did not finish their work, they were subjected to severe flogging, tied to a flogging stand with their hands and feet tied apart, and flogged mercilessly. Due to these atrocities, prisoners are said to have committed suicide in the prison.

The prisoners made desperate plans to escape from the prison, from Barry's tortures. It is said that once 251 prisoners were successful in escaping from the jail but 88 of them were recaptured and brought back to the jail, while the rest got killed by the aborigines in the forest. Out of the 88 prisoners recaptured, one committed suicide, and the rest 87 were hanged to death on charges of trying to escape.

After this episode, the prisoners in Cellular Jail were tortured even more and they were put into rigorous labour. The jail became an inferno on earth. The atrocities of Barry went on increasing and the prisoners tried to go on strike. But the jail authorities succeeded in suppressing the strikes.

There were hospitals in the Settlement to treat the sick. As per the Imperial Gazetteer 1909, there were four district and three Jail hospitals in charge of four medical officers, under the supervision of a Senior Medical Officer of the Indian Medical Service.

Ullaskar Dutt, Prisoner 31552, was a freedom fighter who was transported to the Andamans. He was tortured, declared insane due to malarial infection, transferred to the island's lunatic ward at Haddo, and was held there for 14 years. He writes in his memoir 'Twelve Years of Prison Life' about the atrocities in the Cellular Jail. According to him, "I have myself witnessed a case in which they got a convict tied hand

and foot to the cross bar, while the others dragged, simply because he happened to lag behind a little and could not keep pace with them. It was indeed the most pitiable scene to witness thus a human being treated by his fellow human beings, his whole body scratched and bleeding all the while, as he had to go rubbing and scrubbing against the floor, in spite of himself. This is indeed the very type that goes to prove what Wordsworth wrote in his memorable line 'And much it grieved my heart to think, what man has made of man', even in these much-vaunted days of our Twentieth Century Civilization."

ADMINISTRATIVE DIVISION OF THE PENAL SETTLEMENT:

The Headquarters of the Penal Settlement was on Ross Island. For administrative purposes it was divided into two districts, and four sub-divisions. The sub-division remained constant while the distribution between the districts varied from time to time. Within the sub-divisions, the labouring convicts were kept in stations while the free settlers and self-supporters lived in villages. As per the 'Imperial Gazetteer of India, the following were the division of districts in the Settlement[33]:

EASTERN DISTRICT

1. **Ross Sub-division:**
   Stations: Ross, North Corbyn's Cove, Middle Point, Mount Harriett, North Bay, Rutland Island, Madhoban
   Villages: South Point, Aberdeen
2. **Haddo Sub-division:**
   Stations: Phoenix Bay, Haddo, Tea Garden, Navy Bay, Rangaching, Garachérama, Minnie Bay, Pahargaon

Villages: Chatham, Phoenix Bay, Janglighat, Niigaon, Birch Ganj, Bumlitin, Tayleribad, School Line, Garachérama, Protheroepore, Austinabad, Pahargaon, Lamba Line, Dudh Line.

WESTERN DISTRICT

1. **Viper Sub-division**:

    Stations: Viper Island, Dundas Point, Port Mouat, Naminaghar, Elephant Point.

    Villages: Mitha Khari, Namunaghar, Ograbaraij. Chauldari, Port Mouat, Dhani Khari, Homfray Ganj, Manglutan, Baghélsinghpura, Nawashahar.

2. **Wimberley Ganj Sub-division**:

    Stations: Shore Point, Goplakabang (including Middle Straits), Kalatang, Jatang, Bajajagda, Bindraban,

    Villages: Bamboo Flat, Stewart Ganj, Wimberley Ganj, Kadakachang, Mathura, Bindraban, Anikhet, Cadell Ganj, Hobdaypur, Tusonabad, Manpur, Temple Ganj, Alipur.

ARRIVAL OF POLITICAL PRISONERS AT THE SETTLEMENT:

After the Great Indian Mutiny, the government sent the political prisoners in batches to Andamans, to segregate them from their fellow mutineers. The first batch of prisoners was brought between 1910 to 1914, the second batch was brought between 1914 to 1920 and the third batch of political prisoners was brought between 1932 to 1938.

The accounts that these political prisoners and their memoirs narrate about the Cellar Jail are too scary and blood curdling. R. C. Majumdar in his book 'Penal Settlement in Andaman' recounts those sufferings and describes the Cellular Jail having dark and dingy cells, without light and air and causing suffocation. The prison was designed in such a way as it could suck the very life blood of those who entered into those black holes. The coir pounding made the palms of hands to bleed and if the work was not completed on time, led to severe floggings tied to a stand. Slowing of work brought more beatings, and the prisoners suffered greatly. After work, they were served scanty food of coarse rice and chapatis with dal. Sometimes it would contain dead worms, and vegetables resembling grass used to be served. The most painful part was the solitary confinement from dusk to dawn in the dingy cell, lying on wooden boards on cold floors. These floors were infested with scorpions, centipedes and other poisonous insects and mosquitos causing malaria. The rain water used to be dripping through leaky roof and there used to be very small quantity of drinking water, often full of worms, injurious to intestines. Even the salt water provided was insufficient for washing purposes in the morning. As a result of all these, the prisoners suffered from dysentery, constipation, skin diseases etc., and there was no proper arrangement for medical treatment.

By 1912, the information about the atrocities being executed in the Cellular jail had started spreading out, and the Indian newspapers started publishing stories about it. Soon Port Blair came to the limelight of the nation and it was also noticed by the Home Department. The political prisoners were denied even the basic freedom, which were being allowed to ordinary convicts. The Home Department felt the need to set up a Jail Committee to look into the real situation of the settlement. In 1914, the prisoners went on strike, pressing their demands.

The Jail Committee that visited the islands was puzzled to note so many political prisoners at one place. The prison and the settlement were in terrible condition. Accordingly, the Committee submitted its report recommending for the closing down of the settlement and demanded the end of self-supporter system. It also suggested to deport all female convicts to Indian jails and to decrease the prisoners in Cellular Jail. But, due to the First World War which commenced from 1914 to 1919, no action could be implemented till 1920.

During 1920s, the government brought more volunteers to Andamans from the prisons on the mainland. People of a tribe called 'Bhantu[34]' were brought over from the United Provinces of mainland India. Moreover, groups of Karens were also brought from Burma to work in the forest land. Over the passage of time, the construction of barracks, stores and roads were started and the settlement gradually expanded with the convict families.

The Penal Settlement started growing in size, and it spread outside of Port Blair. Jungles were got cleared and coconut trees, banana, paddy, and vegetables were planted. Some of the 'Self-Supporter' convicts worked in the Forest Department in North Andaman, others in the small dockyard at Phoenix Bay. Some became overseers in-charge of gangs building roads, while others were assigned as domestic servants to British officials. They got a small wage, drawing rations from the government commissariat and lived in one-roomed wooden quarters in the compound. Thieves and forgers were rarely employed as house-boys, cooks or gardeners.

In 1921, the government decided to abolish the penal settlement on the recommendations of the Jail Committee's report. But due to the Moplah revolt[35] in 1921, about 1133 Moplah convicts were transported to Port Blair. The government had to justify its stand by stating that the Port Blair penal settlement was abolished, but it would continue to be an open voluntary settlement. Many steps were also taken to make it an open settlement, such as: The prison terms of fourth- and third-class convicts were reduced, volunteers from other jails were motivated, wives and relatives were also given the fare to join their husbands, Prison uniforms for self-supporters were ended, wages for extra-mural work were fixed on a descending scale, the controls were relaxed and restrictions on the following of religious festivals were also removed. The construction of temples and mosques was allowed and *Taccavi* loans were also relaxed and the rules were revised to grant tenancy rights after five years of tenure as an occupant at willingness.

In December 1925, the Jails Committee again visited to make its recommendations. It was surprised to find that the earlier 1168 numbered self-supporters had increased to 4377 numbers, and realised that its recommendations had been totally ignored!

When the matter was pointed out, the government had to accept that it was a hasty decision to abandon the penal colony. It also pointed that it would not be right to send the self-supporters back to prison for the duration of their sentence. Moreover, the government was concerned about the future of the 3000 local-born[36] population, who knew no other land, except the Andamans.

Most of the political prisoners were from well to do sections of the Indian society and in the penal settlement they were subjected to severe hardships and toils. The inhuman tortures in the prison caused some of the prisoners to end their lives while some others became insane. There was a prisoner named Nani Gopal Mukherjee, just 18 years old, who was transported to Andaman in the Alipore Bomb case. He was dead against the abusive language used against the prisoners by the jail authorities and their beatings. He protested against it and stopped working. He was tortured more for that, by pulling his hair, kicked, beaten and even food was denied to him. He went on a strike and the jail authorities tried to forcefully feed him, but they failed. It is said that after few days, the boy discarded his clothes and his fellow prisoners called him 'Sadhu'. He did not give up and after struggling for two months, he gave up his life in the Cellular Jail.[37]

The environment of the settlement was scary and the prisoners were whipped mercilessly for the slightest hiatus in their duty. When the tortures became unbearable, the prisoners sent petitions to the authorities regarding their living condition in the prison and demanded for books, writing materials and light in the cells during night. They demanded newspapers facilities for reading, writing and receiving letters to their families and better quality of food to keep up their health. Then they went on a hunger strike in favour of their demands from May 12, 1933.

It is said that on the fifth day of the strike, the authorities started forcefully feeding the prisoners. They arranged louts from the sepoys who forcefully put in the rubber tube through the mouth to stomach of the strikers. This caused the milk pipe to get into the lungs of the strikers and three prisoners- Mahavir Singh (an associate of Bhagat Singh, (Lahore conspiracy case), Mohit Maitra (convicted in Arms Act Case), and Mohan Kishore Namadas (also convicted in Arms Act Case) died in the tussle. The news of the tragic death of three prisoners was published in newspapers at the national level and this led to fury and resentment across the country and the government was forced to accept the demands of the convicts and on 26 June, the hunger strike was called off. Soon the prisoners were provided with improved services at the jail.

After about a year, when the authorities returned to the old ways, the inmates of the Cellular jail again went on a hunger strike from the 24th July 1937 with 177 strikers. The strike gathered impetus and it is said that a few days before the strike ended, 230 prisoners out of 290 in the Cellular Jail had joined the strike.

In support of the prisoners on strike at Cellular Jail in Andamans, a large number of political prisoners from various prisons in India started sympathetic hunger strikes in their own prisons. The news of hunger strike in Andaman had spread across the country and great leaders of the country also got involved. It is reported that Mahatma Gandhi sent a telegram on August 28, 1937, on behalf of himself and Rabindra Nath Tagore, to the political prisoners of Cellular Jail requesting them to end the strike, and to have faith in non-violence as the assurance would be supportive to him personally. The strikers accepted the appeal of Gandhiji and other leaders, and ended the strike. The government is said to have brought the matter to the house, but the motion received 55 votes out of 62, causing defeat of the government.

REPATRIATION OF POLITICAL PRISONERS:

Finally, on 14 September, 1937, the order of the repatriation of political prisoners was issued by the Government of India. In the first slot, thirty-six prisoners were sent to jails of Madras, Punjab, Assam, Delhi and Bihar. Then 26 prisoners were sent to Bengal and by the end of September, 72 prisoners had been deported from the Andamans to Indian

Jails. The last batch of political prisoners left the shores of the Andamans on January 18, 1938. With their exit, the chapter of the sufferings of political prisoners from in the 'penal settlement of Kala-Pani concluded.

EDUCATION IN THE PENAL SETTLEMENT:

In the Penal Settlement, there were arrangements for educating the children of settlers and convict parents. According to letter no. G 830-946, dated Port Blair, the 16 November 1876, published in the Home Dept. Proceedings, February 1877, para 3, it is stated that 'The number of children now attending the Settlement Schools is 292, viz., 224 boys and 68 girls, and the average monthly fees collected during the past seven months is Rs. 31-8.'

In the same letter a statement showing number of children in attendance at school according to the last return is also provided which is as follows:

Number	Name of School	No. of Boys	No. of Girls	Total
1	Ross Higher European School	2	—	2
2	Ross Higher Native School	17	—	17
3	Ross Elementary School	47	13	60
4	Aberdeen-One Elementary School	23	3	26
5	South Point Elementary School	20	—	20
6	Navy Bay Elementary School	5	4	9
7	Haddo Elementary School	18	12	30
8	New Clearing Elementary School	15	8	23
9	Protheroepur Elementary School	15	2	17
10	Hope Town Elementary School	10	6	16
11	Bambooflat Elementary School	2	4	6
12	Port Mouat Elementary School	16	7	23
13	Viper Elementary School	34	9	43
	Grand Total	224	68	292

We learn about the Education pattern of the Settlement only through the Census reports and some official documents. The census report 1901 states that 'the Local born population is better educated than is the rule in India, as elementary education is compulsory for all self-supporter children: girls up to 10 and boys up to 14. The sons of the local born and of the free settlers are also freely sent to the schools but not the daughters – fear of contamination in the latter case being a ruling consideration in addition to the usual conservatism in such matters. The girls do not retain much of what they have been taught but many of the boys are really literate in the vernacular. A fair proportion become sufficiently proficient in English for clerkships. Provision is also made for mechanical training to those desiring it, but it is not largely in request, except in tailoring, and there is a fixed system of physical training for the boys. Sewing is taught to the girls.'[38]

Inspection Report[39] of the Penal Settlement of Port Blair by Major H.N. Davies, Secretary to Chief Commissioner, British Burmah for the year 1869, states 'There are three schools at Ross Island, one for the children of Europeans and Eurasians, another for Asiatic children of free parents, and a third for the children of convicts.' Fee was collected in the schools, the Burmese School charged fees of Rs. 5/- and the Government Schools charged Re. 1/-

Imperial Gazetteer of India[40], Andaman and Nicobar Islands, states 'Native employees of Government use the local schools for primary education of their children. Six schools are maintained of which one includes an Anglo-vernacular course, while the others are primary schools. In 1904-5, these contained 152 boys and 2 girls of free parents, and 55 boys and 40 girls of convict parents; and the total expenditure was Rs. 5,360.'

The records of the Proceedings of 'The School-Committee Meetings' from 1936-1940 reveals that there was an Education Department, which was under the control of the Education Advisory Committee. The Deputy Commissioner was the president of the Education Advisory

Committee as well as the High School Managing Committee, while the Head Master of High School was the Secretary of this Committee. The Chief Commissioner was responsible for all the developmental activities regarding education in the Settlement. This included appointment of teachers, opening of schools, providing scholarships etc., which were all decided and approved by the Chief Commissioner.

In the beginning convicts with some educational backgrounds were selected and given the necessary training to help in the office work. Later on, the British Government started imparting education to the convicts who had minimum education. Then they managed to impart education with convict teachers as well as student teachers, who had got education in the settlement schools. There were vernacular schools and Urdu was the major language taught. By the early twentieth century, there were more than 20 schools in the Penal Settlement.

Due to the pressing demands from the Moplas, the Karen settlers and the Burmese convicts, who insisted for education in their mother tongues, schools with Malayalam, Karen, and Burmese as media of instruction were also opened in the settlement.

There was a high school, with English as the medium of instruction and Urdu as a major language. In the meantime, a Girls school was also established which was later on combined with the High school. With the passage of time, as the convict population spread to the interior of the Andamans more primary schools were started to cater to the needs of their children.

The high school at Port Blair was first affiliated to Rangoon University, but with the separation of Burma from India, this affiliation was transferred to Calcutta University in 1936.

SCHOOLS IN THE SETTLEMENT AS PER SCHOOL COMMITTEE (1936-1940):

As per the information in the proceedings of the School Committee Meetings held between 1936-1940, there were Schools with the following names in the settlement:

High School	Delaneypore School
Middle Point Primary School	Burmese School at Middle Point
South Point School	Calicut School
Birch Ganj School	Beadon Abad School
Dhani Khari School	Ferrar Ganj School
A Burmese School, Cosgrave Myo in Garacherama	Benington School with Ranchi children
Namunaghar School	Kenny Line School
Wimberly Ganj School	Muslim Basti School Ograbraj
Webi Boarding School	Burmese School at Namunaghar
3 Malayalam Schools	

SCENARIO AFTER DEPARTURE OF POLITICAL PRISONERS:

After the departure of the political prisoners from the Andamans, the penal settlement was still growing with the settlers and the free population. C. F. Waterfall was the Chief Commissioner of the settlement, whose official residence was at Ross Island.

According to B.B. Lal[41], "A large number of Indians were residing in Ross Island along with the British Officers. Most of them had their own houses in the island itself, and there was no restriction for civilians to visit Ross Island, as regular ferry services were plying between Ross and Aberdeen and other jetties in the harbour. The Ross Island was the centre of many activities and all sorts of social activities including sports and games were organised there regularly. A contingent of 'Gora Regiment' was also stationed there which was subsequently replaced by 'Gorkha Regiment'......... A large number of British and Indian officers were employed to run the different Government Departments under the Chief Commissioner. The structure of the Civil Administration was, Chief Commissioner (Head), Deputy Commissioner, Settlement Assistant Commissioner, Revenue Assistant Commissioner, Tahsildar, Patwari, Choudries and Chowkidars, so far as Revenue Administration was concerned. The other departments such as Forest, P.W.D., Marine and Shipping, Medical, Education, Supply, Law and Order, Transport, were under the charge of a British Officer as the Head of Department with other infrastructural staff."

Thus, the penal settlement of the Andaman and Nicobar Islands was a full-fledged settlement, with offices and schools, and all the office work going on in a systematic manner. But the general public and the British were unaware of the huge calamity that was to strike soon on the Andaman and Nicobar Islands in the form of Japanese occupation of the islands!

Chapter - 26

A GLIMPSE OF JAPANESE RULE IN THE A & N ISLANDS

After the departure of the political prisoners from Andamans in 1942, it was being thought that the sufferings of the Cellular Jail had almost ended. But it was a mistaken conception and the peace of the islands ended shortly as the Japanese forces soon occupied the Andaman and Nicobar Islands.

EVACUATION OF THE SETTLEMENT:

At the global scene, World War II had started and the islanders were unaware of it. But the British already learnt about the global conflicts and the happenings of the Second World War. After the Japanese attack on Burma, there was a surmise that the Andaman Islands might be attacked, and the British government started making arrangements to evacuate the penal settlement.

B. B. Lall[42], in his book A Regime of Fears and Tears reports that towards the end of December 1941, the Administration made a formal announcement to the general public, to keep themselves ready at Chatham Island, in case they wanted to leave the islands, and on the arrival of the ship, they all would be evacuated to the mainland.

Accordingly, many people gathered at Chatham Island and they were evacuated on 2 January 1942 by the passenger ship *SS Maharaja*, that left the shore, packed to its capacity with people. On January 9, a Naval ship called *Alanga* rescued more people from the island. Even after the departure of these two ships, large number of people were still left behind for want of space in the ships. There was sorrow and disappointment on the faces of people who were left behind! *SS Maharaja* was supposed to make one more trip to the islands to rescue the remaining people, but the Japanese had started their invasion and sealed the waterways, which made it impossible for the ship to return.

There were also the local born population left behind who had lost all connections with their relatives in the mainland, and had no place to go!

It is said that on 6 January, 1942, the Japanese submarines started fathoming the Andaman Sea. This was followed by air raids on the islands on February 1, and on February 16, 1942. When the Japanese intensified their air raids and attacks by sea, immediate blackouts were carried out in the city which terrified the residents. On February 24, 1942, the British made announcements to the residents to vacate their houses immediately and soon many people left their houses and went to the interior villages for shelter, to stay with their relatives and friends.

The British were worried about the safety of the Gorkha Regiment that was stationed at Ross islands, lest it should fall into the hands of the enemies. On March 1, 1942, the Gorkha Regiment was sent back by a naval ship with all its arms and ammunitions. On March 13, 1942, all the British officers vacated the islands and moved back to Calcutta, except the Chief Commissioner Sir C. E. Waterfall, and his assistant Major A. J. Bird, who had opted to stay back.

Thus, the people who were left behind on the islands were the Chief Commissioner, his assistant and some subordinate officers, along with about 6000 convicts of whom some were in the Cellular Jail, and about 12,000 people of the local born population.

JAPANESE OCCUPATION OF THE ANDAMAN ISLANDS:
The British had already planned to immediately blow up the Wireless and telegraph office, Marine Workshop and the Chatham Saw Mill, in case of Japanese occupation, so that the Japanese would not be able to lay their hands on them. It is said that on the midnight of March 23,

1942, a Japanese naval ship fired its first salvo, and soon the Wireless and Telegraph office was blown up by its in-charge, which shook the entire town of Port Blair, but the Marine workshop and Chatham Saw Mill were not blown up by the concerned officer-in-charge, thinking of the many people who earned their livelihood from there. Then the Japanese fired a second salvo and when there was no rejoinder from the shore, the ships touched the harbour, and within hours the Japanese soldiers entered the islands from various points. They could be seen walking in the town of Port Blair in squads, holding the Japanese flag, and the leader of every platoon had a map of the islands. They had all arrived well prepared to capture the islands!

ARRESTING OF THE BRITISH OFFICERS:

After the Japanese landed on the islands, the first work executed by them was the arrested the Chief Commissioner C. F. Waterfall along with his subordinate officers from Ross Island, who were then brought to Port Blair, and made prisoners of war. It is said that, Waterfall was pulled out of his car and made to trample and walk on the British Flag and he was humiliated by making him to walk through Port Blair town. Colonel Bucho, a Japanese Officer was appointed as the Civil Governor and he set free all prisoners imprisoned in the Cellular Jail. Then he packed the Cellular Jail with British officers. It was ironic to see that the Cellular Jail, constructed by British to incarcerate the Indian prisoners, was now packed with the British officers. Indeed, time is more powerful than people!

ASSASSINATION OF ZULFIQAR ALI:

The Japanese were very brutal in executing their punishments. First, they caught Ooty, the Officer-in-charge who had blown up the Wireless and Telegraph Office and tortured him cruelly. He was brought to the bungalow of the Deputy Commissioner and inflicted severe injuries. They made him to climb the stairs, and then threw him down from the top of the stair. This procedure continued till he died. This was the first warning to the islanders about the fate of those who tried to support the British!

The Japanese soldiers soon became masters of the islands and moved around Port Blair freely. They entered houses and took away whatever they wanted and even molested the womenfolk. The people of the town lived in fear of their life, trying to protect their womenfolk from the ruthless Japanese soldiers.

The next incident of violence was perpetrated on a young boy named Zulfiqar Ali alias Sunny, who was just twenty years old. He was the son of Akbar Ali, a resident of the Aberdeen village. It is said that soon after the Japanese entered the islands, their soldiers went around looking for women. When they tried to enter the house of Zulfikar Ali, he tried to defend the womenfolk of his house from the Japanese soldiers. He got an airgun and fired at the soldiers. Then he went into hiding, and nobody from Aberdeen village gave any clue about him. The enraged Japanese threw bombs which caused fire at Aberdeen village and houses were burnt down. In order to avoid further destruction, Zulfikar was handed over to the Japanese soldiers, who publicly inflicted brutality over him.

The Japanese soldiers captured Zulfikar and cruelly killed him in front of the residents of Aberdeen Village. According to eye witness, it was March 25, 1942. At 9.45 am., the Japanese soldiers brought Zulfikar to the Maidan of Browning Club. The residents were invited to watch the punishment. First of all, the boy was subjected to Ju-Jut-Su, which is a kind of torture for breaking the joints of his body. When the Ju-Jut-Su was over, the Japanese soldiers kicked and forced the half-dead body of Zulfikar to stand up. When he cried for a 'glass of water' as his last wish, they bluntly refused him. There was pin drop silence among the audience who were watching the punishments in utter fear. Then the firing squad of 12 soldiers fired rounds of bullets at Zulfikar, and the boy fell down dead, and his body lay in a pool of blood. Then the Japanese handed over his body to his family. Even today, the grave of Zulfikar could be seen at Aberdeen village, which gives mute witness to the atrocities of the Japanese.

After Zulfikar's murder, eminent people of the islands met Major Hira-Kawa, who was a Japanese officer and explained to him about the atrocities of the Japanese soldiers and soon order was brought out restricting the Japanese soldiers from entering the houses of civilians.

BEHEADING OF MAJOR BIRD:

The Japanese displayed another act of brutality on May 5, 1942 to intimidate the people of the settlement. It was the beheading of Major A. G. Bird, the Assistant to Chief Commissioner on charges of attempting wireless contact with the enemy. It is said that a convict named Pushkar Bagchi had borne false witness against Major Bird of being a spy, and settled his old scores with Bird.

Chris Pratt-Johnson, the grandson of Major Alfred George Bird, after collecting documents from the Cellular Jail National Monument Library Archives and meeting the eye witnesses from local population, writes about the last days of his grandfather, "Major Bird dressed in white was handcuffed and paraded through the Aberdeen Bazaar to the Browning Club in a most humiliating manner. The local population, including young children, were ordered to attend the execution. The Japanese touts jeered, insulted and abused the 6' 4" tall composed and cool Major Bird, he showed no sign of embarrassment or fear at the harassment or the fate that awaited him. Major Bird was placed standing in front of a trench across the square of the *Browning Club* (located 100 feet from the World War I Memorial the *Aberdeen Clock Tower*), whilst Pushkar Bagchi read the charges levelled against him. Major Bird stood unruffled but was not given the opportunity to say anything in his defence. Bagchi declared that the charges being brought against him were so serious that under Japanese law death was the only punishment. There was silence from the people assembled there as they anticipated the fate of major Bird. The firing squad was ready with rifles pointed when the worst brutality imaginable occurred. A Japanese soldier came forward caught him by the ankle and twisted it until it snapped. He beat him with his fist and hit him in the stomach a number of times until he collapsed, the soldier then began to kick him in the face. He was in unbearable pain and agony but uttered no sound as he was forced to sit in front of the trench his neck and arms twisted and broken. Major Bird asked for some water, a young boy brought some to him, but the Japanese Naval Officer Lt. Mitsuki Hirakaw standing with sword in hand behind Major Bird took the water and poured it on his sword and *beheaded him with one stroke*. He wiped the blood-smeared sword on his dying body and shouted "An enemy must be killed like this". Another soldier charged the body with his bayonet and pushed it into the trench. Major A.G. Bird died gloriously upholding the dignity of his race and his country. He neither cried nor asked for mercy although suffering terrible pain. A gloom descended on the people who witnessed this barbaric act, every man and child were saddened by the event that had just taken place to a kind and generous man who was well known and very well-liked by the local population.

Prior to the Japanese Occupation, Major A.G. Bird owned some land about 5 miles outside of Port Blair Township S.E. of the airport. He had bequeathed this land to his faithful cook, and as a lasting memorial to Major Bird the village of some 3 shops, a Church and a Temple has been named *BIRD LINE*."

These incidents displayed the brutality of the Japanese and terrorised the people of the islands. Everywhere, people lived in an uncertain atmosphere, with no safety of their life.

MILITARY ADMINISTRATION OF THE JAPANESE:

In May 1942, the military administration of '*Gunseisho*' was set up in the islands and the Commandant of the Naval Forces, Colonel Bucho was made the Civil Governor and the administrative head. He soon took control of the Assistant Commissioner's office, the Police Station, Jail, Supply Office, Schools and Hospitals. This office was wound up in December 1942, and replaced by the 'Miniseibu', which was set up in February 1943, with the same administrative organization.[43]

TEACHING OF JAPANESE LANGUAGE IN SCHOOLS:

The Japanese were particular about teaching the Japanese languages in the schools of the islands. They confronted problems in interacting with the islanders and so decided to start a school to train the islanders by teaching them the Japanese language. Soon a school was started at Ross Island, where students from different communities were enrolled and training was provided to them to learn the Japanese language. After the training was completed, those trainees were posted as interpreters in different offices under Japanese officers. It is said that this school was then shifted to Bambooflat.

According to some elderly local people, after occupying these islands, the Japanese administration made learning of the Japanese language compulsory in schools and the medium of instruction in the schools was changed to Japanese. This led to many children leaving the schools, and many schools were closed down.

CONSTRUCTIONS FOR FORTIFICATION OF THE ISLANDS:

Though the Japanese had occupied the islands, but they constantly felt a threat from the Allied Forces. They started works of fortification of the islands, to save themselves, in case of a battle from the Allied Forces. They fenced the entire coastal area from Marine to Rangachang with barbed wires, and constructed Pill Boxes, and the Japanese Bunkers at vital points along the sea shore. They also built big trenches along the sea shore and installed anti-aircraft guns to destroy the naval ships and submarines of Allied Forces. To meet the shortage of work force, they brought labourers from Malaysia and Indonesia. Those labourers are said to have suffered from beriberi and blood dysentery while the Japanese were only concerned about extracting work from them. They extended the airport at Port Blair by adding a new strip to it. They also started constructing another airport at Hathi Tappu, which was later abandoned. While the fortification work was carried out, the labourers underwent extreme hardships and many of them died, but this did not bother the Japanese.

COMFORT GIRLS FOR THE JAPANESE SOLDIERS:

It is said that the Japanese officers were very much concerned about the sexual comfort of their soldiers. Since the soldiers were away from their families, the need to satisfy their sexual starvations was considered by the officers, for their better performance. In the beginning with the help of some notorious fellows, the Japanese officers tried to satisfy the soldiers' carnal desires with local girls. Girls were getting abducted and people had to hide their daughters inside drums or tins, to protect them from the Japanese soldiers. People raised voice against this atrocity. When the problem could not be solved locally, the Japanese officers decided to arrange for Comfort girls from Korea for the Japanese Garrison.

Soon comfort girls from Korea were brought to the islands and they were kept in the barracks of South Point where the government school used to function during the British occupation. It is said that some of those Korean girls were also kept in other villages for the Japanese soldiers who were stationed in other villages. The Korean girls were forced to sexually entertain the Japanese soldiers, and they were treated like animals. The life of those Korean girls was very miserable and they lived their life as if in a hell.

OPERATION BALD HEAD:

Before leaving the Andaman Islands, the British had planned a secret mission of forming a spy ring, in case the Japanese occupied the islands. McCarthy, a British Commandant was assigned that task. After leaving the islands McCarthy was secretly working on the mission. It is said that between 1942-43, after the Japanese occupation of these islands, the British managed to land commando missions-under the code name 'Operation Baldhead' and there were 5 Operation Bald Heads by the British.

Denis McCarthy was the Superintendent of Police of Port Blair and he had been evacuated just before the Japanese invasion. He is said to have returned to the islands with his associates, in a submarine, with the Commando Mission. He landed a few miles off Flat Island, at the west coast. He along with his group moved through the thick forests and reached Ferrargunj, and made a hideout there. He set up radio contacts and started sending messages to the Allied Forces about the Japanese. He then contacted the Village Headman, other Burmese Headmen and Loka[44], the Head of the Andamanese tribe and drew a detailed plan to beat the Japanese. McCarthy soon started transmitting messages to the Allied Forces about important places of the Japanese Military Installations to be targeted, and in turn, Allied Bombers too attacked those particular places. The Japanese were unable to trace out the Spy group as MacCarthy and his group kept moving from place to place. It is said that once the Japanese soldiers spotted the group, but soon they escaped in the submarine.

The anger of the Japanese was triggered when just before entering the port, all their cargo and naval ships were attacked by the Allied bombers and sunk in the sea. The events of Allied bombers accurately targeting the Japanese Military Installations made the Japanese believe that the islanders were involved in espionage for the Allied Forces. They soon started arresting the islanders and torturing them on spy cases.

SPY CASES ON THE ISLANDERS:

From January 1943, the Japanese started mass arrest of the islanders, on false charges of espionage, for spying for the Allied Forces. It is said that the 6th wing of the Cellular Jail was packed with the islanders with false spy cases. The people were forced to accept the charges against them and those who tried to resist were tortured till their death.

A number of heart wrenching incidents of the tortures by the Japanese has been recorded in the annals of history of the Andaman and Nicobar Islands. One such instance is the story of Doctor Nawab Ali, that made the islanders to weep. It is said that Dr. Nawab Ali was arrested on charges of spying. He was tortured and asked to sign his confession document that he was a spy of the British. But Nawab Ali resisted to sign it stating that the allegations placed on him were false. When the man did not give in to the tortures, the Japanese decided to break him by torturing his daughters. In the words of Dr. Nawab Ali, 'They brought his two beautiful daughters, Saira and Sofia before the father, stark naked, with their legs forcibly stretched. Then the Japanese lighted newspapers and placed them under their open thighs. The father covered his eyes out of pain and his helplessness. The daughters shrieked and cried to their father saying, "Abba Jan, bol do han! Abba Jan, bol do han!" (Please dear father, say yes!) The torture of the girls went on, and the girls were crying and lamenting their fate, when finally, seeing the unbearable condition of his daughters, Nawab Ali said 'Yes, I am a spy', and he signed his confession.' Later on, he is said to have died in the prison.[45]

Hundreds of people were tortured similar to Nawab Ali, which made the islanders terrified and they lived in fear of the Japanese!

JAPANESE METHODS OF TORTURE:

The Japanese followed very brutal methods of punishments to torture the people of the islands. Chronicles give vivid descriptions of such tortures which could terrorize people. According to B. B. Lal, in his book 'Regime of Fears and Tears' at page 48-49, states 'the suspected person would be stripped and made naked. Then he used to be forcefully tied to a flogging stand, with his feet and arms stretched out so that he wouldn't be able to move. Then the vicious flogging would start that used to continue till the person became unconscious. Then water would be poured on him and he would be brought to consciousness and the flogging would be continued, till he confessed.

The second stage of torture would be by thrusting red-hot pin into the tips of the fingers and toes of the victim. If the person refused to accept his crime, his arms and legs used to be pierced with knife, causing wounds and making him bleed, and then salt used to be sprinkled on the wounds and it would be burnt with candles.

There was another type of cold-blooded torture in which the accused would be stripped. Then he used to be forcefully made to sit on two small concrete blocks, with his legs spread apart. Then burning candles used to be applied to the soft portions of his body, including his genitals.

These tortures used to be so severe and unbearable that people used to cry out loudly, while Hashida and his mobsters used to mock and laugh. The captured people were made to sit opposite to each other in a line and the baton used to be passed through their folded knees, while their hands used to be stretched upwards having loads of registers. Even a slight movement on their part would invite flogging which would go on till they fainted. Then the fainted persons used to be dragged into their cells and locked. The victims used to lay on the bare floor of the prison, with their suppurating wounds giving out foul smell, while they groaned and wept in pain and no one was there to listen to their cries!'

JAPANESE OCCUPATION OF THE NICOBAR ISLANDS:

Along with the Andaman Islands, the Japanese also got hold of the Nicobar Islands. We learn about the terror of the Japanese in the Nicobar Islands from the memoirs of Bishop John Richardson.

It is said that while the British were leaving Andamans, they had withdrawn all their officers from Car Nicobar. By then, John Richardson, had assumed his duties as Assistant Commissioner at Nicobars. In the morning of 4 July, 1942, Richardson noticed a vessel with the Japanese flag, approaching the coast. Soon an armed contingent of soldiers landed on the coast, and they moved around the island, carrying swords in their hands, enquiring the headman about his nationality. They also wanted to know if there were any British on the island and after confirming that there were none, they gave a short speech to the Nicobarese about their triumph, then they left the island by evening. The next day, Richardson went to the Asst. Commissioner's office, and burnt all the important documents there, so that it should not fall into Japanese hands.

The Japanese returned to the islands on 2 August, 1942 for the fourth time, and they occupied the island. It is said that Captain Ueda of the Japanese Navy moved in with a force of 300 soldiers, and soon after started the construction of a Jetty at Mus. About a 1000 Nicobarese were used for the work which was completed in a record time of four weeks. Once the base was ready, they brought in landing crafts, heavy weapons, ships and troops and raided the island.

On 24 December 1942, the Japanese rounded up 500 men from the Nicobar Island and took them to Port Blair to work at the air strip. It is said that they also took 300 pigs in exchange for 100 bags of rice. In March of 1943, they again returned and took another 500 men.

At the beginning the Japanese behaved well with the Nicobarese, but when the Allied Forces started bombarding the air strips, they started spy cases against the Nicobarese as well and many people were tortured to death. The Japanese ordered all the captains of villages to surrender the Union Jack given to them, and everyone followed the orders, except the Captain of Arong village. He had buried the flag and the Japanese tortured him, but he did not give in. After two years the Japanese found the flag, and the Japanese tortured the captain of Arong again and put him to death.

It is said that once a Japanese vessel was anchored on the coast and three bombers of the Allied Forces, drowned it by bombarding the vessel. This infuriated the Japanese and they arrested all headmen of the villages and put them in concentration camps, on charges of giving information to the British. The Japanese created havoc in the Nicobar Islands. The able-bodied men were taken away, first 1000, then in hundreds and they went on stripping the islands of able men. All the buildings at Mus were pulled down and the timbers were used for air-raid shelters. Tamaloo village too was destroyed. The Concentration Camps were moved deeper into the island. Many hundreds of Nicobarese had been taken away from the camps and they were never seen again. At the camps they were beaten and tortured and were given just a bowl of rice with water, due to which men started dying of starvation.

Richardson says that anyone who was educated was taken away and Richardson was the last prey of the Japanese, who was handcuffed and interrogated day and night. They wanted to know where he had hidden 300 rockets and when they did not get any answer, they threatened to kill him. The next day, Richardson was taken to be beheaded, when suddenly the emperor's message was received to stop the bloodshed, and Richardson was set free.

With the abrupt end of war, tyranny came to an end in Car Nicobar. The good part of the episode was that the outside traders had all fled from Car Nicobar during the war, and the land that the Nicobarese had mortgaged to the traders, were returned to them.

DUGONABAD MASSACRE:

At the Andaman Islands, there came a time when the Japanese took the islanders on round-ups and killed them mercilessly. The first such case was witnessed in Port Blair, on March 30, 1943, when seven men were selected for 'Death Sentence', on charges of espionage. The men were- Narayan Rao, Attar Singh, M.A. Khalique, Dr. Surendra Nath Nag, V. Gopalkrishna, Suba Khan and Chotey Singh. All the seven men were taken in a truck to Dugonabad village. There, they were all made to sit under a tree and all seven people were shot dead by the Firing Squad. Then orders were given to the close relatives to conduct the last rites of all of those killed, under the strict supervision of Japanese officers.[46]

With the passage of time, the Allied Air Force planes intensified their air raids which angered the Japanese even more, and they tortured the islanders by further arresting them in spy cases.

MURDER OF DR. DIWAN SINGH:

ON 23rd October 1943, another spy case was started at Port Blair by the Japanese and innocent people were arrested and packed in Cellular Jail. They were cruelly tortured and compelled to confess their crimes.

When they did not give in, it is said that the wives of those men were also arrested in order to make the husbands confess their crimes. But even that trick failed.

Dr. Diwan Singh[47] was a renowned doctor and he was also a social worker. He was recruited by the Indian Medical Department and in April 1927, he was posted from Rangoon to Port Blair in the Andaman Islands as a civil doctor. He took over the charges in Cellular Jail on 20 October 1927. With his efforts, he was able to lay the foundation stone of the New Gurudwara at Port Blair on 1st of August 1937. Dr. Diwan Singh became President of the Indian Independence League (IIL) in April 1942. After the Japanese occupied the islands, they tried to vacate the New Gurudwara in order to accommodate the Korean comfort women, but they had to face strong protest from Dr. Diwan Singh. By then he had become the President of the Indian Independence League. On 23-10-1943 the Japanese arrested Dr. Diwan Singh on charges of being the Gang Leader of the spy group. He was inflicted severe tortures but he did not oblige to the Japanese. His reply always was that if all the innocent people would be released, he would take all the blame on himself. This frustrated the Japanese who perpetrated further tortures on the captives, but could not break them.

N. Iqbal Singh in his book states 'The Japanese tortures did not rest even after reducing Diwan Singh's body to pulp. They went still further. They subjected him to the ultimate indignity that can be inflicted on a devout Sikh. His hair and his beard were forcibly shorn. Even then his spirit was not broken. But there is a limit what flesh can bear. Within a few days he was dead. He passed away in the dead of night on 14 January 1944.'[48]

The historic Dr. Diwan Singh Gurudwara at Port Blair is named after Dr. Diwan Singh and perhaps it is the only Gurudwara in the country, which has been named after a person other than the Sukh Gurus.

ARRIVAL OF NETAJI SUBASH CHANDRA BOSE:

The Japanese had set up a Provisional Indian Government in Singapore on 29 October 1943, and proclaimed Netaji Subhash Chandra Bose to be its Head. Premier Tojo made an announcement to this effect in the Japanese Parliament in Tokyo and also declared that the Andaman and Nicobar Islands would be handed over to the Provisional Indian Government. Netaji was pretty happy with the announcement as he thought that the Andaman and Nicobar Islands would be the first part of India to be liberated from the British rule.

On December 29, 1943, Netaji was brought to Port Blair in a special Japanese airplane. Then, with due honour he was taken to the Chief Commissioner's residence at Ross Island. On 30th December, Netaji hoisted the Tricolour at the Gymkhana ground and addressed the islanders. Then Netaji was taken by the Japanese Admiral and the Civil Governor to Cellular Jail, but they were very careful not to take Netaji to wing 6, where the islanders had been confined for false spy cases. The members of the Indian Independence League met Netaji, but the Japanese also did not allow the islanders to have a free talk with him. Netaji was supposed to return on 31st December, but due to some safety reasons he was sent back on 1st January. After the departure of Netaji, the members of the Indian Independence League were arrested and imposed with severe punishments.

THE HOMFRYGUNJ MASSACRE:

Soon after the departure of Netaji Subhash Chandra Bose, the Japanese came into action to torture the islanders for spying for the British. It is said that the Japanese officials selected 44 islanders for a death sentence. On January 30, 1944, they were all loaded in trucks and taken to a place called Homfrygunj, which is located about 18 km from Port Blair. On reaching the place, the hapless men were brought down from the trucks and were made to climb a hillock on gun points, which was the selected site for their assassination. An L shaped trench had already been dug and was kept ready on the hillock. Then, fourteen of them were made to sit in the trench, in two batches. Black badges were pinned on the shirts of those men, on their left chest, and the firing squad of 14 Japanese soldiers fired on the black badges of the men, and they were all killed and their bodies were pushed inside the trench by charging bayonets on them. The remaining 16 men were not in a position to move, and so they were carried on stretches by the Japanese soldiers and killed by the firing squad, at the same place. Then, their bodies were pushed into the trench and the trench was filled with mud and those unfortunate men got a mass burial!

THE I.N.A. AND THE JAPANESE:

As per the announcement of the Japanese Premier, the Azad Hind Government was supposed to take over these islands. Netaji had delegated a team of I.N.A. officers, under Colonel Loganathan and it is said that he took charge on March 21,1944 and announcements were made that the Civil Administration had been transferred to the Azad Hind Government but the Defence and Means of Communications were still to continue with the Japanese Military. The Azad Hind Government was not given any power to deal with public matters, and it was essential for them to first get clearance from the Japanese. It is said that the Japanese officers were not in good terms with the I.N.A. officers, and on 22 July 1945, the Azad Hind Government was withdrawn by the Japanese government.

HAVELOCK MASS MASSACRE:

In the meantime, the Andaman Sea was blocked by the Allied Forces and the Japanese were unable to get the essential provisions for Andamans. There was an acute shortage of food grains and other essential provisions in the islands and the buffer stock left behind by the British for the civil population had also been exhausted. Such being the situation, the Japanese decided to cut short the population by mass massacre.

As the days passed, the situation worsened. There were no food supplies for the people, and the available commodities were too expensive for the common man. It is said that people started dying due to diseases like blood dysentery and Beri-Beri, etc. It is also said that there was no cloth available and people had to cover themselves with gunny bags. Since the civilians were forbidden from going to the sea-shore, so even fish and salt were denied to them. The only food available to the masses was grass, leaves, wild fruits and roots. Some elders say that they had to mix the husk of rice with some rice powder, make rotis with it and swallow it with water. The people who had farm lands were not allowed to take their yield from the land, till the Japanese soldiers had taken their quota. The Japanese soldiers entered into houses and carried away whatever they could get. The sufferings of people were increasing day by day and People started dying due to starvation. Life had become miserable for the islanders!

Many memoirs reveal the tragic incidents of mass massacre carried out by the Japanese to cut down the population. It is said that around 700 people were rounded up and they were told that they would be taken to a new island for starting fresh cultivation. On August 4, 1945, around 7 pm, all the 700 people were packed in three boats and the boats left the shores. It was the season of monsoon, and heavy rain and strong gale shook the boats. After sailing for about 6 to 7 hours, when the boats were in mid sea, about a kilometre off the Havelock Island, the Japanese soldiers, at gun points, started forcibly pushing the prisoners into the turbulent sea.

There was a total pandemonium of screams and cries, as the men who were drowning in the sea were crying for help. Some prisoners willingly jumped into the stormy sea to save themselves from the Japanese soldiers, while some others were not willing and were crying piteously while the soldiers pushed them forcefully into the sea. It was one of the gloomiest nights and most of the people perished in the sea that night. When some of them started swimming, the Japanese soldiers gunned them and buried them in the sea forever. In spite of all this, some men were able to reach the shore and most of them were killed by the aborigines and some others were bitten by snakes. It is said that later, about ten of them were caught by the Japanese soldiers and they were tortured and later on killed. Some memoirs say that two men, Saudagar and Govardhan were able to survive this incident and they lived in an island for about 29 days. In the meantime, the British had reoccupied these islands, and both of them were rescued by a ship, and a white man who came in a canoe, took them on board.

MASSACRE AT TARMUGLI ISLAND:

Just before the Japanese surrender, about 300 people from various villages were taken away by the Japanese for a round up, and they were all kept under strict supervision in huts, in Garacharama Village. There were men, women and children in the group and they were neither given food nor any other things to pacify their hunger. On 13 August, the third day of their detention, they were all loaded in trucks and taken to Tytler Ghat that is about 13 miles away from the place. Then from there, they were all taken in boats to Tarmugli Island. All the 300 people were lined up and gunned down there, with machine-guns and none of them survived.

It was said that about 300 police men were left behind by the British while they evacuated the islands, and those policemen had been providing information to the Japanese about each family and the files were maintained by the Japanese. The people condemned the policemen for torturing people during the trials of spy cases. Moreover, it was also said that the property of those people who had been killed, were shared between the Japanese and those policemen. The morale of the people had become so low during the Japanese rule, that even young children, who had learnt the Japanese language, became informers to the Japanese.

Chapter - 27

REOCCUPATION OF THE ISLANDS BY BRITISH

At the global level, the unconditional surrender of Japan was signed on September 2, 1945, by the representatives of the Allied Forces and the defeated Japanese officers, which finally brought an end to the Second World War.

But, in the Andaman and Nicobar Islands, there was no change in the scenario, as the Japanese Admiral at Port Blair was not ready to surrender to the Allied Forces. Soon the Allied Air Force planes started dropping leaflets about Japan's surrender. The news of Japan's surrender soon reached the islanders and on the morning of October 7, 1945, they were happy to see the British Mercy ship being escorted by a Japanese motor launch, which was anchored between Ross Island and Aberdeen Jetty. A senior Japanese Admiral was sent by the Japanese High Command to Port Blair, to carry out the formal surrender before the Allied Forces.

SURRENDER OF JAPANESE IN ANDAMANS:

N. Iqbal Singh in the Andaman Story gives a vivid description of the surrender of the Japanese[49]. It is said that the infantry of Naval Brigade landed on the island on October 8, 1945. They rounded up the Japanese on the same day and on October 9, the formal surrender of the Japanese took place at Gymkhana grounds. Brigadier H.J.L. Addison was the overall in-charge of the administration, but it was Brigadier Salomon who took the surrender ceremony. According to Arafat Ahmed Khan, an eyewitness, a table had been laid facing the Andaman Club and Brigadier Salomon was seated on the other side of the table. All officers were gathered there, while the military was in-charge of the situation. Then a car drove up, carrying 'Shereikan', the Commanding Officer of the Japanese naval forces. He was in complete uniform and was carrying his sword. He got down the car, and was accompanied by two assistants. The Japanese Admiral saluted the Brigadier and Salomon stood up and shook hands with him. Then the Japanese Admiral took out his sword from the sheath and surrendered it to Brigadier Salomon. Then he unbuckled his belt and stripped himself of all other decorations and badges of honour and surrendered it. Then, a document was read out, and it was signed by Brigadier Salomon and the Japanese Admiral on behalf of their governments, while the gathered crowd burst into cheers of happiness. On the same day, Loka, the head of the Andamanese Tribe was also honoured in the presence of the public for the valuable services rendered to Mcarthy and party during their mission 'Bald Head'.

The Japanese soldiers were divested of all their arms and they were given wooden staff in its place. They were further ordered to move at least four miles out of the city limits. Disarmament had been carried out throughout the islands by the end of October 1945. There were 18,846 soldiers of the Japanese troops waiting for evacuation and about 112 Japanese were held in custody as war criminals.

The British sailed a troopship to Car Nicobar on 17 October 1945 and Car Nicobar was re-occupied by the British on October 18, 1945.

REOCCUPATION BY THE BRITISH AND THEREAFTER:
The British were aware of the pitiful state of the islanders, and they had brought sufficient provisions for the islanders including food stuff and clothes on the ship 'Dilwara'. Without loss of time, all the things were downloaded and distributed among the people.

Brigadier Salomon found the Andamans in an appalling condition. During the 1941 Census, the population of the islands was around

34,000. But, after reoccupation of the islands, within a span of about three and a half years, the population had reduced to approximately 18000. The population was in a very bad shape as far as health and nutrition was concerned, and people were suffering from starvation and malnutrition. There were literally no consumer goods available in Port Blair and people wore gunny bags or rags for cloths. The prevalence of malaria was very high, and beriberi and the epidemic of scabies was spread throughout Port Blair. However, the British found that the Nicobars did not suffer as Andamans, and rehabilitation work was much easier there.

Apart from the pathetic condition of the population, the sanitary conditions were appalling. Moreover, heavy destruction had been done to the infrastructure of the islands, such as roads, drains, buildings, marine dockyard and the saw mill etc. Two wings of the Cellular Jail had been demolished by the Japanese and the materials were used for fortifications, while the third wing had been destroyed in the bombarding.

According to Patterson, from the day of their arrival, i.e. 8 October 1945, their entire energy was focused on immediate relief work. The civil population fully cooperated with the military administration. All the government servants who were still in the islands, were immediately reemployed by all the Departments. A great advantage at that time was the presence of about 10,000 Japanese soldiers, who were used as labour force.

It is said that by February 7, 1946, all the Japanese forces had been deported and necessary evidence for the trial of war criminals had also been obtained. Later on, the naval commander responsible for mass killing was hanged along with the chief of the police.

The British re-established the Civil Administration without any loss of time, with the help of the government employees who had accompanied the British Army at the time of re-occupation and along with those government servants who had survived in the islands. The schools that had been shut down by the Japanese Forces were soon reopened. Soon the British government proposed to develop the islands' fisheries, timber and agricultural resources by employing former inmates. In turn, the inmates were assured to be granted return passage to go to their homes on the Indian mainland. They also were given a choice and the right to settle on the islands.

There were 6000 odd convicts who had been detained in the islands due to the Japanese occupation in 1942, and they were all given remission for their balance years and were allowed to return to their homes, if they desired. Around 4200 convicts accepted the offer and they were sent to their homes. The prisons were not reopened again by the British and the penal settlement was abolished. The Japanese were taken as prisoners of War and sent to different camps set up by the Allied Forces.

At the end of the Second World War the British government announced its intention to abolish the penal settlement.

On February 7, 1946, the military administration was ended in the islands and N.K. Patterson handed over charges to Inam-ul-Majid, of the Indian Civil Service, who was appointed as the first Indian Chief Commissioner of the islands. He made arrangements for the repatriation of hundreds of prisoners from Dutch-East Indies, Malaya and Singapore who had been brought by the Japanese to work as labourers in the islands.

On August 15, 1947, when India gained its independence, the penal colony was eventually closed.

PRESENT SCENARIO:

The Cellular Jail, Ross Island, Viper Island, the Homfry Gunj Martyr's Memorial, Duggnobad Memorial, Havelock Island, Tarmugli Island, the Japanese bunkers and the entire Andaman and Nicobar Islands with the surrounding waters of the sea, stand testimony to the atrocities of British and Japanese rule in the penal settlement which have been recorded in the annals of history. Tourists today love to visit the historical places and enjoy the scenic beauty of these islands and return back with fond memories.

Now, in the Andaman and Nicobar Islands, people of all faiths - Hindus, Muslims, Christians, Sikhs, and people speaking all languages like Hindi, Bengali, Malayalam, Tamil, Telugu, Punjabi, Nicobari etc., live together in complete peace and harmony. Inter-religion and inter-regional marriages are common here. For this amazing racial and cultural mix, the A&N Islands are aptly described as Mini-India.

The lives of the aborigines of the Andaman and Nicobar Islands have changed entirely. The Great Andamanese are settled in Strait Island, and their children are admitted to schools at Port Blair to receive education. They are gradually joining the main stream of life, and some of them also work in government offices. The Nicobarese have joined the mainstream of culture and are educated and also occupy high government positions. There are also many doctors, engineers and teachers from among the Nicobarese who work in different islands. The Onges of Little Andaman too have schools but they are not as developed as the Great Andamanese.

Prior to early 1990s, people had to go to North and Middle Andamans by seaways, but later the Great Andaman Trunk Road was constructed through the reserved Forest and it became easy for people to transport by roadways to North and Middle Andaman from Port Blair. People see Jarawas while travelling by the ATR, and they are no more naked, but they lead a hunter-gatherer life. The Shompens of Great Nicobar still lead a hunter-gatherer life, but they do visit the Settlements at Campbell Bay. The Sentinelese live a secluded life and do not come out of their islands, and do not allow the outsiders to enter their 'North Sentinel Island'.

While telling the stories of the British and Japanese rule to his children and Amma, Abba used to become very emotional. He considered himself to be a part and parcel of these islands and serving the people of the islands was his religion. His service motto was to do the greatest good to the greatest number of people.

PART 5

PINNACLE

ABBA IS PROMOTED AS ASSISTANT COMMISSIONER

While staying in Junglighat, Abba was working as Treasury Officer. Though Abba was in a government job, but life was not a bed of roses for Abba and Amma as they were unable to manage the expenditure of the family with Abba's single earnings. Sheryl had completed her schooling and was admitted to the Government College at Port Blair. The other two younger children were in schools and the youngest child was still an infant. Life was moving slowly with struggles. But during holidays and now and then when relatives and acquaintances would visit Abba and Amma, they used to have some good time.

It was February 1979 and Port Blair was getting ready for a national function, and on 11 February, the Cellular Jail was to be declared as the 'National Memorial[1]' by the Prime Minister Morarji Desai. Abba was given responsibilities for the arrangements for smooth conduct of the programme which he accomplished it to the utter satisfaction of his senior officers. Abba also took his children to witness the gala function. Much later, Sheryl wrote about Cellular Jail and showed it to Abba. Abba was happy. He appreciated his daughter!

THE CELLULAR JAIL

I am the much-celebrated National Memorial
With tourists across the world
Thronging at my premises

Paying their tributes
To the unsung heroes of freedom struggle!
But I stand forlorn and dejected
With a sea of memories
A testimony of brutal atrocities
Inflicted over the ages on innocent lives
A Century has passed at a snail's pace
But the wails and whimpers of yesteryears
Still echo in my ears and rake my heart!
Don't look at my stone walls
I too have a heart
Which weeps during lonely nights!
The British had visualized a jail at Port Blair
To enforce obedience at the penal settlement
I was born after ten long years
Of uphill struggle
Rendered by the prisoners
Transported for life at the Black Waters
With seven wings spread around
And with 668 cells, I was unique
Each cell and wing of mine
Was sealed by iron grills
All the wings culminated in the central tower
The guards kept vigil from this high tower
Each wing faced to the back of the other
And no soul could reach or see one another
The carnage of Jailor Barrie
Still makes me tremble
He inflicted brutality on the prisoners
And considered himself to be
The Lord of the Prison
Escape from the prison was not viable
Suffering silently in the cells

Away from families and friends
Many had terminated their lives!
While some became insane!
Some others tried to revolt
While some secretly joined hands
With the Authorities!
After the British, it was the Japanese
They were a step ahead in bloodshed and torture
And buried many in a common grave!
The gallows in my premises are mute witness
To those brave souls
Who had laid down their lives smilingly
I have seen the youth grow grey
Within the prison walls
I have seen the strong men stoop and bend
I have seen Death
Lurking around to smite life!
Today I am a legendary monument
Bubbling with life and happiness!
But the past reminiscence
Torment me even today
And I well know
That my today is only due to my Past!

-Author

Once while Abba had gone to his village, one of his neighbours came to meet Abba and requested him to find a job for his son in the Andamans, as the boy had completed his graduation. Abba assured him that after he would return to Andaman, he would try to find a job for the boy and would let the neighbour know, and then he could send his son to Andaman. But after Abba and his family reached Port Blair, within a month, the neighbour's son arrived at Abba's house with his baggage. Abba couldn't help the situation. He was living in a two-room apartment and it was not sufficient for his own family as his children had grown up. Yet he told the boy that he could stay in his house till he found a suitable job.

It was a burden for Amma to feed one more mouth and she wanted that the boy should get a job soon. She even insisted Abba to find a job for him. Finally, Abba found a job for him in a private firm as an accountant. The young man was not happy to work in a private firm and he was looking for a white-collar job in the government. He joined the firm but within a fortnight he left the job. Abba found another job for him but he was unwilling to join. Abba couldn't find any government job for the young man. He stayed in Abba's house for about six months and then one day he told Abba that he wanted to go back to his village. He also blamed Abba for not showing any interest in finding a government job for him and blamed that if Abba had wanted, he could have easily found a job for him!

After the young man left, the second son of Abba's cousin arrived and later Abba's nephews also arrived and they all stayed in Abba's house. Abba took care of all of them and somehow managed his family. It was not only Abba's relatives but there were many other people living in Andaman and Nicobar Island who came to see Abba for some or other help, and Abba tried his level best to help them all.

In April 1979, Abba received his transfer order to Campbell Bay. He had been promoted as Assistant Commissioner of Campbell Bay[2] vide CC's order no. 1786 dt. 26.4.79, and Abba had to accept it, as it was a promotion transfer. Abba was not very willing to go to Campbell Bay as Amma and the children would have to stay in Port Blair due to the education of his elder daughter, and his family would not be able to accompany him. Abba was also worried about Amma and her ailment. Soon the entire house was busy packing things for Abba to take to Campbell Bay. One fine day after a lot of advice to the children, Abba left for Campbell Bay in a steamer. Abba had made arrangements for domestic help for Amma. The peons at Abba's office had told Abba not to worry as they would go home after office hours and help Amma in case of any need.

Campbell Bay is a town in the Great Nicobar Island, which is also the largest in the Nicobar group of Islands. One could reach Campbell Bay only by steamers and it used to take 5-6 days to reach there. Moreover, the steamers were scheduled just once a month. On reaching the island, Abba joined his office on 14. 5. 1979, as Asst. Commissioner Campbell Bay.

Abba was an industrious man. He was very innovative and brilliant in doing his work. He always respected the law but also believed that the law was a facility to help people in enhancing their living conditions and not to trouble them. He put in his best efforts to do the greatest good to the greatest number of people. After reaching Campbell Bay, Abba took all efforts to help the people and the Ex-servicemen settled on the island.

Under the Government of India's Rehabilitation Schemes of 1969, ex-servicemen from Punjab were brought with their families and settled here. Later on, from August 1977-1980 Ex-servicemen and their families from various states such as Chhattisgarh, Kerala, Tamil Nadu, Andhra Pradesh, Maharashtra, Bihar and West Bengal were also brought in batches and settled here. The places of this island have been named according to their distance from the main town such as Six kilometres, Twenty kilometres, Forty-five Kilometres etc. Each Ex-servicemen family had been allotted 5 acres of paddy land, 5 acres of hilly land and one acre of residential land by the government, in order to settle down and earn their livelihood.

Abba used to visit all those settlements scattered up to 46 kilometres in Campbell Bay and looked into the needs of the people. He was like a family member in those settlements.

During the summer vacation of 1979, Abba made arrangements for Amma and his Children to visit Campbell Bay and spend their summer holidays there. When Amma and the children arrived at Campbell Bay by a steamer, Abba was at the jetty to receive them and he took them to his quarters in his office jeep.

The Assistant Commissioner's bungalow was in the heart of Campbell Bay town. It was a wooden building with an independent campus and a beautiful garden. Abba had planted varieties of plants in his garden and there was also a kitchen garden in the backyard. An Adivasi Ranchi man was Abba's cook and he cooked delicious dishes. His speciality was 'Phulka' Roti, made on burning coal. At night he would cook vegetables, chicken and Phulka which everyone used to relish.

Abba informed Amma and his children that Campbell was the tahsil headquarters and there were many villages in the tahsil which included-7KM Farm, Joginder Nagar, Afra Bay, Alexandra River, Anul, Bewai, Chingam, Campbell Bay, Gandhi Nagar, Shastri Nagar, Govinda Nagar, Henhoaha, Lafal, Laxmi Nagar, Makahu, Indira Point, Katahu, Kokeon, Lanaya, Patisang, Pattiya, Pitayo, Pulloullo, Pulobha, Pulomilo Island, Pulopanja, Shompen Hut, Shompen Village-A, Shompen Village-B, Trinket Bay and Vijoy Nagar.

Abba had visited every settlement in Campbell Bay, including Shompen Huts and Indira Point[3]. He told his children about the giant coconut crab, Megapode and Nicobar pigeon found in the island. Those crabs used to eat away the coconut kernel on the trees and the empty shells would be left. From February to December, the Leather Back Turtle, which is the largest turtle in the world, nests here.

Behind the Assistant Commissioner's quarter there was the dense forest and behind that was a beautiful beach. The peons said that the long beach was strewn with varieties of shells for miles, and plastic materials, toys and buoys could be seen floating on the sea there. On hearing that the children wanted to explore the beach and they asked Abba's permission to go to the beach. Abba advised his children to be very careful on the beach as it was an open sea with high waves, not like the beaches of North and South Andaman, and it could be very dangerous at times. The children insisted Amma to join them but Amma was not ready to walk all those miles. She was afraid of her convulsions and did not go with the children. Amma couldn't join them but she packed snacks for the children to have on the beach, and they left to explore the beach with their bag-packs.

The children walked through the forest by the trail, watching birds and talking all the way. They enjoyed watching the tall trees, the varieties of birds chirruping on trees, monkeys squeaking and jumping from branch to branch, the small brooks flowing through the forest and the orchids and creepers and vines twining on those tall trees. They crossed all those miles through the forest and finally reached the beach.

The virgin beach lay strewn with different types of shells, conch, plastic toys and a variety of plastic materials. The waves were very loud and high, not like the calm waves found in the other beaches they had visited in Andamans. The Children could not enter the waters due to the very high waves, but they enjoyed playing on the beach, collecting shells and plastic materials and toys. There were such varieties of plastic materials and they wanted to take everything with them. There were buoys, different types of balls and toys, chairs, plastic racks etc. When they were tired, they had their snacks and rested for some time. Then they walked around and explored the beach and finally reached the other end of the town, near the jetty, carrying all the shells and plastic toys they had collected. Abba's driver was there for some work and when he saw Abba's children, he brought them home in the jeep.

Abba told his children that all those plastic toys and materials found on the shore were from Indonesia as it was hardly 110 miles from Campbell Bay. The companies there used to discard the plastic products that had some flaws in them and used to throw them away into the sea, which in turn were carried by the waves to the shores of Campbell Bay. Many toys and other plastic materials used to be in good condition and people used to collect them and used it in their houses.

One day Abba brought five Shompen men home and told Amma and the children that the 'Shompens[4]' are an indigenous tribe who are also known as Great Nicobarese. Once upon a time they were savages and the outsiders landing on the islands were got killed by them. H. Busch in Journal of a Cruise among the Nicobar Islands at page 41 states "On enquiring about our native friends from the Little Nicobar, we were told that the interiors of Great Nicobar are occupied by a widely different race of savages, who are always at war with those on the sea-shore: who are always armed with bows and arrows; and about their cruelty many tales are told."

It is said that once upon a time, before the arrival of settlers, the Shompens were the sole inhabitants of the Great Nicobar Island. They belong to the mongoloid stock and live in deep jungles in huts on stilts, made of bamboo and leaves. They lived in the interior jungles ahead of river Galathea and river Alexandria. In their settlements, they usually did not wear clothes. The government tried to befriend them by providing them with fruits, rice, clothes etc., and gradually they started to contact the civilized society in Campbell Bay. Whenever the Shompen men would come to the small town of Campbell Bay, they would have covered their loins with pieces of clothes provided by the government officials. Abba said that when they would enter their, jungles, they would throw away all their clothes, and used to return to their dwellings, in their natural state.

The Shompen men used to bring honey collected from the jungles and they used to barter the honey for rice and grains which they used to take back to their settlements. They did not eat their food raw, but cooked their food and were great hunters. They hunted boar, snake and even crocodiles and ate the meat. The females were very less in numbers compared to the males. A few Nicobari families had also settled in Campbell Bay in a village called 'Chingam', and the Shompens were in regular contact with those Nicobarese and they used to go to them to barter their things. Sometimes they used to go and stay with the Nicobarese and worked as bonded labourers and instead they got food and other eatables. They did not know Hindi and whenever they came to Campbell Bay, people communicated with them through signs.

The Shompens had come to the Assistant Commissioner's Office where they were given free rice and clothes. Abba thought that Amma and the children would be happy to see the aboriginals, and so had brought them home. The Shompens were brown and stout and were not very tall. They had thick black brown hair that was long and matted.

Their teeth were stained by excessive eating of beetle nuts which were found in abundance in the jungles. Some men had pierced their earlobes and wore pieces of bamboo sticks in them. Abba told Amma and his children that people used to tell that those men who had their earlobes pierced and were wearing bamboo pieces were married while the others were yet to get married.

At home, Abba made the Shompen men to sit on chairs but they preferred to sit down on the floor and laughed. They mimicked every word spoken by Abba and laughed merrily. Abba told Amma to serve them food but Amma was scared to go near them. When food was served, they did not know how to eat. Abba showed them how to pick up the food with the hands and eat, but they could not eat. Then Abba picked food and ate in front of them, but still, they couldn't eat. Though they tried to copy Abba but were not very successful. They spilled the food everywhere and laughed. A little food went into the mouth while the rest spilled out and got scattered. They somehow finished their food and Abba sent them back in his office jeep.

One day Abba took Amma and the children to see the settlements in Campbell Bay. There were lots of monkeys and they could be seen sitting in groups on the roads. Whenever a vehicle would pass, the monkeys would follow and chase it to some distance, and then would give up. The settlers complained to Abba that the monkeys would come in a crowd and uproot the plants and pluck coconuts and areca nuts and destroyed their plantations. People complained that the monkeys even entered houses and took away things, and people were helpless. Whenever the jeep stopped near a settlement, people crowded the jeep and they had so much to share with Abba. They also complained about the monkey menace and the giant crab problems.

After a few days Abba made arrangements to take his family to visit Indira Point, which is also the southernmost tip of India. To reach the place they had to cross the river Galatea. When Abba and his family reached the spot, it was raining profusely and the river was flooded and was overflowing its banks. Abba waited there for about two hours for the rains to stop and the river to calm. But the gush of the water went on increasing and it was impossible to cross Galatea in the boat. The yellow water of the river was flowing in all fury, carrying logs and trees on its way. More and more logs were being pulled into the current of the water and it appeared very dangerous. Abba decided to drop his plan, as venturing into the flooded river could be very dangerous as the boat could be easily capsized!

When the summer vacations were nearing its end, Abba accompanied Amma and the children to Port Blair in the steamer. The steamer stopped at various islands. First, it halted at Kamorta Island. Abba told his family that INS Kardip[5] was commissioned in 1973 at Kamorta Island to stop unauthorized intrusions by foreign vessels. Many times, foreign boats and poachers had been noticed and reported in the territorial waters. Hence the Indian Navy decided to establish a forward operating base under the joint services of Andaman and Nicobar Command located on Kamorta island, for the safety of the islands and its people. Abba had good friends at the Headquarters of INS Kardip. Some officers had come to the jetty and when they met Abba and his family on the ship, they offered to take Abba and his family to their Headquarters, and insisted on it. Abba could not refuse them, and accompanied by Amma and the children, visited the Naval base. The place had been well-developed and neatly maintained. Abba and family were taken around and good hospitality was shown by the officers there. They also provided lunch to Abba and his family and then with due respect, they dropped them back at the jetty in their jeep, where the steamer was ready to set sail again.

The next day the steamer reached Katchal[6] Island, which was known as *'Tihnyu'* in the earlier times. It is a beautiful island with pure white sandy beaches, inhabited by indigenous Nicobari Tribes, people working in government offices and Tamil settlers who had been brought from Ceylon to work in the Rubber plantation under Shastri-Srimao Bandaranayaka Pact in 1964. The tropical forest of Katchal is abundant with monkeys, wild boars and many pythons and is very dangerous. The hills of Katchal are composed of calcareous sandstone and marble slates.

The island falls under the township of Nancowry of Katchal Tahsil. It is also the largest island of the central group of islands and has about thirty villages, of which six are main villages - E-Wall, Meenakshi Ram Nagar, Japan Tikrey, Sallo Tikrey, and Upper Katchal. Mildera is yet another village in the island, inhabited by non-tribal people.

Abba told Amma and the children that Nicobar was once a part of the Chola kingdom of Tanjore and there are historic evidences for it. In 1869, the British took possession of these islands from the Danes. The Government of India had declared the Nicobar Islands an Aboriginal Tribal Reserve Area (ATRA) on 2 April 1957. Because of this, the Nicobar Islands have become inaccessible to outsiders and now even Indians need a special tribal pass to visit the islands.

When the steamer stopped at Katchal Island, Abba, Amma and the children got down from the steamer by a gangplank and went around the Island in a jeep which was arranged by Abba's office staff. Lunch had also been arranged for the family by Abba's friends. Many people who were working at the rubber plantation came to meet Abba and they discussed their problems faced on the island. Then, when it was time, Abba along with his family returned to the steamer. In the evening the steamer left for its onward voyage to Car Nicobar.

Car Nicobar[7], also known as *Pū* in the Car language, is the northern most island of the Nicobar group and is the district headquarters. It is a very beautiful island and the next day the steamer reached Car Nicobar. The white sandy beaches of the island glistening in the morning sun, could be seen from the steamer. There was a small pier and no harbour, so the steamer could not berth and was anchored in the sea away from the island. People from the steamer got down onto a pontoon along with their goods. Then the pontoon was towed and taken to the pier or dock where people would disembark and then goods were carried up the dock. During the monsoons and stormy weather, it used to be very difficult for people to climb down the steamer. Incidents of people falling into the sea from the pontoons were also heard many times. Abba told his children that the Nicobarese people are very cheerful and friendly in nature and they lived in villages and there was a Captain in every village who looked into the internal problems of the village. Abba also spoke to some Nicobarese people who were on the ship. The whole day Abba's children were watching the passengers going down from the steamer and coming up to the steamer. In the evening the steamer left on its onward voyage.

The next morning Abba told Amma and the children that the steamer was heading towards Hut Bay in Little Andaman[8] Island. It is the fourth largest island in the archipelago of Andaman and Nicobar Islands, and belongs to the South Andaman District. As the steamer entered the Ten Degree Channel, the steamer was tossed by huge waves. The children felt sea sickness. It remained for a few hours, till the steamer crossed the Channel. After a few hours, the steamer safely reached Hut Bay. The island is low-lying and has widespread rainforest, sandy beaches, bewitching waterfalls and several rare species of marine turtle. This island has become a tribal reserve since 1957. Hut Bay or Kwate-tu-Kwage is the largest settlement in the island.

Abba told the children that the Onge[9] aborigines are one of the ancient tribes of the Andaman and Nicobar Islands. They call the islands *Egu Belong.* Once upon a time they too lived a life of hunter gatherers, but now they had been settled in Dugong Creek. Till early 1960, Little Andaman was exclusively the dwelling place of the Onge tribe. They belong to the Negrito racial stock and when their number started decreasing, they were settled here in Little Andaman during 1976-77. Now, the Administration provided them food, clothes, medicines etc. They had also been provided with houses. A primary school had also been established for the Onge children in 1978.

Settlers from Bengal and other places also live in this island. There are also Nicobari Settlements in the island. Dugong Creek, Netaji Nagar, Rabindra Nagar, Ramakrishnapur and Vivekanandapuram are the main villages of the island. Butler Bay Beach, 14 km from the Hut Bay Jetty, is a popular beach among tourists due to coral viewing, surfing and other marine activities.

Abba took Amma and the children around the island in a jeep. They also saw a few Onge people on the way to the small market and came back to the harbour on time as the steamer was ready to sail. While going around the island, many people came to meet Abba and they all showed great respect to him.

Amma and the children enjoyed their trip thoroughly to Campbell Bay and back. They were mesmerized by the green islands against the blue sea and azure sky. Amma and the children were very proud of Abba as wherever they went, Abba was received with high respect and admiration. They were happy to see that Abba was very popular among the common people in all the Settlements of the islands. Throughout the voyage Abba spent some valuable time with Amma and the children, enriching their knowledge about the geography and history of the islands. That day evening the steamer reached Port Blair and all were happy to reach home safely!

The next year Abba received his transfer order. He was relieved from the office of the Asst. Commissioner, Campbell Bay on 20-7-1980 and he set sail to Port Blair.

Chapter - 29

ABBA VISITS HIS BROTHER'S FAMILY IN SRI LANKA

It was the year 1980. About a year ago, Abba had got news of the demise of his eldest brother who was settled with his wife and four children in Negombo[10]. Then Abba couldn't make arrangements to visit his brother's family due to his posting in Campbell Bay, but Abba was very concerned about his brother's family. A friend of Abba from Andaman had gone to Sri Lanka to visit his relatives and he happened to meet Abba's brother's family there. While having a casual talk, the friend of Abba told them that he was from Andaman and they told him that they had relatives in Andaman and they told Abba's name. The man told them that Abba was a friend of his, and he knew Abba very well. While the man was leaving, Abba's brother's family sent a letter for Abba. After coming to Port Blair, the man met Abba, handed him the letter he had brought and told him about the hardships faced by his brother's family in Colombo.

Abba read the letter that was written by his nephew and the letter described about the difficulties faced by the family. After reading the letter Abba became very emotional and worried about his brother's children. He told Amma that he wanted to go to Sri Lanka and meet his brother's family and help them with some money. Amma too agreed to it. Abba's third brother was living in Port Blair with his family. Abba met him and told him about the problems faced by their eldest brother's family in Sri Lanka and also told him that he was going to meet them. This brother of Abba had four sons. They had a daughter, but the child had drowned in a well in Mannarpuram village, when she was very young. It was a very tragic incident which no one could forget. Abba's sister-in-law told Abba that they would like to adopt a daughter of the eldest brother and if possible, Abba should try to bring the eldest daughter of the brother with him from Sri Lanka. Abba was very happy to hear that, as now he had one more cause to go to meet his brother's family.

Abba arranged for money, booked his tickets and one fine day left for Colombo. He had the address of his brother's house and went to Negombo city on the west coast. He bought sweets and fruits for the children and as per the custom, he also bought a sari for the widow of his brother. When the family saw Abba, they were very happy. The family was struggling financially, with the eldest son working with fishermen. He went for fishing with them in their boats or he went for day labour. The second daughter was at home helping her mother and the younger children were in schools, the youngest child was hardly five to six years old.

Abba advised his sister-in-law to return with the children to India, to their ancestral village, and to live there peacefully. But the sister-in-law did not agree to it. She wanted to spend the rest of her life with her children in Negombo, and in her old age, after her death, she wanted to be buried by the side of her husband, in the same soil. Abba insisted his sister-in-law to at least send Bella, her elder daughter with him to Andaman as his brother's family wanted to adopt her. Abba assured and promised his sister-in-law that he would take utmost care of the child as his own daughter. After much persuasion, Abba's sister-in-law agreed to send Bella with Abba. Abba gave some money to his sister-in-law to take care of her children. Then after staying there for about a week, Abba left for India, with Bella. While returning from Colombo, he brought a Citizen watch for Sheryl.

One fine day Abba returned to Andaman and brought Bella with him. Bella was about sixteen years old and she was very fair, beautiful and a happy child. Abba's brother and his family, Chithi and her family, all came to see Bella. They were all happy to see the child who was Abba's eldest brother's daughter and who had come from far off lands. She was a very cheerful child and spoke Tamil with a Sinhalese accent. Abba told his bother that he would send Bella to their house after a few days. Bella stayed with Abba and his family for about four days and then Abba told Amma to take her to his brother's house, who also stayed close by at Junglighat. Amma and her children took Bella to her new home and leaving her there, they returned home. Henceforth Bella was supposed to live with Abba's brother's family. Abba and Amma expected that Bella would be happy in her new home as there were four boys and no girls in the family and the sister-in-law would take good care of her.

Bella was warmly welcomed by Abba's brother and sister-in-law. Their four sons, were happy to have a sister and took great care of her. Though the family bought many things for Bella, but she was not happy in her new home. Most of the time Abba's brother used to be drunk and would be sleeping. When sober, he used to be the most affectionate and loving person. But if drunk, he would be a totally different person, shouting and screaming in a changed tone. The younger sons used to go to school in the morning and would return only in the evening. The eldest son of the family had discontinued his school and used to help his mother who was running a bar in the house for a livelihood.

Abba had tried many times to help this brother of his with money so that he would start his own business. He was a tailor and Abba had given him Amma's sewing machine and also bought clothes for him to stitch so that he could earn a livelihood and take care of his family in a respectful manner. But he sold all the clothes and with the money bought liquor for himself. Abba was worried about this brother of his! Abba seldom went to his house but would enquire about the well-being of the family from Amma who used to visit them once in a while.

Since there was no way of earning a livelihood, Abba's sister-in-law had taken to that trade. Her husband was not doing any work, and she had to take care of her sons and shoulder the family responsibility. She made money in that business and had also bought land and property for her family. Abba had urged his sister-in-law many times to start some other work as she was financially stable then. She too used to assure Abba that she would soon give up that trade and start some other business. But when Bella came to the house, the bar was open and the trade was still going on. Men were coming to the bar for drinks and sometimes they would be foul mouthed, shouting and there would be a bad scene. Bella did not like it at all and the family atmosphere made her very sad. She did not want to stay there and wanted to return to her own family. But she was helpless and did not know what to do!

After about two months, one evening Amma visited Abba's brother's house to see Bella. When Bella saw Amma, she ran into Amma's arms and started crying loudly with great sorrow. She begged Amma to take her back with her. She told very clearly that she did not want to stay in that house. Amma was bewildered and did not know what to do! She had just come to find about the well-being of Bella in her new home, but what she saw was shocking for her! Since Amma was a very soft-hearted person, and couldn't see anyone in sorrow, she also started weeping with Bella. Amma tried to talk to Abba's brother and sister-in-law, but they were not willing to say a word. The sister-in-law told Amma to take Bella with her, if she wanted to go. When Amma asked Bella again, she started crying pathetically and shook her head in agreement. So, without a second thought, Amma told Bella to collect her belongings and she brought Bella back home.

In the evening when Abba returned from the office, he was surprised to see Bella at home. Amma told him that Bella didn't want to stay in Abba's brother's house and also described all that had happened in that house. Abba was very sad about the entire episode. He said to Bella, "Do not worry child, I am here in your father's place. I have two daughters and you would be my third daughter. If you want anything or if you have any problem, do let me know, and do not hesitate. From now on consider this to be your own house."

An additional member in the house was a burden for Abba and Amma, but they managed their household well. Since Bella was not going to school and was at home, she was a great help to Amma in all the household chores. But the children of the house were not very happy. They were jealous of Bella as Abba was very affectionate towards her. Whenever Abba would be kind to Bella, the children would get angry. Jason was very possessive of Abba and the house. He used to say that the house belonged to him. At home, on many occasions, he would not even allow Meryl to sit on the chair and he used to push her from the chair saying that it was his chair and Meryl would sit on the floor and weep. She was a silent child and would never complain about it to anyone. After Bella's arrival, Jason found many reasons to fight with Meryl and Bella! He would not directly fight with Sheryl as she was elder to him. Abba and Amma ignored all the behaviours of Jason thinking that he was very young and once he would grow up, he would change!

Chapter - 30

ABBA IS POSTED AS CONTROLLER, ANDAMAN LABOUR FORCE

In 1980, Abba was transferred from Campbell Bay and he returned to Port Blair. In the same year, on 20-7-1980, he was conferred with DANICS. It was a very proud moment for Abba and his family. The acronym DANICS stands for "Delhi, Andaman & Nicobar Islands Civil Service".

DANICS is a 'Group A' Civil Service post of the Government of India. Officers of this service are recruited directly through Civil Service Examination and are responsible for the diverse administrative functions of the National Capital, Delhi and the Union Territories. They form a feeder cadre to the Indian Administrative Service.

Abba had become a DANICS officer by virtue of his hard work and promotions and it was a great achievement for Abba. Abba and Amma were very happy and as always, they counted their blessings and thanked God for His mercy on their family. Abba also remembered the beginning days of his service and the officer who had advised him to join the Revenue Department, due to which Abba could become a DANICS officer. He got a pay hike and with the arrear money, Abba bought a refrigerator for home, and Amma was very happy.

After arriving at Port Blair, Abba received his order of posting and he was posted as Controller of the Andaman Labour Force. Abba reported for duty on 29th July 1980 at his office at Haddo Wharf. The islands had 8 major ports, 15 minor ports, 1 airport and 3 defence airports. The present job of Abba was full of challenges as the labourers used to pose a lot of problems at the harbour. Suddenly there used to be labour unrest and work would be stopped at the port. The labourers would not allow any work to be carried out at the port. When ships would berth and containers would arrive with goods, many goods would get stolen at the port itself. Ships would not be allowed to berth on time by the labourers and passengers would face a lot of difficulties. The inter-island ferry services also used to be affected every now and then due to labour unrest. All these posed a lot of complications to the administration as well as the general public.

On assuming the charge of Controller of Andaman Labour Force, Abba started revamping his office and its system of working. He started listening to the labour problems seriously and learnt that all the problems were due to delay in payment of salaries and non-regularisation of services of the labourers. Abba started streamlining the pending cases of salary of the workers, regularising the service of temporary workers, sorting out pension cases and compensations, medical reimbursements etc. He used to be very close to his workers and took care of them as his own family. He used to personally go with the salary file of the workers to the higher authorities and to the Pay and Accounts Office and got the salary bills passed. With a lot of effort, and with the help of his superior officers, Abba could get the services of temporary workers regularised. He also focused on 'Welfare Committee Meetings' of the workers. He regularly called those meetings and the problems of the workers were discussed in the meetings in detail and solutions were also found. The leader of the workers could raise genuine issues in the meetings, and Abba also tried to solve those issues.

The workers of the labour force were very happy on getting their service regularised. Many of them were working for more than ten years on temporary basis. They considered Abba to be their God and adored him and they were ready to do anything for him. Once the workers were satisfied, it was easy for Abba to make them work for the welfare of the department.

Since most of the problems of the workers were solved, soon their confidence also got boosted up. Due to that, the output of the Department also increased and at the same time the ships plying between mainland and inter-islands were streamlined and they started moving on time. Within a year, all the labour problems were also resolved.

The same year, in July 1980, Abba's eldest daughter Sheryl had passed her Bachelor of Arts and Abba was elated. He was so happy that he wept with joy! His ardent desire to go to college could not be fulfilled due to his family's financial conditions and now he felt his dreams being fulfilled through his daughter. Though Abba was very intelligent and had good knowledge of doing any official work but many times he used to feel very low as the new recruits, the younger officers, were graduates or postgraduates. He used to tell Amma that the new recruited officers were all degree holders and that he felt so low in front of them. During such times Amma used to encourage Abba saying that those officers could have degrees, but Abba had vast knowledge and experience, more than any of those new officers. It was true as Abba himself had felt it many times!

Abba was very proud of his daughter who had become a graduate. Whenever someone would come home, Abba would proudly tell them that his daughter had passed her graduation. He told Amma to cook special dishes to celebrate the occasion. He also advised Jason and Meryl to study very well and score good marks and become graduates one day.

During September of the same year, Abba got an administration seat for Sheryl for B.Ed. That seat had been allotted to another girl, but as she was not willing to join the course, she had surrendered her seat. When Abba learnt about it, he applied for the seat and managed to get the seat allotted to his daughter. He booked ship tickets for Sheryl and himself and one fine day Abba took Sheryl to Chennai to admit her for her B. Ed. training in Annamalai University. With a lot of advice, he left her at the university hostel and returned back to Andaman. He regularly sent money orders to his daughter for her studies. When

Sheryl completed her training, Abba brought her back to Port Blair in 1981. Within a few days she got appointed as a teacher in a government school on temporary basis. The whole family was happy and celebrated the occasion. Abba was very happy thinking that since his daughter had got a job, his family would become financially stable with one more earning member!

But that did not happen. Just like Abba joined his job at the age of 20, Sheryl too joined her job as a teacher when she was just 20 years old and Abba was very happy. Soon Abba started receiving wedding proposals for her. But Abba was not prepared for her wedding so soon, as financially he was not very sound. From his salary, he had been sending money orders for his daughter's higher studies and also had to see to the needs of his other three children and the family expenditure. Abba had emptied his provident fund and at any rate, he was not ready for his daughter's wedding!

A family had seen Abba's eldest daughter in the church and the family members were willing to seek Abba's daughter for their son. They wanted to visit Abba's house formally to see the girl, and they also sent words to Abba about it. But Abba didn't know what to say!

On a particular evening, the family formally visited Abba's house to see Abba's eldest daughter. On that day Amma had prepared special sweets and savouries. Abba also returned from his office on time. When Sheryl came back from school, she was surprised to find the house decked up and guests were at home. Abba and Amma knew about the family's visit beforehand, but they had kept it from their daughter. When Sheryl arrived, Amma told her to serve coffee and sweets to the guests and Sheryl obeyed. There was some formal talking about both the families and their villages at the mainland, and the family told Abba that they liked his daughter and wanted to have the wedding soon. But Abba told them that he would talk to his daughter and inform them later. So, after some time, the family left.

After the family left, Amma told Sheryl about the marriage proposal and wanted to know whether she liked the boy who had come to see her along with his parents. But Sheryl was not happy about the marriage proposal and she told Amma very clearly that she was not interested in that alliance. Amma was annoyed and inquired whether she liked somebody else. To Amma's great shock, Sheryl told that she was in love with a young man who worked with her as a teacher. This left Amma speechless! Amma was very upset on hearing that. She asked her daughter about the man whom she loved and Amma learnt that the man her daughter loved did not belong to their community and that he was a Keralite. Amma was afraid to tell Abba about that as Abba would be very angry! She knew that there would be a war in the house if Abba would learn about his daughter's wish. She prayed to God that the problem should be settled peacefully!

But the matter did not settle so peacefully! After the guests had left, Abba told Amma to ask Sheryl's opinion about the boy, and Amma also left the place to talk to Sheryl. Abba was waiting to know Sheryl's views, and he called Amma to find about it. Amma was very frightened and did not know how to tell Abba about Sheryl. Somehow, gathering courage, she told Abba that Sheryl was not interested in the alliance. Then Abba wanted to know the reason and asked Amma if she wanted to marry someone else! Amma was surprised at Abba's question and told him that Sheryl told her that she was in love with a young man who was a teacher and was working with her. Abba was totally shocked and stunned. He was unable to believe his ears. He sat there petrified for some time, his whole body going limp! He was still unable to believe what Amma had told him. He again asked Amma what Sheryl had told her. With trembling heart, Amma narrated the entire conversation that she had with her elder daughter!

Then, Abba's anger started mounting up slowly and he burst out like a volcano, seething, shouting, screaming, abusing, and was very furious. He had never expected such a behaviour from his daughter! She was his favourite daughter and how proud he used to be of her! He felt betrayed and devastated at her behaviour. In his anger, he called out to Sheryl, and when she came in front of him, he slapped her and beat her hard. Amma rushed to protect her and she too got beatings. Abba drank a lot of liquor that night and was mournful about life. He kept on lamenting, shouting and screaming about the unfaithfulness of his daughter, who had not thought about her parents even once, before deciding about her future! He screamed at her loudly saying that she was very selfish and had no respect for her parents. He lamented where he had gone wrong in his parenting! Then he sat there and wept bitterly about the betrayal of his daughter. No one in the house had ever seen such a face of Abba! Amma and all the children in the house were in great fear of Abba and no one wanted to have food or talk or smile. The entire household was sunk in gloom and silence engulfed every heart!

The next day Chithi came home with her husband and they learnt about the previous day's happenings from Amma. Chithi and her husband tried to convince Sheryl to agree to the wedding proposal but Sheryl was too adamant and told them straight away that if she would get married, it would be to the man whom she loved. Chithi's husband understood that Sheryl would not change her mind and so he spoke to Abba to get her married to the man of her choice. But Abba was not pleased with his advice. He told Chithi's husband that he had cast-off Sheryl from his life and that she was no more his daughter and if he was so interested, he could get her married to whomever she wanted!

Days passed slowly and Abba's household dragged on cheerlessly. Abba had forgotten to smile. Amma and her children were very silent. Chithi and her husband regularly visited Abba and Amma and had long discussions for hours.

After about four months Abba finally agreed for the wedding of his daughter with the man of her choice, but with the condition that he did not have any money to spend on her. Sheryl could take the jewellery made for her and he would also arrange for the wedding reception, but Sheryl should not expect anything else from him. Sheryl agreed to all the condition of Abba. But she had started her M.A. evening classes, and told Abba that she wanted to complete her studies first and then she would get married. But Abba did not agree to her. He told her to get married first and then she could continue her studies.

Thus, at last the wedding was solemnized in the Catholic Church at Port Blair. Abba arranged for the wedding feast and also invited all his friends and relatives and everybody was happy.

Though Abba had been very hurt by his daughter's behaviour, and he had arranged for the wedding as a duty, but when the wedding was over and while Sheryl was departing with her groom, Abba told her that if she faced any problem in her life, she could always turn to him for help and he would always be there for her!

Chapter - 31

AMMA'S MOTHER BREATHES HER LAST!

The boat of life was moving with ups and downs for Abba and Amma and they were trying to maintain a balance with the tide. Abba's elder son Jason had completed his schooling and Abba tried to get a BE seat for him in Chennai. Abba visited many colleges and universities with Jason, but the donations demanded were beyond his pocket and so he had to return back unsuccessful. Then, Jason started his graduation at the Government College, Port Blair. Meryl was still in high school.

After about a month of Sheryl's wedding, Sheryl and her husband got regular jobs as teachers and they were posted at Long Island[11]. Soon they left for Long Island to join their duties at their place of posting. Before they left for Long Island, Abba and Amma came to their daughter's house and advised Sheryl and her husband to be dedicated in their duties as teachers, since teachers were the nation builders. Abba also told them that life would not be very easy always and they should overcome the problems of their life together. If they wanted any help, they could always inform him and he would be there for them. Amma blessed them for a happy married life!

Long Island is a small island in the Middle Andaman and it could be reached only by steamer. Mark Bay, Lalaji Bay and Guitar Island are popular islands with beaches close to this island. Long Island belongs to the East Baratang Group of Islands. For Sheryl and her husband, the journey through the mangrove creeks by boat was very thrilling and mesmerizing. Long Island was surrounded by beautiful islands and pristine virgin beaches. When they landed on the island, they found that there were no roads on the island and there were only footpaths to go around. Few people owned bicycles but otherwise, everyone had to walk for going from one place to another. The water was hard and people would eagerly wait for the rains to have soft water. During the rainy seasons, every household would collect rain water and store it for cooking and drinking purposes. Electricity was supplied for a few hours. There were no pipe lines and water had to be carried from wells. During rains, it appeared as if all the centipedes of the planet rush out of the dark bowels of the earth to occupy the island. You can't walk on roads at night as thousands and thousands of those black and brown creatures would be wriggling and jostling to eat those flying ants that fly out during rains. They were of black and brown colour and people had to find footholds by jumping from stone to stone to reach their houses, as there were no roads. Outside the house it would be terrifying to see the centipedes in thousands, jiggling everywhere, and one could not go out in the night. Life was really difficult in Long Island!

It was about eight months after Sheryl's wedding when one day Abba received a letter from Sheryl stating that she was with child, and was on her family way. Amma was elated as she was to become a grandmother. But Abba was still not very happy with his elder daughter and son-in-law. Amma wanted to meet her daughter so Abba decided to send Amma to Long Island with Bella to take care of her for some days.

When Amma reached Long Island with Bella, she once again had those seizures. The journey by boat had made her tired. In Long Island, since there were no roads or vehicles, Amma had to walk from the Jetty to Sheryl's quarter which was on a hillock. This made her exhausted. But Amma was very happy to see her daughter and son-in-law. The next day after Sheryl and her husband had left for school, Amma thought of cooking some special dishes for her daughter. After she finished cooking, Amma went to take a bath. After some time, Bella heard a loud noise from the bathroom and she called out to Amma. But there was no reply. Bella started banging on the door, still there was no reply. On hearing the noise, the women of the neighbourhood, who were housewives, came to see what had happened and Bella told them that Amma had gone for a shower but was not replying. Then they all made a young child who was about four years old to climb through the ventilator and get into the washroom. The child reached inside and opened the latch of the door that Amma had bolted from within. The women found Amma lying on the floor, in an unconscious state, her mouth frothing and her face, neck, arms and leg muscles were jerking. Her entire body had turned cold. The neighbourhood women were all afraid and somehow managed to carry her to the bed. Then they sent words to Sheryl and her husband about Amma's condition and soon they rushed back from school and found Amma lying unconscious on the bed.

There was a hospital in Long Island but it was on a hillock and it would not be possible to carry Amma there. The neighbours suggested to carry Amma to the hospital but Sheryl told them that Amma would be fine after a few hours. And after a few hours, Amma indeed recovered and came back to her senses and was very upset. She lamented that she had come to take care of her daughter but had created problems for her daughter and son-in-law. Amma stayed with her daughter and son-in-law for a fortnight and then returned to Port Blair with Bella. During her stay at her daughter's house, she prepared special dishes of sea food and chicken for her daughter, and was very happy.

After returning to Port Blair from Long Island, Bella told Abba that she wanted to go to her native place in Sri Lanka. Abba tried to convince Bella that he was looking for a suitable groom for her at Port Blair but she did not agree to that. She told Abba that she did not want to be in Andaman and she wanted to go back to her mother and siblings, and she would be happy to spend her life with them. So, Abba arranged for tickets and requested Chithi's husband to take Bella back to her homeland and he too agreed. Abba got a gold chain, and new clothes for Bella. He also gave some money to her and sent her back to her hometown. Abba was very sad as he could not keep his words with his sister-in-law and could not do anything for Bella!

It was the end of April 1983, and Amma's mother had taken ill and was hospitalized. She had been staying in Babu Lane with Chithi for the past six to seven years. She was just 64 years old but appeared to be above 80, as throughout her life she had undergone many hardships and struggles to raise her daughters. When Amma went to see her mother in the hospital, she confided to Amma that she wanted to go to Amma's house and stay with her during the last days of her life. She said to Amma, "Take me to your house." Amma expressed her mother's wish to Abba and he agreed. At the hospital, the doctors told Abba that the condition of Amma's mother was very critical and she would not live long. They told Abba to take her home. Soon Abba got her discharged from the hospital, and brought his mother-in-law to his house at Junglighat.

So Amma's mother was brought to Junglighat quarters. Abba and Amma took good care of her but her condition deteriorated day by day, and the medicines did not work on her. Chithi and her husband visited her regularly. Gradually Amma's mother stopped eating and was put on liquid diet. On the 14th of May in the evening, she seemed to be better and she even asked Amma for something to eat. She enquired about Jason who had completed his graduation and was in the mainland for his training. She loved her grandson very much! On that night she slept well. But by midnight Amma heard some strange sound and woke up. She found her mother calling out to her and she wanted water to drink. Amma gave her water and she drank just one gulp. With that, her eyes closed forever. Amma was totally shattered and burst out wailing!

That evening Chithi did not go back to her house. She had some strange feelings and had stayed back with Amma. On hearing Amma's cries, Chithi and the whole household woke up. Everyone was sad to see that Amma's mother was no more. Throughout the night Amma and Chithi remained awake, weeping and lamenting their mother's death. Next morning the news of Amma's mother's demise spread out and all the relatives and neighbours gathered to grieve. As per Amma's mother's wish Abba had already arranged for flight tickets for the next day for Jason to come from mainland. Early next day, on 15 May Jason arrived, and the funeral of Amma's mother was held on the same day. There was sorrow on every face. When the coffin was lifted, Amma, Chithi and the children burst into wailing and Amma almost collapsed. The entire household was drowned in sorrow!

Chapter - 32

ABBA IS POSTED AS SECRETARY, PORT BLAIR MUNICIPAL BOARD

The 9th Asian Games were held in Delhi from 19 November to 4 December 1982. It was an amazing moment for the people of Andamans as they were able to watch the live telecast of the Asian Games on Television sets. Till then people only used the radios to hear the live commentaries. Abba also bought a black and white TV set, that was the first TV in the colony. Children of the whole colony used to gather at Abba's house to watch the programmes on DD. It used to be such a gala time for everyone. Sometimes the elders too used to join the children, and there used to be a lot of talking and laughing, all enjoying the TV programmes. Soon, other households also got their TV sets, and life started taking a different course. Earlier people used to sit with each other and chit chat but now people started being confined to their houses, to watch the T.V. programmes!

In May 1983, Abba was transferred from Andaman Labour Force and was posted as Secretary, Port Blair Municipal Board. He had been granted six advance increments vide Administration order 2546 dated 19-5-83 and Abba and Amma were happy.

Abba was given a warm farewell by the staff of Andaman Labour Force and many of them were in tears as Abba was leaving them. Abba consoled them all saying that he would be in Port Blair and his house was always open for them and they could always come to him if they needed any help. Abba joined his new office on 24th May 1983, as Secretary, Port Blair Municipal Board.

After assuming his new office Abba became very busy with his work. Many local leaders also started visiting Abba for various help. The Municipal Councillors regularly visited Abba seeking his advice and help in solving the municipality-related problems of their wards in Port Blair Municipal area and Abba was always ready to render a helping hand in their needs. As Abba was very interested in gardening, he decided to refurbish the Marina Park of Port Blair and give it a new look. Working day and night with the workers, finally the Marina Park got a facelift due to Abba's efforts.

On 23-3-1984 Abba was confirmed in Grade II DANICS, which was another achievement in Abba's life. He was very happy and thanked God for all the blessings. In the same year, Abba was allotted a type-IV quarter in Junglighat opposite to the milk booth. It was a big house with an independent campus. Soon Abba developed a beautiful garden in front of the house and a vegetable garden too was developed on the sides. At the back of the house, a shed was constructed and Abba bought a cow and there was no dearth for milk or curd at home. A man was hired to milk the cow and Amma would collect the cream from the milk and extract ghee out of it. Soon the plants grew and started yielding vegetables and Amma was happy to get vegetables from the garden. Life was going smoothly for Abba and Amma!

While working at Port Blair Municipal Board, Abba had to be always busy with the VVIP visits and their civic receptions. In February 1984, Prime Minister of India, Mrs. Indira Gandhi visited the Andaman and Nicobar Islands and Abba was in charge for making all arrangements for the civic reception. Abba did his job very well for which he was highly appreciated by the Lt. Governor of the islands. Abba was very impressed by the personality of Mrs. Indira Gandhi. When she visited the Nicobar Islands, Abba accompanied the officers' group and saw her concern for the tribal people of the islands. After the Prime Minister's departure, Abba got time to relax. He told Amma that though Indira Gandhi was called an iron lady as she was very bold and daring, but she also had a kind heart with a lot of compassion for the poor and deprived!

Sheryl and her husband were in Long Island and when it was time for Sheryl to deliver the baby, she and her husband came to Port Blair, to Abba's house. But Abba did not talk to them properly. Sheryl delivered a baby boy at the hospital and later when she brought the baby home, Abba did not want to see the baby or take him in his arms. Amma was very sad at Abba's behaviour and wept silently. She expressed her sorrow and inability to her daughter. Abba always seemed to be busy with his office work and meetings and would come home late. Sheryl was very sad at Abba's behaviour and felt that she should not stay in her father's house for long and create more problems to him. So, when the baby was about two weeks old, she left for Long Island with her husband.

Abba's second daughter Meryl was studying in 2nd year of BA when Abba found a groom for her from his own community. Abba advised Meryl to get married and then to continue her studies after her wedding. But Meryl did not want to marry then, but only after completing her graduation. This infuriated Abba as he was afraid that she too would find a boy after her heart, like her elder sister. He told it openly to Meryl and she couldn't oppose Abba and finally Meryl agreed to the wedding. Abba made all arrangements for the wedding and Meryl's wedding was solemnized in the Catholic Church at Port Blair in 1984 and Abba forgetting his anger, invited his elder daughter and her family to the wedding.

After Meryl's wedding, Abba couldn't find a job for her immediately as she had not completed her graduation. It was an ache in Abba's heart as he had not allowed her to complete her graduation. Abba saw to it that Meryl completed her graduation. Once she completed her B.A., Abba got a job for her in the Social Welfare Department. When Meryl reported for her duty as a Mukhya Sevika, Abba was the happiest person on this earth and felt relieved of his burden!

Chapter - 33

ABBA IS POSTED AS
ASST. COMMISSIONER SETTLEMENT

During May 1985, Abba got his transfer order. He was transferred from the office of Secretary Municipal Board and posted as Assistant Commissioner Settlement. Abba assumed his charge at the new office on 31-5-1985. It was a parent department to Abba and he knew every employee there. He had started his career from that office and had worked in various capacities in the office as Revenue Inspector and then as Tahsildar and now he was the Assistant Commissioner. The staff members of the office were very happy to see Abba back in the office, as its Head of Office. But Abba was very humble and never felt proud of his position. His relationship with his staff always remained the same as it was during the initial years of his service, and he treated his staff as his co-workers and not as his subordinates.

In the Settlement Department, Abba had a lot of work to do. He was assigned a special task of regularizing the land records and it was a mammoth task. Abba knew that the job was time-consuming and laborious but he accepted the work as a challenge. His officers were happy and they believed in Abba's ability.

The basic duties of the Assistant Commissioner Settlement were the maintenance and updating of Land Records with reference to Records of Rights (ROR), survey records of maps, classifications etc. The survey maps of land had to be updated and checked with proper latitude and longitude positions on the location, with the boundaries. The village boundaries also had to be fixed, government land and common land for use of the villagers had to be classified, and forest land had also to be marked. Apart from that, the position of roads and drainages had to be updated from time to time.

Records of lands of people living in the village and people who had purchased or sold lands all had to be updated. There were surveyors, Patwaris, Revenue Inspectors, Tahsildars etc. to work in the department but still much work had been pending and needed to be updated. Abba had a mountain of task in front of him!

In 1984-85, after the visit of the then Prime Minister of India, a policy was adopted by the government to regularise the prior 1978 encroachments of land in Andaman. Abba was also given this assignment by the senior officers and Abba took it as a challenge. This task was time consuming as there were thousands of encroachment cases pending. Each encroachment case had to be recorded, ROR to be prepared, map of land had to be prepared and the file had to be approved by the councillors of the particular area of the Pradesh Council. Then the file was to be sent to the Lieutenant Governor to get approval. Once the approval was granted, then the licence had to be prepared.

Once the work of regularization of land started, Abba became very busy. He would work with his office staff till late at night and on weekends too Abba went to office. In the meantime, many people started thronging Abba's office as well as home with their land related problems.

Abba used to calmly listen to people's problems and dealt with them kindly. He would advise them to submit all their documents in his office. Many office staff working in various designations in the office, also started bringing cases of land encroachments to Abba for regularization. Most of those cases used to be of their relatives, friends or acquaintances.

While the encroachments were being regularised, one day Abba received an application along with a file of an encroachment case on his table. Abba read the file and kept it aside. The application was from a man having the same name as Abba's son-in-law. Abba considered the application to be of his son-in-law, and was very angry with him for submitting a false encroachment case. When the particular application was turned down more than three times by Abba, the surveyor who had prepared the file met Abba personally with the file. Abba got angry and told him that it was a false case. The surveyor was surprised and asked Abba if he personally knew the person. Abba became very angry and told him, "Don't I know my family members?" The staff then told Abba that it was a genuine case and the applicant was standing outside and was waiting to meet Abba. With permission the applicant entered Abba's room and on seeing the man, Abba became very embarrassed as it was not his son-in-law. Abba realised his mistake and felt sorry. Soon, license was prepared for that man. This story spread among the settlement staff and one peon told the story to Amma as well.

While the encroachment cases were being regularised, a few office staff of Abba's office got their own encroached land regularised. Some staff got the land of their relatives and acquaintances regularised. Some councillors also made money as documents of the encroachment cases had to be got signed by them. Some also got money in the name of Abba from people for getting their land regularised and Abba was unaware about it all, but sometimes his office staff used to bring malt bottles for Abba as a gift.

Being in the Settlement department, Abba could have easily acquired acres of land in his name. He could have bought land for his children, but his conscience never allowed that. He always tried to help others, particularly the poor, to get their land regularised. Even Amma used to tell Abba to get a piece of land in his name. But Abba used to quote the Bible and tell Amma, "Foxes have dens and birds have nests, but the Son of Man has no place to lay his head." (Matthew: 8:20)

Then Abba used to tell Amma, "When the Son of God did not find a place to lay his head; I am nothing, just a common man. How much land does a man need? Just six feet! What are we going to carry with us after death? Don't trouble me about land and property." This used to be the regular refrain of Abba whenever Amma talked about purchasing land and Amma would become silent.

A few years back, when Abba was working as a Tahsildar and he had gone on a holiday to his village, the office staff had moved a file for allotment of a house site for Abba at Pathargudda. The file also got approved but then another Deputy Tahsildar, who had taken charge in place of Abba, got the land allotted in his own name. Once again, the settlement staff selected a house site for Abba at Bathubasti and that file was also prepared, but this time a surveyor got the land allotted in his own name. When Abba returned after holidays, the office staff informed Abba about it, and Abba had simply smiled at them!

Later on, whenever Abba used to travel via Bathubasti or Pathargudda with his family, he would very innocently show those particular plots of land to Amma and the children and say, 'that land was originally allotted to me,' and Amma and the children used to smile at Abba's innocence. Abba couldn't identify the real faces of people. He considered everyone to be like him and trusted everyone!

It was the year 1989 and the work of regularisation of encroachment was almost over and Abba had got his work completed. A programme was arranged by the settlement department for the distribution of licences of land to the owners and the Lt. Governor of the islands distributed the licences to the land owners in a gala function. Abba was well praised by everyone for his great efforts in accomplishing the work on time!

On 15th August 1990, Abba was awarded the prestigious **Lt. Governor's Commendation Certificate** for his services in regularising the land records and preparing licences. His hard work had finally been paid and it was a great honour for Abba!

During the Lok Sabha General Elections of India 1984, Abba was assigned with Election duties, and he shouldered his duties very well. He went to each and every populated Island in the Andaman and Nicobar and conducted Trainings to all the Polling Officers. Abba was so responsible in his work, so meticulous, and so punctual in finishing the work on time that during the Lok Sabha General Elections of India

1989 Abba was appointed the ARO, and during the 1991 Lok Sabha Elections Abba was appointed as the Returning Officer for Andaman and Nicobar Constituency, by the Election Commission of India.

Soon Abba got geared with the new assignment. A Returning Officer is responsible for supervising the election in a constituency, as directed by the Election Commission. The Returning Officer's duties include accepting and scrutinising nomination forms, publishing the affidavits of candidates, allotting symbols to the contesting candidates, preparing the list of contesting candidates, training polling personnel, designating counting centres, and counting the votes and declaring the result. Then there were postal ballot votes, model code of conduct, Election expenditure monitoring, dispatching of polling materials to polling stations, receiving of materials after polling is completed, safety of the poling materials etc., and Abba knew his duties well.

Abba used to read the handbook of Returning Officer and note down the sequence of the work to be done. The most tedious work was visiting all the islands and providing training to the polling officers and the assistant officers. Abba would go away to the other islands for few days and Amma could be seen packing Abba's bag with 2-3 pairs of clothes. Abba was indeed very busy. When the elections got over smoothly, Abba was appreciated by everyone for the way he had imparted the trainings, and accomplished his work so smoothly. Abba's officers were very happy with Abba's work!

Chapter - 34

ABBA ASSUMES CHARGE OF DIRECTOR TRIBAL WELFARE

Abba was an earnest and devoted officer who was much admired by his superiors. His hard work had not only earned him a good name in the Andaman & Nicobar Islands, but it also got him a number of promotions in his career. On 19-8-87 Abba assumed the charge of Director, Tribal Welfare. In the same year, he was also given the additional charge of Director Transports. He also had the office of Asst. Commissioner Settlement and one could see him shuttling between all those offices.

The office of Tribal Welfare was functioning for the welfare of the aboriginal indigenous people of Andaman and Nicobar Islands who had been dwelling in these islands for centuries, leading a hunter-gatherer lifestyle. They are the Andamanese and the Nicobarese. The four Andamanese tribes belong to Negrito group, while Nicobari tribes, belong to Mongoloid group. Studies reveal that the Negrito tribes must have arrived on these islands from Africa about 60,000 years ago while the Mongoloid tribes would have come to these islands from the Malay-Burma coast several thousand years ago. Abba had already met some of those tribesmen in his career.

After taking charge of his new office, Abba started reading all the available literature related to the tribes of Andaman and Nicobar Islands. He focussed on the various welfare schemes that were being carried out for them and used to call them the 'Noble Savages'. He used to educate Amma and children about these aboriginals and used to share a lot of information about them.

Abba also used to talk about the life and culture of the natives that he would have read from various books or heard from the local elders. During the British occupation of these islands, the British had classified the tribes of the Andaman Islands into twelve groups, each with its clearly defined locality and run with its own language, and to a certain extent had its own separate habits. The following descriptions of the natives have been taken from the Census Reports of India, the Andaman and Nicobar Islands and other books, and the reference is quoted.

The tribes of Andamans from north to south are: Chariar, Kora, Tabo, Tere, Kede, Juwai, Kol, Bojigyab, Balawa, Bea, on the Great Andaman. The Onge-Jarawa occupies, with its Jarawa division, the interior of the South Andaman, the North Sentinel, and parts of Rutland Island; with its Onge division parts of Rutland Island and the Little Andaman.[12]

The tribes were said to be living separately, but between 1875 to 1880, due to the efforts of Edward Horace Man, the British administrator, it could become possible to make the natives acquainted with each other's existence.

THE TRIBES OF ANDAMANS:

In the ancient times, the Andamanese tribes lived all over the islands of the Andamans. The Andamanese traditionally believe that due to a great Deluge, a greater part of the islands was submerged, due to which they were all divided, and spoke different languages. The 12 tribes of Andaman natives belong to three divisions- the North Andaman group of tribes, the South Andaman group of tribes and the Onge group of tribes. They were further divided into septs and each sept had its own leader or headman. However, the aborigines of Andamans were grouped into two categories-*Arioto,* the coast dwellers and *Eremtaga,* the jungle dwellers and their main difference was in the way they collected food. The *Ariotos* got their main food supply from the sea and hence were expert swimmers and divers, skilful in fishing and shooting with the arrows. On the other hand, the *Eramtaga* were experts in finding their way through the jungles, and had more knowledge about the flora and fauna and had expertise in hunting the pig.[13]

The Andamanese are fond of fishing, and use harpoons to fish turtle, dugong and large fish. They also use bows and arrows to catch fish and for hunting. They make their own canoes by carving it out of tree trunks, and are expert canoeists. They are said to be bad fighters and never attack until certain success. They do not know agriculture, but had always been hunters and food gatherers. They did not domesticate animals, till the British introduced the dog to them, as a pet. They do not eat raw but cook their food. It is said that they did not know to use salt or sugar in their food but they loved honey.

The Andamanese were nomads and kept moving from place to place, due to the monsoon or scarcity of food in a place, throughout the centuries. The 'Kitchen Middens[14]' had been found scattered all over the islands, and it is supposed that about 30 people lived in the group.

Frederic J. Mouat in his book 'Adventures and Researches Among the Andaman Islanders' at page 295, states "Children among the Andamans are never weaned. As long as the bountiful source of nourishment provided by nature can supply them with sufficient to allay the calls of hunger, the mother is expected to sustain her children, until utter exhaustion renders it necessary to have recourse to other means of support. As no clothes are at any time used by the aborigines, who go about in a perfectly naked state, no sort of garment is provided for newly-born children, who also remain naked from the first day of their existence."

CEREMONIES AND RITUALS OF THE ANDAMANESE TRIBES:

The Andamanese, while celebrating and feasting, could go on dancing for about three to four days at a time. Marriage ceremony is very simple, and when the elders learn that a young couple is interested to get married, they take the would-be-bride to a newly built hut and make her sit there. By then the bride-groom runs away, and he is persuaded and brought back, and made to sit in the bride's lap. That makes the marriage ritual complete.

They are strict monogamists and the husband and wife stressed on being faithful to each other. Divorce is unknown in the tribe. The child is named even before it is born, while in mother's womb. When the young girls attain puberty, during their menstruation, they are given names of flowers, particularly, name of whichever tree blooms at that time.

The burial customs among the Andamanese natives were strange. A dead child was buried under the floor of the parents' hut, while the grown-ups were usually tied in a bundle and the body used to be placed on the top of a tree, on a platform. The tree used to be marked with cane leaves and left for about three months and no one went to that place. During mourning, which used to be for three months, the relatives and friends of the deceased used to cover themselves with grey clay and no festivity was observed during that period. After the end of the mourning period, the remains of the corpse used to be brought down from the tree, the bones used to be washed and then broken into pieces and were used as ornaments. It was believed that it had healing values and the touch of it could stop pain and also cure diseases. In some cases, the bodies used to be buried, and after the mourning period, the body used to be unearthed, and the same used to be done with the bones of the deceased.

It is also said that the Andamanese did not know to make fire and so they used to conserve fire by keeping it burning and also carried it wherever they went, by sea or on shore. In case the fire died, it used to be considered to be a great disaster. Dancing is the main entertainment for the Andamanese, and almost every night they would dance. After a hunt, they love to sing and dance at night.[15]

THE ONGES OF LITTLE ANDAMAN:
The Onges have lived in the Little Andaman Island for thousands of years, and the kitchen middens with fossilized shells found in the place proves it. The kitchen middens of Little Andaman also revealed use of

pottery and pigs in their dwellings. They also believed in the legend of Deluge like the Andamanese, which separated them from their native people of the Great Andaman Island. The Onges built temporary shelters as well as permanent huts and they were more elaborate than the huts of the Andamanese. The huts were circular with water-proof mats used as roofing. The roofs of their huts looked like huge umbrellas resting on poles. Inside the huts there were no partitions and on the floor at the centre of the hut, a fire was kept burning. Even the Onges had the same belief about the fire as the Andamanese. Beds were made on four strong poles dug into the ground and sticks spread on it, that looked like a platform. A piece of wood was used as headrest, while all the members of the family slept with their heads towards the centre. They loved to decorate their body with clay mixed with water. They drew patterns using clay or red ochre mixed with turtle or pig's fat.

The Onges harpoon the fish or shoot it with bow and arrow, and also catch molluscs, crustacea, lobsters, crayfish and crabs. If they catch a turtle, they cut it into pieces while still alive and put it in boiling water or roast it alive. They also like to eat cicada and collect the pupae as they come out of the ground, and then roast them.

Like the other Andamanese tribe, the Onges too didn't use salt or sugar, but they loved honey. When they find a hive of bees, they marked the tree and established ownership. They collected honey in a very interesting way. They climbed the tree bare bodied, chewing 'tonjoghe' leaves that grow abundantly all over the Little Andaman Island. They smeared its pulp all over their body, even on their hair, and also spit it on the bees, which provided protection. In the forests they sucked the stems of 'Lianas' for water, or else they used to drink water like animals, lying flat on their stomach.

During the marriage of the Onges, the bride and the groom were painted with white clay, and an elder addressed and enjoined them to be a good husband and wife to each other. The rest of the ceremony was similar to that of the Andamanese. The ceremony of a girl attaining puberty was held in a very elaborate manner.

The Onges were skilled in making canoes out of tree trunks. Launching a canoe was a great ceremony, and the canoe was decorated with ochre, like their own bodies. They also made their own bows and arrows. The bows were made from trunk of large trees while its string was made from long thin strips of a particular bark, which was twisted together, while the arrows were made from bamboo. They loved to sing and dance, holding hands and going round and round in circles.

THE JARAWAS:

Compared to the Andamanese, the Jarawas are a hostile tribe. They are nomads who live a hunter-gatherer life, moving from place to place. The Jarawa tribe's actual name is 'Ang'. Ironically, they came to be known as Jarawas since the British occupation in the islands, and the word in Great Andamanese language means 'Outsider'.

They inhabit the western coast of South and Middle Andaman Islands. The Jarawa tribe is known to live self-sufficiently on these lands. The Jarawa hut is called *Chadda*. They hunt pig, turtle, fish through their arrows, and gather honey and fruits from the forest.

The Jarawas had attacked on the Settlement a number of times to take away tools and clothes. Records reveal that they had killed British officials as well as policemen and other people of the settlement a number of times.

THE SENTINELESE:

The Sentinelese live on the North Sentinel Island and they are not in contact with the outside world. They are considered to be very savage. They live in huts with slanting roofs and tend to have fire outside their huts. They build small canoes and use it to fish and harvest crabs in the shallow reefs. They lead a life of hunter-gatherers. They also carry bows and arrows; spears and knives; and their tools and weapons are tipped with iron, which they probably find washed ashore, and they use it for their needs.

THE ANCIENT ABORIGINE CUSTOMS[15]:

The Census Report 1901, states that 'Among the Andamanese, the duties of the husband chiefly consist in hunting, fishing, turtling, collecting honey and constructing canoes, building the better kind of huts, and manufacturing the bows, arrows and other implements needed in his various pursuits; he must also assist his wife in looking after his children, in keeping up the fire, and in providing the materials in making their weapons, and utensils; only in cases of stern necessity he will condescend to procure either wood or water for the family requirements; being considered purely feminine duties and derogatory for the lords of creation.'

Every woman is supposed to be proficient in shaving, tattooing, and scarifying; she has to prepare the red-ochre paint, the strings to fasten the weapons, making of ornaments etc., which are duties of women; along with that procuring certain kind of food, cooking, providing the water and fuel required for the family.

It is the duty of those men and women who stay at home to attend to the sick, infants and others who are in a dependent position, to look after the fire in various huts, to protect the property of absentees. Migration and other events are arranged by the chief and elders; while on the march women are expected to carry the heaviest loads: as men would be unable to shoot or pursue any animal which might cross their path. Children learn from their parents. Young boys are given miniature weapons according to their age and later, they accompany men in fishing and hunting. Girls are taught by mothers and females to fulfil their various duties.'

THE TRIBES OF NICOBARS[16]:

The details of the Nicobar tribe have been taken from 'In the Nicobar Islands' by George Whitehead.

THE NICOBARESE belong to the Mongoloid group of people. Their language has similarities with the languages of Burma, the

Cambodians, and the tribes in Malaya and Sumatra. The Nicobarese of the Nicobar group of islands can be divided into – 1) Car Nicobar, 2) Chowra, 3) Teressa and Bompoka, 4) (a)- Central (Camorta, Trinkat, Nancowiy, Katchall), (b) Southern (Great and Little Nicobar, Kondul, Pulo Milo), and 5) in the interior of the Great Nicobar is a separate tribe, the Shorn Pen.

The Nicobari people are a peace-loving race, quiet in spirit, and honest in their demeanour. All the villages lie near the coast- the 'village hall', the burial ground and the dead-houses are always right on the shore, and are known as *el-panam*; the birth-huts are generally there too. The native houses are built in small groups, generally two to eight houses, each group (called a *tu-het*) belonging to one man, in his personal capacity or as representative of his sept.

The ordinary dress of the Nicobarese man contains a small piece of cloth, such as a 'loin-cloth', with long strings which is tied round the body and hangs down behind as tails. This relates to the origin of the story that the Nicobarese were a naked people and had tails. The women wear their traditional colourful HILA and INYUT (Lungi and blouse) which largely resembles the Burmese dress.

The ancient houses of the people were very much like bee-hives, raised six to eight feet above the ground, on great stakes. The door way used to be in the floor, using a light ladder which could be easily drawn up when wanted. Cooking was generally done outside, or in a special cook house; but the fire-place was always on the floor in the house. A *tu-het* is always kept neat and clean and used to be lit up at night by burning the half-shells of the ripe coco-nut. Apart from coconuts, yam and pandanus are their favourite food. The yams are cooked, and eaten with pork, or fish, or anything else that may fall their way.

The Census Report of 1901 states that there were foreign traders doing trade in Nicobars and over 75 per cent of them were Burmese. There was an average of one shop in a village. Most of the Indian shops belonged to large firms having their headquarters in Colombo, Calcutta and Bombay. Sometimes, one or two Nicobarese used to go away with the traders to the island of Manicoi, or to the Laccadive or Maldive Islands. They would stay there for two or three years, and when came back professed Moslems, and would wear Moslem dress.

The chief amusements of the Nicobarese are canoe-racing and dancing and they find amusement in everything in their life, their work, their religious festivals, and even in their funerals. The Nicobarese are fond of music and song. Of all their songs the most popular are in praise of the canoe or the pig. Their dances are kept up for many hours, night after night, when it is fair and the moon is bright, and on certain festivals dancing is kept up the whole night.

The marriage among the Nicobarese is a solemn function. The bridegroom will give presents to the father of the bride, and there would be a feast on the occasion. A piece of pork would be sent to each house, informing about the marriage festival of the two parties being held. A larger number of people attend the later functions of birth, infancy, or death. During the last two months of the wife's pregnancy, and also for some time after the birth, both parents must abstain from certain kinds of food and from certain actions. When the prospective mother goes down to el-*panam,* her husband goes along with her in order to be ready at all times to wait on his wife. There are always a number of women and their husbands living in el-panam and they usually do not leave for their own homes for three to six months after the birth of the child.

A child is named after the woman who first receives it into her hands, if a female; after her husband's name if it is a male. After three to six months, when the parents and relatives bring the baby to the village; they must leave behind them everything they have been using whilst they had been staying in el-panam —including clothing, mats, cooking pots, and whatever else they may have had —for these things are considered to be 'unclean'.

The religion of the Nicobarese is animistic and consists in the propitiation or compulsion of evil spirits, which are credited with possessing power to cause sickness, damage property, and generally harm individuals. To discover and frighten away the iwi or (evil spirits), the Nicobarese erect "scare-devils" which differ considerably in form and number in the Northern, Central and Southern Groups.

The Nicobarese think that the spirit can go away on its own travels, leaving the body behind, and that this is the cause of dreams. For this reason, they do not like to awaken suddenly any sleeper, lest the spirit might be away at the time, and might get flurried by the interruption, and never get comfortably home again; in which case the results might be very serious. They believe in the spirits of the dead, spirits of the ocean and sky, of rocks and trees. There are the *menluana*[17] or witch-doctors, who are skilled and have the knowledge and power and can coax and please, or thwart and check, terrify and punish the evil spirits; and all sicknesses and accidents are due to the action of malicious or capricious spirits. Whenever there is a great deal of sickness in the island, they have special ceremonies to banish it. The witch-doctors are the wise men who have found out the secrets by which they can compel the spirits to yield to them, and so they are highly reverenced.

Rev. John Gottfried Haensel in his 'Letters on Nicobar Islands' at Page 51 states, "The inhabitants of the Nicobar Islands believe, that all dangerous diseases proceed from the devil, who is nevertheless under the control of their sorcerers, or Paters. If, therefore, these men cannot cure a disorder by their tricks and enchantments, by which they pretend to catch the devil and drive him off the place, then they are sure, that he has entered into some man or woman, sitting in his or her house, and by witchcraft, sucking all the power of healing out of the patient's body. The sorcerer then proceeds to discover the witch, and finds no difficulty in fixing upon someone he hates. The word of such a wise man is, of course, taken by all for the voice of truth, and the poor person accused is murdered without further inquiry."

The Nicobarese naturally love the sea, and canoes. In the Nicobar only small canoes could be made and the larger ones have to be purchased from Chowra Island. Public canoe races take place after the acquisition of a new canoe, or after a trip to Chowra, and there are also frequent private canoe races. Canoe races also form part of the last funeral feast, at the conclusion of which those in mourning and ceremonially unclean become purified again, and put on new garments. On these occasions a fowl is killed in sacrifice, its head is cut off and a little warm blood is dripped on the canoes.

The spirits of the canoes are also fed with the blood of pigs or fowls, at the annual 'Harvest Festival' (*Kun-seu-ro)* or after a visit to Chowra, and on many other occasions. The greatest events of the year in the ordinary life of the Nicobarese are the visit to Chowra, which is the holy island, some forty miles south of Car Nicobar. The small uninhabited rocky islet of Batti Malv lies half-way in the course, and serves as a beacon to the men who make the journey to this dangerous land. Only canoes purchased through the Chowra people as brokers can go on this trip, for they forbid all other canoes to land there.

When young boys go for the first time to Chowra; they sacrifice, by cutting the throats of some cocks, and they let the blood drip on the heads of the boys who are going for the first time. After this they all feast together in a house on the beach in el-panam —and they eat the flesh of the fowls which have been sacrificed. Then they sing songs in praise of the canoe whilst waiting for the tide to begin to ebb. All who are going on the trip wear garlands made of the ripped-up young banana leaves, which are plaited and they also wear round their necks a cord from which hangs a small packet of an odoriferous root something like ginger. When they reach Chowra, the people of the island come down to the shore to meet them, and some of them will come off in small canoes to greet old friends and anticipated customers. A house on the beach is placed at the disposal of the visitors, who immediately set about to carry up all their things. The young lads are duly introduced by their fathers to those with whom they trade, and the blood of fowls is again rubbed on their bodies, and fowls' eggs are broken on their heads. They tie to the masts baskets made from chamam. They have some sour brinjals, limes, wild oranges, in the canoe, strung together, as a protection if there should be many great fish; for they will throw those at the sharks and porpoises which may come around them, and which might so easily upset the canoe, or break the bamboos which keep the outrigger in its place, when the canoe would at once become unmanageable.

When the people of Car Nicobar want to return, they collect their things —the pots they have purchased, and the necessary food, and a delicacy called kui-loi, as a treat for their friends at home. While at home, the people of Car Nicobar keep a keen look-out southwards in their canoes, expecting their return home. They take out their long lines for fishing, and will have with them plenty of coco-nuts to drink. When the voyagers get back to their own village, all the people go down to the beach to meet them. They also heat water for their al-fresco bath in el-panam, and they take down food for them. For two or three days those who have been upon the trip will remain in el-panam and they go through the ceremonies of purification —which is to free them from all unholy influences of the spirits, both those of Chowra and of their own land, and also from the spell of the magicians. The young boys who have now accomplished their first trip to Chowra, and been initiated into the company of true men, are decked out, and have silver wire wrapped round their arms and legs, like the ma-a-fai. Seeds of pandanus are also threaded and put on them as necklaces.

The Census Report of India 1901, at page 210 describes Chowra as the holy land of the Nicobars, the cradle of the race where the men are wizards. It also describes about 'Devil Murderers of Nicobar and they occur on Chowra, Teressa and the Central Group. 'They commit a murder, when there is a necessity for it. They are true ceremonial murders of men and women and sometimes even of children undertaken for the public benefit by a body of villagers after a more or less open consultation to get rid of persons considered dangerous and obnoxious to the community. But the root cause is always spirit-possession, the victim is bad and dangerous because he is possessed. The orthodox method is very cruel. The legs and arms are broken or dislocated so that the victim cannot fight; he is then strangled and his body sunk at sea. But there is a good deal of variation from this practice in actual fact. The victims are usually taken unawares, but sometimes they make a fight and struggle for life.'

The Census Reports of 1901 at page-208-9 states that the funeral customs followed at that time, were different in north and south Nicobar group of islands, but extravagant grief is displayed at all deaths due to fear of angering the ghost. In the Central and Southern Groups, all friends and relatives are expected to be present at the funeral ceremonies with presents in order to appease the ghost. The eyes of the dead are closed to prevent the ghost from seeing, the body is laid out, feet to the fire place, head to the entrance of the hut, and washed in hot water continually. Then follow eight obligatory duties:

- Removal of all food, as it is tabued to the mourners till after the ceremony of purifying the hut, only hot water and tobacco being allowed.

- the destruction of the movable property of the deceased and placing the fragments on the grave as a propitiatory sacrifice to the ghost.

- the collection of a little food at the head of the corpse for the ghost, the 'remains' of this are thrown on its removal to the dogs and pigs.

- the construction of a bier made out of the deceased's or a mourner's broken up canoe.

- the digging of the grave five feet deep and putting up the two head posts and the foot post.

- the making of the fire to 'bar the ghost' on the ground at the hut entrance out of chips from the bier and cocoanut husks:

- the completion of the grave by placing the sacrificed articles on the ground or in the deceased's destroyed basket:

- the throwing of the pig-tusk trophies, some kareau and pictures [henta-koi) into the jungle.

The deceased is buried with all the clothing and ornaments possessed in life to appease the ghost, and 'ferry-money' is placed between the chin-stay and the cheek. The corpse is entirely swathed, except as to a small portion of the face, in new clothes of any colour, except black, presented by the mourners for the purpose. Burial takes place at sundown, before midnight or early dawn in order to prevent the shadows of the attendants from falling into the grave and being buried with the corpse. The priest (menluana) exhorts the ghost to remain in the grave until the memorial feast and not to wander and frighten the living. When in the grave the body is pinned into it by special contrivances to prevent the mongwanga or body-snatching spirits from abstracting it. The spirits even of those present are finally waved out of the grave by a torch and it is quickly filled in. After the burial the family return to their hut, in which they are bound to sleep, and about 24 hours after the interment, the hut is purified by mere brushing and washing, and the mourners by bathing, anointing on the head and shoulder by the priest, and the waving of a lighted torch to drive away the spirit. The family then disguise themselves by shaving the head and eyebrows and assuming new names, with the object of deceiving the ghost of the deceased. They then take a meal in silence with all the mourners, consisting of every variety of food procurable, in order that each person present may then and there choose the article that is to be tabued for him, till firstly the enloin feast, three to seven days after, and secondly the laneatla feast, two to three years later. At the laneatla feast the skeleton is exhumed and thoroughly cleaned, together with the ferry-money and silver ornaments, and reinterred, a custom which is a survival apparently of the still existing Northern custom of reinterment in communal ossuaries.

The Chowra customs were quite different. The same census Report at page 209 states, 'On Chowra and Teressa the dead are swathed in cloths and leaves and put into half a canoe cut across for the purpose and placed in the forks of a pair of posts about 6 feet from the ground. These canoes are in Chowra kept in a cemetery in a thick grove about 50 yards from the 'public buildings' of the village, in Teressa on the sea-shore till they fall out and are partly devoured by the pigs. The bodies rapidly decompose and become skeletons without apparently much effluvia arising from them. Children are put into small half canoes. Every three or four years the bones are thrown at a feast into a communal ossuary.[18]

THE SHOM PENS of the Great Nicobar Island belong to the Mongoloid group and live in the interior jungles of the island. In the Census Report of 1931[19], we learn that 'The Shom-Pens are divided into a number of small communities or septs, each sept living within its own territory and rarely leaving it except when bent on a raiding expedition. Constant feuds have been maintained for generations between the coast people and these inland tribes, and have resulted in the evacuation of the East Coast of Great Nicobar by the Nicobarese. They are as nomadic as the Andamanese and move from one place to another directly for the supplies of game and fruit in their vicinity are exhausted; yet they keep strictly within the territories of their sept.

The Shompen huts are much coarser than the huts found in Nicobar. For a short stay they build huts raised three or four feet from the ground and thatched with long leaves of the areca palm. But a permanent house is built on posts some eight or nine feet from the ground, and its access is by means of a ladder. The sites for permanent habitation were always well chosen for defensive purposes and were surrounded by a slight stockade, which also helps safety from attacks by the coastal Nicobarese on their inaccessible villages in the interior. A third type of hut is also found built in trees and was noticed on the Dagmar River and on the Galathea River by Boden Kloss.

There is no segregation of sexes in the huts or at meal times. Within the huts reed mats were observed and short lengths of wood which probably served as pillows. All cooking is done either within the hut or in a neighbouring shelter constructed for the purpose. The cooking pot is made of stout bark. Lengths of bamboo with pierced inter-nodes are used for the storage of water. Beneath the hut a fencing is often erected to act as a cage for any wild pig captured. Recently, owing to greater contact with the coastal people, domestic pig and dogs have found their way into Shom-Pen encampments.

Both men and women are now in possession of loin-cloths obtained from the trader through the coast inhabitants, but formerly both sexes wore a species of bark-cloth around the loins. The Shompen method of cultivation is of an extremely crude and primitive type. Yams, edible roots, a coconut tree or two, pandanus, areca and plantain trees are planted, and a small fence is erected around the yams and edible roots to protect them from pigs. Betel is much chewed by both sexes, causing a prognathic deformation and blackening of the teeth. Lime is obtained by burning shells collected on the sea-shore.

The Shom-Pens have small canoes made by themselves and it is 6 to 10 ft in length, and they use them only on the rivers and never venture out to sea. The canoes are roughly made possessing neither the technique nor the finish of those made by the coast people. They do not know the bow and the cross-bow used by the Nicobarese. The only weapon is a wooden pointed spear of areca wood which is notched on the upper parts to serve as barbs. Of late years iron has been obtained to make these spear heads, and they are able to obtain dahs by trading.

The chief diet of the Shom-Pen is turtle, snakes, frogs, birds, lizards, crocodiles, fresh-water fish, shell-fish, honey, yams, bulbs of the caladium, spathes of the areca, fruit of the nipa palm, plantain, pandanus, coconut and above all wild pig. Pigs are either staked and speared or hunted down with dogs, while birds such as the megapod are snared. Fish are either speared or caught by means of a network of bamboo placed across the stream at low tide, enabling the fish to be easily secured. Another very common method is to poison the water with the bruised bark of a forest climber, thus stupefying the fish. They also use bird-line to catch birds.

Less is known about the Shompen customs. There is mention about existence of a 'meluana' or witch doctor, due to the influence of coast people. Marriage as a rule is arranged by the parents, and the girl is handed over to the parents-in-law after she is weaned. This information was gathered by the Census party that the Shom-Pen sell their children to the coast people for a dah and three fathoms of cloth per child. The child grows up with the family but assumes the position of a servant and in most cases subsequently marries into the family.

Among the Shompens, the dead are buried in a siting posture with the hands lashed together near the mouth in which pulp of pandanus is placed. The body is not subsequently disinterred as among other Nicobarese. A year later a large feast accompanied by dancing is held, lasting some six to eight days to which all neighbouring septs are invited. The camp is immediately deserted and never occupied again; all septs being informed of the fact; it is however re-visited so that any ripe fruit from the plantations may be collected.

The Shom-Pen who came to the coast in search of iron and cloth were aggressive, attacking any village when the menfolk were away, killing the remaining inhabitants, and plundering the huts. Each village is however on friendly terms with some sept of the Shom-Pen with whom they barter for rattan and obtain permission to make canoes in the jungle. The rattan is purchased in bundles from the Shom-Pen and forms the chief export of Great Nicobar not only to the rest of the Nicobars but to Penang and Singapore where it commands a high price. The practice of selling their children has caused the tribe to come much more in contact with the coast people of recent years, and it is not unusual to find several Shom-Pen at Kondul and in the coast villages of Great Nicobar.

According to S.A. Awaradhi[20] Honey plays an important role in the Shompen life. Apart from consuming it, they also use it to barter for other things. The Shompens are said to grow bees in the forest in their own natural way. When Shompens locate trees with hollow trunks, they would cut an opening into the hollow trunks and leave it for the bees to occupy and build a hive. It is said that in due time, when the bees locate such hollow trunks, they build their hives in it. After some weeks, when the Shompen comes to the place again, and if he finds the bee-hive in the hollow trunk of the particular tree that he had cut open, he could claim his right over the honey, and could also mark the hollow tree that he had located. On seeing the marking, the other Shompens would not harvest honey from such identified trees.

After reading all the literature about the aborigines, Abba used to share his knowledge with his children and Amma.

The Administration and the Tribal Welfare Department used to arrange friendly contacts with the aborigines and gifted them with bananas, coconuts, food items, cloths etc. While discharging his duties as the Director Tribal Welfare, Abba used to be part of those friendly contact trips who went to meet the aborigines. He used to tell Amma and the children about the stories of the life of those tribal people whom he had seen or met during those friendly trips.

It was the year 1986. Abba's elder son Jason had already graduated and soon after, he also had got a job. Abba was happy and his family life was moving smoothly. Jason had been posted on an interior island in the Nicobar group of islands and Abba was very much worried for him as Jason was facing difficulties for his food. Abba wanted to get Jason married soon, so that he could also settle down in his family life.

The next year, Abba and Amma went to their village to find a bride for their son Jason. Abba was very particular that the girl should be well educated. He got many alliances and selected a girl from a neighbouring village of Kallikulam, to be the bride for his son. Abba decided to have the wedding during the summer vacation as his daughters and their families would be able to attend the wedding then. Abba invited his daughters and their families to the wedding. A day was fixed for the family to formally visit the girl's house and the date for the wedding was fixed.

Everything went well at the bride-seeing function at the girl's house and both the boy and the girl liked each other. Finally, the wedding was well solemnized in June 1988 in a church in the bride's village. Abba had invited all his relatives to the wedding. He also arranged a grand feast for the people of his village. There was music, fun and happiness everywhere. Amma and Abba were very happy for Jason.

After the holidays got over, Abba and Amma returned to Andaman with all their children and grandchildren. After coming to Andaman, Abba and Amma took very good care of their daughter-in-law. They treated her as a princess and provided her with everything to make her happy. But the girl always remained forlorn and desperate in memory of her family in the village.

After the wedding of Jason, Abba soon got a job for Jason's wife as a teacher. There were servants at home to help Amma with the household chores. Amma used to do all the work for Jason's wife. Every morning when the girl would get ready for her duty, Amma would serve her hot breakfast on the table and also packed her Tiffin. Many times, Amma even used to wash her clothes! But when Amma's daughters used to come with their families, to see Amma and Abba, the daughter-in-law would not show much interest. She always used to be very formal in her behaviour or she would conceal herself in her room. Amma was not very happy about it but she could not say anything to her daughter-in-law, lest she should be misunderstood!

One day Amma and Abba came to know that Jason's wife was on her family way and they were very happy. They started taking more care of Jason's wife, and Abba even used to get special food packed from hotels for her. For lunch, Amma would send hot meals to her school through the peons. Thus, Jason's wife had no other work but to eat good food, relax and enjoy her life. When it was time for her to deliver the baby, she went to her parent's house on the mainland and there she delivered her son.

Amma and Abba were overjoyed and distributed sweets to everyone. Abba applied for leave and Abba and Amma with their youngest son visited their village during the summer holidays. They visited their daughter-in-law and blessed the child. Though Abba was modern in his thinking, but he strongly believed that the family line was carried forward by the male child only. Abba loved all his grandsons, but Jason's son was the apple of his eye, why not, Abba considered him to be his progeny!

Sheryl and her husband had got their transfer from Long Island to Port Blair and Meryl and her family were also staying in Port Blair. Abba's daughters used to visit Abba and Amma with their families on holidays and weekends. During holidays Abba would arrange for family picnics to some or other beaches or picnic spots such as Wandoor, Chidiya Tapu, Burma Nallah etc. Abba used to invite the families of his daughters too for those picnics. It used to be a such happy time for Abba and Amma to be with their children and grandchildren!

In the office, Abba used to be so busy with his work that he was not getting proper rest. The increasing tension of work made him a BP patient. His blood pressure always used to be at the higher end. He did not get good sleep at night and due to that, he had to take sleeping pills at night. All that worried Amma. She kept telling Abba to take leave, to take rest but Abba would say that he knew what to do. One day while Abba was in his office, his blood pressure shot up very high and he almost fainted. The good office staff immediately rushed him to the hospital and when the doctor checked Abba's pressure, he straightaway ordered to admit Abba to the hospital. Soon the office peons came home and informed Amma that Abba had been hospitalised, and she was shocked!

When Amma and the children went to see Abba, he kept telling them that he was all right and that the doctors had purposely admitted him. Abba told Amma and his children to return home. Though the doctors insisted that Abba stayed in the hospital for a week, but Abba stayed in the hospital only for two days. Abba wanted to go home and he requested the doctors to discharge him. Finally, considering his request, the doctors discharged Abba, and advised him to be at home on medical rest for a week. Though Abba agreed to take rest, but after coming home, he asked his staff to bring his office files home. So, Abba had set his office at home now. Amma was not happy to see all that. Abba hardly rested for three days and soon joined his office.

Abba was under medication now. Morning, afternoon and evening he would bring out his medicine pouch and he could be seen sitting with it and having medicine before meals and after meals. At home, Amma became very conscious about Abba's health and started focussing on his diet. She stopped using salt for Abba and served him plain boiled food. Abba always liked to have spicy food but now he felt helpless and couldn't say anything to Amma. He simply obeyed her as she was the boss now!

Abba and Amma loved their youngest son Ethan more than all their other children. Since he was born twelve years after their third child, so all his elder siblings pampered him. This made him a spoilt brat. Since a small child, he saw to it that he was the pet child of Abba. He would complain about his elder siblings to Abba so that they got scoldings. He was very careful about his money since his young age. The money he used to get from Abba or his siblings, he used to save and lend it out on interest, and would be very careful in collecting the interest. Whatever he demanded, Abba used to fulfil it, and that made him stubborn and arrogant.

At the home front, Abba's grandsons were growing and had started nursery classes. Usually, after school and when the children used to have holidays, Sheryl and Meryl used to leave their sons with Amma and she too loved taking care of her grandsons and feeding them. Ethan was about seven years elder than his nephews and so he was the leader of the boys group.

The two nephews would always be seen running after Ethan like little elves calling 'Mama, Mama', meaning uncle. He would make them do all odd jobs for him. The boys loved to obey his orders, and sincerely followed his words. After school hours, the children would come to their grandparent's place and stay there till their parents would come to pick them after their duties got over. Amma would feed the grandsons and take care of them and Ethan would be seen with the kids always.

One day, when the children were about 4-5 years old, Amma was shocked to see Ethan showing foul behaviour towards his young nephews. He was thirteen years old and his games with the children had taken a different course that no one had noticed at home. He started playing bad games with his young nephews, and began sexually abusing the children. The little boys without understanding anything, simply did whatever was told to them!

It was a holiday for the children's school and Amma's daughters had dropped their sons at Amma's place. The children were playing and Amma was busy cooking. Though she would always keep an eye on her grandsons, but since Ethan was at home, she did not bother much. That day, when Amma didn't find any movement of the children in the house, she went to check on them. She entered the bedroom and was shocked to see the children with Ethan in the bed, and they were not playing any good game! Ethan was abusing his young nephews. When Amma saw that, she was stunned. She couldn't believe her eyes! She shouted at Ethan and told her grandsons to get out of the bedroom and play outside, and the children ran out of the room. Then after shouting at Ethan, Amma walked out of the room, questioning to herself since when such dirty games had been started by her younger son, and lamented to herself as how she had missed such activities in the house!

When Abba returned from his office, Amma told Abba about Ethan's dirty games with his nephews, but Abba was too busy to listen. He was in the middle of some important office work. However, he advised Amma to keep an eye on Ethan when the children were at home. When Sheryl came home, Amma told her about Ethan's behaviour and also advised her to be very careful with the children when they were with Ethan!

In 1989 Abba was transferred and posted as General Manager, Andaman and Nicobar Islands Integrated Development Corporation Limited (ANIIDCO) and Abba joined his office on 29-6-1989. The Corporation was started on 28-6-1988 under the companies Act 1956, and hence was a new venture of the A & N Administration.

Chapter - 35

ABBA IS APPOINTED AS DEPUTY COMMISSIONER CAR NICOBAR

It was the year 1990, and Abba received his Selection Grade in DANICS on 24th May 1990. It had been such a great moment in Abba's life and Abba was very happy to share the news with his family. Though Abba had scaled great heights in life, yet he always remembered his humble beginnings. He used to constantly talk about this with his children and grandchildren.

It was the month of June 1990, and summer vacation had started for Abba's youngest son, so, Abba and Amma went to their village to spend their holidays there. Whenever Abba used to go to the village, he used to relish every moment of his stay there. Abba would buy chicken, fish, vegetables etc. for Amma to cook lavish lunches, so that it could be relished by his sisters and their families.

Abba's two elder sisters lived on either side of Abba's house and every morning they would visit Abba and all would have their morning coffee together, chatting about their village and early days of life. Abba's sisters used to take breaks and go to their houses but would soon return. Then the chitchat would go on and on in a spiral about the past and the present world and the ups and downs of their lives. Amma in the meantime would cook lunch for all and Abba would compel his sisters to have lunch with them, which they normally used to accept.

Whenever Abba visited the village, most of the people of the village used to come to meet Abba. They would talk about their family problems or financial problems expecting Abba to help them, and Abba too never disappointed them and helped them in whatever ways he could.

The village priest and nuns also used to visit Abba for donations and Abba would generously donate to the village church and school. Sometimes the nuns used to approach Abba for the higher education of children in their orphanages and convents and Abba used to help those children by sending money orders every year. In fact, Abba was helping a number of such children to get education and become able to get jobs, while those children did not know about Abba and they had never met him. But the nuns used to write to Abba about those children who had completed graduation or who got jobs etc. Abba used to be happy that at least he was able to help some children to get education.

Every year before going to the village, Abba used to withdraw a considerable amount of money from his provident fund, and also would take salary advance from his office. A part of this money he used to spend on charity works and Amma was a good wife, who always supported Abba in all his work!

After the holidays were over, Abba and Amma returned to Port Blair and they got new dresses for their children and grandchildren. When Abba reached Port Blair, there was a pleasant surprise awaiting him. When Abba went to the office, he received an order stating that he had been posted as Deputy Commissioner, Car Nicobar. It was the greatest honour Abba had ever received in his career. It was a great moment in his life. That day Abba returned home and shared the news with Amma and his children. All were overjoyed and congratulated Abba. All were very proud of Abba. Then it was celebration time at home. After all, Abba had reached the pinnacle of his career! Even on that day Abba remembered his first posting as a clerk and thanked God for all the wonderful works He had done in his life!

After a fortnight Abba left for Car Nicobar by the steamer. He assumed his charge as Deputy Commissioner on 18-7-1990. He left back Amma and his youngest son at Port Blair as he was studying in class 7. After a few months of the same year Abba came to Port Blair and took Amma and his younger son to Car Nicobar and Ethan was admitted to a school there.

Car Nicobar is the headquarters of the Nicobar group of islands. There are many legends about the origin of the Nicobarese race. The stories of origin of Car Nicobar and the coconut trees are stated in the Census of India Report of Andaman and Nicobar Islands, 1901, at page 211.

"According to a legend, a man arrived there from some unknown country on the Pegu-Tenasserim Coast with a pet dog. By her he had a son, whom the mother concealed in her *ngong* or cocoanut leaf petticoat. The son grew up, killed his father, and begot the race on his own mother. The end of the long bow tied round the foreheads of young men is to represent the dog ancestress's ears, and the long end of the loin cloth, her tail. They treat all dogs kindly in consequence, where perhaps we may trace a lost totemism among them.

At Car Nicobar, too, cocoanuts originally grew out of the head of a man who was beheaded for pouring water out of his elbow by magic. Water is scarce in Car Nicobar. The people, however, were afraid to touch a cocoanut till one was given to a dying old man who at once recovered. Cocoanut trees are therefore valuable spirit scarers and at every death some are cut down, the nuts placed in the graveyard and the leaves round the house, and the body is washed with the milk— all to scare the ghost."

One more legend says that the first Car Nicobarese was the child of a Burmese woman who was blown by a storm to the shores of Car Nicobar Island, where the first village originated, and he is said to have spread his race incestuously through his mother.

Trinket Island too tells a similar legend of its origin, with a Burmese woman who had children from a non-Burmese father. Whereas Katchal Island tells the tale of a Chinese to be its first marooned inhabitant of the island. There is yet another legend that gives credit to worms that had endured a great flood and later evolved into human beings. However, it is also said that the Nicobarese symbolize an ancient Mongoloid race who have been isolated by time and space.

A *Tuhet*, in Nicobar, includes all the family members, including grandparents, uncles etc., of the family line. Land is not divided among the family members, but cultivated by various members of the family, and each member can take the fruits of his labour. The Head of the family has to contribute during feasts, while others are free to keep their incomes from their pigs, vegetables or coconut trees.

The Nicobar group of Islands are out of the purview of the Panchayati Raj Act and the Tribal Council is functional here, which is constituted by elections. Every village in the tribal area has a Village Council which is headed by the 1st captain and he is assisted by a 2nd and a 3rd captain. The captains are elected democratically by secret ballot usually for tenure of 5 years. Every island group has a Tribal Council, which is constituted by the 1st Captains of Village Council falling in their jurisdiction. These 1st Captains then select Chief Captain & Vice Chief Captain of the Tribal Council. The Nicobar district, has seven Tribal councils namely Car Nicobar, Katchal, Nancowry, Kamorta, Teressa, Chowra and Pilobhabi. The Village Councils play an important role and are a link between the Local Administration and the tribal people of the island.

Abba told his children that in Nicobar Islands, in the very ancient times, there used to be death punishments for crimes such as theft, adultery and murder. The offender was pierced on a sharp post or was stoned to death and then buried without funeral-rites. Later on, they started settling the quarrels by whipping or making payments in pigs, which was the common property of *tuhet,* and thus they shared the shame of the culprit. The pig was then consumed by the whole village. However, in the present time, punishments are decided and carried out by the village council in a fair manner.

The Nicobarese use different methods to catch fish. During fair weather, they use fishing nets from their canoes or from the shore when the tide is retreating. During low tide, at night, they torch coconut leaves and attract the fish to the light and then spear the fish. They also catch fish in an amazing way, by sprinkling the powdered seeds of Barringtonia speciosa which stupefies the fish, and then it's easy to catch.

In the Nicobarese life, in all the rituals, feasts and ceremonies, the pig is very important. A man is considered wealthy by the number of pigs he has. The kanaha-un is celebrated as a thanksgiving festival in the islands. Singing and dancing is a part and parcel of their life and no communal activity is complete without it. Toddy is brewed from coconut palm and is a part of feasts. Men and women equally participate in the work of cultivation, rearing pigs, building the dwelling and making articles for everyday living. In Chowra island women make pots. Women are not considered lower to men in any way as we see that the Chief Captains of Nancowry have been women.[21]

Marriages in Nicobar takes place within the *tuhet*. The boy courts a girl and he has to win her consent and only then the family takes up the matter of their marriage. In Chowra and Teressa islands, gifts such as clothes, pigs, coconuts and fowl are given as a bride price at the time of the girl's wedding. As per the family circumstances, the boy and girl decide about their dwelling after their marriage and when the family is short of males, the boy could stay with the girl's family, and help with the work. The pregnant mothers who are about to deliver babies are separated from families and kept in the birth house. Women of the household help in the child birth and the mother and baby are confined to the birth house for two to three months. In the island of Chowra where there is no birth house, the would be mother is sent to jungle for delivering the baby and she is attended to by her husband, smearing her with blood of pig, to keep her healthy.

Death is a community affair among the Nicobarese. After the death of a person, the corpse is removed to the death house for cleaning. In the ancient times, the body was buried with all the belongings of the deceased, which is not practised any more. Relatives and friends who handle the corpse are considered unclean and they are not allowed entry to the village for seven days. In Nancowry, Katchal and kamorta, the burial is conducted in the presence of a witch doctor and the belongings of the dead are hung on a tree near the grave while the relatives take a vow of abstinence from certain food and drink, which they follow till the memorial feast that used to be held after three years.[22]

The Nicobarese life moves around festivals associated with their belief of the evil spirits. All-important festivals are connected with the pig, canoe and the sea. Many thanksgiving festivals are organised by the village tuhet, when food is plentiful. The kanaha-un is an ossuary festival which is marked by pig fights, drinking of toddy and a celebration of feasting on ham and pork.

Abba had already worked as Asst. Commissioner in Campbell Bay and then he had visited the Nicobar Islands several times on duty. But now it was different. He was the District Collector and had got an opportunity to work for the upliftment of the tribal people of Nicobar. The office of the Deputy Commissioner is situated at Car Nicobar, which is the Head Quarter of the District of Nicobar. This office has the Central Control over the District Administration and it provides service in the form of numerous developmental activities for the of people. The office also controls the Tehsils of the District i.e., Car Nicobar, Nancowry and Great Nicobar. The District of Nicobar came into existence on 1st of August, 1974, prior to this, it was a part of District of Andamans. The district office has 2 sub-divisions- Car Nicobar and Nancowry. But for the smooth functioning of the administration, it is divided into three circles under the supervision and control of Assistant Commissioners (A C) who work directly under the Deputy Commissioner. A C Head Quarters is for Car Nicobar, A C Nancowry having headquarters at Kamorta for Kamorta, Katchal, Nancowry, Trinket, Chowra, Teressa and Bompooka islands and AC Campbell Bay having headquarters at Campbell Bay for Great Nicobar, Little Nicobar, Kondul and Pilobhabhi islands.

All the Assistant Commissioners function as Executive Magistrates in the area of their jurisdiction. They are aided by Tehsildars, BDO's, Extension Officers and Village level workers. The Asst. Commissioners are also the in-charges of departments like Supply, Shipping, Transport etc. in addition to Revenue, Development & Law and order in area of their dominion. The region has been designated as Integrated Tribal District. The Deputy Commissioner is also the Ex-Officio Chairman of Integrated Tribal Development Project (ITDP). The various Programme sponsored by Ministry of Rural development is implemented through District Rural Development Agency (DRDA), which is also headed by Deputy Commissioner. The Deputy Commissioner is also the District Magistrate and District Collector of the district.

After assuming his charge as Deputy Commissioner Car Nicobar, Abba started his work for the welfare of the Nicobarese people. He learnt about the Nicobarese culture and their life style. He came to know that the Nicobarese people living on different islands speak a different dialect of the Nicobarese language and are usually classified as the Car, Chowra, Theressa and Bambooka languages. They use the Roman script for writing their language. Abba visited all the islands of the Nicobars under his jurisdiction and saw the office work carried out there. He saw to the basic problems of the people and tried to alleviate it with his personal efforts.

The captains of different villages used to come to meet Abba with their problems and Abba used to solve their problems on priority basis. On many occasions, they used to tell Abba about their ancient traditions. Abba was told that in ancient times, the Nicobarese were animistic in nature and then they used to believe in spirits and ghosts and considered them to be the cause of storms, diseases or natural disasters.

Now Christianity is the most followed religion of the Nicobarese and Bishop John Richardson was the man who educated the Nicobarese in their language by producing the first Nicobarese Primer. He also translated the New Testament into the Nicobarese language. He emerged as a great leader during the Japanese occupation of the Nicobars and eventually reached the ranks of Bishop. Each village has a school, church, playground and a burial place.

In the ancient times, the Nicobarese did not know currency, but they used to barter coconuts or pigs in exchange of whatever goods they wanted. Abba told a heart-warming story of Edward Ku-chat, who was the Village Chieftain of Kakana village. During the Japanese occupation, Ku-chat was the Captain of Kakana village and had a large area of land. The Japanese with forced Nicobarese labour, built a large air strip on the land of Ku-chat, by clearing hundreds of coconut trees from the place. His brother Solomon, was the first Nicobarese to be killed by the Japanese. In his memory, Edward Ku-chat had built the first coral church on the island. It is said that after Indian independence, when Edward Ku-chat, was the Head of the Tribal Council in Car Nicobar Island, the government was in need of additional land for the expansion of the airfield. When Ku-chat was approached, he was reluctant. However, Nehru, the then Prime Minister of India, invited the tribal leader Ku-chat, to New Delhi in the late 1950s, and in a party, Nehru requested him for the land and he couldn't refuse. When Ku-chat was asked what price he needed for the land, instead of a quantum of money to settle the deal, to everyone's surprise, Ku-chat asked for the 'achkan' (jacket) that the Prime Minister was wearing. The guests assembled there were quite amused, and the prime minister accepted the deal with delight. The coat was kept safe in Ku-chat's house for generations!

Christmas is celebrated with great fervour in the Nicobar group of islands. The celebrations begin in Car Nicobar on the first Advent Sunday and it goes on till mid-January. Music is the heartthrob of the Nicobarese and during the Christmas season, the whole island of Car Nicobar comes alive with music and singing of carols by cheerful smiling people in their colourful dresses. The fragrance of Christmas could be felt in the air and the place turns into a fairyland.

In the evenings carol groups of a church visit the other village churches in trucks, jeeps and cars with their guitars, candles, lanterns and stars for participating in the carols. They also carry their music systems and loud speakers to make the celebration more effective. Then the celebration begins with the singing of carols with guitars and drums. The carol singing goes on for a long time, sometimes till the next morning. There may be demands for particular carols which are sung by the carol groups. There is a lot of fun and frolic and music everywhere.

The carol singing concludes by wishing everyone a Merry Christmas and a Happy New Year.

After the carol rounds are over, a lavish and extravagant dinner is served to all by the village church which includes cakes, pork, varieties of seafood, chicken, Biryani, traditional foods, sweet dishes from Pandanus, Tapioca, banana etc. After dinner sometimes the group returns home by the next day morning and they get geared up for the next round of carols in the evening. Each member of the carol group is also given a gift from the host village according to their pockets, whatever they are able to get.

The Nicobarese are great sports persons and canoe racing, pig fighting, football and wrestling are a few of the popular sports which they enjoy playing. The staple food of the Nicobarese is coconuts and Pandanus, the breadfruit. They love to eat fish, turtles, octopus, Chicken, pig, yam, banana etc. and these are quite popular among the Nicobarese. Toddy is a popular alcoholic drink made by fermenting palm sap. It is popular among men and women and is also consumed during ceremonial rituals.

After taking charge of his office, Abba started beautifying his office and bungalow. He developed beautiful gardens in his office premises and bungalow, with varieties of flowers which was a sight to see. He presided over the meetings of the Tribal Council and pressed on his ideas for the development of the tribal people. He also participated in all the community celebrations of the Nicobarese with Amma.

Abba's elder daughter and son's family too visited Car Nicobar during Abba's work period. They were mesmerised by the beauty of the place. The pure white beaches, happy people moving around in colourful traditional attires singing on their way, was a common sight. People could be seen working all day to keep their surroundings neat and clean by uprooting the grass around their houses. Even during noon time, they could be seen holding an umbrella and cleaning their surroundings. Women folk sitting together, scrapping coconut with Kurz, the natural, thorny cane scrappers was a common sight. Then they could be seen pressing the scraped coconut kernel in their traditional equipment called 'Kintan tavi-i, to get coconut milk, which they boiled to extract oil. The Children diving in the waves, catching small fish and eating them raw were other common sights on the beach!

Abba's children got a chance to visit the traditional Nicobari huts and houses. The place appeared to be a paradise on earth, so serene and so peaceful. Women moving about in colourful *Hila* and *Inyut* were a delight to the eyes!

Abba told his children that Bishop John Richardson was a native Nicobari who rose to the ranks of a Bishop. Abba had read a write up about Bishop John Richardson by M.D. Srinivasan in the book 'Sons of the Light, The Story of Car Nicobar.' He had gathered a lot of information about Bishop John Richardson. John Richardson was sent to attend school at S.P.G. Mission in Mandalay in Rangoon and Richardson became the first Nicobarese to be ordained as an Anglican priest. Later he returned to Nicobar in 1912 and worked in many capacities such as a catechist, the Government Agent with first-class Magisterial powers, Tahsildar, and Teacher. He was a great footballer and it is said that he had introduced the game to the Nicobarese in 1912, and now it has become the most favourite sport of the Nicobarese. He preferred to be a priest and loved to spread the Word of God. He devoted his time in shepherding the Christians, and in spreading the Gospel among the non-Christians on Car Nicobar.

On Sunday the 15th January 1950, John Richardson was consecrated as Bishop in St Paul's Cathedral, and in 1952, Bishop Richardson was nominated to represent the Andaman and Nicobar Islands in the Indian Parliament at New Delhi, a unique distinction for a Bishop of the Christian Church. He served in this capacity for five years. Bishop Richardson was instrumental in building Churches in all the villages of Car Nicobar and other islands of the Nicobar, and bringing people to Christianity. He received Padma Shri in 1965 and Padma Bhushan in 1975. He was the man who instituted village councils and tribal councils in the Nicobars. Bishop John Richardson left this world on 3 June 1978.

In memory of Bishop John Richardson, a hospital in Car Nicobar has been named 'Bishop John Richardson District Hospital'.

The following note on the recurring seasonal religious ceremonies[23] observed by the Car Nicobarese, written by Bishop John Richardson.

January- Fa-nang-nya el pan-am (fa-nang-nya is the abstract noun of the verb 'fang' to burn. El pan-am is simply the beach where public buildings, grave yard, dead house, and birth houses are.)

In the month of December rattan leaves are stuck across the el pan-am to keep off the evil spirits which bring sickness to the people during the N.E. Monsoon.

In January these leaves are pulled up and gathered in a heap on the beach, where they are burnt.

On that occasion the leaves which are used as medicine are displayed hung in the houses at el pan-am, in honour of the events.

February- In this month the spirits of the dwelling houses are honoured. Fishes are caught from the sweet water ponds in the interior. Small fishes are stuck on sticks, and placed over the entrances of the houses. ('Ke-la-kapa-ti'. i.e., to put the fish for the houses.)

March- 'Ke-la-ok pa-ti', the putting of young coconuts in the houses. On this occasion the spirits of the sea fishes are honoured. In the night men go out in several canoes to catch the curve fishes. The fishes are attracted by the light of the torches, and when they come alongside the canoes they are speared. In the morning everyone brings his catch to el pan-am on the beach with several young cocoanuts and tender leaves of the coconut palm. The fishes are cut up into small bits and stuck on the young cocoanuts with the leaves. In each hut three of these young cocoanuts are to be hung.

This is the offering to the spirits of the deep, in order that they may not get angry, and send sickness through the eating of the fishes.

This is the calmest of the months, and trips to Chaura Island can be taken twice; and people go far out to sea to catch fish by lines and hooks.

April- In this month fire festival is held. When the moon is waning, the whole night is lighted with cocoanut shells. Dancing goes on the whole night; followed by wrestling in the morning.

After this performance no light should be shown at el pan-am till about the waning of May, when the harvest festival will be held.

May- In this month 'Kun-seu-ro' or the making of pudding is held. Yams, ripe and green plantains are scrapped. First of all, cocoanuts are scraped, and oil is extracted. When the oil is refined, the yams and the ripe and green plantains are put in the Chaura pots. The pudding has to be stirred the whole night till it is quite cooked, in order that it may not stick on the side of the pot. This has to be done at el pan-am under the houses.

The next morning each family has to kill a pig. The village is decorated with tender cocoanut leaves, which are wound round the top of a stick, and over them some young cocoanuts are cut crosswise and put on the stick; then pig's blood is sprinkled on the cocoanut leaves, and pudding kept on the young cocoanuts.

All the best produces of the land are hung among the decorations in the houses, such as the largest size of yams, cocoanuts, pineapples, jackfruits as well as some of the puddings.

The men who hang up the decorations in the house will shout out, "May this season be a prosperous one; plenty of pigs, cocoanuts, yams etc., and may a pretty girl be willing to wed with me," and so on.

The next day is a day of rest. In the evening the boys will go to el pan-am where they start the game of spearing the young cocoanuts which were stuck on the decorations. They are collected in one place and the boys stand in a long line; a man throws each young cocoanut in front of the boys, and as the nut rolls on the ground the boys try to hit it. When they have done that at el pan-am they will go into the village to perform the same thing.

Next day is a hunting day for the wild pig.

June- No ceremony in this month.

July- The bad spirits are driven away and put on a raft. The spirits of the dead have rendered help, and so they are honoured. Each relation of the dead has to provide anything that is demanded of them; kill chicken and pigs. These are handed to the Ta-mi-lua-na, or the seers, who are the only persons that can approach them. They are Ma-a-fai before they become Ta-mi-lua-na.

August- The first festival of fishing with line and hook after the rough weather. The usual offerings are put in the house; three young cocoanuts are hung with bits of fish, and ferns are placed on the wall of the house all-round the house, with bits of fish each.

September- Second festival of fishing with line and hooks. This time they go to the west coast for the first time. (Offering as in August.)

October- The putting on of banyan leaves at the el pan-am to change the direction of the wind from S. W. to N. E.

November- Driving of the bad spirits as in July; but are not sent away on a raft as the wind is contrary. They are simply killed by the Ta-mi-lua-nas, and thrown into the sea.

The spirits of the dead are not fed either.

December- The putting up of the rattan leaves on the beach to keep off the bad spirits which brings sickness generally at this time of year.

'Tabus' and ceremonies in connection with the annual trip to Chaura for the purchase of the earthenware cooking pots made there. This is contributed by Bishop John Richardson.[24]

'Several things are tabu'd or forbidden when a canoe is newly bought from Chaura, e.g., bats are not to be eaten, - reason their wings might blind the eyes, and people will not be able to find their way to Chaura. Octopus fish should not be eaten as it is bad for those travelling on the sea, as it is known to have attacked ships. Splitting of wood is forbidden to prevent the canoe from splitting of itself; and many other things. These are observed for months, even for a whole year before the canoe takes its first trip to Chaura and back.

When a boy is taken to Chaura for the first time the blood of a chicken is sprinkled all over his body before the starting from Car Nicobar and after the arrival at Chaura.

After coming back from Chaura there will be a canoe race, and then strips of pork are tied up and hung over the body of the boy for about one or two hours. After that raw eggs are crushed on his head. This continues for one or two days. Silver wire is wound round both his arms and legs, like a ma-a-fai. Seeds of Pandanus are stringed and hung on him. The boy keeps a stick to keep off the other boys from getting the seeds. Several boys would hang about him trying to snatch the seeds without being caught.'

While in Nicobar, Abba used to be invited to be the chief guest for various celebrations. On some occasions, Amma too was invited to give away the prizes etc. In the beginning, Amma used to be very hesitant to attend those functions but with Abba's encouragement, she became confident and started attending the functions.

In 1991 Abba received his transfer order to Port Blair and he was posted as Director of Transports. Abba was happy that he could serve the Nicobari people while in office.

PART 6

THE EXODUS

Chapter - 36

ABBA FACES CBI INQUIRY AND IS ACQUITTED

Abba had a great love for his elder son Jason. Since childhood, Jason had a distinct place in Abba's life and he was taken special care of by Abba and Amma. During the childhood days of the children's life, even when there would be less milk in the house, Jason used to get his share of milk and the same was with other eatables. Not that Amma and Abba considered the girls to be inferior but they were not so well off to buy sufficient milk and eggs needed for all children and the son was a priority as he had to carry on the family line!

It was a Saturday and Abba was at home. It was evening and Abba had some work in Aberdeen Bazaar. Abba asked Jason to take him to the bazaar on his bike. Abba had bought Jason a motorbike a few years ago. Abba did not know to ride a cycle or a motor bike. Jason got ready and took Abba to the bazaar on his bike. While they were crossing Gandhi statue near Aberdeen bazaar, suddenly a lorry came from the opposite direction and hit the bike. The bike was careened to a side and Jason and Abba fell down and were pulled under the moving lorry. While Abba was under the lorry, he tried to push out Jason so that the tyre would not come on Jason and crush him. As a miracle, the driver could apply the brakes and stop the lorry and it was a narrow escape for Abba and Jason. When they both returned from the Bazaar, Amma saw the condition of their soiled clothes and was much worried. She wanted to know the reason for such a condition of their clothes!

Abba narrated the whole incident to Amma and said, "Due to the accident, we both got under the lorry, while it was still moving. I thought that we both would be killed. I was praying to God and with all my strength I tried to push Jason out so that he could be saved. I am an old man now, but Jason has to live a long life. Somehow the lorry stopped and God saved us!"

This was the pure love of Abba for his son Jason. But whether Jason could ever pay this love back to Abba is a big question mark!

In the year 1991, the Barren Island, which is a volcanic island, suddenly erupted after a period of 140 years. The Barren Volcano started exploding and throwing out lava that flowed out and reached the sea. The Andaman and Nicobar Administration arranged trips for officers, scientists, school children and other people to visit Barren Island to see this wonder of nature. Abba too visited the Barren Island and saw it seething, fuming and throwing out huge quantity of lava. He marvelled at nature's fury. On returning from the trip Abba told Amma and his children about the Barren Island volcano, and described its intricate details!

Barren is an uninhabited island and the only inhabitants of the island are a large herd of goats, that could be seen on the slopes and cliffs of the island. It is said that a score of these animals was left in 1891 by the station steamer from Port Blair, and they had flourished in that island. In the ancient records of 'The Andaman and Nicobar Gazetteer, we find descriptions of the Barren Islands. Captain Blair, who passed near the island in 1795, writes about enormous volumes of smoke and frequent showers of red-hot stones, thrown from the Barren volcano.

During the year 1991, after Abba had regularised the land records and licences had been issued, complaints had been filed by some people to CBI against Abba for having taken bribes for regularising the encroachments of land. Abba's well-wishers from the office informed Abba about it. Soon Abba also received a notice from the CBI informing about the case and he was saddened. He told Amma about it and Amma became much worried. But Abba told Amma not to worry as he had not taken any bribe from anyone and so nothing would happen to him and he would be acquitted as innocent very soon. He also told Amma to pray so that truth would be brought to the forefront and those allegations would be proved wrong.

Soon the local newspapers started tossing the issue of the CBI inquiry and Abba became the talk of the town. Abba and his family members were very depressed as whoever came home, only talked about the stories being spoken in the islands, by people against Abba. The truth was that those people who had actually taken bribes were peacefully sleeping in their homes while Abba and Amma had lost all their sleep. Amma kept praying to God that Abba should be acquitted from the case. The name that Abba had earned all those years in the Andamans was being tarnished and Abba and Amma felt very miserable.

The CBI officials conducted a detailed inquiry into Abba's case. They sent summons to Abba to attend the interrogation sessions. Abba attended all the sessions and faced the interrogations boldly. He answered all the queries put to him. The officials enquired Abba about his bank balance, property etc., which Abba provided to them and all were cross-checked.

The CBI officials also visited Abba's quarter at Junglighat and ransacked the entire house. Amma was very frightened and sat in a corner praying silently. After searching the whole house, the CBI officials could not find anything. There was some cash from Abba's salary kept for the house expenditure and some jewellery of Amma. The officials noted down all the details and did not get any proof against Abba. They had to return empty handed.

Then the officials also went to Abba's village to take stock of Abba's house and property but couldn't get any wealth there. Abba had constructed a two-bedroom brick house with a terrace and he had a piece of farmland which he had received from his father.

But the news about the CBI inquiry spread far and wide, across the islands at lightning speed and those people who were jealous of Abba were enjoying the news thoroughly. At the home front, Amma and the children were very much worried for Abba and prayed that Abba should be acquitted from the case.

The interrogation sessions by CBI officials were going on and Abba was being called for interrogation every now and then and Abba felt the harassment. Finally, after about two years the CBI submitted its reports stating that the charges and allegations filed against Abba were found baseless and false. There was no evidence against Abba for having taken bribe as Abba had no money in his bank account and he did not have any wealth. He had not bought any property during that period either. At last, Abba was acquitted as he had been found innocent in the case.

When the CBI investigations started, Jason advised Abba to apply for a voluntary retirement as Abba just had a few years of service left. But Abba did not agree with him. Abba told him that he had not done anything wrong and so he was not afraid, and he would complete his service as he knew that God would give him justice!

Abba said, '*The mill of God grinds slowly but surely. I have faith in God.*' Finally, Abba had proved himself right.

Abba had been acquitted of all the charges by CBI, but the entire event left a deep scar in Abba's heart. He knew many officers who used to accept bribes and had acres of land and property but no case had ever been filed against such officers. On the other hand, he had always been so honest in his work, and he had not even acquired a house site for himself or for his children, yet he was victimized. He had always tried to help the poor and the needy, but charges were laid against him to be a corrupt officer. CBI officers had raided his house also and Abba also felt very sad about that. During that entire period, Abba and Amma tried to console each other saying that God knows the truth and they need not worry about anything.

At the home front, Jason had got married, and Ethan was very happy to get a sister-in-law, as his both elder sisters were already married and lived in their own houses. But after his sister-in-law came to Port Blair, she always remained aloof and did not like to mingle freely with her husband's family members. The sister-in-law and brother-in-law relationship could never be genial. Though Abba and Amma used to pamper Jason's wife, but the new bride always considered Ethan as her arch rival in the house. Ethan gradually started feeling irritated and angry with his sister-in-law for being so arrogant and egotistical. Every now and then the sister-in-law and brother-in-law duo used to find fault with each other and there would be such anger and irritating situations in the house that would make Amma very sad, and finally Ethan used to get scoldings or beatings from Abba.

Jason's wife was a teacher and after Jason's wedding, Abba and Amma had thought that she would take care of Ethan's studies but that never happened. Though Amma used to do all the household work but Jason's wife never showed much interest in teaching Ethan. If the boy would ask for any doubts in the lessons, sometimes she would clear his doubts, but generally she tried to evade the situation. Amma used to feel very sad about her such behaviour, but could not tell her anything!

Amma was very timid in nature, and was basically afraid of her daughter-in-law. Normally Jason's wife used to be good at home, but when things would not happen according to her wish, then she used to shout and crate a scene. Amma never wanted to get caught in such a scene with her and so usually kept silent. But when her daughters would arrive, Amma would tell them about it all and lament that though she and Abba tried to treat Jason's wife very affectionately, but the girl never showed any consideration to them or their house.

One day Ethan and his sister-in-law were back from school and Abba had not returned from the office yet. As usual, the sister-in-law said something harsh about Ethan and he too replied to her in the same coin. Their arguments grew louder and louder, while Amma was busy in the kitchen getting the food ready for them. She also heard the loud verbatim, and decided to remain silent. She thought that after some time the duo would calm down. But the arguments didn't stop. Ethan was a young boy in the 9th standard and he was thoroughly enjoying that word war. Answers like bullets were being shot out of his mouth against the blames poured on him by his sister-in-law, and soon the argument and blame game turned into a noisy brawl which soon changed into physical assault on each other, the elder person in a fit of anger pulled out the sandal from her foot and hit the younger one, while the opponent instantly replied with a punch, landing right on her face, a reflex action to the situation!

Ethan had a punching bag in the shed at the backyard of the house and every day he used to practice on it. When he gave a punch, it hit his sister-in-law very hard, in the left eye, and she started shouting, crying and abusing loudly and Amma came running out of the kitchen to find out what had happened. Amma was shocked to see the condition of Jason's wife, and Amma shouted at Ethan. But he told Amma that first he had been hit with a sandal and Amma was speechless. By the time Ethan realized the whole situation, there was total mayhem in the house and he escaped from the scene and ran away to his elder sister's house which was close by. There he narrated the whole story to his sister and brother-in-law and they scolded him for his behaviour. They also told him that his behaviour was not right and asked him to return home immediately. But Ethan did not want to return home. Instead, he went to his younger sister, who pampered him very much, and spent the night in her house.

When Abba returned home from office, he found total silence in the house. He wanted to know where Ethan was and Amma narrated the entire incident to Abba and Abba was shocked. Ethan was not at home so Abba could not talk to him. But Jason's wife came out of her room with a severe black eye! Abba was shocked to see her in that state, and tried to console her. But she went on weeping, shouting and at the same time complaining about Ethan. She even shouted at Abba and questioned him, "What a son you have raised and what values you have given him?" Abba and Amma were speechless to hear Jason's wife talking in that tone. Amma silently prayed that the matter should be solved peacefully! But Abba was not happy with the behaviour of his daughter-in-law!

The next day Meryl brought Ethan home with her and she too saw the black eye of her sister-in-law who had all complaints against Ethan. Everyone at home compelled Ethan to say sorry to his sister-in-law and he complied. When Abba came to know about it, he told Amma that the daughter-in-law should not have beaten Ethan with her sandal! After a few days the situation became normal in the house, but not in human hearts!

But Amma once again started having those seizures. The turmoil inside the house did not give her peace. She was very unhappy with the home atmosphere and the anger and brawl among her children. Those thoughts made Amma very unhappy. One day evening, while she was walking in the colony with those thoughts in her mind, she had her seizures and fell down on the road, and she became unconscious. The passersby carried her to the side of the road, got water from a nearby house and sprinkled it on her face. Someone in the crowd recognised Amma and they sent words to Sheryl, who lived close by. She immediately rushed to the spot, and found Amma unconscious and arranged to take Amma home!

Chapter - 37

ABBA ASSUMES CHARGE OF DIRECTOR TRANSPORTS

After returning from Car Nicobar, Abba joined the office of Director Transports and assumed his charges as its Director on 12-7-1991. It was not a new department to Abba as he had the additional charge of this office earlier. He knew most of the staff members there. Even otherwise, in which ever office Abba had worked, with his friendly behaviour, he soon used to make all those employees his friends.

The Transports Department was a major department of the Andaman and Nicobar Administration. It dealt with the road transport of all the islands, which was the lifeline to commuters and Director Transports was a very responsible post. There were many problems in the department. A number of bus accident cases were pending and many drivers and conductors had been suspended on charges of reckless and careless driving. Apart from that, there would be sudden strikes by the transport employees that would cause a lot of trouble to the commuters and it was a major issue to be handled. But Amma knew that Abba would be able to tackle the problems and bring the Department to smooth functioning, and Amma was right in her thinking.

After assuming his charges, Abba got geared to confront the challenges of the Transport Department. He worked very hard, day and night, reading each pending file, writing comments and quoting rules to clear the files. He took personal interest in the cases of drivers and conductors. He argued for them with his higher authorities, solved the cases, got the salaries released and within a few months he also brought the drivers and conductors back to work for the Department.

The employees of the Transport Department became great admirers of Abba. They had got an officer who cared not only for them but also for their families and children. If there was any problem with any staff, Abba took it as his own problem and would work day and night to get it solved. If there was an ailing member in any family of the workers of transport department, Abba would see to it that the person was immediately referred to mainland India for treatment. He also would get the medical advance drawn for the worker from the administration so that the person would not face financial crisis. Abba was very particular in making payments to his employees on time and also to clear all their medical reimbursements without fail.

Once a driver's wife came to office and she complained to Abba that her husband was addicted to alcohol and that he used to spend all his salary on liquor and never brought his salary home. The driver had four children and his wife was helpless and did not know how to manage her household. Abba called for the man and spoke to him and tried to convince him about the evils of drinking. Abba advised him to give his salary to his wife and to take care of his family. But the man was not convinced. That day he went home and beat his wife brutally for complaining against him. The next day, one of the office staff who was living next door to that driver's house, told Abba about the happenings in that driver's house. Abba asked his office staff to call the wife of the driver to office and when she came to office with her children, Abba got a written complaint from her and then he sent for the driver. When the driver came, Abba told him that from then on, his salary would not be given to him but it would be given to his wife as she had given a written complaint against him. The man was very upset but he could not do anything. Later on, the man understood his mistakes and changed his behaviours. Such used to be Abba's dealings!

Soon more family issues were brought to Abba and in most cases, men were addicted to liquor or gambling and did not give money at home. Abba used to call those staff members to his chamber, and try to counsel and guide them. Some men used to understand the situation and tried to rectify themselves, while others used to be angry with Abba and would argue in a quarrelsome mood. Abba never bothered about the consequences but would see to it that justice was done to the family of the staff. In many cases, wives of the workers could be seen visiting the office on the salary day, to receive the salary of their husbands.

One day while Abba was in his office, he got angry with one of his staff members for not doing his duty properly and he severely reprimanded the man. The man instead started arguing with Abba in a loud voice, which Abba had not expected. Abba's blood pressure shot up, and he got very angry with the employee. At the same time, he also felt pain in his chest. He sent the man outside his chamber and called for the peon. When the peon came in, Abba was already collapsing into his chair. The peon called the other officers and Abba was rushed to the hospital. The doctors gave him medicine to calm his BP and advised Abba to take proper rest.

Abba returned home but he was not feeling well. Early the next day morning he felt severe pain in his chest and he told Amma to call the driver. By the time the Jeep came, Abba was almost down with pain. Abba was rushed to the hospital, but on the way to the hospital, Abba became unconscious. At the hospital, Abba was taken to the ICU and he was given emergency treatment and it was found that he had a massive heart attack. The sister at the ICU gave him CPR and also a heart-saving injection. By the grace of God, Abba's life was saved but he was not yet out of danger. Abba had been kept in the ICU for two days, under strict observation and then he was shifted to the nursing home. Doctors had strictly advised Abba not to talk. Amma and the children were very much worried and they visited the hospital to take care of Abba. But Abba would always be surrounded by his office staff who stayed with him 24 x 7. Finally, after five days Abba was discharged from the hospital and he was referred to Chennai for further treatment. When Abba came home, he appeared very tired, weak and worn out!

Abba came home with a bag full of medicines and a long list of instructions and precautions. He had been referred to Chennai for treatment but he was not fit to travel. Doctors had advised him to wait for a week, and when his condition would improve, he would be able to travel by flight. Abba was on complete medical rest!

After taking rest for a week, Abba went to Chennai all alone and there he went to a government hospital where the doctors asked him to go for a check-up. After the check-up, the doctors checked the reports and advised Abba to undergo an open-heart surgery as soon as possible!

Chapter - 38

ABBA UNDERGOES OPEN HEART SURGERY

After seeing the medical reports of Abba, the doctors became apprehensive as Abba had multiple blocks in his heart. They also told Abba about the multiple blocks and that he should immediately undergo an operation. Abba didn't know what to do. He told the doctors that he had come to Chennai all alone and he wanted to consult his family before the operation. The same day, after returning from the hospital, Abba called Amma over phone and told her about his medical reports and the doctors' advice. He had to undergo an open-heart surgery soon and, in that case, he would need an attendant at Chennai, to be with him during the operation. He discussed with Amma as who could be his attendant. Amma was shocked on hearing about Abba's operation and became speechless. Abba thought that Jason had nervous attacks at one or two times, and Abba thought that Jason should be at home, to take care of Amma. Then Abba suggested that Jason could stay back at home to take care of the family in his absence and he would call his elder son-in-law to Chennai, to be with him during the operation. As always, Amma too thought that Abba's decision was right and agreed to Abba.

Abba soon contacted his elder son-in-law over the phone and told him about the operation and the doctors' advice. He also asked his son-in-law if he could come to Chennai immediately as he might have to undergo a heart operation soon. Then Abba called Amma over the phone and told her to inform Jason that he wanted him to be at home with

Amma, taking care of the family in his absence, and that he had also told his son-in-law to be his attendant during the surgery. He thought that it would be good for all if his elder son-in-law was with him during the operation.

When Abba called his son-in-law and told him about the heart operation, his son-in-law did not go for a second thought. He immediately applied for leave and the very next day left for Chennai by the first available flight to attend on Abba. Amma felt relieved and was happy that her son-in-law had gone to take care of Abba!

At Port Blair, Sheryl was left with her children and her responsibilities increased in the absence of her husband. At Abba's house, when Jason and his wife came to know from Amma that Abba had asked his son-in-law to be with him during the operation, they both became restless and annoyed. They were angry as why Abba had called his son-in-law and not his son to be with him during such a critical operation! The close friends of Jason and his wife were giving them evil ideas as the son-in-law would inherit Abba's all property. Unaware of the brewing of a storm in the house, Amma was very sad and worried thinking about Abba's health and his approaching heart operation!

After Sheryl's husband reached Chennai, he accompanied Abba to Apollo hospital for a check-up. There too the doctors told Abba that the reports showed multiple blocks in his heart and that Abba should immediately undergo a Coronary Artery Bypass Graft (CABG). The CABG involves taking a blood vessel from another part of the body (usually the arm, chest or leg) and attaching it to the coronary artery above and below the narrowed area or blockage in the heart.

From Chennai Sheryl regularly got updates from her husband about Abba's health condition and the progress of Abba's treatment. On the fourth day, her husband informed Sheryl that Abba's operation had been fixed for the next day and that the doctors had made all arrangements for the operation. Abba had already been admitted in the hospital and he also told her to inform Amma about the operation and to pray for the success of Abba's operation.

After talking to her husband, on the same day evening, Sheryl with her sons, went to Abba's house to apprise Amma and Jason about Abba's operation that was to take place the next day. When she reached Abba's house, she saw Amma sitting in the Veranda while Jason and his wife were talking to her in a very loud voice. It did not sound to be a pleasant conversation! The moment Jason's wife saw Sheryl coming with her children, she was out of her control and came running out of the house, up to the gate, and stopped Sheryl and her children from entering the campus. Jason and his wife were mad in their anger as Abba had asked his son-in-law to be with him during the operation. Amma was watching the drama in a shock and she thought to herself, "Are Jason and his wife really so worried about Abba's health?" Their behaviour appeared so comical to Amma. She thought that Abba had gone to Chennai all alone after a massive heart attack! Then Jason and his wife were not at all concerned, then why were they so over reactive then, Amma could not understand!

Sheryl was in tears. Her husband had gone as an attendant to take care of Abba in the hospital and instead of taking care of her and her children, her brother and his wife were fighting with her on the road, blaming her and her husband. The scene became worse when neighbours and passers-by stopped to find out the reason for the commotion taking place on the road, outside the house!

Sheryl felt so insulted that tears swelled in her eyes. She took hold of her children's hands and turned back to go away from there, without entering Abba's house. Amma started crying, and called out to Sheryl to come inside the house, but Jason's wife was standing at the gate, blocking the way and pouring words of fire. So, Sheryl silently left the place. Amma was heartbroken at the behaviour of Jason and his wife towards Sheryl, her whole body was trembling and she felt so helpless!

In Chennai, as instructed by the doctors, Abba had been admitted to the Apollo Hospital two days prior to the heart operation. In the meantime, Abba's son-in-law was with Abba to take care of all his needs. He then arranged to send a fax to the Lt. Governor regarding Abba's treatment and the hospital expenses and soon the amount was released from the Andaman Administration. On the appointed day Dr. Girinath of Apollo Hospitals performed the heart operation for Abba.

The bypass surgery is a major surgery which is done through a long incision in the chest while a heart-lung machine keeps the blood and oxygen flowing through the body. The centre of the chest is cut along the breastbone to spread open the rib cage to expose the heart. The heart is usually stopped for 30-90 minutes of the 3-6 hours of surgery. The heart-lung machine allows the surgeon to work on a still heart. Once the surgery gets over, the surgeon and perfusionist restart the heart. Abba was given the anaesthesia and got ready for the operation. During the operation, Abba's heart too had been stopped and he was put on a heart-lung machine, which was later successfully restarted. The heart operation went on for six long hours. With the grace of God, the operation was successful and Abba was shifted to a private room where he lay unconscious, like dead, for two days. When slowly he regained consciousness, he was unable to tolerate the pain. His whole body was in severe pain. His legs ached a lot as the veins had been removed for the bypass. He lay on the bed groaning and moaning and the doctors gave him painkillers to ease his pain, but the medicine could not bring him relief!

The doctors needed blood for Abba and Abba's son-in-law donated blood for him twice. He was like a shadow with Abba seeing to all his needs. Abba was unable to tolerate his pain, but he did not want to show his pain to anyone. Gradually with medicines and proper care, Abba's health conditions improved and his pain decreased.

In the meantime, Jason too reached Chennai to see Abba. He had been advised by his wife and well-wishers that he was the elder son of the family and he should be the one who should be with Abba during that critical moment. He went to see Abba in the hospital but Abba was in the ICU and all were not allowed there. He did not have the courage to go inside and meet Abba. He checked on Abba from outside through the glass door and after a couple of days, he returned to Port Blair.

After about two weeks of the operation, the doctors told Abba that he could travel, and Abba returned to Port Blair with his son-in-law. The news of Abba's advent had spread everywhere and soon Abba's friends, office staff, and relatives started pouring in to see Abba and to inquire about his health. All were happy to see Abba back. But Abba needed rest. He was feeling severe pain in the ribs. While walking he felt his legs had lost all its energy!

Abba told Amma and the children that after the operation he was unconscious and did not know what happened to him, but his son-in-law took good care of him in the hospital, like his own son. Abba showed the scars on his chest and legs which appeared like centipedes crawling. All were pained thinking how Abba must have endured the pain of the operation. Amma wept for Abba and his pain!

Abba's son-in-law told Amma that after the operation Abba was unconscious for two days. Those were very critical days and the machines were monitoring Abba's pulse, heartbeat and BP. After Abba regained consciousness, he was in severe pain for days. Even after coming home, Abba felt a lot of pain inside his chest. He had been advised by the doctors not to smoke or take liquor, as it might be dangerous. Abba had been addicted to smoking for many years, but after the operation Abba quit his smoking habits. Instead, after a few years, he started chewing paan with tobacco. Amma told everyone that Abba had got a new life and thanked God for His mercy!

Abba was a very keen observer and he could feel the environment inside the house was not very genial. Jason and his wife were like the touch-me-nots, shrinking away from everyone. whenever Sheryl and her husband would come to see Abba, they would get inside their room like snails crawling back into its shell on finding intruders!

While Abba was at home on medical rest, Amma took good care of him. She almost stopped using salt in the dishes and cooked plain food for Abba. She was worried to see Abba in such a lot of pain. She would often weep on seeing the pain of Abba and tell her children, "Abba has done so much good to so many people, then why God has given so much pain to Abba!"

Since the behaviour of Jason and his wife was very strange at home, Abba asked Amma what had happened behind him. Amma was trying to evade the topic, but after a few days, in a quiet moment, Amma told Abba about the row in the house between Jason and his wife and Sheryl, while he had gone for the operation. She told Abba how the son and daughter-in-law did not allow Sheryl and her children to enter the house and were so brutal in their allegations on Sheryl and her husband, thinking that Abba would give away all his property to Sheryl and her husband. Abba became very sad on hearing that. Jason and his wife knew that one day Amma would tell Abba about their fight as Amma never kept anything from Abba!

Jason's wife had always wanted to lead an independent life and had been waiting for an opportunity to leave the house with her husband and sons. Now she got that opportunity that she had been waiting for all those years. On the pretext of Abba being more considerate towards his daughter and son-in-law, she started insisting that they should leave the house. One day, by evening, Jason and his wife left Abba's house with their sons and all their belongings. Amma was at home and she pleaded Jason and his wife not to go, but they shouted at Amma, blaming and accusing her and Abba for differentiating among the children! Amma could not believe her eyes as how could her beloved son change so much. She remembered all those sleepless nights she had spent for him, when he was sick as a child, with both of his legs affected by eczema. She had carried him from church to church, praying for his good health. Now the same son did not consider the tears of his mother!

Abba had joined duty and was in his office when the incident happened. Amma was in tears and she requested her son and daughter-in-law to stay back till Abba returned from office so that they could amicably talk and solve their differences. But Jason was obstinate!

Amma tried her level best to stop them, but they did not listen to her. Amma was weeping and pleading in front of her son, but her tears could not melt his heart, that had become so hard for his mother. Amma was shattered when Jason left the house. She helplessly sat on the sofa and wept bitterly!

In the evening when Abba returned from his office, Amma broke the news to Abba that Jason and his family had left the house. Abba was very hurt, but he remained silent. Later that evening when the daughters came to see Abba with their families, they were also shocked to hear about Jason's departure from the house. It was a critical moment in the family as Abba had just undergone a major operation. Abba and Amma needed the help of their son then, at that time, more than at any other time in their life. Abba told Amma that maybe since he was nearing his retirement, they had left him as they did not want to take care of them in their old age. Whatever be the reason, Abba and Amma were totally devastated. Jason and his sons were Abba's heartbeat and he loved them beyond words could express, but now they were all gone! This made Abba sadder, he felt a void in his life, that could never be filled!

After returning from the hospital Abba was constantly complaining of severe pain in his chest. He would tell Amma and his daughters and sons-in-law that while sleeping or when he turned sides in the bed, he felt as if his heart was rolling from one side to the other. Moreover, during rain or cold weather, the wires that joined his ribs got very cold and gave him a lot of pain. This became an everyday complaint of Abba, and all would sympathise with him, but no one could help to reduce the pain of Abba. Abba used to joke on the situation and tell "Nobody can carry your cross; it has to be carried by you, yourself, and so is the pain of a person!" Amma would not say anything but used to weep silently asking why God had given so much sufferings to Abba!

Days rolled by and it was time for Abba's retirement.

Chapter - 39

ABBA POSTED AS DEPUTY SECRETARY, PRADESH COUNCIL

Though Jason had left Abba's house, but Abba regularly gathered information about his elder son and shared it with Amma. He would ask his office staff about Jason and his family and they regularly gave information to him about Jason. Abba was much concerned about his son, but was trying to accept the facts and heartaches of life. Abba's both daughters were settled in their family life and Abba had no worry about them. They had government jobs and all were doing well.

Abba's worry was for his younger son Ethan, who was still in school. Abba and Amma poured all affection on him as he was their child of old age. They would try to provide him with whatever he desired. He had completed his Secondary exams and was in his senior secondary classes. Ethan told Abba that he needed tuitions in all subjects but Abba clearly told him that he did not have money to spend on his tuitions, rather he should concentrate in his classroom teaching. The boy was upset. When Sheryl and her husband came to know about it, they felt bad for him. They both were teachers, and Abba's son-in-law had good contact with the other teachers. He told Abba not to worry about it as he would arrange for Ethan's classes. Accordingly, he also arranged for his coaching classes.

During those days, after his open-heart operation, Abba was constantly feeling pain in his chest, and was regularly complaining about it. So after about six months of his operation, Abba again went to Chennai for a check-up. His second son-in-law was in Chennai then, and he told Abba that he would accompany him to the hospital.

Abba and his son-in-law went to the hospital. After all the check-ups, doctors found that the ribs that had been wired after the operation had got opened and hence Abba was feeling a lot of pain. Since the ribs were opened, so while sleeping, whenever Abba turned his sides on the bed, the heart moved and that gave him severe pain. Abba was indeed right about his moving heart!

Once again Abba was admitted to the hospital and the operation was performed. This time doctors saw to it that the ribs were wired properly. Abba returned to Port Blair after a week and he felt that the pain had subsided much.

In 1993 Abba received his transfer order and he was posted as Deputy Secretary of the Pradesh Council. Abba joined his new office and soon became busy with his work.

During the British era, and also after Indian independence, the Chief Commissioner used to be the administrative head of the Andaman and Nicobar Islands. In 1982, the Chief Commissioner's post was replaced by the newly created Lieutenant Governor's post as the Head of the Administration. Accordingly, a 'Pradesh Council' with Councillors as representatives of the people was constituted to advise the Lt. Governor. Thus, a 30-member indirectly elected Pradesh Council was constituted by the promulgation of the Andaman and Nicobar regulation 1979, to advise the Administration.

The members of the Pradesh Council were local leaders who knew the various problems faced by the people of the land. These representatives were from the islands who belonged to different states and religions, speaking different languages but their main focus used to be the welfare of the people. There were representatives for different departments such as Education, Health, transport, forest etc. and they saw to it that the problems faced by the concerned departments assigned to them were solved soon.

After Abba joined his office, the Andaman and Nicobar Islands Panchayats Regulation 1994 came into effect on 23rd April 1994, repealing the A & N Islands Administration Regulation 1979. Thus, the tenure of the Pradesh Council expired on April 1994 and a new Pradesh Council with Municipal Board Regulation came into existence.

Abba too proceeded on superannuation on April 30, 1994, after successfully completing 38 years of his service in the islands. Farewell functions for Abba started much before his retirement, by the offices where Abba had served earlier. On 30th April 1994, a formal farewell function was arranged for Abba by his own office. On that day Abba returned home with a lot of garlands, bouquets, gifts and sweets. The office staff from Abba's office had also accompanied Abba home to show their love and respect towards Abba.

In the meantime, Jason and his family who had left Abba after the operation, had started paying short visits to Abba and Amma. So, by the time Abba retired, they became regular visitors to Abba's house. Amma and all children were very happy for Abba. Amma also cooked special meals for the whole family on the occasion and there was a gala gathering at home!

Chapter - 40

ABBA PROCEEDS ON SUPERANNUATION

On 30 April 1994, Abba superannuated from his service. When Abba retired, Abba did not have any land or property in Andaman to build a house or to stay back in the islands. Ironically, he had been regularizing the lands and allotting land and house sites to people in Andaman & Nicobar Islands. Abba decided to return to his village Mannarpuram and settle down there. But Ethan was in his 12th standard and so they had to wait till Ethan's examinations would get over in March 1995.

Days were rolling for Abba and Amma in a pleasant way, as every day, some or other friends or relatives would come to meet Abba and Amma. But they looked forward to the evenings as their children and grandchildren used to visit them in the evenings. It used to be a happy time at Abba's home, since all his children with their families would be assembled there and there used to be a lot of talking, fun and frolic. Sometimes Abba used to make plans that during the next summer vacation the family should go on a trip to some places. Abba wanted to visit St. Alphonsa's grave at Kottayam. St. Alphonsa[1] was beatified at Kottayam, on 8 February 1986 by Pope John Paul II during his apostolic pilgrimage to India. It was a long pending wish of Abba. But every year Abba used to make programme for a family tour, and it would never be carried out. When Abba would start making plans, Amma would smile as she knew that in the morning all plans too would vanish like the night stars from the sky. Sometime, Amma would tease Abba about his plans of the previous evening, and Abba would then say, "It would need money and we don't have extra money for visiting places! What is the harm in making plans and talking about the trips. Just enjoy it!"

Sometimes they all would play cards, rummy, donkey or 28 and have a lot of fun. Sometimes they all used to sit together and chat for long hours, and would have meals together. Abba and Amma enjoyed that period of time very much! Old parents do not need children's wealth, they just want to spend their time with their children, and that was what Amma and Abba were doing.

Abba had received his pension benefits and he decided to gift some gold ornaments to his daughters from his pension money. He told Sheryl and Meryl that he would be gifting each of them gold chains of two Sovereign and they could select their designs for the chain. The daughters were happy and thanked Abba. Though Abba was not happy with his daughter-in-law for all her behaviour, but along with his daughters, he ordered a similar gold chain for her also. Abba always tried to give equal share of things to his daughter-in-law, just as his daughters, but she could never understand it throughout her life!

After his retirement, Abba received his gratuity and the lump sum pension benefits. Chithi's husband was a renowned businessman by then and had scaled great heights in his business. Then he was the Treasurer of the Andaman Chamber of Commerce. Earlier he used to insist Abba that after his retirement Abba should help him in his business and that they both would work on some new startups together. He also assured Abba that he would make a chamber for him in his shop itself and Abba could work from there.

Accordingly, after retirement, Abba went to Chithi's husband, and told him that he had retired, and wanted to invest a part of his pension money in business with him. But by then Chithi's husband had changed his mind. He told Abba that he was not in a position to start any new business and he was not in need of any money from Abba for investment in his business. Long back, Abba had given some money to Chithi's husband as a deposit, and now he returned back that money as well to Abba.

Abba felt sad about the whole matter and left the place. He did not know what to do with his pension money and the money that Chithi's husband had returned. There was a jeweller who was in good terms with Abba and he had a gold jewellery shop. The man came to know that Abba had some pension money, and he met Abba and told him that Abba could invest the money with him and he would give him monthly interest for the amount invested. He also assured Abba that later on, whenever Abba would need the money, he would return it, and then Abba could get it from him immediately. Abba was convinced by the words of the jeweller and Abba gave the money to the jeweller which was returned to him by Chithi's husband.

The jeweller to whom Abba had given his money, was in the good books of Abba as he frequently visited Abba's house. He used to tell Abba that he was like his father. Whenever he used to come home, he would kneel down and get blessings from Abba and Amma. So, Abba thought that his money was in safe hands. Moreover, he would be getting monthly interest and whenever he would need the money, he would be able to get it back. Such was the trust Abba had on that man!

But the jeweller turned out to be a cheat. He paid interest money to Abba for 3-4 months. Later he stopped giving the interest money and when Abba asked about it, the man started making excuses. He started telling stories about his business loss and Abba was not happy with his behaviour. Abba told the man to return his money, but he did not give any response to Abba's words. Abba even visited his shop a number of times, but the man tried to avoid the situation and did not return the money. With no other option, when Abba was leaving Andamans, he told Jason to collect the money from that jeweller, whenever and however possible. In his life Abba could never enjoy the money he had earned with so much hard work!

Since Abba did not have any land or property in Andamans, he decided to purchase a house site for Jason, with a part of his pension money. Abba found a plot at Prem Nagar, near Kali Bari and purchased the house site for Jason in his name. Then he told Jason, "This is my gift to you and this much only I can do for you. You and your wife both are working, and you both have a handsome salary, so you can easily get a bank loan and build a house. Rest of the money I need for Ethan, Amma and myself." Jason was very happy to get a gift of a house site in his name as he would be able to build his own house soon!

In March 1995 when Ethan's Examinations were over, Abba got all his luggage packed and sent it to his village house at Mannarpuram. As the day for Abba's departure for his village neared, people started pouring in to bid him farewell. Everybody had good words for Abba. Many people wanted Abba to stay back in Andamans. Abba told them that he did not own a house in Andaman and so it was not possible for him to stay back in the islands. Then many of Abba's friends offered Abba their apartments and told that Abba could stay there as long as he wanted, but Abba thought that it was not right and he did not agree.

On the appointed day, Abba and Amma left Port Blair for good. Abba's all three children with their families had come to the airport to see off Abba and Amma. Amma was very emotional as all her elder children lived in Andaman, and now they won't be able to visit her every day, as they used to do all those years. She told her children to visit them in the village during summer holidays without fail and the children too promised Amma to visit her every year.

Abba had come to serve in the Andaman and Nicobar Islands when he was in his twenties, and now after about forty years of his working there, he was leaving the islands, and he was not very happy. But since he had no house of his own, he couldn't stay back. He had decided to spend the rest of his life peacefully in his village. Abba expected that if Jason would build his house in Prem Nagar, then Abba and Amma could think of coming back to stay with him, but he was not sure what the future had in store for him!

Chapter - 41

ABBA RETURNS TO HIS VILLAGE FOR GOOD

In 1995, Abba and Amma with their youngest son returned to Mannarpuram village. Since Abba had a house there, so there was nothing to worry about. Abba had always wanted to go back to his village and now finally he was in his village for good, and he was happy!

After reaching the village, Abba and Amma tried to settle down in their life as per the conditions of the village. The kitchen was cleaned and set and the pantry filled. The refrigerator was always full of vegetables, fruits, fish and chicken. Abba's two sisters lived in the same village along with their families, and every day they would come to Abba's house early in the morning and have coffee with Abba and Amma. Abba's sisters' children would also visit Abba and Amma every now and then to help Amma in the household chores. There used to be such a lot of talking and laughing and Amma used to be cooking for them all. From Andaman, Abba's children regularly called them over the phone and Abba and Amma were happy.

Abba soon got a hand pump fixed at the backyard of his house. He had brought coconut saplings from Andamans and planted them around the house. He also arranged for some ornamental plants for his house, and also planted them. He started spending some of his time in grooming his garden and taking care of his plants.

In June the result for class XII examination was out and Ethan had passed with good marks. The Andaman & Nicobar Administration had quota seats in various fields of Engineering, Medicine, Teaching,

Management etc. for the aspiring students of the islands. Since Ethan and Abba were in the village, so on behalf of Abba, his elder son-in-law attended the counselling, completed all the formalities, and got an engineering seat allotted for Ethan. He signed the security bond and collected the documents and sent them all by courier to Abba at his village address.

When the documents for admission for Ethan were received in the village, both Abba and Amma were overjoyed. They went to the church at the village and thanked God for all the blessings received in their life. Then they took Ethan to the Engineering College in Madurai and got him admitted in the college as well as in the hostel. Abba advised him to study well so that he could get a placement and Ethan too promised Abba to study well. Then Abba and Amma returned to the village. Madurai is about 215 km. from Mannarpuram village and would take about three to four hours of bus journey to reach the village, so Ethan could come to the village on weekends and holidays! Abba and Amma were very happy.

After Ethan's admission to college, Abba and Amma settled down in their village life. During weekends and during long holidays Ethan used to visit the village and stayed with them at home. Amma used to cook special meals those days. Abba was receiving his monthly pension and life started moving smoothly for Abba and Amma, with a new routine.

At Port Blair, the then Member of Parliament of Andaman & Nicobar Islands had sponsored Abba's name to the Executive Committee of the Coir Board. The Coir Board is a statutory body established by the Government of India under legislation, enacted by the Parliament namely the 'Coir Industry Act 1953' for the promotion and development of the Coir Industry as well as for the export and marketing of coir and coir products in India as a whole.

Regular meetings of the Executive Committee of the Coir Board used to be held and members had to attend those meetings that would be held in different parts of the country. For attending those meetings, the members were entitled to payments of travelling and daily allowances at the rate admissible to Grade-I officers of the Government of India.

Abba soon received a letter from Coir Board, stating that his name had been sponsored to the Coir Board and he was happy. Now he would be able to attend those meetings, and meet people from different parts of the country and he would not have to spend money from his pocket. He could also come to Andamans to submit his reports.

During 1993, Meryl's husband had got transferred from Andaman. He was earlier posted at Calcutta but he found it difficult to manage his food and life there, and he had been trying for a transfer to his native place. After some years, he got a transfer to Nagercoil, in Tamil Nadu and soon joined his duty there.

Nagercoil is about 75 km from Abba's village. Meryl was at Port Blair with her son and she was finding it difficult to manage her life single handedly. She was thinking of taking a long leave and going to Tamil Nadu to stay with her husband, but she was concerned about her son's education. She wanted to leave her son at her elder sister's house at Port Blair. Abba was then at Port Blair and he strongly disagreed to Meryl. He told her that children should always be with their parents and Meryl should take her son with her. Thus, Meryl decided to take her son with her.

In 1996, Meryl applied for long leave and along with her son, came to stay with her husband at Nagercoil. That was a great support for Abba and Amma as the place was close by and they were happy. Sometimes Amma and Abba used to go to Nagercoil and Ethan also used to join them there during his holidays. Meryl and her husband used to take great care of Amma and Abba and also used to arrange for trips to the nearby places of interest and they all enjoyed the holidays. Sometimes they used to go to Kanyakumari[2] or to Kutralam[3] waterfalls and enjoyed those trips. Life was going peacefully for Amma and Abba.

On 19-7-1996 Abba's elder brother passed away in Port Blair, Andaman. Abba received the news of his brother's demise and was very sorrowful. After about a few weeks of his death, Abba decided to leave Amma in the village and visit his elder brother's family in Andaman.

Accordingly, by the end of August 1996, Abba visited Andaman and stayed with Sheryl's family in their quarters. This was the first time Abba was staying in their house and Sheryl and her husband were very happy. They took good care of Abba. Sheryl used to cook Abba's favourite dishes and Abba too was very happy. He used to call Amma over the phone and tell her, "Your daughter has cooked my favourite dish and I am enjoying my days here." He used to share every bit of news of Andamans with Amma.

Abba visited his brother's house in Junglighat, gave clothes to his sister-in-law as per the custom and mourned his brother's death. The sister-in-law was very sad about her condition. Abba comforted his sister-in-law saying that God is there and she should not worry much.

The news of Abba's arrival at Port Blair had spread around and Jason also came to know about Abba's arrival. He came to Sheryl's house along with his wife to meet Abba. Abba was not very happy with them but spoke a few good words and replied to the questions asked by Jason. After spending some time with Abba, Jason and his wife left. Later that same day Jason met his sister and brother-in-law, and requested for financial help. Abba had bought him a house site before leaving Andaman, and now he wanted to build a house. He told them that he had no money. He wanted his elder sister and brother-in-law to speak to Abba to lend him money and he would return it after getting a bank loan.

Abba stayed in Port Blair for about ten days and every evening Jason and his wife visited Abba. Then after two days they requested Abba for money to build the house and Abba was silent. Jason told Abba that he had applied for a bank loan and assured that once the bank loan would be approved, he would return Abba's money.

Sheryl and her husband also spoke to Abba in favour of Jason and requested Abba to help him. But Abba was not convinced. Abba told Jason that both he and his wife were working and they also earned a very good salary, and should also be having good savings. Abba wanted to know what had happened to all their earnings, as till the time they stayed with Abba and Amma, Abba had been taking care of the entire expenditure of the family. Jason and his wife hardly ever spent for the family. Abba said that he had been a single earning member and had taken care of his own family and Jason's family as well, till they left the house. Already he had bought him a house site and now the money left with him was for Ethan's studies and it was for Amma and himself, and for their expenses, in case of any medical emergency. Abba also felt it very strange as why Jason could not get a bank loan till then!

But Jason and his wife did not give up their efforts to persuade Abba. They visited Abba regularly and requested him for financial help. In the beginning Abba denied to help him, but finally, before leaving Port Blair, Abba's heart melted and he decided to help Jason. On the last day, before leaving for his village, Abba gave Jason a cheque and told him to withdraw the money and start the construction work. He also clearly told Jason that he had parted with all his pension money to Jason, and told him again and again that he should apply for loan immediately and return the money to Abba as soon as possible!

Before Jason was leaving the house, Abba once again told Jason that he had emptied his bank account and insisted that he should return the amount as soon as his bank loans were approved. But then Abba did not know that Jason would never return that money!

PART 7

REPATRIATION

Chapter - 42

ABBA CONTESTS PANCHAYAT ELECTION

After returning to his village, Abba spent his whole time with Amma and his relatives. Villagers used to come to Abba to discuss with him various issues such as their land and revenue problems, problems related to their village or their family-related problems etc. Abba would listen to them patiently and suggest solutions to them. In case of land and revenue matters, if anyone was in need of help, Abba would accompany them to the Taluk office at Nanguneri and meet the officers there and talk to them and try to solve the problems of the villagers. Sometimes he would accompany the villagers to the district headquarters at Tirunelveli, to talk to the officers there to solve their problems. Regarding family issues, whenever someone sought his help from the village, Abba used to give his advice and also used to spend his time counselling the people on the importance of family values.

The villagers admired Abba for his vast knowledge on revenue matters and his speaking skills and convincing the authorities to help solve their issues. More villagers started coming to Abba seeking his advice on various matters. Whenever the villagers would face any problem regarding land, Abba would go with them to the Taluk Office to resolve the issues. Abba was slowly becoming popular in his village and officers at the taluk level and district level started recognising Abba. Amma was very happy with all those developments as those works kept Abba busy!

Earlier after Abba's retirement, she had seen Abba sleep talking, ordering office staff, giving dictations, talking about meetings etc. Then Amma used to feel very sad for Abba and used to share those with her children. Now she was happy to see that Abba had become busy once again.

It was the year 1996, there was a notification from the Tamil Nadu Government about the elections to local bodies and the elections were to be held in October. Abba's relatives and villagers advised Abba to contest the elections. Abba was confused. But the village people started visiting Abba regularly and requested him to contest the Panchayat election. Abba was popular in the village as he was always ready to help the villagers and solve their problems. Abba spoke to Amma about that and as usual, Amma had no opinion of her own. She told Abba to think and take decision, as he had always done and she would support his decisions. Finally, Abba decided to contest the Panchayat election!

On an auspicious day, Abba accompanied by a few village elders and relatives, went to file nominations in the Taluk Office at Nanguneri. After the nomination was filed, there was a lot of enthusiasm among all. Abba with the village elders and his relatives returned home in the evening. Amma made coffee for everyone and gave them sweets. They all sat there talking about the elections till late. Every day, the village elders started assembling at Abba's house and they used to spend long hours talking about the elections and about the various progress work to be undertaken for the development of the village. Amma regularly served them coffee and snacks!

The election that was to be held, was a Panchayat election and there was one seat for 7 to 8 nearby villages. Abba also visited the nearby villages along with the village elders for canvassing. The village elders convinced Abba that they too would canvass for Abba personally in the nearby villages and Abba need not worry. Abba had spent an amount of his money kept for the emergency fund, for the election campaign.

On the appointed day, the election was held peacefully and the whole village went to vote. When the counting was started, there was a lot of tension among the people of the village. Finally, the results were declared, and Abba had lost the election. Abba could not get many votes but his opponent who was in politics for many years had won the election. The village elders had played a double game, by speaking to Abba in his favour, and at the same time, supporting the opponent. Abba was a simple man, an honest worker and a leader but not a politician. Moreover, he did have much money to spend lavishly to lure his voters. So, Abba's aspiration to contest elections came to an end! Though he had lost some money, but he had learnt a lesson and also gained some experience of politics.

In a quiet moment, Abba told Amma that he should not have entered into politics as it was not his cup of tea. Amma just smiled and kept quiet. She would never advise Abba on money matters as she thought that Abba was earning his money and he was wise enough to spend it as well.

Meryl had taken a long leave from her service and was staying with her husband in Nagercoil. Abba was worried about Meryl's job. He wanted to get a job for her in Tamil Nadu, so that she could be with her husband. After coming to the village, Abba had made some good friends who were also leaders and politicians at the high level. Abba met them and spoke to them about his daughter who was working as a Mukhya Sevika in the Social Welfare department in the Andamans, and wanted to know about the possibility of finding a job for her under the Tamil Nadu government. He pursued the matter day in and day out, and finally he was assured help. There was a rule set by the Tamil Nadu Government according to which 'People of Tamil Nadu origin, who had been working in other states, their children could be considered for appointment in the state of Tamil Nadu, provided there was vacancy.'

Abba met those leaders a number of times and also went to Chennai dozens of times with his application to meet the Ministers. Finally, Abba was told to submit a new application for his daughter along with documents of Abba's origin, his daughter's work experience, place of posting etc., to be considered for appointment. Abba soon submitted the application with all needed documents. Within a year, Abba could get the appointment order for Meryl and she got an appointment in the same cadre of job that she was working in Andamans. Abba was very happy. He had been very harsh towards Meryl in her childhood, and there was always a guilt in his conscience about it. After getting a job for Meryl, Abba's great burden vanished from his heart and finally he felt peace!

After getting her appointment letter from Tamil Nadu Government, Meryl came back to Andaman, in 1997, to render her resignation from her job. She joined her duty in her office and also submitted her technical resignation. Then in November 1997, she joined the same cadre of her duty under Tamil Nadu government. She had to write an exam in Tamil, for further promotions, which she qualified. It was a happy time for Amma and Abba as Abba had finally succeeded in getting a government job for Meryl under Tamil Nadu government!

That summer vacation Abba's all children visited the village and Abba and Amma were very happy. Abba planned to take his children to Velankanni[1] church. Abba told his children that during 1500s several miracles had happened and Apparitions of Virgin Mary had appeared in Vailankanni, India. The Apparitions of the Virgin Mary is known as "Our Lady of Vailankanni" or "Our Lady of Good Health." Abba booked a van and on a fine day with his family left for the Shrine. This shrine is often referred to as the Lourdes of the East!

A story is told about a shepherd boy whose name was Tamil Sankaranarayanan. It was a hot summer day and the boy had to walk from Vailankanni to Nagapattinam to deliver milk to his master. Tamil was feeling tired and he lay down under a banyan tree beside a pond to rest, and he fell asleep. When a strong gust of wind began to blow, he woke up and was startled to see an apparition of Mary standing before him, holding a child in her arms. Both Mary and the child had a glow of light emanating from them. Mary asked Tamil if he would give her son some milk to drink, and Tamil agreed. The child then drank all of the milk that Tamil offered from his pot, and Mary thanked Tamil before they disappeared. When the boy reached Nagapattinam, which is a coastal town, his master was angry at him for the delay. Tamil apologized and explained why he had been delayed. His master became angry thinking that Tamil had given away some of the milk, he was supposed to deliver. But when Tamil and his master looked inside the pot to check how much milk was left over, they saw it miraculously filling up. The pot kept filling up until the brim and milk started spilling out. Astonished, Tamil and his master ran back to the pond, and Mary and the child appeared to them there as a vision before disappearing. Thereafter, the pond became to be known as Matha Kulam or 'Our Lady's Pond'.

There is another legend of a crippled boy who supported himself and his widowed mother by selling buttermilk to thirsty travellers at work at a place in Vailankanni. Suddenly the boy saw a bright light appear with two figures inside the light: Mary holding a child. Both Mary and the child wore white clothes that scattered a dazzling light. Mary asked the boy for a cup of buttermilk for her son, and the boy handed her a cup and watched as the child drank it all. Then Mary thanked the boy for being generous. Afterward, Mary asked the boy to go to Nagapattinam to tell a certain Catholic man living there that she and her son had appeared in the area, and that he should build a church there to commemorate the apparition. The boy told Mary that he would like to go, but he couldn't walk on his own, so he had to wait for his mother, who would arrive at the end of the day and carry him there. But Mary urged him to try, and when he did, he realized that he had been miraculously healed of his disability. The boy then ran to Nagapattinam and found the man. When he talked to the man, he told the boy that Mother Mary had appeared to him in a dream the night before and told him to expect the boy's visit. The man built a chapel where the apparition had appeared and placed a statue on the altar of Mary holding Jesus Christ as a child. The statue became known as Our Lady of Good Health.

There is also a legend of 17th century, about a Portuguese ship sailing from Macao to Ceylon which was caught in extreme weather in the Bay of Bengal. The terrified sailors prayed to the Virgin Mary under her title Our Lady, Star of the Sea. The raging storm suddenly subsided and the entire crew of 150 on board the ship was saved from capsizing. This incident happened on 8 September, the Feast Day of the Nativity of Mary. In thanksgiving the sailors rebuilt the shrine, and continued to visit and donate to the cause of the shrine whenever their voyages brought them to that area.

On the way to the Basilica, Abba updated the children with all those legends about Velankanni. When they reached the church, it was evening. They got a room and all refreshed and went to the church and marvelled at its beauty. The church showcased a unique blend of Gothic and Indian architectural styles, and it was a true marvel to behold! The Velankanni Basilica is adorned with exquisite sculptures and artwork that depict various scenes from the life of Jesus Christ and the Virgin Mary. Intricate carvings, vibrant paintings, and delicate murals can be found throughout the church, creating an atmosphere of awe and reverence. These artistic masterpieces are a feast for the eyes and inspire a deeper connection with devoutness!

The place of the shrine was crowded and more and more people were arriving from far and near, in cars and buses to seek solace, offer prayers, and experience the divinity that surrounds the church. After attending the evening service and offering prayers, Abba and his family went around the place. There were hundreds of shops selling curios, medals and fancy items. Abba's children bought some curios and then they all had dinner in a nearby restaurant. While they were returning, they saw hundreds of people sleeping in front of the church, on the bare ground. Abba told his children that he too wanted to sleep there, and soon found a place and lay down to sleep. Following Abba, all the others too lay down in front of the church and slept peacefully there. The next day, they left for the village, carrying good memories.

They returned via Madurai and Abba showed his children the school where he was studying for his pre-degree course. Talking about the history of Madurai, Abba told his children that Madurai is a temple city and is probably the oldest city of Tamil Nadu. It is situated on the banks of River Vaikai. The history of the place is associated with the

Pandya Kings, and Madurai was the site of the Pandya capital during 4th–11th century. The Meenakshi temple is at the centre of this ancient temple city and it is mentioned in the 6th-century texts of Tamil Sangam literature. Then Abba went on to tell the story of Kannagi[2] who burnt Madurai.

Kannagi was the daughter of a merchant and she was married to Kovalan, whose family were sea traders. Later, Kovalan had an affair with a dancer named Madhavi, and he lost all his wealth to the dancer. At last, penniless, Kovalan realized his mistake and returned to his wife Kannagi, who forgave him, and also accepted him in her life. Kovalan hoped to go to Madurai for trade. Since the couple had no money, Kannagi offered Kovalan to sell her only possession- a precious pair of anklets that contained rubies. She removed one of her anklets and handed it to Kovalan. Kovalan hesitated to sell it, but he had no other choice. Madurai was ruled by Pandya king Nedunj- Cheliyan-I in those days. When Kovalan tried to sell one of the anklets of Kannagi in the market of Madurai, the vendor thought that it was the lost anklet of the queen and immediately took Kovalan to the palace. Without a second thought, the Pandya King, Nedunj-Cheliyan ordered the execution of Kovalan on account of the theft of the Queen's anklet.

When Kannagi was told about the execution of Kovalan by the Pandya king, on the accusation of the theft of queen's anklet, she became furious, and taking her anklet in her hand, she set out to prove her husband's innocence to the king. She walked into the court and looked at the king with fiery eyes and asked for justice from him. With that she threw down the anklet in her hand, and broke open the anklet seized from Kovalan and the rubies spread everywhere. Kannagi argued that the queen's anklets contained Pearls and accused the king for having killed her husband without knowing the facts. The king realized his blunder of having caused such an injustice, and he committed suicide in shame. Kannagi uttered a curse in her grief and anger that the entire city of Madurai be burnt. Soon the capital city of Pandyas' was set ablaze resulting in huge loss, due to the curse. No one could pacify her anger, so

Goddess Meenakshi descended from heaven and requested Kannagi to stop the fire! The story forms the core of the Tamil Epic-Silappatikaram.

Abba narrated the lines from Silappatikaram, and all were amazed at Abba's vast knowledge of the Tamil Literature. He was equally good at English Literature, and would recite from Shakespear and Keats! Amma and the children were very proud of Abba!

When they all reached the village, they had made some very good memories and had spent some quality time with each other. After a week, the children all returned to their places of work and Amma and Abba were left in the village.

Chapter - 43

ABBA FACES FINANCIAL CRISIS

mma and Abba were leading a peaceful life in the village. During summer vacations, every year, Abba's children from Andamans used to visit them with family and it used to be a happy time for all. Once, during the summer vacation, when Abba's children visited the village, Abba and Amma planned out a trip to visit the famous Church of Our Lady of Red Sands, which is known as 'Manal Madha Church'[3]. They packed food, booked a cab and went to see the church. As the car was nearing the place, they found the area deserted with hardly any house, but the whole place was covered with red soil. When they reached the church, they found that it was underground, deep under the soil. A new church had been built above, on the top. They all went to the church underground, prayed and came out. Abba told the children that there were many legends associated to the church. It is said that in ancient times, that place was known as 'Kanakkan Kudieruppu', and numerous families lived here in the Kingdom of Pandiyas.[4]

It is said that St. Thomas[5], one of the disciples of Jesus, when he came to India during the 1st Century, happened to visit this kingdom of Kandhappa Raja, and went to meet one of Pandiya Chieftains to spread the Word of God. He happened to see the wife and daughter of the Chieftain possessed by demons, and he drove out the demon from them, due to which the king was so impressed that he got baptized as a Christian. It is also said that a devotee of that place had a dream of Our Lady, who asked him to build a church for Her, and the devotee built the church. In 1339, the church was consecrated and the statue of Our Lady was installed there. The same statue is still venerated as '*Athisaya Madha*' or Miraculous Mother.

This church is said to have been frequently visited by St. Francis Xavier[6] in 1548, when he visited Manappadu and Periyathalai, both towns in South India, to preach the Gospel of God. During one of his visits to this church, he is said to have brought back to life a dead young man, by praying hard to Our Lady.

There is yet another legend which says that there lived a poor pious widow in Kanakkankudiyiruppu, who was a faithful devotee of Our Lady. She used to feed and take care of the cranes in a nearby lake. Instead, the cranes used to throw fish for her in the courtyard of her house and she used to collect those fish and sold it in the market, and in that way, she made a living. Some people of the village were jealous of the woman and spread immoral stories about her character and accused that the fish were not given to her by the cranes, but her illegitimate husband.

Those days the place was ruled by King Thuravi Pandian, and when the matter about the widow's immoral character was brought to him, the king without investigating the matter, gave a hasty judgement, to burn her alive by pouring oil into the holes drilled in her head. When the poor widow was burnt and her cries filled the whole place, soon a heavy torrent of red sandstorm shook the whole place and covered the whole village. Soon everything was buried in the red sand, including the church, houses, market etc. The town disappeared and it appeared as if the curse of the widow had destroyed the entire community.

Soon, the place became a desert, roved by wild animals. In 1798, a shepherd boy was grazing his cattle there when he stumbled on a piece of wood, and he started digging. He found that it was a cross and the shepherd boy ran to the nearby village of Sokkankudiyiruppu and informed about it to the villagers. Soon people rushed to the place and started digging. After several weeks of excavation, the church was unearthed. The church was still underground, but when the doors of the church were opened, people were surprised to see a lamp burning inside the church. So, the church got its name of '*Athisaya Manal Madha Church*'.

Abba and his family were very happy to visit the church. The entire place was a deserted land of red soil. They ate their packed lunch and left the place with good memories!

Days were rolling by for Abba and Amma in the village, and it was the year 1998. Ethan was in the third year of his college education and during weekends and long holidays, he regularly visited the village and spent his holidays with Abba and Amma. Abba was somehow managing Ethan's college fees with his pension money.

Once when Ethan came to the village, he told Amma that he wanted a motorbike. In Abba's house, whenever the children wanted something, they wouldn't ask Abba directly. They would convey their need to Amma and instead she used to convey it to Abba and would also get their work done. But this time Amma knew that there was not much money in the bank, except Abba's pension money. She told Ethan that Abba did not have money as he had given the major portion of his pension to Jason to build his house. She promised Ethan that once the money would be returned, then she would make Abba to buy him a bike. But Ethan was not willing to listen to Amma. He went on a hunger strike and did not eat his meals and Amma did not know how to resolve it. When Amma shared the problem with Abba, he became much concerned. He felt helpless as he was financially held up. He told Amma to ask Jason if his bank loan had been approved and when he would return the money.

When Amma called Jason over the phone and told him that Abba was in need of money and he wanted to know when he would return the money, Jason told Amma that he had started the construction work of his house and himself was in a financial crisis. He also told Amma that he needed more time to repay Abba's loan. Amma informed Abba about Jason's reply and Abba did not know whom to ask for help.

After a few days, Ethan returned to his college, but from then on, whenever he came to the village, he constantly pestered Amma for a motorbike. Once he even threatened Amma and told her that he would sell his kidney and with that money he would buy a motorbike. When he started threatening Amma about selling his kidney, Amma became very frightened and depressed, and wept at her inability. She shed many tears for her son who was not able to understand the family conditions!

Amma told her daughters about Ethan's behaviour and his demand for a motorbike, which Abba was unable to fulfil and the son was threatening to sell his kidney and buy a motorbike. It was a hard time for Amma and the daughters were very sad for Amma and Abba!

In the meantime, Abba started receiving notice for attending Coir Board meetings and Abba willingly attended those meetings. He used to get TA and DA for attending those meetings and he was a bit relieved. He used to bring the money and give it to Amma asking her to save it. Abba and Amma also started cutting short on their expenditures and started saving money from the monthly pension bit by bit.

Finally, after about a year Abba was able to buy a motorbike for Ethan and the boy was very happy, without understanding the sacrifices Abba and Amma had made for him, in their old age!

The same year Jason completed the construction of his house at Port Blair and invited Abba and Amma for the housewarming. Abba and Amma were very happy and they reached Port Blair few days before the housewarming. Abba had got new clothes for all his children and their families. Jason and his wife were very happy!

The housewarming function was well arranged and Abba and Amma thoroughly enjoyed it. Abba's daughter and Chithi also attended the function with their families. Abba could meet some of his old friends, and refresh his memories with them about the good old days! There was a room for Abba and Amma in the new house. So, Abba and Amma stayed with Jason. They enjoyed the time spent with their grandsons. Sometimes Abba's daughter used to visit Abba and Amma with her family and that used to be a happy time for Amma and Abba. Abba used to tell stories about Andaman and his village and he used to be very happy!

While in the village, Amma had a domestic help, to help Amma in the household work but the basic cooking was done by Amma. But after coming to Jason's house, there was no work for Amma as the daughter-in-law did all the cooking. So Amma relaxed and spent her time with Abba and her grandsons, reading books, playing cards, watching TV or telling the prayers. Life was going on smoothly.

At Jason's house, Amma was amused to watch her son's wife doing all the household work in the new house. She had a part-time maid, but she used to clean the house and washrooms herself. Amma used to smile at that as while she stayed with Amma and Abba in the quarters, she never bothered about any work, leave cleaning. Amma thought that now it was her house and so she was being very careful about cleaning every nook and corner of the house. Maybe she had never considered Amma and Abba's house as hers!

After staying with Jason for about two months, Amma and Abba returned to their village. They had got adjusted to the life there. Whenever they wished they would pack their bags and leave for Meryl's place and spend some time there. Meryl and her husband used to be happy to serve the old parents. There they used to visit all the nearby churches and offer prayers for their family and children. Time was rolling by!

Chapter - 44

ABBA AND AMMA SHIFTING RESIDENCES

One day Ethan came to the village and informed Amma and Abba that he had got a placement in a Multi-National Company. Abba and Amma were overjoyed. Their fears about the future of their youngest son had been cleared. They went to church with their son and thanked God for His blessings. Soon after college, Ethan joined the Multi-National Company for a training. He completed his training within the period and also joined the company at the Chennai office.

Amma and Abba were in the village and were growing old. It was their time to take rest and live peacefully. But the sad part was that Amma was still struggling with her household chores and Abba was looking for relatives and friends to talk to and spend his time with!

Once Abba's elder son-in-law had gone to Chennai on a duty. He happened to meet Ethan there. After learning about his whereabouts, he advised Ethan to bring Amma and Abba to Chennai and keep them with him as they were growing old. He told him that they would feel happy and he too would be in the company of his elderly parents. He also gave him money to get a house on rent and bring Amma and Abba from the village. Accordingly, Ethan got a rented house at Kodambakkam in Chennai and soon brought Amma and Abba from the village. Thus, Amma and Abba came to stay in Chennai and they were happy to be with their youngest son!

Life had once again taken a new course for Abba and Amma. At Chennai, there was a part time maid to help Amma in the household work. Every morning Amma would prepare breakfast and Ethan would leave for his office after having breakfast. He used to have lunch at his office and would return only in the evening. During day time, Amma and Abba would prepare lunch for themselves and after having lunch, they used to spend their time chit-chatting, watching TV and having a short afternoon nap.

Evenings would begin with a cup of tea and snacks and go on with watching TV, praying the rosary, cooking dinner and waiting for Ethan's return from his office. Abba and Amma would have their dinner early and wait for Ethan to return. Only after his arrival, they would go to bed. Sundays used to be fun days as Ethan would be at home and Amma and Abba used to cook special dishes. Then they all would have lunch together and watch movies!

It was the year 1999. One day Amma was not feeling well, her body temperature was rising and she had fever. Though Abba gave her medicines, but the fever did not subside. It was over a week and Amma still had fever and Abba became worried. Abba and Ethan took Amma to a nearby hospital and met the doctor there and the doctor advised for a blood test. The blood test was done and after seeing the blood report, the doctor told Abba that Amma was suffering from severe jaundice and it had affected her liver!

Abba was much worried. There was no one at home to take care of Amma. Abba and Ethan were taking care of Amma as much as they could. During those days, Amma's sister Chithi had come to Chennai with her husband and they visited Amma and Abba. When they saw that Amma was very ill, they told Abba to shift Amma to a family friend's house with whom Chithi and her husband were then staying. He was a businessman in Chennai, and when he came to know about Amma's illness, he too came to see Amma and requested Abba to shift Amma to their house. Abba had no other option and he was obliged to accept the kindness of the family friend and shifted Amma to his house. Abba stayed in their house with Amma for more than a month. His wife and Chithi took good care of Amma and Abba felt relieved.

Though Amma was taken good care of and she was also taking her medicines regularly, but her condition did not improve much. Her eyes and her whole body had turned pale. She felt weak and remained confined to the bed. Abba did not know what to do! He prayed silently for Amma. One day a priest, who was also a close friend of Abba called Abba over the phone and wanted to know about their whereabouts. He was a Priest of the Pilar congregation and knew Abba from Andamans. He had come to Chennai and wanted to meet Amma and Abba. Abba told him that they were put up in a friend's house and also informed him about Amma's illness and expressed his fears and worries!

Amma was lying pale and weak in the bed and was worried about her illness. She was anxious for Abba who had to stay in other people's house to take care of her. She was lost in her own thoughts and did not listen to Abba talking over the phone. Suddenly she saw the green bottle flies flying into the room through the window. Soon there was a swarm of them around her. Their numbers were increasing and Amma got worried. Her mind was filled with fear and evil forebodings! She knew that those green flies usually moved around dead and decayed things. Amma started thinking that her end was very near. She doubted if she would ever be able to see her children again on this earth. The pain started growing steadily within her and she felt hopeless and downhearted!

While such thoughts were storming in Amma's mind, the priest who had spoken to Abba over the phone, arrived at the house where Abba and Amma were staying. He had got the address from Abba, and Abba was happy to see him. The priest was pained to see Amma's condition. He sat by Amma's side, took hold of her hand and prayed for her for a long time. He blessed her and also administered 'Anointing of the sick'[7] to Amma and gave her the Holy Communion. Then after about an hour, the priest left. Usually, the 'anointing of the sick' is given to people who are very sick, and at their death bed. Abba was heartbroken and devastated when Amma was administered the Sacrament! Tears swelled in his eyes!

Hardly the priest must have crossed to the next street, and just after about 10 to 15 minutes time, Amma got up and sat on the bed. She felt better and she appeared happy after so many days. Abba thought that it was a miracle and God had saved Amma! From then on Amma started recovering and the critical moment had passed off.

After about a week Abba and Amma returned back to Ethan's rented house. Gradually Amma started recovering from her illness and Abba and Ethan were happy!

After about a year, Ethan informed Amma and Abba that his company had selected him to be sent abroad, to the United States, to work there, and Abba and Amma were overjoyed. After a few months, Ethan left for the US, but he told Amma and Abba to go and stay with his elder brother in Andamans. Abba and Amma also thought that it was a good suggestion and decided to go to Andamans!

When Ethan left for the US, after a few days, they also packed their belongings and left for Andamans. Abba's elder children were happy to know about Abba's arrival and were at the airport to receive them and Abba and Amma were happy to be back in the islands!

Time was passing happily for Amma and Abba as Sheryl used to visit Amma and Abba regularly with her family. There used to be a lot of talking, discussions and laughter, and Abba and Amma thought that their decision for coming to Andamans was right!

But gradually, as the days rolled into months, Abba and Amma felt the old days returning in Jason's house. Jason's wife started becoming irritated when her children spent more time with their grandparents. The children always took the shelter of Amma and Abba when they were scolded or told to study. The mother wanted her sons to be in their room, studying and doing their schoolwork which they were avoiding now and then. Months were passing by and Abba and Amma spent much time with their grandchildren. Sometimes relatives, friends or acquaintances used to visit Amma and Abba, and they used to enjoy those visits. Sheryl would invite her parents to stay in her house and they too used to visit their daughter's house, but by the end of the day they would return to their son's house.

It was Easter Sunday. Sheryl invited Abba and Amma and Jason's family to her house for the Easter celebration, but Jason and his wife were unwilling. So, Abba and Amma also decided to celebrate Easter with Jason and his family. But Sheryl told Amma that she would send them Easter breakfast and they too agreed to it. On that day Sheryl prepared Appam[8] and chicken curry early in the morning, then she packed it in a hot case and sent it to Jason's house. When the breakfast arrived, Abba and Amma invited Jason and his family to have breakfast with them. But Jason and his wife told Abba that they had already had their breakfast. Abba told Amma to serve him the Appam and chicken curry while it was still hot, and also invited his grandson to join them for breakfast. The child joined them and all three of them had the breakfast together.

After they had finished eating breakfast and while Abba and Amma were relaxing in their room, they heard loud voices of shouting. Amma and Abba came out only to find that Jason's wife was screaming and beating the child for eating Appam and chicken curry that had been sent by his father's sister. When Abba tried to stop her, she burst out at him shouting, "Don't we provide you food! Are you not satisfied with what we are providing you? Should you be sent food from your daughter's house?"

Jason's wife was screaming at the height of her voice in a country style, with no respect for the elderly in-laws and Jason did not speak a word. He concealed himself in his room and did not come out at all. Then, while Amma and Abba were still standing there petrified, the lady went inside her room and slammed the door on their face!

Amma and Abba were filled with sorrow. They went to their room and stayed there full day, gloomy and sad. As it was Easter Sunday, they expected Jason and his wife to call them for lunch. Though the Easter Lunch had already been prepared in the house, but neither Jason nor his wife came out of the room to call them for lunch and the whole day

Amma and Abba remained hungry. Thus, Easter Sunday passed for the old parents, without a lunch in their beloved son's house!

They say that during old age, people always feel hungry due to the taking of medicines and they need to eat their food on time. But Abba's son and daughter-in-law were not bothered about the old couple! The next day when Sheryl came to meet Amma and asked about the Easter celebration at their son's house, Amma told her that they did not have any lunch on Easter Sunday and narrated the whole story to Sheryl, with tears in her eyes. Abba was sitting there looking gloomy, but did not say anything. Sheryl wanted to talk about it to Jason, but Amma stopped her saying that it would spoil the peace of the house! 'But is there any peace in the house?', Abba asked Amma!

This type of unhappy behaviour was regularly displayed in Jason's house and Abba and Amma were not very happy to stay there. But their love for Jason did not allow them to leave the house as well. Even though they would spend money for the household goods and buy things for their grandsons, but in their life, they could never make Jason's household happy! Days were rolling on for Abba and Amma in Jason's house but the happiness that the old parents should feel living with a son's family had disappeared. Food was cooked on time and kept on the table for them but Abba and Amma were not able to relish their food! All work related to the parents was done in the house as a routine, just as a duty, and that Abba could feel!

Slowly Abba and Amma started spending much of their time in their room, with their grandsons. When Jason's sons would return from school, they would rush to Abba's room and enjoy the company of their old grandparents. The children became so attached to Abba and Amma that they seldom wanted to be with their own parents. Abba was fulfilling all their demands and their inclination towards their grandparents went on increasing. Jason used to be busy in his office and would return home late. The children did not want to listen to their mother and always took the protection of their grandparents. This irritated and angered their mother very much.

One day Abba had gone out for some work and Amma was at home. The boys had returned from school and were having fun with Amma in her room. The TV was on and there was much laughter in the room. Amma was also enjoying and playing with her grandsons. Soon the children's mother stormed into the room, and she was very angry. She shouted at the boys to go to their room and change their uniform and do their work. When they did not budge from their places, she shouted at Amma saying, "Why do you pamper the children so much? You would spoil their life. Why don't you go and stay in your house in the village and give us some peace?"

On hearing such words, Amma was totally shattered. She had never expected such words from Jason's wife, asking them to go back to their village. She sat there on the bed, pondering if she had really heard what her daughter-in-law had said or was it her imagination!

But then Amma saw the children being beaten up and being told to go to their room to study. Amma knew then that she was not imagining. She felt a desperate pain rising in her heart. Her hands started twitching, her whole body was jerking and she lay down on the bed, with tears rolling down her eyes. So many thoughts were storming in her mind. She remembered the house site purchased by Abba for Jason and how Jason had borrowed Abba's money for building the house. Hardly a few months had passed of their arrival in their son's house, and the daughter-in-law advised them to leave her house and go back to live in the village. Amma felt that they had committed a big mistake by coming to stay with Jason!

When Abba came back from his work, it was late evening. He found Amma lying on the bed and her body jerking. She was not in her real self. Usually, Amma was a happy-going person who was always cheerful. Abba asked Amma what had happened and Amma tried to hide her pain. But Abba could read Amma's face and understand that something had happened in the house. Abba gave Amma her medicines so that she does not have fits. He told her to sleep and decided that he would talk to Amma the next morning.

The next morning Amma got up late. The son and daughter-in-law had gone to their office and the children had already left for school. Breakfast was on the table. After having the breakfast Abba asked Amma what had happened the previous evening. Amma told Abba that they should soon go back to their house in the village. When Abba insisted, Amma told him about the happenings of the previous evening and that they should soon return to their village!

Hearing that Abba became silent. He was very upset. He told Amma that he would talk to Jason about it as the house was built with his money and Jason should immediately return Abba's money. Amma was not happy with that. She thought that it could start a new row in the family and again their son would drift away from them!

Amma begged Abba not to say anything to Jason. After many requests, Abba agreed to keep quiet. But when Sheryl came to meet Amma and Abba, that evening, Amma narrated the entire happening of the previous evening to her. This made Sheryl very sad and she requested her parents to stay with her, in her house. But Abba did not agree to that.

When Jason came home that evening, Abba asked Jason when he would return his money. Jason told Abba that he had applied for a loan and that soon he would try to repay it. But that was the refrain he always used to sing whenever Abba asked him for the money. Abba and Amma had intuitions that they would never get back the money they had given on loan! How helpless they were in their old age!

After that incident, within a fortnight Abba and Amma decided to leave for their village. Abba had thought that he and Amma would spend their old age with Jason's family but that did not happen. Jason kept quiet as if he did not know what had happened between his wife and his parents. Soon Abba and Amma bought tickets, packed their bags and once again left for their village!

In Andamans, so many friends and acquaintances used to come to meet him. You could not walk with Abba in the market or bazaar as on the way, so many people would meet him or talk to him. He knew so many people there. Many people revived Abba's memories of his work and years spent in Andamans. But after returning to the village, Abba and Amma felt left alone. They went back to their old routine! Ethan was in the US and would contact his parents over the phone to know about their whereabouts. When he learnt that Abba and Amma had returned to their village, he became worried for them!

Chapter - 45

THE TSUNAMI-ABBA VISITS ANDAMANS

Life was going on in a routine manner for Abba and Amma in the village. During the holidays Meryl and her family used to visit Amma and Abba, and they all used to have a good time. Later during summer vacation of the following year, Jason and his family visited Amma and Abba and it was a happy time for the old parents. Even Sheryl and her family visited Amma and Abba for a few days and the parents were very excited. Amma would become busy cooking special dish for her children, and the daughter used to help Amma in cooking. At night all the children used to sleep on the open terrace, talking and telling stories. It used to be so hot that sleeping inside the rooms would be next to impossible. During evenings, Abba would arrange to get the terrace cleaned and then pour water on the floor of the terrace, so that it would become cool and would become possible to sleep there during the nights. Sleeping under the stars, talking, telling stories, and making plans for the visits to nearby places would all be so entertaining for Abba's children. Even Abba and Amma used to join their children on the terrace and spend some good time, talking and reviving memories!

After a few years, Meryl had got transferred to Dindigul, a town near Madurai and she was settled there with her family. Abba and Amma used to frequently visit her. They used to stay with her for one or two weeks and then in between they also used to visit their village. In September 2001 Ethan returned to India on a holiday trip to meet Amma and Abba. He had saved money and he purchased a plot for building a house at

Valsaravakkam, in Chennai. He took Abba and Amma with him to show them the land. Abba and Amma were very happy. After the registration of the land was over, Ethan flew back to the US to join his duty while Amma and Abba returned to their village.

As time passed, Ethan wanted to start the construction work of his house in Chennai. He talked to contractors in Chennai for building the house. Then he told Abba that he would send money to him for building the house and also requested Abba to supervise the construction work. Abba had no work in the village and so he agreed to help him with the work.

Soon the construction work of Ethan's house was started and Abba and Amma came to Chennai. They used to stay in the Andaman House for a few weeks and from there Abba used to go to the construction site every day and see the progress of the work. In between Abba and Amma would go to their village and after a few days, they would again return to Chennai to supervise the work. This was the new routine of Abba, and Amma followed him to wherever he went, like his shadow!

The construction work of Ethan's house was in full swing and so was the flow of the money. Ethan had been regularly sending money and Abba too was shifting between the bank to withdraw money, and to the construction site to supervise the progress of the work. The building had taken a shape and it was a duplex building. In 2002, while the final works had to be started, Ethan told Abba that he had extinguished all his savings and he did not have money. He also requested Abba to ask Jason or his sisters for a loan and that he would repay the money within a year!

Abba was perplexed. He didn't understand why he should borrow the money for Ethan. Ethan could also ask Jason or his sisters for the money. Abba knew that Jason would not help as he had not yet returned the money borrowed from Abba. Then there were his daughters, but Abba did not like to ask them for monetary help. Abba told Ethan to ask for the loan himself from his siblings. But Ethan told Abba that if Abba would ask, they would not deny and would give him the money for sure. With a lot of confusion in his mind, Abba decided to ask his children to help Ethan.

Abba was a person who had a lot of self-respect and he did not like to borrow money from anyone. Throughout his life, he always knew his income and accordingly he used to limit his expenses. Amma too never spent money lavishly and Abba was never in any debt in his life. Since Ethan had requested Abba to borrow money for him, Abba was considering it for about some days. He was still in total confusion if he should ask for the loan or not.

In the meantime, at Chennai, the construction work of Ethan's house had come to a halt due to lack of funds. So, Ethan again started insisting Abba, and Abba finally decided to ask his daughters if they could lend Ethan money to complete the construction work of Ethan's house. Abba spoke to his daughters and sons-in law, about the problem and requested them to help Ethan with money, assuring them that Ethan would return the money soon. Abba somehow arranged for the required amount of money from one of his daughters and in return he gave a blank cheque to them, saying that Ethan had promised to send the money soon, and once he would receive the money in his account, then he would let them know about it and they could withdraw the amount!

Thus, when the problem of money was settled, Abba soon got the construction work of the house started and also saw to it that the work was completed in a time bound manner. After the work was finished, in September 2003, Abba arranged for the housewarming function for the newly built house and Ethan also came back from the US to attend the function. Abba's elder children also attended the function. It was a happy time for Amma and Abba!

Abba and Amma were very happy as Ethan had got his own house in Chennai. Now they wanted to settle him down in his family life. They stayed with him in the house and also started searching for a bride for Ethan. They soon found a bride whom Ethan too liked and the wedding was fixed for the next year in the girl's village in Kallikulam. In the meantime, Ethan returned to the US, leaving Amma and Abba in his new house in Chennai.

Days were rolling into months and life had taken a new course for Abba and Amma in Chennai. There was a part time maid to help Amma in the house. There was a patch of land in front of the house and according to his passion, Abba started setting up a small garden there. He got a part time gardener and started working on the garden. He visited the nearby nursery and got garden grass and carpeted the landscape. Then he got ornamental plants and got it planted. You could see him watering the garden with the hose line and he loved the work. Soon the garden was set and the patch of land turned green with colourful flowers blooming!

The next year, Abba arranged for the wedding of his younger son Ethan in the bride's village of Kallikulam. The bride had already been seen and both the families had agreed to the wedding. Abba's all children attended the wedding with their families. In the evening, Abba arranged for a community dinner for all his relatives and the people of his village. The whole village came to bless the bride and groom and it was a gala function. Abba and Amma were very happy!

After the wedding was over, Abba and Amma came to Chennai with Ethan and stayed with him in his house. Abba had some good friends in the neighbourhood there to chit chat with, who were of his age. He also used to spend some time in the garden. After a few months Abba and Amma came to know that Ethan's wife was on the family way and they were overjoyed. Abba and Amma took good care of her. A maid was also got to do all the house hold chores and cooking. It was a happy time for all at home.

Christmas of 2004 passed happily and Abba and Amma were in Chennai. On the morning of 26th December Abba received a call from his daughter Sheryl from Port Blair and she informed that an earthquake had hit the Andaman and Nicobar Islands and the tremor was still going on. She seemed much worried about the earthquake. But Abba took it very casually and told her that there was nothing to worry about it as

Andaman is prone to earthquakes and he had seen so many earthquakes while in Andamans. And after some casual talks, Abba cradled the phone!

By evening the news of the Tsunami that had hit Indonesia and many coastal areas in India was on all news channels. When Abba and Amma watched the news, they learned that the tsunami had hit the Andaman and Nicobar Islands too and understood the seriousness of the situation. They became much worried for their children! Abba tried calling his children over the phone, but the lines could not connect and Abba and Amma became much worried. After two days, after trying many times, Abba could connect over to a known friend of his in Andaman for a short while, and he learnt that the Junglighat area, where his children stayed, had been hit by the tsunami waves and people had been evacuated from the shores. Later Abba was able to contact his children over the phone and could talk to them.

Sheryl told Abba that the tsunami waves had reached beyond their quarters and people living on the ground floor had lost all their belongings. But Jason's house was on the hillock at Prem Nagar and they were safe. Near Junglighat play grounds, the force of the waves had opened the doors of houses at the ground floor, and pulled out everything from inside. The ground was submerged in water and belongings from houses such as sofa sets, gas cylinders, plastic chairs, clothes, utensils, furniture etc., were seen floating in the sea water there. People saw the ocean retreating back and were frightened. Then, soon it swelled and rushed back, with more energy, roaring on its way. Thrice it happened and people saw the power of the black waves, carrying logs from Choudhury and Dorri Lal Mills, tossing the buses, cars and trucks parked there. There was a mayhem as people rushed out of their houses and ran uphill towards Rabindra Bangla School, to save themselves. But the waves did not cross beyond Junglighat School. When the waves retreated, people could see fish on the playground, left behind by the waves, and some people also collected those fish. Abba came to know from his children about the damages caused by the tsunami waves in the islands and was very much worried.

Abba was informed by his daughter that due to the tsunami waves, they could not go to their house and had to sleep on the roads for two days, and Jason and his family were with them. There was no electricity, no telephones lines and they were cut off from the world. A deathly silence had enveloped the islands, and its people. Though Abba and Amma were sad to learn about it, but one thing that gave them peace was that both their children were together with their families, at that moment of calamity!

Sheryl also informed Abba that a Relief Camp had been set up in her school on 27th December and victims were being brought there from the Nicobar group of islands. Their condition was pathetic as many were in rags and had not eaten anything for two to three days. The killer waves had taken away all their belongings and they were miserable. Abba was sad to learn about the devastation caused by the Tsunami and he wanted to visit the islands.

In the meantime, Abba also got calls from the Bishop of the Catholic Church in Andamans stating that the Catholic Church was going to initiate relief works in the A & N Islands and they wanted Abba to help them as he had vast experience in administrative work in the islands. Abba had also been the President of the Andaman and Nicobar Catholic Association for about ten years. Abba was happy to know about the offer and he too was willing to work for the church, but for some reasons, that plan couldn't be executed. However, Abba decided to visit Andamans with Amma.

The Tsunami was triggered by the world's biggest earthquake in four decades with its epicentre near Indonesia and it had engulfed lakhs of lives in South Asia. In the Andaman and Nicobar Islands, the Nicobar group of islands was totally ripped off by the tsunami waves, that were almost 30 feet high. It is said that the tsunami of 26th December 2004 was generated by ten earthquakes- four in Sumatra and six in Nicobar. It resulted in devastation, destruction, death and misery proving the vulnerability of human beings in front of nature. Thousands of people had been rendered homeless and were on the roads, shuddering at the fury of nature. Thousands had perished in the waves and many children were left orphaned.

But the amazing bravery, courage and determination shown by people at that time of hazard was praiseworthy. In the Nicobar group of islands, many people showed tremendous endurance and survived without food and water for more than a week, and survived in the jungle among rotting dead bodies. There were also people who had been carried by the huge waves and who were held on to the tree tops and remained there for many days without water or food, till they were brought down by the rescue team after the water had receded. There were also people who had braved the waves to save their loved ones. Then there were also people who had seen their loved ones perish in the sea!

It was the end of January 2005 and Ethan's wife went to her mother's place to deliver her baby. Then Amma and Abba decided to visit Andamans. They bought tickets, and one fine day reached Andamans and they stayed in Jason's house. Amma was hesitant to go to stay there but Abba told Amma that it was his house and Amma shouldn't bother about anything. The earthquake was still continuing, but its intensity had decreased. After reaching Port Blair, Abba visited his old office and came to know about the relief work being carried out in the Andaman and Nicobar Islands. He also visited the relief camp with Amma, at the Catholic Church ground, run by Nirmala School, and met the people in the camp. Most of them had lost their houses and family members in the killer tsunami. Abba and Amma were very sad to see the people in their shattered conditions.

Abba spoke to a few inmates of the Relief camp, who shared their experiences of the tsunami with Abba. *Juber and Salma* of Tee Top village told that they were around 30 members in their family and stayed in the same compound in different houses. Salma was nine months pregnant and was expecting her baby soon. On 26th December, in the morning, when the earth shook and the water started rising, all of their family members ran into the forest. The waves had separated them all but by 1 O'clock in the afternoon; they could find each other in the forest and remained there together, feeding on whatever they could find. On the 28th they reached the airbase and spent the night there. On the 29th the air force plane took them to Port Blair and they were brought to the camp. On 12th January, Salma gave birth to a healthy baby boy and they named him Jhahid which means strong witness. The family had lost everything in the tsunami but were happy as all their family members were safe.

But everybody was not as lucky as *Juber and Salma*. There were many people who had lost their loved ones. *Vimla Kumari* of Kakana village had a very pathetic story to share. She got up in the morning to collect water from the tap when she felt the tremor. She went inside the house and called out to her husband who was still sleeping. He got up from his sleep and feeling the tremor, told her to run out of the house with their baby. But when he opened the back door, he fell down as the tremor increased. He noticed the chimney of the quarter bending and breaking. He took hold of his daughter and pulled his wife out of the house. They sat down on the ground outside their house holding each other's hands to avoid the falling trees due to the severe earthquake. When the earthquake slowed, they went inside the house only to find it filled with water, as the water tank had broken and the water had spread inside the house. While he tried to clean it, there was a roar and they noticed through the backdoor, a very huge wave, some 20 ft. high rolling and gushing forward. They immediately rushed out of the house, followed by a huge wave which washed away their house. A second wave caught them up and also many coconut trees in the surroundings. The family was pulled and separated by the force of the waves. Vimla was wounded in her body and later found herself caught in some creepers and dirt. She heard her husband calling out to her and telling her that their daughter slipped from his hands in the water. She saw her husband in the water and then another huge wave caught him and pulled him into the ocean. Vimla survived the tsunami and later when she came out of the water, she found a group of people who gave her coconut water and took her to their house. They saw the rescue helicopters but they were not spotted by the rescue team. She could never find her husband and daughter who were engulfed by the killer waves. Water was constantly oozing from her ears and she felt totally devastated as she was left alone on this earth.

There was a boy in the camp named Shiva, who was carried by a huge wave, but he got hold of a coconut tree and stayed there for about 4-5 days, till he was rescued. He had lost his entire family to the tsunami waves which had made him an orphan. There were about 2500 people in the camp and each person had a story to share, story of pain and sorrow. Hundreds of stories could be heard from the people in the camp and each story was heart wrenching! Amma and Abba were very sad to hear those sorrowful stories and sympathised with the people!

The earthquake was so powerful that it shifted some of the Nicobar Islands 100 feet to the southwest. In many places, there was much damage and there were issues in disposing of the debris and dead bodies. Many aftershocks were felt which set fear in the minds of people for more tsunamis. By January 2005, the administration confirmed about 2000 people to be dead, another 5000 were missing and about 40,000 were rendered homeless and moved into relief camps.

Car Nicobar was struck thirty minutes after the earthquake in Sumatra. Since it is a flat island and entire villages, and the Air Base was swept off. The Katchal Island suffered great destruction. Some villages there were totally submerged by sea water and many people got trapped there. There was no drinking water anywhere and people had to survive only on banana and coconut. It was said that a group of teachers had gone to the jetty as they heard about the sea retreating and they wanted to see it. While they were in the jetty, suddenly the sea swelled and a huge wave broke over the jetty and took all those people with it. Many of their bodies were never found.

The tsunami had smashed jetties and ships couldn't berth, causing challenges to the supply of relief materials. Babies were born in the jungles and relief camps. In many places, bare dead bodies were floating in the sea without any clothes. Stories were heard of men who were removing gold from the dead bodies! Thousands of stories were being told by the survivors about their sufferings during the tsunami. Abba and Amma were very sad to hear about those people, and were thankful to God for keeping their children safe!

Abba wanted to visit the other islands to see the situations there. His friends were ready to arrange vehicles for Abba but Amma did not want Abba to go on those trips. She was worried about Abba's health. His BP was always at the higher end. Amma thought that if there would be any medical emergency for Abba, how would he manage! Thus, Abba also gave up his plans of visiting other islands. After living in Port Blair for about a month, Abba and Amma returned to Chennai.

Chapter - 46

ABBA GETS A PACE-MAKER

During Abba's visit to Andaman, Sheryl and her husband told Abba that they had bought a house site at Marine Hill and were thinking of building a house there. Sheryl and her husband also took Amma and Abba to show their plot, and Abba and Amma were very happy to see the place. Abba told his son-in-law to finish the construction work soon, as he would like to come to Andaman for the house warming function.

During his previous visit to Andaman, Abba came to know from his earlier office about Govt. of India's order- GOI MHA, Notification, No. 14012/10/87-UTS dated 7-4-1989 about the scale of pay to be fixed in Selection Grade for DANICS Officers. Abba got a copy of the order and wrote an application to his office to fix his pay according to the order. But the officer told Abba, that if he gets a Court order, they would be able to do it easily. Then after reaching Chennai, Abba had moved a petition at the Hon'ble Tribunal Madras Bench regarding his pay fixation, as per GOI MHA order. On 31/1/2005, the verdict came in favour of Abba, directing Abba's pay to be fixed in the Junior Administrative Grade vide MHA Notification from 19/8/1987, while he was working as Director, Tribal Welfare. During his Visit to Andamans after Tsunami, Abba visited his office and submitted the Court order. Soon the files were moved and on 24/2/2005, vide Administration's Order No.724, Abba's pay was fixed from 1987, and arrears was paid to Abba, and he was very happy.

The same year Abba and Amma went to their village and Abba gave money to his nephew to purchase a paddy land for him. Abba had got his pay fixation arrears and thought of investing the money in a proper way. The nephew also told Abba that he would complete all the work and after the registration would be done in Abba's name, he would inform Abba about it. But after a year Abba learnt that the nephew had purchased the paddy field with Abba's money, but he had got the land registered in his own name. Abba and Amma were very sad, but were helpless. When they met their daughters, they lamented about the whole situation!

The year 2005 was moving fast and Abba and Amma were staying in Ethan's house in Chennai. Ethan's wife had gone to her mother's house for the delivery of her child, and Ethan had left for the US.

One of those days, when Abba and Amma were in Chennai, Abba started feeling some discomfort in his chest. He felt difficulty while breathing. He started snoring too much at nights and Amma used to be so frightened to see Abba gasping for breath during his sleep. Night after night Amma watched Abba and it appeared as if Abba's breath would stop any time and he was struggling to get back his breath. In the morning, one day, Amma told Abba about her observations, and his struggle for breathing at night. Abba too agreed that he also felt very uncomfortable while breathing. So, Amma suggested that Abba should consult his doctor.

The next week Abba went to Apollo Hospital and consulted his doctor there. After the check-up, the doctor told Abba that his heartbeat was slow and irregular. He also advised Abba not to worry and recommended to fix a pacemaker that would need just a minor surgery and Abba could leave the hospital the very next day. The doctor also told Abba that a pacemaker is a small device that would be fixed under the skin near the collarbone, on the left side of the chest. Pacemakers work only when needed; if the heartbeat is too slow and irregular, then the pacemaker sends electrical signals to the heart to correct the beat. It helps manage irregular heartbeats called arrhythmias. Pacemakers are also used to treat some types of heart failures!

Abba returned home and told Amma about the doctor's advice to implant a pacemaker, since his heart beat was irregular. He was very upset and worried as a pacemaker would need more than a lakh rupees and Abba had no money in his account! When Amma learnt about it, she immediately called her both sons and informed them about Abba's health condition and the doctor's advice of implanting a pace maker. She strongly believed that her sons loved their father and would immediately come down to Chennai, to help Abba.

Ethan had recently returned to the US after his holidays, when he got Amma's call, he was worried. He soon called his elder brother Jason over the phone and spoke to him about the situation. He told him about his inability to come down to India as he wouldn't get holidays. So, he requested his brother to get a pacemaker for Abba and to take care of the surgery as well. But Jason told Ethan that he was financially held up and he did not have the money for Abba's surgery.

After hearing from Jason, Ethan did not want to waste any more time. He understood his responsibility at that moment, and decided to book his tickets immediately to Chennai via Mumbai. Accordingly, he soon came down to Chennai and the same day he took Abba to Apollo hospital. He got the appointment of the doctor for the next day and admitted Abba to the hospital and the surgery was done for Abba. The pacemaker was implanted for Abba, and the next day Abba was allowed to go home. Then in the same week Ethan also returned to his workplace in the US.

Abba and Amma were very happy for Ethan and his timely help rendered for Abba. They blessed him wholeheartedly for his love and concern and for his quick decision to get the pacemaker for Abba. But at the same time, the parents were very upset with their elder son's behaviour. The boy whom they had loved so much, did not have the heart to help Abba during his time of need! Amma remembered the fuss Jason and his wife had made when Abba had gone for the heart operation with his son-in-law! At that moment they talked about Abba not having taken his son with him. Now when

Amma had asked her son for a help, where had the responsibility and love disappeared! So, everything was an eyewash! Was their care and concern just for Abba's money! Thinking about all that, Amma became sad!

By August of the same year, Ethan's wife returned back to Chennai with her baby and Abba and Amma were overjoyed. They spent most of their time with the child and were happy. In the meantime, Ethan came to Chennai and after staying in Chennai there for a few weeks, he told Abba that he had decided to take his family to the US with him and that he had made arrangements for that. Abba and Amma were happy for Ethan. After a few weeks, he took his wife and son with him to the US.

At Chennai, Amma and Abba were left alone in the big house. There was a maid to help them there, and Abba used to spend his time by caring for the small garden in front of the house and watering the plants. Once in a while he would hire a gardener, and he could be seen instructing the gardener to weed and maintain the garden.

There were a few good neighbours near Valsaravakkam house and they were also elderly retired people like Abba. One neighbour was of Abba's age and he was very friendly with Abba. He used to come to meet Abba and they both used to talk about their days of service. The man was a retired army officer and had many stories to say about his service period. When he learnt that Abba had worked as the Deputy Commissioner of Nicobar Islands, he was very impressed. He wanted to hear Abba's stories of the Andaman Islands. He used to tell Abba that Abba had enough experience of life and now he could entertain himself by chewing the cud, remembering his good old days!

That neighbour was right as most of the time Abba could be seen dozing in his chair. He would read the newspapers, watch news channels, chat with Amma and other times he could be seen sleeping in his chair. It would not be a happy sight to Amma as once upon a time Abba used to be such a busy man, and now his entire energy, intelligence and life was confined to that chair. Amma thought that old age was not a happy phase of life!

Chapter - 47

A FAMILY UNION

It was the year 2006 and Abba's elder son-in-law informed Abba that the construction work of their new house had been completed and the house warming function was fixed for April 2006. As promised earlier, Abba and Amma reached Andaman to attend the function. They got new clothes for all their children, and enjoyed the function. They also stayed in Sheryl's house for two days. They were happy that their son-in-law had built a beautiful house and were happy for their daughter. After staying in Andaman for a fortnight, they returned to Chennai!

Abba and Amma had learnt to manage their life in Chennai. They had a part time maid to cook and also to take care of the house hold chores. She also used to get provisions from the nearby market. Meryl used to visit them whenever she came to Chennai for attending her trainings or office work. Then Jason and his family used to visit Amma and Abba whenever they went to Chennai. Life was moving at a slow pace for them. Ethan was in the US with his family but he told Abba that he was trying to come to Chennai on a holiday trip in 2007. This was a great news for Abba and Amma and they were very happy. Soon they started counting the days for their younger son's return, as per his promise. Every day they received calls from their children and were happy to know that all were doing good.

In March 2007, Ethan returned to India with his family on a holiday trip. This made Abba and Amma very happy. Now their youngest son was with them and they need not worry about anything. They started spending most of their time with their grandson and forgot all worries of life. One day Abba told Ethan to plan a family trip to Andaman and he too agreed. Abba also told Meryl that they were going to Andaman and insisted that she also joined them and Meryl and her family also decided to visit Andaman with Abba and Amma.

Accordingly, by the end of March 2007, Abba and Amma again landed at Port Blair with Ethan, Meryl and their families. Abba's children at Port Blair were overjoyed to see Abba and Amma back in Andamans. Ethan's family stayed at Jason's house while Meryl and her family stayed at Sheryl's house. It was a happy time for Abba and Amma as all their four children were together with them once again, after many years. Evenings used to be a gala time for Abba and Amma as all the children would assemble at Sheryl's house with their families and there used to be such great fun, laughter, eating and merry making.

During that visit, Abba and Amma went on trips to the beaches in Port Blair with their Children and grandchildren. Abba used to become nostalgic and would remember his earlier days of work. Each place they visited brought lots of memories back to Abba's mind and he cherished all those memories. He met many acquaintances at different places of visit and all had high appreciation for Abba as they had received some or other help from Abba while he was in office.

Abba also wanted to visit all the other islands once again. He wanted to refresh his memories of the islands. He asked his son-in-law if it was possible to arrange a vehicle. When the office staff of Abba's earlier office learnt about Abba's wish, they told Abba that they would arrange the vehicle for him. But Amma did not agree to that plan of Abba. She told Abba that he was not very young and he needed to take medicine all three times of the day. How would he manage if he fell ill on the way? Moreover, he had a pacemaker! Abba too thought about it and finally changed his mind.

Those days Abba, Amma and his children visited Ross Island, which was the British Headquarters once upon a time. Now the island was in ruins, and the bygone era could be felt in the air. Sheryl told Abba that she had written a poem on Ross Island, and Abba was happy to read it.

REMINISCENCE OF THE ROSS

The magnificent Ross
Stands silhouetted
Against the rising sun
Pulsating
With a sea of memories
Buried within
Are a million stories
Of the ancient past!
It was the much celebrated
Capital town
Of the penal settlement
Known as 'Paris of the East'
During the British regime!
The lovely Island
Was then alive
With exotic people
Who lived in grandeur!
The swimming pool,
Water treatment plant,
Clubs, tennis courts
Ball floor, bakery,
Barracks, market, church
Offices, school, the press
And the power house!
There was luxury all around
With illuminations
The Island appeared
A paradise on earth!
Today the island
Stands on the ruins
Of the celebrated past
Time has come to a halt here!

The debris tells its tale
While roots of ancient trees
Creep around
Like silent snakes
Devouring the desolation
And spreading its fangs
On everything on the way!
The quiet cemetery
Echoes wails and whimpers
Of the loved ones!
The garrulous sea breaks
On the shores
Telling the tales of yore!
The smell of ancient times
Lingers in the air
The still trees
Stand as mute witnesses
Of churning time
After British rule
The Japanese atrocity
Exploded the island
But Ross has stood
As a brave sentinel
Enduring bombs,
Earthquakes
And Tsunami!
Today the island is crowded
With peacocks, deer
And thousands of tourists
But are they able to feel
The Reminiscence of the Ross?

-Author

The family went around the island watching the deer, peacocks and the ancient trees, twining around the ancient buildings. After spending half a day, they returned home by a steamer.

Abba's visit to Port Blair had spread far and wide and many people came to meet Abba. Many people advised Abba not to go back to Chennai. Abba just laughed at their care and concern.

Abba and Amma wanted to make that trip to Andaman a memorable one. They decided to arrange for a family dinner. Abba wanted to invite all his relatives living in Port Blair, as he also wanted to meet them personally. He spoke to his elder son-in-law about his wish and he agreed to make the arrangements. Abba and Amma were happy!

According to his wish, Abba invited all his relatives who were living in Port Blair to a dinner. Apart from Abba's children, there were Chithi and her family, Abba's brother's family, his nephew and his family, and also Abba's cousin's sons and their families were there. The arrangements were made at Sheryl's house and Abba and Amma enjoyed it thoroughly. The food was good and all relished it. After a long time, Abba could spend some quality time with his relatives who were staying in Andamans. Everybody was happy to see Abba and Amma amidst them. There was a lot of chit chat and fun in the air.

But Jason was not at all happy. He was quite apprehensive about the gathering and the celebration. He became very superstitious as Amma and Abba were old people and such gatherings could cast an evil eye. He also talked about that to Sheryl and her husband. But then the family dinner was going on and all were enjoying the party!

After spending about two weeks in Andaman, Abba and Amma left for Chennai with Ethan, Meryl and their families. Amma told her children that maybe it was her last visit to Andaman, but her children told her that she should not talk like that and that they would visit her in Chennai and she should not worry about anything. Abba and Amma had made some good memories during that visit and felt that they could cherish it for the rest of their lives!

Since Ethan had come to Chennai, he was thinking of permanently shifting to Chennai. Abba and Amma were staying with him in his house at Valsaravakam. He was also thinking of resigning from his job at the MNC and to start his own business. With all those plans in his mind, he finally left for his place of work with his family. But he assured Amma and Abba that within a year, he would return to Chennai, and Abba and Amma were happy.

When Ethan left for his place of work with his family, Amma and Abba were left at Chennai house. Sometimes Amma and Abba would sit and talk of the good old days spent in Andamans. They wanted to go to Andaman but where to stay was a problem for them. Their elder daughter stayed in Andaman and she used to invite them to come and stay with her. They knew that she would take great care of them but they did not want to stay in their daughter's house as it was against their tradition. The love for their elder son was in their blood and soul, in spite of the fact that the son was so helpless and was unable to bring his parents to stay with him!

PART 8
THE SEPULCHRE

Chapter - 48

ABBA LEAVES HIS VILLAGE FOR GOOD!

It was the year 2007, and Abba decided to go to his village, and attend the village festival. Abba's second sister had passed away in 2003. But his eldest sister was in the village and she was very old, above 90 years, and Abba wanted to meet his sister. When he told this to Amma, she too agreed. Soon they packed their bags and set out to their village in a car.

After reaching the village, it was a happy time for Abba and Amma as they were always surrounded by relatives. Abba's elder sister was very happy to see Abba and Amma, and she used to spend much time with them. Many villagers who had been working in other cities and states had come to the village to meet their near and dear ones and to attend the village festival. Abba was happy to meet those young men whom he had known as young children, and now they had grown up and become family men. They called Abba 'Thatha' or grandfather and told him about their places of work. Abba was happy to hear all their stories and thought that indeed his village was flourishing!

It was a gala time for Abba and Amma in the village during the festive season. The fun and frolic of the place with relatives and friends coming and going, boisterous laughter, church prayers, special food in every house etc., could be enjoyed in the village. But as soon as the ten-day festival got over, people started returning to their place of work, one by one. The village soon became silent and returned to its normal pace.

After the village festival was over, Abba and Amma started leading a silent life. Amma was no more so energetic to cook food and maids were not available in the village. Some relative girls used to come to clean the house or wash the dishes out of goodwill. Abba's sister's children were married and some of them were living in the village. They were a great help to Amma and Abba. Abba used to give them money to buy food for Amma and himself. Sometimes Abba's sisters' family used to cook food and bring it for Abba and Amma.

Days were rolling very slowly for the old couple. Now and then Abba and Amma used to go to the town to withdraw money from the bank for their expenditure. Though their needs were not much, but one needs money for food and basic essentials. When you cook food at home, it is different as the groceries are in stock at home and only the vegetables or fish and poultry are to be bought. But when you are unable to cook for yourself, and you are dependent on others to provide you with food, at such a situation, money is needed for everything. Since Abba had arrived in the village, his nephews and niece or their children used to regularly come to ask Abba and Amma if they needed anything. Abba and Amma considered it as a great favour and used to give them money and they too used to buy the essential things for Abba and Amma.

One of those days, Sheryl and her husband had gone to Bhubaneshwar for submitting their Ph.D. thesis. After their work was over and while they were to return to Andaman, they decided to visit Abba and Amma and meet them in the village. It was about 3.00 pm when they reached Abba's house and when Abba and Amma saw them, they were overjoyed. They were happier to learn that they both had submitted their Ph.D. thesis. Abba was very proud of his daughter and son-in-law. He always appreciated their passion for education.

Abba and Amma were very excited on seeing their children and did not know how to take care of them. Amma couldn't cook as in the early times, and their own food was at the mercy of the relatives, and now the children had come after a long time!

Soon the news of the arrival of Abba's elder daughter and son-in-law spread in the village and Abba's elder sister came to see them and she hugged Sheryl and her husband. Then Abba's nephews and nieces who were staying in the village also came to see them. Abba went to his room and got his purse. He took out few hundred-rupee notes from his purse and gave it to his nephew and told him to get some snacks and coffee for all, and he left the place. After sometime, the coffee and snacks arrived and Sheryl served it to everyone. Later Abba again gave a thousand rupees to his nephew to buy food for all. When the food arrived, Amma and Abba had food with his son-in-law, daughter and sister. Then they all sat down talking.

Since their arrival, Sheryl and her husband had been silently observing Abba and Amma, and they could understand the routine of their old parents in the village. They were very sad to notice how dependent they had become on others for their very basic needs including food. Age had pulled them down in body and strength. Abba was no more able to walk briskly and he trembled while walking. He had become an old man! Amma too couldn't walk steadily and hobbled while walking. Their mirth and strength had been swapped by anxiety and helplessness!

Sheryl and her husband were much worried about Abba and Amma's condition. Old age had made them so dependent! Amma couldn't even prepare a cup of coffee, as her hands trembled so much! They had to look up to others for every small need of theirs. Sheryl's husband asked Abba why they should be living such a miserable life in the village. For even a cup of coffee, they had to look to others. He told Abba that they were leaving for Chennai the same night and insisted Abba and Amma to pack up their belongings and go to Chennai with them.

Abba immediately agreed to his son-in-law. It appeared as if he had been waiting for one of his children to come and take them back from the village. Abba asked Amma to pack up the bag as they were leaving for Chennai. Amma was happy to hear that and she immediately started packing the bag with the few dresses they had brought with them.

Abba sent words to his sister through his nephew that they were leaving for Chennai that night. He then told his younger sister's son to get a cab to go to the railway station at Vallioor. The moment Abba's sister came to know that Abba was leaving, she rushed to meet Abba and wanted to know if Abba and Amma were really leaving. She was totally perplexed and did not know what to say or what to do. She dawdled here and there with deep sorrow on her face. Just an hour ago, all of them were so happy and cheerful! And now everyone assembled there appeared to be in a state of total bereavement! Abba's sister was very old, above 90 years and at that age, no one could say if she would meet her brother again! The environment was becoming more sorrowful with every passing minute, and all were in a desperate situation. Abba's sister had tears in her eyes. She hugged Abba, and could not speak anything. She loved Abba very much as he had been very kind towards her and her family throughout their life. Since he started his job, he had never denied any help to her. All were very sad!

It was about 8 p.m. and Abba and his family had to reach Vallioor to board the train by 11.30 p.m. Soon the cab arrived. Abba slowly walked out of his house, trembling and wavering at each step. There was a storm of emotions whirling inside his mind. As he walked out of the gate, he noticed the word 'MALARAGAM' inscribed on the gate, and appeared sad. He got down the few steps, and turned back and saw his house. Then he moved slowly, finding every footstep heavy. He felt that he had suddenly grown very old. He reached the car as if moving in a trance, and with a burdened heart, got into the vehicle and closed the door. Amma and the children were already seated in, and the cab left the village. The relatives standing there were waving their hands while Abba's sister was watching the departing car with tears of sorrow in her eyes!

Abba was very sad while leaving his village. He looked at his sister through the window of the car. The car started moving, and he saw sorrow on her face. Abba was leaving his house and his village for good. He did not know if he would ever come back to his house or visit his village again. Going away from one's own soil could cause such a lot of pain; Abba was able feel that pain then. All those years whenever Abba visited his village and when he used to depart, he used to feel sad, but he also used to have hope about his return to his soil soon. But now the conditions were very different. He was old and could no longer travel alone. He needed someone to hold his hands and support him while walking. The life that he had spent in the village since his childhood rolled in front of his eyes like a film and he felt numb. Even in the darkness of the night he saw his house and his people, the streets and the church, the fields and gardens, all were running back, as the car rushed forward!

Abba was going away from his village, but the village would always remain alive within him, in his memories. Time and space would never be able to separate his village from him. He remembered the hug of his mother, he remembered his father's voice, he remembered running on those streets as a child, how carefree he was then from the burdens of life! Abba felt a lump in his throat and his eyes started swelling! He turned his head away!

Suddenly the cab stopped, as the railway station had been reached. All got down from the cab. Sheryl's husband paid the fare to the cab driver and bought tickets for them in an AC sleeper coach to Chennai. The Kanyakumari Express was to arrive soon and they had to reach the platform. Since it was late at night, there were very few passengers at the station and all were rushing to their particular platforms to board the train as per the compartments allotted to them on their tickets.

Abba and Amma started walking towards their particular platform along with their children, but Amma and Abba were not able to keep to their pace. It was time for the train to arrive and they were yet far away from their platform. Sheryl and her husband took hold of Abba and Amma's hands and started walking with them towards the platform. Abba's legs were trembling and he was finding it very difficult to take each step. A similar condition was also that of Amma. The man who used to walk all those miles so briskly, through the woods or marshes, smart in his suit and boots, had been slowed down by age. He could no more wear shoes, but had confined to his slippers, tumbling at every step that he took. He felt that he had indeed grown into an old man! Somehow, they reached the platform.

Vallioor is a small station and the train would stop there just for ten minutes. Abba and his family had reached near the AC coach platform. The train arrived at the platform on time and people were rushing to get into the train. Soon the train would leave. But Abba and Amma were unable to climb into the coach. With great difficulty, panicking every second, with the elderly parents' physique trembling, Sheryl and her husband somehow managed to get Abba and Amma into the compartment and they too got in, and at the same time the train also left the platform. Abba and Amma were panting, their whole body shaky due to exhaustion and old age. The sleeper berth was located and soon, with some difficulty, Abba and Amma were settled in the berth. Abba laughed at his condition and in his usual jovial tone told his daughter and son-in-law, "Old age is a terrible condition of life and now I am experiencing it!"

The train reached Egmore Station at Chennai in the morning by 10 a.m. As Abba got down at the station, he remembered his first journey to Chennai made in 1956, when he was a young boy, just 20 years old. He felt how life had slipped away so fast, in a twinkling of an eye!

Sheryl and her husband took Amma and Abba to Ethan's house at Valsaravakkam. The next day they both left for Andaman and Abba and Amma stayed in Chennai.

When Ethan came to know that Abba and Amma had arrived at Chennai, he was happy. He called them over the phone and told them that he had got his transfer to Chennai and he would soon return to India. Amma and Abba were very happy and started counting the days for their younger son's return from the US.

Chapter - 49

AMMA HOSPITALISED: BREATHES HER LAST

After a few months, Ethan returned to Chennai on transfer and also reported for duty at Chennai Head Office. Abba and Amma were happy and spent much time with their grandson. The child had started speaking, and Amma started teaching him the prayers, which he used to repeat after Amma and she used to be happy.

Since his last visit from Port Blair, Ethan was obsessed to have a sea-facing house. He had been fascinated by the sea-facing houses of Sheryl and Jason in Andaman. Soon he arranged to sell his house at Valsaravakam and told Amma and Abba about it.

Within a few months, he sold his duplex apartment and also made a good profit out of the sale. Then, very soon, he bought a sea-facing plot at Injambakkam in Chennai, after his heart's desire.

After selling his duplex, Ethan shifted to a rented house in Kottivakkam along with Abba and Amma. In the meantime, he started his private business and quit his job in the MNC. He started making vestments with help of tailors and embroiders for the churches and started selling church related goods online. Amma and Abba used to help him in packing the rosaries and small curios. They saw that he was making good money out of his business and were happy for him.

Within a few months, Ethan started the construction work of his new house in his recently purchased sea facing plot. This surprised Abba as he was waiting to return the borrowed money that he had got for constructing Ethan's house. The enthusiasm he had shown to make

Abba to borrow the money, was not seen in him for returning the money. He remained unmindful about it. Abba and Amma were not happy and asked him as why he was not returning the money, but he told them that he would return it. But Amma started feeling that he was not doing the right thing!

Amma and Abba's life was going on smoothly. Amma would never sit idle. She would help Ethan's wife with the household chores and spend her time with Abba and her grandson. Abba and Amma would sit together and watch TV serials, play rummy or tell their prayers and rosaries together. Sometimes they would also fight on silly matters, but the anger would vanish soon. Then again, they would play rummy or watch serials.

It was the year 2008. Amma and Abba were staying with Ethan and his family in Kottivakkam, in the rented house. Abba's children used to visit Abba and Amma whenever they got holidays or during their summer vacation. Since Meryl was staying in a nearby district, she and her family used to visit Amma and Abba regularly during their holidays. Abba's grandsons were in colleges and they too used to visit their grandparents. Whenever the children or grandchildren visited them, Amma and Abba used to be very happy!

During the summer vacation, Sheryl and her family visited Abba and Amma for a week and they all had a happy time. Sheryl told Abba that the 'Golden Jubilee' celebration of her school would be held on 8 December, and she invited Abba and Amma to attend the function. Abba too agreed and promised that they would surely attend the celebration.

Soon the holidays were over, and Sheryl and her family had to leave for Port Blair the next day. It was still pitch dark but Amma had woken up early in the morning to see off her daughter and had also prepared a cup of coffee for her son-in-law. When they came out with their baggage to bid her goodbye, Amma hugged Sheryl and was very sad. Sheryl could feel Amma's body quivering and there were tears in her eyes. With trembling hands, she gave her a pair of gold earrings, but Sheryl refused to accept it. She told Amma to keep those earrings and to wear them as they belonged to her. But Amma told her that Abba couldn't give her anything during the wedding and insisted to take the earrings. She forcibly kept the earrings in Sheryl's hands. Sheryl promised Amma that she would take it from her later, and gave back the earrings to Amma and Amma stared at her very sadly, helpless. When Sheryl saw tears swelling in Amma's eyes, she asked, "Amma why? what happened?"

Amma said, "I am 72 years old now. At this age, I don't know if I would be able to see you the next time!"

Sheryl kept comforting Amma and told her that she should not think in that way and that they would surely visit her during their next holidays. When they left the house, Amma was standing there at the gate, watching them go, with tears in her eyes!

During August of the same year, Amma suddenly fell ill. It appeared as if she had delusions and behaved as if she was not in a good state of mind. Her talks became irrelevant and sometimes she behaved as if she did not recognise anyone. Abba became much worried at Amma's condition and soon admitted Amma to a hospital. He called Meryl over phone and informed her about Amma's condition and told her, if possible, to take leave and come to take care of Amma. Meryl soon applied for leave and rushed to Chennai to attend on Amma.

At the hospital, after the check-ups, the doctors told that Amma had hyponatremia, that occurs when the body has an abnormally low amount of sodium in the blood. This had altered her personality.

When Meryl came to the hospital, she was shocked to find that Amma's hands and legs were tied to the cot with supports. She wept at the dismal condition of her mother. Meryl requested the hospital nurses to untie the riggings, but they did not agree to it. They told Meryl that Amma would become violent and she would be out of control and so they had to tie her to the bed. They told her not to worry as they had started medications and had also given sedatives to Amma to put her to sleep and she would recover in a few days.

After few hours when Amma woke up from her sleep, she saw Meryl standing beside her. On seeing her daughter, Amma started weeping bitterly like a small child. She started complaining about the hospital workers and requested Meryl to untie the supports. Amma wanted to know why she had been tied to the cot and whether she had become insane! Meryl too started weeping with Amma and tried to convince her that she was very weak and needed rest. She took great care of Amma as if she was a small child. She used to feed Amma, comb her hair and be by her side all the time. Gradually Amma's condition improved and when she became normal, the nurses untied Amma's supports.

The next week Amma was brought home and Meryl stayed back to take care of Amma. Amma was not very normal yet. She was very tired and would become irritated for no reason. Once due to some reason, her irritation flared up and she started complaining about Abba to Meryl. She called Abba by his name loudly and complained that Abba was very proud and arrogant and that she was very upset. Meryl was surprised to see such a behaviour of Amma as she never called Abba by his name! Abba was sitting in the adjacent room and he heard Amma calling out his name and telling Meryl something about him. Later Abba tried to ask Meryl what Amma had told about him, but Meryl simply smiled and evaded the topic. After a few weeks when Amma's condition got improved, Meryl returned to her place of work to join her duty.

Two months later, in October, one day, Amma fell off the bed while sleeping at night! She was on the floor, crying and was unable to get up. She felt severe pain in her hip. Her cries woke Abba and he found Amma on the floor. He was unable to help Amma and lift her to the bed. He lamented at his own inability. He called out to Ethan and when he came, they somehow managed to lift Amma and made her to stand up, but she had great difficulty in standing and walking. Then they laid her on the bed and the whole night Amma kept crying and groaning in pain!

The next day Amma was taken to the hospital. After X-ray and check-up, doctors said that she had a hairline crack on her hip bone and she had to take proper rest and care. Abba informed Meryl about Amma and soon she applied for leave and came to take care of Amma. After the treatment, Amma was brought home. But within a few days, she once again fell off the bed, and her condition started deteriorating. So Amma was again shifted to the hospital.

Ethan called his elder siblings over the phone and informed about Amma's illness and that she was admitted to Apollo Hospital. Immediately both of them rushed to Chennai with their families. When they went to see Amma in the hospital, saw was in a bed in the ICU and a number of machines had been fitted to her body. Her long hair had been cropped and made very short, that came up to her shoulders. Amma had thick long hair and it used to come up to her knees. The children used to be so proud of Amma's hair. Since, the staff at the hospital could not manage her hair, they had cropped it. Amma's cropped hair and her condition made her children to weep!

It was 25th October when the children came to see Amma in the hospital and it also happened to be Amma's birthday. Amma became very excited after seeing all her children on that day! She started calling out to the nurses there and proudly introduced her children to them. Then she asked her children to get her a cake and sweets as she wanted to distribute it to the sisters. Though Amma was asking for cakes and sweets but nobody got any cake or sweets for Amma's birthday.

Since the beginning of their family life, after their children were born, Abba and Amma always used to celebrate their children's birthday as per their ability, by cooking some special dish, or buying a new dress. But the children never ever thought of celebrating their parents' birthday. Even at the hospital, when Amma asked for cakes, none of them thought of getting a cake for her! But yes, Abba and Amma celebrated their wedding Anniversary every year, by preparing special meals on that day. During that year's summer vacation, Amma had told her children that on May 9, 2010, they would be completing 50 years of their wedding, and they should celebrate the 'Golden Jubilee' of the wedding anniversary in a grand manner, and the children too had agreed. But now, in October 2008, Amma was in the hospital!

The children stood there petrified, looking at Amma's condition, not knowing what to do. In the evening Abba also came to the hospital to see Amma and he was very sad. There was fear in his eyes, fear of losing Amma! He walked slowly, his whole-body shuddering and he reached Amma's bed and stood by her side, startled and terrified. After some time, Ethan took Abba home and Abba walked in a stupor, as if he was totally lost. He was in that phase of life where death was the only truth! But how to face that phase, Abba neither knew, nor had the courage!

The next day Amma was moved out of ICU and shifted to a room in the hospital. Amma's both daughters stayed with her to take care of her. As Amma was with her daughters, she felt very free and started talking to them cheerfully, as she used to talk to them when they were young children. She told about her childhood stories that how she always used to be laughing and she was quite famous for her fun and mirth. She was sad that Abba could not do much for the daughters as he had spent all his bank balance on Jason. Amma also was worried about Ethan's behaviour, who had made Abba to borrow for him and he did not bother to return the money. She lamented saying that Ethan had sold his house and still he did not want to return the money he had borrowed. The daughters told Amma not to worry too much about all those matters and to take rest. But Amma was skeptical about Ethan. She thought that her younger son was going to bring a bad name to Abba! That thought worried Amma night and day!

That night Amma told Sheryl and Meryl that she had some gold ornaments, bangles and chains and she had kept it for them. After her, the daughters should get those gold ornaments. She lamented and confessed that she had not done much for the daughters, and what she was going to carry with her then! Both Sheryl and Meryl told Amma that they were well off in their life and she should not bother herself about those ornaments, and that nothing would happen to her!

In the evening, Abba came to see Amma and Jason and Ethan had also accompanied Abba with their wives and children. Abba appeared totally shattered and broken. He was lost and forlorn. Suddenly he appeared very old, stumbling at every step!

On seeing Abba, Amma became very happy and her face brightened up like the morning sun. Abba told Amma that she was lucky as all her children were around her, and they had left their work and had come all the way to see her. Amma was also very cheerful and spoke a lot with everyone. She also told Abba to pray for her by keeping his hands on her head. She insisted and Abba prayed for Amma. Abba was worried to see Amma talking so much. Usually, Amma never spoke too much in front of Abba but now she was talking without any stop! This was giving worries to Abba and he felt that it was a clear sign of the approaching disaster! The fear could be seen on Abba's face. Somewhere in Abba's mind, there was a doubt that Amma would not survive long!

After a few days, Sheryl and Jason along with their families returned to Andaman, but Meryl stayed back to take care of Amma. After some days, Amma was discharged from the hospital and brought home. Soon Meryl also left for her place. While Amma was discharged, the doctors advised Ethan to bring Amma back for a check-up, after a week.

It was 20th November and Amma was feeling better. It was the day she had to be taken to the hospital for a check-up. But Amma was not at all willing to go to the hospital. She told Abba that she did not want to go for the check-up. She wanted to be at home and thought that she was well. But Ethan told Amma that the doctors had insisted to bring her for a check-up. He also called for the ambulance and when it arrived, Amma was panic stricken. Tears rolled from her helpless eyes and she was very apprehensive. She again requested Abba and Ethan that she did not want to go to the hospital. But Ethan insisted and Abba could not say anything. Then Amma was moved to the ambulance to be taken to Apollo hospital. Helplessly Amma left home, with tears in her eyes. While parting from Abba, her eyes were pleading, not to let her go! She did not know if she would see Abba again or return home alive!

Abba stood there devastated and broken-hearted, watching the ambulance leave the house with Amma. He felt a part of himself going away from him. He was traumatized and felt his whole-body shivering. He took support of a nearby chair and sat in it. He did not speak to anyone. He waited for Ethan to return with Amma and did not want to eat anything!

On reaching Apollo hospital, Amma was changed into the hospital gown, and she was shifted to a room for the check-up. The room had a number of machines on all sides. To Amma they appeared like huge monsters that would tear her down. Amma became terrified. She lay there on the bed, praying to God. She was caught by a stark terror, and her fear started increasing within her, while her pulse started dropping and her heart became instable. She could see that the doctors there were giving orders to the nurses who were rushing here and there. They brought Oxygen cylinders and thin tubes were put to Amma's nostrils and oxygen was administered. Soon a number of tubes and wires were attached to her body and Amma trembled from within!

With every passing moment, the fear was taking a deeper grip on Amma. Her pulse was fluctuating as was her fear. She looked at every activity of the hospital with doubt and dreadful eyes. The machines and wires in that room were so terrifying and Amma felt it would strangle and kill her. As the fear got a deeper hold on her, she trembled and shivered. She remembered Abba and her children and felt the pain of separation. She was all alone in the hospital bed, with machines around her, and tubes and pipes fitted to her body, which traumatized her. She wanted to go home, to Abba, but he was nowhere to be seen. She felt so helpless. There was no one to hear her voice. She wanted to pull out all those tubes and wires and run away from there. She moaned and cried for Abba to come and help her out of the place! But Abba was not to be seen anywhere! She panicked about her condition. She prayed to God to take her out of the pain. There was a battle going on in her mind, a battle of life and death. The graph at the cardiac monitors started running crazily up and down which made the doctors to rise up and run from their comfort zones. They rushed to check on Amma, but her pulse had started sinking and within the blink of an eye, the lines on the ECG monitor became a straight line which showed that Amma had breathed her last!

Ethan was at the hospital, standing outside and waiting to know about Amma's results after the checkup. He was worried as the doctors had not told him anything about Amma till then. He was apprehensive with all evil forebodings. Just then a doctor came out of the room and informed Ethan that Amma had breathed her last. Ethan was shocked to hear about Amma's death. He could not believe his ears. Just a few hours ago, Amma was fine and now she was no more. How was that possible! He wept bitterly like a small child. He remembered that Amma was not willing to go to the hospital and he had insisted and brought her for a check-up. Amma was so scared of the hospital! He felt lifeless and did not know what to do! Then he remembered that Abba must be anxiously waiting for his call to know about Amma's results. But he did not know how to tell Abba that Amma was no more! He stood there petrified for some time, but then gathered courage and with trembling heart, he called Abba over the phone, and informed him that Amma was no more. He was crying over the phone while at the other end Abba sat horrified, unable to believe his ears, tears rolling down his eyes. Then Ethan called his siblings and informed them about Amma's demise!

The news given by Ethan gave Abba a terrible shock. His whole body was trembling and he felt a void widening within him. He was unable to accept the bitter truth of life. His fears had after all come true! He could not believe that Amma was no more! He felt devastated. Amma was the link connecting him to his children. Whenever children needed something, they would never tell Abba but would tell Amma. Then, Amma would very obediently become their guardian angel, and speak for them to Abba and tell him about the children's requests and persuade Abba to get their work done. Abba suddenly felt cut off from his lifeline, from his children, from his family and the world. Life appeared to be a hollow truth. He felt an emptiness within him which could never be filled!

Abba remembered Amma's sufferings in her life. After delivering their first child, the pain and agony that she had undergone, were indescribable! She was a perfect companion to him, always supporting him in all his work. Though he had been very harsh towards her on some occasions, but she had always respected him and stood by him during his difficulties. Tears were rolling from Abba's eyes and he did not know how he would live his life thereafter! But the truth was that Amma had left him!

After a few hours, the ambulance arrived and Ethan brought Amma's body home which was covered in a white shroud. A cold box had been arranged at the house and Amma's body was shifted to it. A pall of gloom engulfed the household. Throughout the night, Abba and Ethan remained with Amma's body, awake while Amma slept peacefully in her cold coffin!

Abba was sitting in a chair, near the coffin, his thoughts wandering around Amma. She had always wanted to die before Abba. She used to say that she wanted to depart as a married woman, and not as a widow. Abba used to tell Amma that he had blood pressure, heart problem and what not and so he would depart from this world before Amma. But Amma would challenge him and tell, 'Let us wait and watch as who is departing first!'

So Amma had won the challenge and had departed first. Abba thought that Amma had gone peacefully, but she had left Abba behind, to face life alone! Abba felt it to be a great chastisement to live without Amma. He couldn't imagine his life without Amma! Abba passed the whole night, drifting in his thoughts of Amma!

The next day Amma's elder children would arrive with their families and they all had confirmed about it to Ethan. There was a deathly silence in the house. Abba did not move from his chair and was sitting motionless, as if he had turned into a stone! Ethan sat by the coffin of Amma and waited for the day to dawn. His tears had almost dried up!

Early next morning, Meryl arrived with her family. On seeing Amma's body she broke out weeping and lamenting, which made the others also to weep and cry. Then Abba's sister who was living in Chennai reached with her children. The arrival of a family member or a close relative caused the sorrow to surge and blow up which went on for some time. By 10 O'clock in the morning, Sheryl and Jason also arrived with their families and the wails could not be controlled. All the four children of Amma were crying and lamenting, and they were unable to console each other. They stood there bereft, orphaned and deserted! When Amma was alive, she was their guardian angel. When they had any need, they used to tell their mother and she used to tell Abba and try to get the work done. Now their mother was sleeping peacefully, sleeping her eternal sleep, with serenity on her face, as if happy to get rid of the sorrows of life! Amma's children stood there looking at their mother. Each one of them had so many things to share with their mother, but now all those unspoken words were left within themselves, and they felt the burden of those unspoken words and feelings pulling them down! Now they had to live with that burden, throughout their lives!

After some time, Chithi and her husband also arrived from Andaman. Wails and whimpers filled the room. There were tears in every eye. Abba sat there broken and totally shattered. He sat there, his head hung, as if he could not face those sad looks and sympathies of family and friends! He felt orphaned without Amma! Friends and acquaintances, whoever got the news of Amma's demise, started calling to convey their condolences. More and more condolence messages were being received. There was pain and sorrow on every face, and all were sad!

When his elder children arrived, Abba was sitting in the veranda in utter silence, unattached to anyone. Sheryl and Jason came to Abba and sat by his side, holding his hands and they started crying. Abba only said, "All is over!" Then he became silent again. There was a forlorn look in his eyes, the looks of a person who had lost everything in life!

More and more people were coming to pay their last tribute to Amma. Relatives were coming all the way from Abba's village. There were Abba's nephews and nieces, their children etc. They were all very attached to Amma. Just like Amma's children, they too used to approach Amma for help, before approaching Abba. Moreover, Abba's help always reached them through Amma. Abba would never give money or things to his relatives by himself. He would give it to Amma and ask Amma to give it to them. He never shared any relationship with his relatives without Amma! Abba had always kept Amma's dignity in the forefront, in front of his relatives and family!

Time slipped by with the wails and whimpers of family members and soon it was time for the funeral. Someone called out and told that it was time to leave the house. Soon Abba got up from his chair, stumbled in a daze, and moved towards the coffin. He looked like a desperate child from whose hands his precious possession had been snatched. He stood by Amma's side while she was shifted from the cold box to a wooden coffin. She looked so serene and beautiful, sleeping peacefully, unaware of the mayhem around. Amma's wedding saree that Amma had been keeping safe all these years for this moment, was also placed in the coffin along with a rosary. Abba was devasted!

When the coffin was lifted, the whole house shook with cries and lamentations from family members, relatives and friends. Abba who had been so silent all that time, burst out wailing. He tumbled towards the coffin and started crying loudly, telling, "Amma, you are going away! Why have you left me alone? What'll I do now?" Hearing Abba's cries, all started crying, and soon the coffin was carried out of the house. Abba's children got hold of Abba, lest he should fall down, and tried to console him, but Abba could not be consoled!

The hearse left the house with Amma's coffin, followed by a number of vehicles in the funeral procession. Rose petals were being thrown all the way and the procession reached St. Antony's church at Palavakkam in Chennai. The casket was carried to the church by Amma's sons and grandsons, where a funeral mass was held and all prayed for the departed soul. After the service, the casket was carried to the vehicle and the procession moved towards the cemetery. More rose petals were being thrown on the path, throughout the way, till Amma was taken to the cemetery, while people and vehicles followed Amma in a slow march. They finally reached Mandavally cemetery where the burial was to be held. There was a good crowd of relatives and friends there. Lastly, the priest said the prayers and blessed Amma and the grave. All family members were asked to come forward to see Amma's face for the last time. One by one the family members came forward and made a sign of cross on Amma's forehead. When all had seen Amma for the last time, the coffin was nailed and lowered into the grave. The priest, Abba, Amma's children, relatives and friends all threw handfuls of soil in the grave and the grave was closed with the prayers-

'May the angels lead you into paradise
May the martyrs come to welcome you
And take you to the holy city,
The new and eternal Jerusalem.'

Soon friends and relatives started dispersing. Leaving Amma in the grave was a painful moment for Abba and his children. Abba didn't want to go from there. While leaving Amma's grave, Abba turned again and again and looked at the grave of Amma, as if he was worried for Amma, as he was leaving her alone! He seemed totally shattered! Abba's whole body was shaking and he was unable to walk. Abba's children took hold of his hands and helped him to come out of the cemetery. Abba felt as if his life had come to a standstill. All were very sad and a pall of gloom covered the hearts of Abba and his children. When they reached home, each one of them was sad. The family had been full with Amma, but now a void had been created by Amma's death, which would never be filled!

Amma's children lamented their mother's death and each heart was heavy. They considered their mother to be a true saint. They felt the pain of separation from their mother. Sheryl wanted to cry out loudly. So many things she had to tell to her mother, but all was over. She silently lamented while words were rushing and gushing in her mind -

Amma!

You were a saint on this earth

A true mother

An epitome of love

Your sacrifices to mold our future

Your silent sufferings

To give us comfort

Your cheerfulness

On seeing us scaling heights

Your prayers to God for us

You were the golden thread

Binding us all together

So gentle, so kind

Loving and caring!

In you, we found solace and peace

Today we stand shattered and orphaned

Oh, Amma! We were so selfish

We could never give you anything

Even we couldn't express

Our love to you!'

But what was the use of such lamentation! It has been said by great philosophers that the person who leaves the world, leaves in peace, but people who are left behind, have to carry the burden till their end. So, Amma had left in peace, leaving the pain of her departure in the hearts of Abba and her children!

Chapter - 50

ABBA'S LONELINESS

After Amma's funeral was over, Abba, his children and grandchildren returned home, with an emptiness in their hearts. The relatives had parted from the cemetery. A veil of stillness lingered around the family members and everyone was silent.

The house had been thoroughly cleaned by some workers. Food was ordered but no one wanted to eat. It was late evening and Abba was sitting alone at the dining table when he called out to all his children, to come out, including his daughters-in-law and his sons-in-law. All came and sat around Abba. Abba was holding a bundle in his hand. He looked very sad and distressed. He showed the bundle to his children and then told that it was Amma's jewellery and that he wanted to distribute it among them. Then with trembling hands he tried to open the bundle, but couldn't, and broke down, and wept bitterly like a child. All eyes were wet and Abba's children tried to console him, and everyone there started crying.

Abba's elder son-in-law told Abba to keep Amma's jewellery back and that it was not needed then, but Abba set him aside. He untied the bundle and gave two gold bangles of Amma to Sheryl, two gold bangles to Meryl and two bangles each to his two daughters-in-law. Then he started taking out the other jewellery, but, Abba's elder son-in-law took the bundle from Abba's hands and told him that it was enough for his daughters.

He then handed the bundle to Ethan to keep it, as he had taken care of Amma all those days. Ethan too took the bundle, then his mother-in-law who was sitting behind him, immediately came forward, took the bundle from Ethan's hands and went inside the room to keep it safe. After that, it was time to distribute Amma's saris and that was done by Jason's wife and Meryl.

On the third day after Amma's death, prayers were held for Amma's departed soul. Abba's children and relatives attended the prayers. Then a fellowship meal was arranged for all the relatives and family members. The relatives were talking about how Amma had been so kind and considerate towards them. The children too remembered Amma and her unending love for them. But now she was gone! Gone to the world from where there was no return. Finally, they only had memories of Amma!

Once the rituals were over, Abba's children also started leaving for their houses. They all were in service and had to join their duties. While leaving home, Sheryl asked Abba when he would visit Andaman and Abba told her that he would visit during December as Amma had already told him to attend the Golden Jubilee Celebration function of the school. Even at her last time, with all her sufferings, Amma had remembered the school function and had reminded Abba to attend it. That was Amma!

As promised to Amma, Abba visited Andaman during the first week of December. It was just sixteen days after Amma's death when Abba came to Andaman but he appeared totally shaken and broken. At one instance when Sheryl spoke to Abba about Amma, he broke down and wept bitterly. He lamented that Amma had left too soon, leaving him alone to suffer in this world!

Abba attended the Jubilee function and could meet many of his old friends and refreshed his memories. He felt so proud to see his children all well settled in their lives. After staying for about a week in Andaman, Abba returned back to Chennai to stay with Ethan.

After returning to Chennai, while staying with Ethan and his family Abba started feeling depressed and very lonely. Earlier Amma was there with him like a shadow and took care of all his needs. Every small need of Abba was attended by Amma, when Abba would go for his bath, Amma would keep ready his clothes to change in. But now Abba felt so helpless! Now, if he wanted something he had to tell his son, and he did not like that. He was much concerned about his self-respect and never liked to ask for anything to others, and now the others included his own children!

After a few months of Amma's death, Ethan's wife's grandmother came from the village to stay with them in Chennai. She was an old lady and Abba was not very happy with the lady at home as she always used to talk about rules and regulations related to human behaviour which irritated Abba. One day Abba saw a bottle of chocolates kept on the dining table. He opened the bottle and took out a few chocolates to eat. When the old lady saw that, she told Abba that those chocolates were not for him and it was for the grandson. Abba couldn't withstand such conditions and was hurt by the words. He thought that it was his house and how could an outsider tell him what to eat and what not to eat in his own house. How could a stranger tell him what to do and what not to do! Throughout his life, everybody had respected him and nobody had ever spoken to him in that way!

The words of the old lady haunted Abba night and day. Had Amma been there, she would have diverted Abba's thoughts during such a situation! But no one was there with whom Abba could share his pain. Abba felt so insulted in his own house that he did not want to live in that house any longer. He felt very sad! But when he started giving the incident a second thought, he felt that he was living with his son and that the house belonged to his son, and not to him. In a way the lady was right and he had no right to eat the chocolates without his son's permission. He felt so heartbroken and injured with his own thoughts that he decided to leave the house!

Abba took a bag with two dresses in it and silently left the house. Nobody noticed him going out. He walked slowly, minding each step, lest he should fall, moved out of the confines, and reached the railway station. There he managed to get the help of a porter who bought him a ticket to Dindigul in the AC coach. The man also located the compartment and made Abba comfortable in his berth. Abba gave him some money and the man was happy and blessed Abba. After about 6 hours, the train reached Dindigul station and Abba got down at the station with his bag. Then he got a cab and reached Meryl's house and pressed the calling bell.

Meryl opened the door and was amazed to see Abba there. She had no intimation of Abba coming to her house. She looked outside, to check if Abba was accompanied by her sibling, but nobody was there. She took Abba's bag and led him inside the house and made him comfortable. She was surprised at Abba's sudden arrival and wanted to know why Abba had taken the risk to travel all alone!

Abba sat down in the sofa and sadly narrated to Meryl about his decision to shift to an Old Age Home! Maryl was upset to hear that and wanted to know the reason. Abba sadly told her that, he did not want to live in the house that belonged to his son. Then he started narrating the incident of the chocolate, just like a child would complain to his mother, as how the old lady had rebuked him for taking the chocolates!

Abba didn't want to go back to Ethan's house again. He was seriously thinking of going to some old age home. Meryl and her husband tried their level best to convince Abba to forget such insignificant matter and return to Ethan's house, but Abba couldn't be convinced and he told Meryl that if they did not want him to be in their house, he would leave their house as well. He was adamant to go to some old age home and spend the rest of his life there peacefully.

Those days, Jason had gone to Chennai for some work and when he went to his younger brother's house, he came to know that Abba was not there. Moreover, he was told that nobody knew where Abba had gone! Jason was surprised on hearing that and wondered how Ethan could be so callous about Abba and he did not even bother to find out about Abba's whereabouts. He thought that may be Abba had gone to Meryl's house and contacted Meryl over the phone. To his relief, Meryl told him that Abba was in her house. Jason informed Ethan that Abba was in Meryl's house, and then, he took a bus to Dindigul and reached Meryl's house. On reaching there, he tried to convince Abba to return to

Chennai. But Abba was adamant and wanted to go to an old age home. After much persuasion and requests, Jason finally brought Abba back to Chennai to stay with his younger brother. Somehow Abba started living with Ethan, but not wholeheartedly!

After coming to Chennai Abba had no work. He badly felt the absence of Amma. He used to remain silent and ponder about his life. He tried to engage himself by spending his time with his grandsons.

In the meantime, construction of Ethan's new house had got completed, and Abba was worried about his words given while borrowing money for building Ethan's first house, along with a blank cheque. The boy seemed to have totally forgotten his promise of returning the money within a year, and now many years had passed. Abba felt that he had made Abba a scapegoat to borrow the money! With all those worries in his mind, Abba told Ethan to fix a date for the housewarming as he wanted to invite all his children for the ceremony!

Chapter - 51

FAMILY GATHERING

It was 30th August 2009, the day fixed for the housewarming of the new house of Ethan. As Abba had desired, all his children were present for the function with their families.

On the day of the housewarming, all got ready early in the morning, as the traditional boiling of milk of the new house was to be held before sunrise. Abba had shaved, taken bath and was wearing new clothes. His children were happy to see Abba in his usual happy mood. They joked with him saying that he looked like a young groom, all fresh! Abba too laughed with his children and joked about himself. His children were seeing Abba in his usual jovial mood after about nine months, after Amma's death!

The only person that Abba missed was Amma. He even told his children that Amma should have been there! For a second, Abba became emotional, but then he controlled himself and did not talk about Amma.

After the prayers and boiling of the milk, all were served milk and breakfast. Abba's sister who was staying in Chennai had come with her family and Abba took them around, to show the new house, and he seemed very happy.

Around 11 am. Abba's elder children, told Abba that they wanted to go to buy gifts for their younger brother's new house, and told Abba that they would return soon, and they left for the shops.

Abba spent his day talking to his elder sister and her children and other relatives who had come to attend the house warming function. Abba was very cheerful on that day! He withdrew money from his bank account and distributed money to all the workers working in Ethan's factory. Though Abba only had his pension money in his account, but he felt happy in helping those workers. Then during lunch time, Abba personally saw that food was served to all properly and that all ate to their satisfaction. when all the relatives and friends had finished their lunch, they all left. Then Abba sat at the porch, waiting for his children to return.

By the time the children returned from the shopping, it was already past 3 p.m. in the evening and all guests had already left. Abba was not very happy. He was tired of waiting. He scolded his children saying, "Why are you wasting your money on shopping? How much shopping is needed for a person? Every time you people come, you go for shopping and waste your money!"

The children kept quiet and did not reply back. After sometime Abba calmed down. He called the children and made all of them to eat their lunch. After they finished their lunch, Abba went to have a nap. In the evening when Abba got up, he was a bit sad. He told his children, "My duty on this earth has been accomplished as all my children are well settled and I have no more responsibilities or worries. God has been very merciful towards me!"

Abba's children expressed their displeasure to Abba for talking like that. Sheryl said, "Who knows about the end time Abba? Anybody can be called by God, anytime. Maybe I would go before you!"

But Abba rebuked her immediately saying, "You are not like me. You are very young now. You have so many responsibilities on your shoulders. Your children are still young. All my duties are completed on this earth and it's time for me to depart."

Sheryl knew that she could never win an argument with Abba and so she kept quiet.

Abba had a few pegs of whisky in the evening and chatted with his children and grandchildren merrily. The talks moved from one topic to another and they all enjoyed the chit-chat. Then his elder children told Abba that they were leaving the next morning, while Meryl told Abba that she and her family would leave by afternoon. This made Abba gloomy. But he knew that his birdies had their own nests and how long could he bind them! They had to go as they all had their duties to attend to.

The same evening Ethan shifted some of his belongings to the new building and all stayed in the new house that night. While talking, Sheryl wanted to know from Abba as when he would visit Andamans. Abba assured her that he would visit them for Christmas. Sheryl was happy to hear that!

At night the whole family had dinner together. Abba believed that a family that prayed together and ate together always stayed together. During dinner, Abba talked a lot and cracked jokes, having fun with his children and grandchildren. At that time the children did not know that it was the last supper they were having with Abba!

The next day, on 31ˢᵗ August, Sheryl and Jason had to leave early in the morning, with their families. They all got ready to leave for the airport as the flight was at 5.00 in the morning and they had to be at the airport at 3.00 am. It was still very dark and the children went to see Abba to take leave of him, but to their surprise, Abba was not in his bed. When they came out, they found Abba sitting outside in the porch. He had got up so early to see them off! Usually, whenever the children would be leaving the house, Amma used to wake up early, to see them off. But now Abba had taken up the duties shouldered by Amma all those years and he was sitting there, alone, to bid them goodbye! Seeing Abba sitting there alone, made the children sorrowful. They felt that Abba was trying to fill up Amma's emptiness in their life!

While the children were leaving the house, they felt sad to see Abba, who appeared to be so desperate and broken. They knew the loneliness faced by Abba and felt bad for him. But they were helpless and could not do anything! They did not know that they were seeing Abba for the last time!

Chapter - 52

FATEFUL NIGHT: ABBA BREATHES HIS LAST

It was 1st September 2009. Since morning Abba was not in a happy mood. He felt dejected and forlorn. His three elder children had departed with their families two days back, but none of them had bothered to make a call to inquire about him. Those thoughts nagged Abba and he thought that maybe, his children felt that Abba was now the responsibility of his youngest son and so the others were not bothered about him!

In Ethan's new house, life had taken a normal course and all got busy with their daily routine. Abba on the other hand did not have any routine or work. He woke up as usual, completed his ablutions and then got confined to his chair. When Ethan invited him for breakfast, Abba obliged. After breakfast, he again occupied his chair and soon started dozing. Abba wondered for how many more days he had to live his life like that! He felt totally dejected and disappointed with his life!

When Ethan saw Abba dozing in the chair, he told Abba to go and sleep on the bed, but Abba told him that he was not sleeping and was fine. Ethan left the place with a smile. This was his regular practice. When Amma was alive, she used to tell to her children with a smile that though Abba appeared to be sleeping but was not really sleeping. He had the ears of a snake and could hear all their talks. And Amma used to be right, as later Abba would relate to their talks and comment on that! At that moment too, Ethan thought that Abba was sleeping, but Abba's mind was soaring in its own thoughts. He felt annoyed at being disturbed!

These days, after Amma's death, Abba usually passed his time by sitting in a chair and dozing. When it would be lunch time, he would have his lunch and then he would have a nap during day time. In the evening, he would get up and again sit in his usual chair. The chair had become his permanent companion. He was no more interested in watching TV programmes or NEWS. Every now and then he could be seen dozing in that chair.

In Ethan's house, Abba did not have many people to talk to, and there were only his younger son, daughter-in-law and his grandsons. The son used to come to him now and then informing him about the day-to-day work or that the meals were ready. The meals would be cooked and kept on the table and Abba could eat whenever he felt hungry. Sometimes they all would have their meals together. Sometimes his son would talk to him, but those talks were just small talks, not the talks that would boost one's knowledge and intellect, which Abba liked so much!

How Abba loved to have those intellectual conversations! He wanted to know so many things about the world, its systems, about science etc., and many times he used to look for such people who would boost up his intellect and with whom he could share his knowledge! But those were stories of the past. Now everyone was busy with their work and Abba was left alone, to his chair and to his thoughts.

The last day of Abba's life was very painful. He felt totally depressed and dejected. When Amma was alive he used to vent out his anger and irritations on Amma, but now there was no one with whom he could share his feelings. Of course, he had four children, sons-in-law, daughters-in-law and grandsons, but they all were busy with their own life. He had been waiting to hear from his children for two days, but he did not receive their calls. He did not have a mobile phone of his own. He had to be at the mercy of Ethan to make a call!

When Amma was alive, Abba had asked Ethan to buy a mobile phone for him, but he just denied stating that Abba had a pacemaker and it could be dangerous to have a mobile phone. Even he told his siblings not to entertain Abba with a mobile phone, as it could be harmful for him. Abba could not say anything against Ethan. Now Abba felt dejected and thought that no one had time for him and he had become a vestigial member of his family!

After the housewarming of Ethan's house, Abba felt that he had accomplished all his duties on this earth. Now it was time for his return, return to his heavenly abode. Though Abba's youngest son and his family took care of his needs, but Abba always felt a void in his life, a void that couldn't be filled by anyone. He started feeling that his children were all grown up to take care of themselves. They did not need him anymore in their life, and even without his presence, they would survive and lead a good life. He wondered if he should still live on this earth!

Abba didn't want to be a burden to anyone in his old age. It was a constant fear in his heart and when Amma was alive, he talked about that fear frequently, to Amma and his children. One such fear was, suppose he becomes bedridden in his old age, then he would become a problem to his children. He had a heavy body, and this fear was slowly gnawing him from within.

Abba always considered Amma to be very lucky. He had seen that Amma's all children had rushed to see Amma when she was hospitalised. They all loved her and attended her funeral with sorrowful hearts. But within a few days, they all had returned to their homes and got busy with their routine work and soon Amma was only in their memories, seldom remembered.

Abba knew that his children would take care of his funeral and other rituals as well, and soon he too would become a part of their memories. He was ready to die, but he did not want to become bedridden in his old age and become a burden to his children.

Abba started pondering about his life in Ethan's house. He knew that he would get regular meals at the dining table and his grandsons would entertain him with their childish talks, and the days would pass into nights and the nights would roll into another day. But how long should he live such a lonely and meaningless life? He didn't know what to do and he was worried about it.

One thing that was bothering Abba in his final days was about his words which he could not keep. How proud he used to be in keeping his words and promises! But now Abba was confused about his younger son's silence. Along with a blank cheque, he had given his words! But those words had not been respected by his son! He wondered if his younger son too had made a fool of him like his elder son! Abba was very pained that neither he could keep his words nor did he have a bank balance to return the money!

Abba remembered his ever-favourite author 'Shakespeare' and his first-choice book 'King Lear', and the famous line, "How sharper than a serpent's tooth it is to have a thankless child." (*Act* I, Scene 4 of *King Lear*) Now he could understand the true meaning of those words!

Sitting in his chair, with various thoughts storming in his mind, Abba felt no peace. His loneliness without Amma was a heartache which was killing him from within. While he would be seen dozing in the chair, one would think that he was sleeping, but a storm of thoughts was wrenching him from inside, which no one could ever understand!

It was 1st September 2009. That day evening Abba took a few extra pegs and brooded over his loneliness. Dinner was over and all had gone to bed. Abba too tried to sleep, but he couldn't and kept tossing left and right on the bed. There was no sleep in his eyes. He got up and sat in the chair. His mind was very upset. He missed Amma very much. His life reeled in front of him like a film. His village, parents, siblings, church, the house he had built etc. all crossed in front of his eyes. The struggles he had undergone in life, his search for a job, his going to Andamans, his marriage with Amma, his family, his scaling heights in office etc., flashed in his mind. He remembered his days in office and how well he had shouldered all his duties. He also thought about the sufferings of Amma and her steadfast love and support that she had given him throughout her life. He thought about his children, his elder daughter, who had not considered about her parents and the moment she got a job, she had found a groom for herself, and he thought about his elder son-in-law, whom he had despised in the early days of his wedding with his daughter, but during his operation he had taken care of him like his own son. He thought of Meryl who had taken care of Amma so lovingly during her last days and who had been so affectionate to Amma. He also thought about his sons, whom had loved so much and how they had cheated him and proved themselves to be so selfish! He lamented and cried out, 'Vanity of Vanities, all is Vanity!

In his desperate state, Abba called out to his mother and wept. He felt his mother's presence with him there, who had come to comfort him in his moment of grief. He always considered her to be his guardian angel. Now he wanted to sleep his eternal sleep peacefully, in his mother's lap. It was past midnight and Abba sat dozing there drifting in his thoughts. All the while, his pacemaker was supporting his missing heartbeats!

The greatest ache of Abba was that he did not have any purpose in life then. He was a man who loved to talk to people, those intellectual talks, and do work but now he was without any companion or work. Tomorrow the sun would rise in its own time and life would go on in a routine way for everyone on this earth. But he felt that his life had come to a standstill and he had become a burden on this earth. There was no worth of his being alive and he was of no use to anyone, even to his children. He remembered his sufferings and sacrifices with Amma to bring up his children, but now he considered whether those sufferings were really worth it! The more he thought about the life he and Amma had spent in anguish for their children, the more grief engulfed his heart! His present situation without Amma wrenched his inner-core and the pain in his heart grew more and more. A sheer stark pain started rising within his chest, which went on and on, and Abba was unable to tolerate the pain!

The feeling of uneasiness, suffocation and pain in the chest, made Abba to suffer. It was like a tight ache, pressure, fullness or squeezing within the chest. He felt the pain and discomfort spreading beyond the chest, and moving to his shoulders. He was feeling shortness of breath and a sudden cold sweat covered him and he felt chill. He thought that maybe it was a warning sign of a heart attack!

But Abba did not want to wake his younger son. He did not want to give him any trouble. He got up and staggered towards his medicine pouch. He did not bother to switch on the light as he knew his medicine pouch and all the medicines in it. How long had those medicines supported his life! He opened the pouch in the dimness of the night and took out the pills. His hands were shaky and he picked up the pills to be taken. Then searching the pouch, he got a few more pills and gulped it all together with water. Then he moved towards his chair and sat there for some time, but the pain in his heart did not decrease.

Abba was tired of the pain. He thought of his situation and remembered the lines he had read sometime long ago–

'Your children are not your children

They are the sons and daughters of life's longing for itself

They come through you but not from you

And though they are with you, yet they belong not to you

You may give them your love but not your thoughts

For they have their own thoughts.'

(Khalil Gibran: On Children)

Abba wondered if he had demanded too much from his children. Anyhow, he knew that his children had their own life and commitments, why should they bother about an old father!

Abba had taken the medicine and he tried to calm himself. The wine that he had taken earlier, had started intoxicating him. He stood up, shaky, unable to stand properly, but somehow managed to reach the wall bench in the room, which was actually a couch, and he sat there, supporting his body to the wall, trying to forget his pain, knowing that he had to live with it till death. Drifting in his deep mental agony, with the pain in his heart constantly rising, Abba did not know when he fell asleep and when his heart stopped beating. He did not know!

The morning dawned in its own time. It was about 9 O'clock in the morning when Abba's younger son came to see Abba in the room. Usually, Abba was an early bird, who used to wake up early in the morning. But the son found that Abba was not in his bed and he was sitting by the support of the wall, on the couch. He went close to Abba and tried to wake him, but Abba's body had turned cold. Abba had passed away in his sleep. Even his pacemaker could not support his heart!

Chapter - 53

ABBA'S FUNERAL

Ethan was shocked to find that Abba had passed away in his sleep. He immediately called out to his elder siblings over the phone and wept bitterly. He informed them about the sad news of Abba's demise. His two elder siblings who lived in Port Blair informed him that they would take a flight to Calcutta, from there they would take another flight to Chennai and reach home by evening. His second sister who lived in another district informed him that she would arrive as soon as possible.

By the time Abba's all children arrived, it was late evening. Abba's body was kept in a cold coffin where Abba was sleeping his eternal sleep. When the children arrived, there was wailing, crying and weeping. They had just gone for a day and Abba had left them forever. All the children felt orphaned. They tried to console each other, but no words could erase the pain in their hearts!

Somehow the family spent the night, sitting around Abba's coffin. It was the most painful night for the children as Abba was sleeping in the coffin and they were on a night vigil, all mourning the death of Abba. On 3rd September, Abba's funeral was arranged. Relatives and friends started arriving to pay their tributes to Abba. Chithi and her husband also arrived from Andaman to attend the funeral. Whenever a close relative or friend would arrive, a wail of cry would upsurge and all the family members wept with them.

Then it was time for Abba's funeral, and Abba's body was shifted from the cold coffin to a bed where he was clothed with new shirt and dhoti. When the body was lifted, bouts of blood with water gushed from

Abba's mouth and the children broke out in tears! Sheryl thought that may be Abba was alive! But then Abba had passed away in his sleep! When it was time to lift the coffin, each family member and relative of Abba made cross on Abba's forehead one by one, praying for his soul to rest in peace. Jason Kissed Abba on his forehead, and broke down in tears! All were crying and it was a terrible moment with a lot of wails and whimpers!

Abba's body was shifted to a wooden casket, carried by Abba's sons and grandsons and it was placed in a hearse arranged for the purpose. Soon the cortege left the house, followed by family, relatives and friends. Thy reached St. Antony's church and the casket was lifted and brought inside the church, where a holy Mass and prayers were offered for Abba's departed soul. After the prayers, the casket was carried back to the carriage by Abba's grandsons and sons, and the funeral cortege left for 'Mandavelly' Cemetery where the burial had to take place. Throughout the way, rose petals were being thrown, as a mark of tribute to the departed soul. Already a burial place had been found for Abba, near Amma's grave. The land had been cleared, dug and kept ready for the burial. On hearing about Abba's death, a few of Abba's friends had come from far-away places, all the way to the cemetery to pay their last tribute to Abba. The priest told the final prayers and all the family members saw Abba's face for the last time. Then the coffin was closed with the lid and nails secured it.

The priest blessed Abba's grave with prayers,

'May the angels lead you into paradise

May the martyrs come to welcome you

And take you to the holy city

The new and eternal Jerusalem.'

Then with tears and cries Abba's coffin was lowered into his grave. All the family members, relatives and friends threw handfuls of soil on the coffin reminding 'Remember that thou art dust and unto dust thou shall return.' Soon the grave was closed with mud, and everyone left the place, leaving Abba to sleep there, in eternal peace!

Along with Abba, also parted his wealth of knowledge, wisdom, and his own memories! Abba's chapter ended on this earth with seclusion and loneliness! On learning about Abba's death, many people in Andamans also shed tears in his memory thinking about the good deeds he had done for them in their lives. Many considered Abba to be a real saint on this earth!

Sheryl's feelings were all around her father, and she lamented her father's death, thinking-

Dear Abba,

You were a saint on this earth!

A noble soul

Born to help people in need

Service to you was a prayer

Your benevolent help to the needy

Would be remembered by many

Till the end of their lives

Your faith in God

Was so firm

To spread His word

You have toiled hard

Your responsibilities all

You shouldered well

But we your children

In our selfishness and greed

Could never pay you back

The love that you deserved!

On the third day after Abba's demise, prayers were held at Ethan's house for Abba's departed soul. Abba's children, Chithi's family, relatives from Chennai and Abba's village, all attended the prayer. It was followed by a lunch and Abba's favourite dishes had been prepared. After having the lunch, all relatives departed for their homes, praising Abba for all the help he had rendered to them in their lives. The next day, Abba's elder children too left with their families, to their own homes, with an emptiness in their hearts!

Amma and Abba were the binding factors of their family, and always tried to keep their children together. They had lived exemplary lives, and departed from this world leaving memories in many hearts and minds. They were real saints on this earth!

EPILOGUE

The death of Amma and Abba was a sad event in the life of their children, relatives and friends. But it did not make any difference on this earth. Life and death move on its own axis and do not wait for anyone. For Abba's children also life started moving at its own pace and soon they all became busy with their own struggles of life. But sometimes, whenever they would think about their Amma and Abba, they used to feel a vacuum within themselves, which could never be filled by anyone on this earth!

Now, the Andaman and Nicobar Islands, is a favourite destination of tourists who throng the place from different parts of the world. Tourism activities could be seen in the Andaman Islands throughout the year, and a number of hotels and guest houses have come up to accommodate the travellers. Many ancient trees have been cut down, and a number of housing colonies with modern houses have come up, while the wooden houses are gradually vanishing. The Andaman Great Trunk Road now connects the South Andaman to the Middle and North Andaman and people need not wait for ferry boats to visit those far off islands, but can book a cab and reach those islands easily, within a day. There are many flights now, that connect Port Blair to all the major cities of India. The transportation facilities have improved much in the islands with a number of buses and private vehicles. English medium schools have come up in all the islands, and there are colleges with UG and PG courses, a medical college, a law college etc., for the higher education of the children of the islands. Living conditions in the islands is not as difficult, as it used to be during 1956, the time when Abba had first landed on the Islands.

Soon after Abba's death, Abba's sons met their sisters and told them that they had to change the landline telephone and the gas connection that was in Abba's name and that they had to apply for that. They requested their sisters to sign on blank papers, and they too signed it, without thinking that it could be used otherwise. Shortly after Abba's passing away, his sons took possession of Abba's land and property in Abba's village as they were Abba's progeny, but the blank cheque issued by Abba, still lies silently in some remote bag.

Then the sons decided to build a bigger house on Abba's land, and within a few months of Abba's death, without informing their sisters, they got Abba's house demolished. Abba and Amma's dreamhouse, that was built with so much of sweat, love and sacrifice, and that had taken years of Abba's life and hard work, was instantly pulled down and brought to the soil. The belongings of Abba's house were all transported to Chennai, to be shared by both the sons, and some timber and building materials of the house were taken away by Abba's nephews.

The building that stood so notably at the entrance of the village, fascinating the villagers, is no more to be seen there. After the house was destroyed, the land had been left deserted and barren. Many people of the village felt sad about it and lamented how the sons could do such a thing to their Abba, and that too within months of his passing away! The pulling down of Abba's house was like erasing Abba's memories from his village for ever!

Mannarpuram village is still teeming with life. Abba's elder sister passed away after crossing 100 years of age. There are about 350 families living in the village now, with more and more people coming to settle down there. The road from the junction to the village is not in wilderness any more, but many shops have come up there. The huts with mud walls in the village and thatched roof have all been replaced by huge concrete modern buildings. There are many petty shops in the village now. The families of the washer-man, hairdresser and cobbler of the village do not do their ancestral work anymore and their children now work in big cities. Their families go to church, and they are not discriminated by the villagers. Life style and living condition of the people of the village have changed, as many young men have migrated to big cities or to foreign countries. All households of the village use modern gadgets, including TV sets, mobile phones, Wi-Fi connections etc. Pipelines have been allotted to households, and all the houses have washrooms, and people no longer go to the village wells for bathing or collecting water. From every family, children go to colleges in buses or private vehicles. Men folk do not climb the Palmyra trees anymore for their livelihood. The village festival is still a time for reunion of families as people working in those big cities return to their village to celebrate the festival and carry back cherished memories!

The church bell still rings all the three times of the day and people assemble in the church to pray the 'Angelus'. When people pass the streets where once stood Abba's house, they watch the deserted piece of land. The elderly villagers sometimes talk about Abba and Amma and feel sad about the barren piece of land, that once used to be Abba's house, with furniture, carpets, cushions, curtains etc., always bubbling with life and laughter, fun and mirth! But otherwise, people come and go, and life goes on peacefully there!

ACKNOWLEDGEMENTS

'Give thanks to the LORD, for He is good; His love endures forever.'
-1 Chronicles 16:34

At the very outset, I thank God for giving me proper insight and wisdom to write this book, with the memories of my parents. When I started writing this book, there had been a number of instances, when I thought that I would never be able to complete it! But God's love endures forever!

I have an amazing family and I appreciate their love and unconditional support in all my endeavours. I thank my beloved husband Dr. S. J. Mathew, for his constant motivation and support, for sharing his views and interpretations, that has helped me to have better perceptions, enabling me to enhance the quality of my memoir. I thank my loving children Arun, Aashish, Elizabeth, Anu and my darling granddaughter Rebecca, for their constant love and care that has helped me to accomplish my work!

At this juncture I cannot forget my parents, and would like to thank them for being the fountain of inspiration in my life. Though my Abba and Amma have reached their heavenly abode fifteen years ago, but they have been my true motivation to write this Memoir!

Finally, I want to thank all my dear friends and well-wishers who have always encouraged me and expressed their unbiased views and appreciations to my writings, which continuously boosted my morale! Just like in the dark nights, even the tiny stars can help find the way, in the same manner, many of you have shared your thoughts and small experiences about Abba with me, which has been a great help to write this memoir. It would not be possible for me to thank everyone individually here, as the list is too long. But yes, I thank each one of you, from the bottom of my heart, for inspiring and supporting me!

The dates mentioned in this book related to Abba's life and career are from Abba's 'Service Book' from the Government Records!

God Bless All!

Marine Hill, Port Blair   Author
July 4, 2024

NOTES

PART-1

1. Onam is an annual harvest and cultural festival of Kerala, which is a southern state in the Union of India.
2. It is an island country in South Asia, which is historically known as Ceylon and officially known as the Democratic Socialist Republic of Sri Lanka.
3. The Rajapalayam Hound, also known as the Polygar Hound or Indian Ghost Hound, is a southern Indian dog breed. The breed is named after Rajapalayam, a town in the Virudhunagar, Tamil Nadu.
4. Idli is a type of savoury rice cake made by steaming the batter consisting of fermented de-husked black lentils and rice, originating from South India which is a popular breakfast food in South India.
5. Vadai is a popular south Indian breakfast. It is doughnut shaped fried dumplings made with lentils.
6. Pazhaya sadam kanji is made using leftover rice that is soaked in water overnight at room temperature to allow it to ferment and consumed the next morning.
7. Madras- now known as Chennai, the city of Madras was officially renamed Chennai on July 17, 1996. The decision to change the name was made by the Tamil Nadu state government, led by Chief Minister M. Karunanidhi.
8. Paambadam or Thandatti is an earring worn by elderly women in South Indian States such as Tamil Nadu and Kerala during the late 19th–early 20th century. The sheer weight of a paambadam enlarges

the ear lobe, which has to be pierced with a special knife for gradual expression.

9. It is a socio-cultural organization to promote Tamil Culture, History and Heritage amongst the Tamilians of the islands.

10. Kolam is a form of traditional decorative art, originated in ancient Tamil Nadu and is drawn by using rice flour, to welcome friends and guests at home.

11. Uvari is a coastal village, known for the miraculous St. Antony's Church.

12. Mayabunder is a town and a tehsil in the northern part of Middle Andaman Island, Andaman Archipelago, India.

13. Karens were a group of Burmese who had been converted to Christianity. They were brought to the Andaman settlement to clear forest land during the British period.

14. Adivasi refers to the indigenous people of eastern and central India who are recognized as Scheduled Tribes by the Indian Constitution.

PART-2

1. Diglipur is the largest town in the North Andaman Island, Andaman Archipelago, India.

2. Gymkhana ground is the famous ground in Port Blair, where Netaji Subash Chandra Bose hoisted the Indian Tricolour on 30th December 1943.

3. The Angelus is a basic Catholic prayer that praises the Blessed Virgin Mary and invokes the Lord Jesus Christ.

4. Karupatti is a natural sweetener made from palm sap.

5. Kummi is a folk dance, popular in Tamil Nadu and Kerala in India, danced mostly by South Indian women in circle.

6. Chandhai is a Tamil word which means bazaar.

7. Umikari is burned rice-husk, used for cleaning the teeth.

8. Shikakai is a powerful ayurvedic plant that has been used for generations as a cleanser for healthy, long hair, dandruff management in South India.

9. Oppari-the folksong of Tamil Nadu and North-Eastern parts of Sri Lanka, is known as the song of mourning. The practice of women singing oppari is prevalent in the suburban and rural spaces of Tamil Nadu.

10. Paan is an Indian after-dinner treat that consists of a betel leaf filled with chopped betel nut and slacked lime assorted other ingredients, including red katha paste.

11. Mother's younger sister is called Chithi in the Tamil language.

12. A novice is a person who has entered a religious order and is under probation, before taking vows.

13. Strait Island is a small island located 6 km east of Baratang Island. The Great Andamanese, one of the indigenous people of the Andaman Islands are settled here.

14. The Great Andamanese are an indigenous people of the Great Andaman archipelago who belong to the Negrito stock.

15. Operation Chengiz Khan was the code name assigned to the pre-emptive strikes carried out by the Pakistani Air Force on the air bases of the Indian Air Force on the evening of 3 December 1971.

16. The Indo-Pakistani War of 1971 was a military conflict between India and Pakistan that occurred from 3 December 1971 to 16 December 1971.

17. INS Vikrant was India's first flagship carrier. She was built for the British Royal Navy during World War II but was put on hold when the war ended. India purchased the incomplete carrier in 1957 and commissioned it.

PART-3

1. Kanjivaram sarees are a traditional form of silk saree, typically made in the state of Tamil Nadu. They are known for their bright colours and elaborate designs, which often incorporate gold and silver thread. Kanjivaram sarees are usually made from a heavier type of silk known as Kanchipuram silk and it refers to the town of Kanchipuram from where the saree originates.

2. Japanese bunkers or pill box were built by the Japanese between 1942 to 1945 in the Andaman and Nicobar Islands strategically to defeat the Allied Powers.

3. Handia is a common rice beer in Jharkhand. People drink it during festivals and marriage feast.

4. Karens were a group of Burmese who had been converted to Christianity. During the British occupation of the islands, they were brought to the Andaman settlement to clear forest land.

5. Ross Island used to be the Capital of the penal settlement in the Andaman and Nicobar Islands during the British occupation of the islands, and was known as the Paris of the East. On December 30, 2018, the island was renamed as Netaji Subhash Chandra Bose Island.

6. Rangat is a town on the Middle Andaman Island and is also one of the three counties (tehsils) administrative divisions of the North and Middle Andaman district, in the A & N Islands.

7. Villupuram Chinnaiya Manrayar Ganesamoorthy, better known as Shivaji Ganeshan (1 October 1928 – 21 July 2001) was an Indian actor and producer. He was active in Tamil Cinema during the latter half of the 20th century. He was known for his versatility and the variety of roles he depicted on screen, which gave him also the Tamil nickname Nadigar Thilagam.

8. An altar is a table or platform for the presentation of religious offerings, for sacrifices, or for other ritualistic purposes. A home altar is a shrine kept in the home of a Christian family used for Christian prayer and family worship.

9. Jatra is a popular folk-theatre form of Bengali theatre, spread throughout most of Bengali speaking areas of the Indian subcontinent.

10. Villu Pattu also known as Villadichampaatu, is an ancient form of musical story-telling method performed in Southern India, where narration is interspersed with music, an art of southern states of Tamil Nadu. In Tamil villages, performers narrate stories ranging from mythological to social. The main storyteller narrates the

story striking the bow. The bow rests on a mud pot kept facing downwards. A co-performer beats the pot while singing. There is usually another co-singer who acts as active listener to the narration, uttering appropriate oral responses.

11. Panguni is the last month in the Tamil calendar and is celebrated as Phalgun Purnima in North India. The full moon in the month of Panguni is celebrated as Panguni Uthiram.

12. Kavadi (meaning 'burden' in Tamil) itself is a physical burden carried by the devotee, to implore Murugan, the Hindu god of war and victory for help. Worshipers often carry a pot of cow milk as an offering and also do mortification of the flesh by piercing the skin, tongue or cheeks with vel skewers.

13. Vel is a divine spear associated with Murugan, the Hindu god of war. According to legends the goddess Parvati presented the Vel to her son Murugan, as an embodiment of her shakti, in order to vanquish the asura.

14. Kumaraswami Kamaraj (15 July 1903 - October 1975), popularly known as Kamarajar was an Indian independence activist and politician who served as the Chief Minister of Madras State (Tamil Nadu) from 13 April 1954 to 2 October 1963.

15. The Jarawas are an indigenous people, and one of the four tribes of the Andaman Islands in India. They live in parts of South Andaman and Middle Andaman Islands.

16. Mother Teresa was an Albanian-Indian Catholic nun and the founder of the Missionaries of Charity, a religious congregation. Mother Teresa was admired by many for her charitable work. The congregation manages homes for people who are dying of HIV/AIDS, leprosy, and tuberculosis. The congregation also runs soup kitchens, dispensaries, mobile clinics, children's and family counselling programmes, as well as orphanages and schools. On 4 September 2016, she was canonised by the Catholic Church as Saint Teresa of Calcutta. The anniversary of her death, 5 September, is her Feast Day.

PART- 4

1. The Census of India 1901, Vol. III, Andaman & Nicobar Islands, by Lieut. Col. Sir Richard C. Temple, BART, C.I.E. Commissioner of The Andaman and Nicobar Islands, and Superintendent of the Penal Settlement at Port Blair. Published by the Superintendent of Government Printing, India, Calcutta. Pg. 44-45.

2. In The Nicobar Islands by George Whitehead, B.A., With A Preface by Sir Richard C. Temple, Bart., C.B., D.L., CLE Sometime Chief Commissioner of the Andaman & Nicobar Islands, London Seeley, Service & Co. 196 Shaftesbury Avenue 1914, P. 32-33.

3. Kiran Dhingra, The Andaman and Nicobar Islands in the 20th Century- A Gazetteer, Published by Oxford University Press, 2005, Chapter 2, Pg. 33.

4. M. V. Portman, The History of our Relations with the Andamanese, Vol. 1, Published by Office of the Superintendent of Government Printing, Calcutt, 1899, Pg. 81-82

5. Ibid., Pg. 86.

6. N. Iqbal Singh, The Andaman Story, Ch: 4, P. 27. Published by Vikas Publishing House, New Delhi, 1978.

7. Ibid, Pg. 28.

8. Imperial Gazetteer of India, Provincial Series, Andaman and Nicobar Islands Published by Superintendent of Government Printing India, 1909, Pg. 57-58.

9. Census of India 1931, Vol. II, The Andaman and Nicobar Islands, by M. C. C. Bonington, Superintendent of Census Operations, Published by Government of India, Central Publication Branch, 1932, Pg. 39.

10. Local Gazetteer, The Andaman and Nicobar Islands, Published by the Superintendent of Government Printing, India, Calcutta, 1908 (KCW, Chief Commissioner), Pg. 112.

11. M. V. Portman, The History of our Relations with the Andamanese, Vol. 1, Published by Office of the Superintendent of Government Printing, Calcutta, 1899, Pg. 255.

12. Ibid., Pg. 276.

13. Ibid., Pg. 277.

14. Ibid., Pg. 278-9.

15. Ibid., Pg. 280-85.

16. Mount Harriet was the summer headquarters of the Chief Commissioner during British Raj. It is the highest peak in the South Andamans and is 365 mts. high. The park was named in honour of Harriet C. Tytler, the second wife of Robert Christopher Tytler, a British army officer, who was appointed Superintendent of the Convict Settlement at Port Blair in the Andamans from April 1862 to February 1864. On 17th October 2021, Mount Harriet was officially renamed as Mount Manipur by the Union Government of India, as a tribute to the freedom fighters of Manipur.

17. The Chatham Saw Mill was established in 1883 with the second-hand imported machines, to meet the local requirement of timber for construction works. During the colonial period the British used this mill to convert huge quantity of timber for catering the various needs of London, New York and various other cities. During the Second World War, during the Japanese bombardment on the mill on 1942 March 10, many workers were succumbed to death.

18. Kiran Dhingra, The Andaman and Nicobar Islands in the 20th Century- A Gazetteer, Published by Oxford University Press, 2005, Chapter 2, Pg. 59.

19. Local Gazetteer, The Andaman and Nicobar Islands, by KCW, Chief Commissioner, Published by the Superintendent of Government Printing, India, Calcutta, 1908, Pg. 114-15

20. Vedappan Solomon was a catechist who was instrumental to spread Christianity in the Nicobars and is known as the Apostle of Nicobar.

21. Imperial Gazetteer of India, Provincial Series, Andaman and Nicobar Islands, Published by Superintendent of Government Printing, Calcutta, 1909, Pg. 25.

22. Local Gazetteer, The Andaman and Nicobar Islands, by KCW, Chief Commissioner, Published by the Superintendent of Government Printing, India, Calcutta, 1908, Pg page 123.

23. Sher Ali was a Wahabi convict transported for life to the Andaman Islands. On 8 February 1872, he succeeded to kill Lord Mayo, the Viceroy, who was on a visit to the islands, at Panighat while he was returning from Mount Hariot, now known as Mount Manipur.

24. History of Andaman & Nicobar Islands with a study of India's Freedom Struggle' by Dr. L.P. Mathur, Published by Oriental Publishers and Exporters, Delhi, 1985, pg. 50-126.

25. The Census of India 1901, Vol. III, Andaman & Nicobar Islands, by Lieut.-Col. Sir Richard C. Temple, BART, C.I.E. Commissioner of The Andaman and Nicobar Islands, and Superintendent of the Penal Settlement at Port Blair. Published by the Superintendent of Government Printing, India, Calcutta. Pg. 189.

26. Imperial Gazetteer of India, Provincial Series, Andaman and Nicobar Islands, Published by Superintendent of Government Printing, Calcutta, 1909, Pg. 33.

27. The Menluanas or the witch doctors, were the ones who assisted in establishing communication with the spirit world. The priest is also the bearer of traditional wisdom of the Nicobarese.

28. Every village in the Tribal area of Nicobar Islands has a village council headed by 1st captain and who is assisted by 2nd and 3rd captain. The captains are elected democratically by secret ballot normally for tenure of 4 years.

29. Rani Islon was a Nicobari woman, and a British agent. In October 1914, the German warship Emden sailed to the Nicobar Islands and Islon mistook it for a British ship and hoisted the Union Jack. The Commander of the ship Muller thought that there was a strong British presence in the islands, and hastily withdrew and sailed off to Penang. Islon realised that it was a German ship and immediately dispatched a messenger to the nearest signal station to inform the British. Islon's information helped the British to the capture of

Emden. The grateful British conferred on Islon the title 'Rani of Nancowry.

30. Bishop John Richardson was a Nicobri, who rose to the ranks of the greatest leader of Nicobar. He devoted his time to shepherding the Christians, and spreading the Gospel among the Nicobarese. He wrote the first Car Nicobarese Primer using the English script in 1923.

31. The Cellular Jail, was a British colonial prison in the Andaman and Nicobar Islands, now it is known as the National Memorial.

32. Local Gazetteer, The Andaman and Nicobar Islands, by KCW, Chief Commissioner, Published by the Superintendent of Government Printing, India, Calcutta, 1908, page 122,

33. Imperial Gazetteer of India, Provincial Series, Andaman and Nicobar Islands, Published by Superintendent of Government Printing, Calcutta, 1909, Pg. 59-60,

34. Bhantus are a tribe from Central Province. During the period of British, they were notified under the Criminal Tribes Act. Many were exiled to the Andaman Islands.

35. The Malabar rebellion of 1921, started as a resistance against the British colonial rule is also called Moplah rebellion. After the Moplah Rebellion of 1921, about 1133 Moplahs were transported to Andamans in the first phase.

36. The term local- born refers to the community of old convict settlers who were transported to the Andamans by the British and their offsprings born in the islands. They are also officially known as the Pre-42 Settlers.

37. 'Sachindranath Sanyal aur Unke Yug' by Vishwamitra Upadhyay, published by Pragatisheel Jan Prakashan, 1983.

38. The Census of India 1901, Vol. III, Andaman & Nicobar Islands, by Lieut.-Col. Sir Richard C. Temple, BART, C.I.E. Commissioner of The Andaman and Nicobar Islands, and Superintendent of the Penal Settlement at Port Blair. Published by the Superintendent of Government Printing, India, Calcutta. Pg. 401.

39. Inspection Report of the Penal Settlement of Port Blair by Major H.N. Davies, Secretary to Chief Commissioner, British Burmah, Published by Office of Superintendent of Government Printing, Calcutta, 1869, Pg. 8.

40. Imperial Gazetteer of India, Provincial Series, Andaman and Nicobar Islands, Published by Superintendent of Government Printing Calcutta, 1909, Pg. 78.

41. A Regime of Fears and Tears by B.B. Lall, published by Farsight Publishers & Distributors, Delhi, 1992, Pg. 13-19

42. B.B. Lall, the author of the book A Regime of Fears and Tears was 12 years old when the Japanese Imperial Forces occupied the Islands in 1942. In his book he throws light on the atrocity of the Japanese done on the people of Andamans, during their occupation of the Islands.

43. Kiran Dhingra, The Andaman and Nicobar Islands in the 20th Century- A Gazetteer, Published by Oxford University Press, 2005, Chapter 2, Pg. 49.

44. Loka was a native Andamanese chieftain who acted as an undercover agent for the British Army even as he played his native role of chieftain. His knowledge of the islands, seamanship skills and trustworthiness among natives helped him spy on the Japanese and deliver strategic information to the British stationed miles away.

45. The Andaman Story by N. Iqbal Singh, by Vikas Publishing House Pvt. Ltd., Ch. 24, Pg. 271

46. B.B. Lall, A Regime of Fears and Tears, Pg. 49.

47. Dr. Diwan Singh Dhillon, or Diwan Singh Kalepani was one of the leading freedom fighters at the Settlement. Dr. Diwan Singh was posted from Rangoon to Port Blair in the Andaman Islands as a civil doctor. He took over the charges in Cellular Jail on 20 October 1927. He was a poet and a social activist and became President of the Indian Independence League (IIL) in April 1942. During the Japanese occupation of the islands, he fell under suspicion of the Japanese and he was arrested on 23-10-1943, kept in wing 6 of the

Cellular Jail and tortured brutally. On 14 January 1944 he died in his cell.

48. The Andaman Story by N. Iqbal Singh, by Vikas Publishing House Pvt. Ltd., Ch. 24, Pg. 250.

PART- 5

1. Cellular Jail is today known as the National Memorial. It remembers and venerates the invaluable sacrifice of our freedom fighters incarcerated in it. The National Memorial was dedicated to the nation on 11 February 1979 by the then Prime Minister, Shri Morarji Desai.
2. Campbell Bay is a town in the Great Nicobar Island, of the Nicobar district of Andaman and Nicobar Islands.
3. Indira point is the southernmost tip of India's territory and is located at Great Nicobar Island.
4. Shompens are aborigines of the Nicobar group of islands and live in Campbell Bay, in the interior jungles.
5. INS Kardip was commissioned in 1973 at Kamorta Island to stop unauthorized intrusions by foreign vessels.
6. Katchal Island is a part of the Nicobar group of islands and belongs to the township of Nancowry of Katchal Tehsil.
7. Car Nicobar is the district head quarters of the Nicobar district. It is a coral island and is the northern most island of the Nicobar chain of islands.
8. Little Andaman Island is at the southern end of the Andaman chain of islands and falls under South Andaman District, for administrative purposes.
9. Onge is an Andamanese Ethnic Tribe who are settled in Little Andaman Island.
10. Negombo is a major city in Sri Lanka, situated on the west coast. It is one of the major commercial hubs of the country. Negombo is known for its long sandy beaches and centuries old fishing industry. Negombo has a large bilingual (Sinhala/Tamil) population with a clear Roman Catholic majority.

11. Long Island is an island of the Andaman Islands and belongs to the North and Middle Andaman administrative district.

12. The Census Report 1901, page 49,

13. The Aboriginal Inhabitants of the Andaman Islands by Edward Horace Man, Published by the Anthropological Institute of Great Britain and London.

14. The Kitchen Middens are mounts, about 50 feet in diameter, left behind by the Andamanese when they leave a dwelling place and move to another place. Digging the place revealed mixture of ashes and earth, shells, bones etc.

15. The Census Report 1901, page (Page-107-109)

16. 'In the Nicobar Islands' by George Whitehead, B.A., published by London Seeley, Service & Co., Shaftesbury Avenue, 1914, page 196-199

17. Menulanas also known as witch doctors, were the medicine men, contacted immediately when illness occurred, and who used to cure people in the Nicobar group Islands in the ancient times.

18. In the Andamans and Nicobars, by C. Boden Kloss, published by London John Murray, Albemarle Street, W. 1903- Pg. 141-154.

19. Census Report 1931, Appendix-A, Page-87-88

20. 'Master Plan (1991-2021) For the Welfare of the Primitive Tribes of Andaman and Nicobar Islands', by S.A. Awaradhi, Published by Andaman and Nicobar Administration. 1990: Pg. 59-62.

21. Imperial Gazetteer of India, Andaman and Nicobar Islands, Published by the Superintendent of Government Printing, Calcutta 1909, Pg. 39-56.

22. The Nicobar Islands and their People by Edward Horace Man, Printed by British India Press Bombay, 1923, Pg. 123-148

23. Obtained from John Richardson by R.F.L and published in the – Census of India Report-1921, Appendix P.

24. Note by John Richardson on Tabus and ceremonies, Appendix-Q Census-1921.

PART-6

1. St. Alphonsa of the Immaculate Conception, FCC, (19 August 1910 – 28 July 1946), was a nun in the Franciscan Clarist Congregation and an educator by profession. Her tomb is at St. Mary's Syro-Malabar Catholic Church, Bharananganam, and has become a pilgrimage site. She is the first woman of Indian origin to be canonised as a saint.

2. Kanyakumari is a city in Tamil Nadu, and is the southernmost tip of mainland India. The city is situated 20 Km. south of Nagercoil. It is famous for the Vivekananda Rock Memorial, Thiruvalluvar Statue, the Temple of Goddess Kanyakumari and the coastal beach.

3. Kutralam, is a small-town bordering Kollam District. It is famous for its waterfalls on the Western Ghats. With captivating panoramic views, the town is popularly known as 'Spa of South'. It has nine waterfalls in the region which add a charm to its exotic beauty.

PART-7

1. Velankanni is a town in Tamil Nadu, where the Basilica of Our Lady of Good Health, also known as Sanctuary of Our Lady of Velankanni, is located. The shrine is dedicated to the Blessed Virgin Mary.

2. Kannaki is a legendry Tamil woman who forms the central character of the Tamil epic Silappatikaram, who had burnt the city of Madurai with her curse.

3. Athisaya Manal Matha Shrine, also known as Our Lady of Red Sands is in southern Thoothukudi District of Tamil Nadu.

4. Pandyas were one of the three ancient Tamil kingdoms (Chola and Chera being the other two) which ruled the Tamil country from pre-historic times until end of the 15th century. They ruled initially from Korkai, a seaport on the southern-most tip of the Indian peninsula, and in later times moved to Madurai.

5. St. Thomas was one of twelve apostles of Jesus Christ. He is said to have travelled outside the Roman Empire to preach the Gospel,

travelling as far as Mylapore in Tamil Nadu. According to Syrian Christian tradition, St. Thomas was killed on 3 July in AD 72, with a spear at St. Thomas Mount in Chennai. Santhome Church in Chennai, is said to be the tomb of Saint Thomas.

6. St. Francis Xavier was a Spanish Catholic Missionary and Saint, who co-founded the Society of Jesus with Ignatius of Loyola. He arrived in India in 1542 and faced countless challenges. For seven years Francis preached in the streets and public squares, labouring tirelessly across India and the Asian Pacific islands. He is considered one of the greatest missionaries of the Catholic Church. His body is now in the Basilica of Bom Jesus in Goa.

7. In the Catholic Church, anointing of the sick is administered to bring spiritual and even physical strength during an illness, especially near the time of death. It is most likely one of the last sacraments one will receive.

8. Appam is a lacy and fluffy pancake from Kerala cuisine, made with rice, coconut and yeast.

BIBLIOGRAPHY

1. Awaradhi S.A., 1990, Master Plan (1991-2021) For the Welfare of the Primitive Tribes of Andaman and Nicobar Islands, Published by Andaman and Nicobar Administration.

2. Bonington M. C. C, 1932, Census of India 1931, Vol. II, The Andaman and Nicobar Islands, by Published by Government of India, Central Publication Branch.

3. Busch H, 1845, Journal of a Cruise among the Nicobar Islands, Printed by Sanders and Cones, Calcutta.

4. Davies Major H.N, 1867, Inspection Report on the Penal Settlement of Port Blair, Secretary to Chief Commissioner, British Burmah, Published by Office of the Superintendent of Government Printing, Calcutta.

5. Dhingra Kiran, 2005, The Andaman and Nicobar Islands in the 20th Century- A Gazetteer, Published by Oxford University Press.

6. Dutt Ullaskar, 1924, Twelve Years of Prison Life, Published by the Arya Publishing House, Calcutta.

7. Haensel Rev. John Gottfried, 1812, Letters on Nicobar Islands, London.

8. KCW, Chief Commissioner, 1908, Local Gazetteer, The Andaman and Nicobar Islands, Published by the Superintendent of Government Printing, India, Calcutta.

9. Kloss C. Boden, 1903, In the Andaman and Nicobars, published by John Murray, W. Albemarle Street, London.

10. Lall B.B., 1992, A Regime of Fears and Tears, published by Far sight Publishers & Distributors, Delhi.

11. Lowis R. F, 1923, Census of India 1921, The Andaman and Nicobar Islands, published by Superintendent Government Printing India, Calcutta.

12. Lyall C.J. & Lethbridge A.S., 1890, Report on the Working of the Penal Settlement of Port Blair, Printed by Superintendent of Government Printing, Calcutta.

13. Majumdar R. C., 1975, Penal Settlement in Andaman, Gazetteers Unit, Department of Culture, Ministry of Education and Social Welfare.

14. Man Edward Horace, 1883, The Aboriginal Inhabitants of the Andaman Islands, Published by the Anthropological Institute of Great Britain and London.

15. Man Edward Horace, 1923, The Nicobar and Their People, by Printed by British India Press, Bombay.

16. Mathur L. P., 1968, History of Andaman & Nicobar Islands with a Study of India's Freedom Struggle, Sterling Publishers.

17. Mouat Frederic J, 1863, Adventures and Researches Among the Andaman Islanders, Published by Hurst and Blackett Publishers, London.

18. Portman M. V, 1899, A History of our Relations with the Andamanese, Vol. 1, Published by Office of the Superintendent of Government Printing, Calcutta.

19. Report of the Indian Jails Committee 1919-20, 1921, Printed and Published by His Majesty's Stationery Office, London.

20. Singh Iqbal N, 1978, The Andaman Story, Published by Vikas Publishing House, New Delhi.

21. Sinha Bijoy Kumar, 1939, In Andamans, The Indian Bastille, Printed by P. Topa, at the Allahabad Law Journal Press.

22. Srinivasan M. D., Sons of the Light- The Story of Car Nicobar, published under Project Canterbury.

23. Superintendent, 1877, Handbook for the Andaman and Nicobars, Revised up to the 1st April 1877, by Office of the Government Printing, Calcutta.

24. Superintendent, 1909, Imperial Gazetteer of India, Provincial Series, Andaman and Nicobar Islands, Government Printing India, Calcutta.

25. Temple Sir Richard C, 1903, The Census of India 1901, Vol. III, Andaman & Nicobar Islands, Published by the Superintendent of Government Printing, India, Calcutta.

26. Upadhyay Vishwamitra, 1983, Sachindranath Sanyal aur Unke Yug, published by Pragatisheel Jan Prakashan.

27. Whitehead George, 1914, In the Nicobar Islands, With A Preface by Sir Richard C. Temple, Bart., Sometime Chief Commissioner of the Andaman & Nicobar Islands, published by London Seeley, Service & Co. 196, Shaftesbury Avenue.

PHOTO GALLERY

Penal Settlement in the Andmans

Photo Courtesy - National Memorial Museum

Penal Settlement in the Andmans

Tokens used in the Penal Settlement during 1863,

Photo Courtesy -
National Memorial
Museum

Life in the Nicobars

Nicobarese village

Bishop John Richardson Pic

Nicobarese hut on el-panem

Nicobar War Memorial in memory of those who died during Japanese Occupation.

Nicobarese Canoe

Photo Courtesy - Mr. Poppy Penny

Life in the Nicobars

The Nicobarese Youth

Toddy making

Remembrance Festival

Ossuary Celebration

Pig fight

Photo Courtesy - Mr. A. Justin

Andaman & Nicobars

Cellular Jail areal view

Nicobarese dance

Gallows-Inside-Cellular-Jail

A Japanese Bunker

Coconut Scrapping

The National Memorial

Photo Courtesy - IP&T

Tsunami in Andaman & Nicobar Islands

Photo Courtesy - The Catholic Church, Diocese of Port Blair

Abba & Amma

Abba & Amma

Abba's house at Mannarpuram Village

Empty land where once used to be Abba's house!

Abba's grave at Mandavally Cemetry- Rest in Peace

Amma's grave at Mandavally Cemetry- Rest in Peace

www.ingramcontent.com/pod-product-compliance
Lightning Source LLC
Chambersburg PA
CBHW051127130726
47988CB00005B/1741